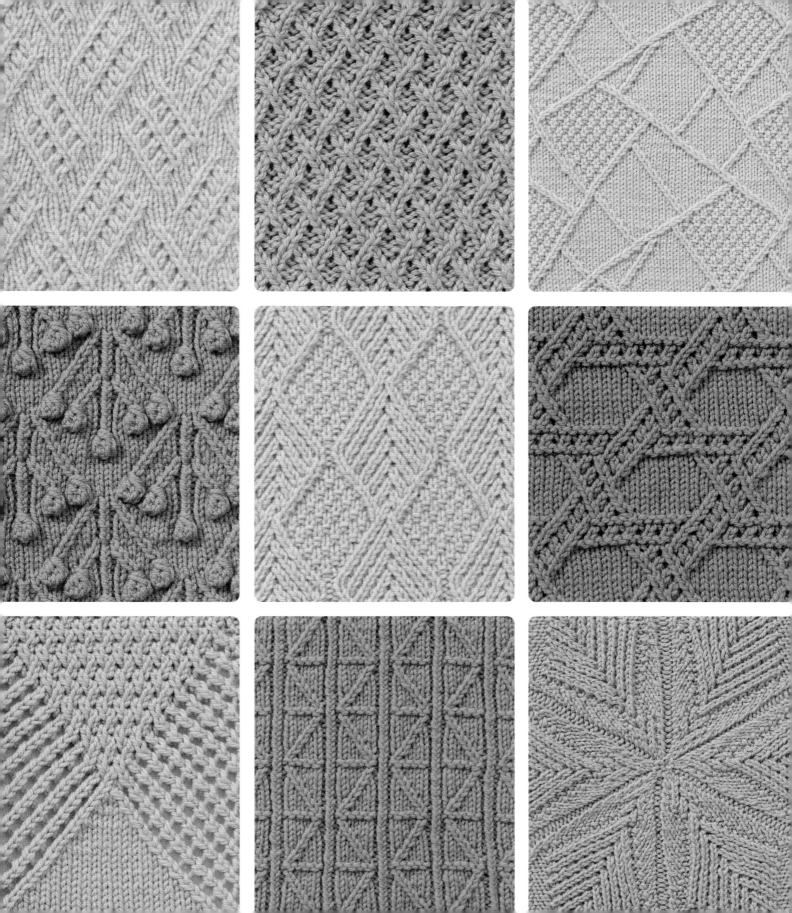

NORAH GAUGHAN'S
Twisted Stitch Sourcebook

A Breakthrough Guide to Knitting and Designing

Abrams, New York

Contents

Introduction

MAKING UP NEW PATTERN STITCHES is my favorite thing to do. I first discovered this years ago, when I was just beginning to design professionally, and my love has only grown since. The "aha!" moment for me came after returning home from a magazine's annual design meeting with memories of a lovely textural pattern from the editor's inspiring slide show. After diving into stitch reference books to figure out where to start, Barbara Walker's Treasuries provided the tools I needed. Twisted stitches were what I needed to build the pattern I was remembering, or what the pattern had turned into in my head. I tested the several ways of making twisted stitches suggested, and the author's favorites became my favorite methods as well. I used these exact ways of forming right and left twists for several decades, only recently adjusting my left twist to more exactly match the right twist (see page 11). Putting my new skills to good use, I began by inventing loads of patterns with twisted stitches. I found it so much fun to rearrange a few simple elements— knit, purl, right twist, and left twist—into new-to-me formations. A few years later my interests broadened to include cables. I credit this early dive into inventing twisted stitches with my love of making up cables and the eventual publication of *Norah Gaughan's Knitted Cable Sourcebook*. While I've incorporated twisted stitches in my work now and again over my career, I recently renewed my devotion to these stitches.

So, just what are twisted stitches? Knitting terms often have different meanings in different circumstances. For instance, the term *twisted stitch* has a few common meanings. When you knit or purl through the back loop of a stitch, that makes a twisted stitch, but not the kind of twisted stitch this book is about. In this book, twisted stitches are two stitches that change places with each other, much like a cable, but worked entirely on the needles in a special way, by working two stitches

together and one of them on its own. While the look is very similar to a cable, these stitches stand out from the fabric in high relief, much more than if the switching of places was worked like a cable, with one stitch held in the front or back while the other stitch is being worked.

Why do I love twisted stitches? As much as I adore cables, it is very satisfying to be able to knit elaborate-looking surface patterns without the interruption of placing stitches on a cable needle or performing the machinations of working a cable without a cable needle. I am intrigued by how much a few simple motions can do. On a very basic level, stacking twists on top of each other makes mini cables, and lining them up makes diagonals, slanting either to the right or left. Combining either or both of these things with knits and purls opens up infinite possibilities.

This book is divided into three parts: "Stitches," "Garments," and "Designing Your Own." Part I, "Stitches," contains 130 stitches, most of which are newly invented and some that are fundamental basics. The number of stitches is actually higher. I cheated a bit in Chapter 3 and knit related small columns in swatches together. The first two stitch chapters, 2 and 3, contain stitches built entirely of diagonal lines. Often, the stitches are shown in a series, with different fills and background stitches aiding in the evolution of one stitch into the next. The next three chapters are defined by the addition of horizontal and vertical elements and then a combination of them all. Next, eyelets and twists worked on the wrong side add further complications. Finally, in the last stitch chapter, repeating triangles of pattern form hexagons, which look as if you were peering into a kaleidoscope.

The second part of this book, Part II: "Garments," contains fifteen knitting patterns: twelve sweaters, two scarves, and a hat and mitt set. The sweaters are written in a full range of nine sizes, to fit chests 30–62"

(76–157.5 cm). Size inclusivity has long been a pet issue for me. The societal pressure to be thin took its toll on me when I was younger, and I am now very happy that wonderful clothing can be found in a much wider range of sizes than ever before.

I also believe it's important for knitters to be able to express themselves with the pieces they knit and wear. Included at the end of each pattern is information on how to switch out the stitches designated for a pattern, replacing them with stitches of your choosing. To make substituting stitches easier, I measured each swatch in the book to see how much the gauge differed from Stockinette knit with the same yarn and needles. Each stitch pattern is labeled with a number indicating how wide that stitch is compared with Stockinette. I call it the Percentage of Stockinette Stitch, or PSS. Many of the garments are very easy to customize using this information. Making changes like these is the first step to designing. Who knows where it might lead?

Part III: "Design Your Own" is a guide for those interested in making up their own new twisted stitch patterns. I talk about how to get started by finding inspiration, and how every new design is built upon those that came in the past. Some helpful tools included are knitter's proportioned graph paper and diagonal grids to help with planning out new stitch patterns. A series of ten lessons range from the basics of pattern design to details pertaining specifically to twisted stitches.

A WORD ABOUT RIGHTS AND DESIGNER USE

The stitch designs in this book are meant to be used by knitwear designers. Feel free to incorporate the stitches in your own work, and feel free to make your own variations. That's how progress happens. That's what the book is for. However, you are not permitted, by law, to use any of the artwork, photos, or charts in anything you sell. Designers must make their own charts and use their own artwork and photos.

As I mentioned in my *Cable Sourcebook*, to my mind, there can be no such thing as an all-encompassing encyclopedia of any type of stitch. This collection of twisted stitches is just a beginning, a jumping-off point for making new discoveries. It is an exciting adventure to which I welcome you.

CHAPTER 1

Essentials

Twisted stitches are easily accomplished. It's amazing how
a few simple actions can create so many different patterns.
Before you get started, it's important to know some essentials,
like choosing yarn, reading charts, and working the twists
themselves, whether you are standard or a combination knitter.

BASICS

Choosing Yarn

My favorite yarns for knitting twisted stitches are made of wool and wool blends; in particular, those with a smooth, round construction. Those of you who prefer to avoid wool or animal products can find some very nice cotton/acrylic or acrylic/nylon blends that are bouncy and light, great qualities for twisted stitches. Whatever the fiber, 3-ply, 4-ply, and multi-ply constructions tend to be round and springy and really show off the mini cables and diagonal lines, the building blocks of all twisted stitch patterns. I tend to avoid 2-ply yarns when I'm working with twisted stitches, because the results are pebbly and the extra texture doesn't enhance these pattern stitches. However, single-ply or roving yarns can also be great choices. When it comes to color, solid shades are best. Semisolids can also work well, but too much color contrast within the yarn fights with the twisted stitches for visual dominance, and neither wins.

The multi-plied yarns I used for the swatches are among my very favorites. I chose them because of how well they showed off the multitude of stitches in each chapter.

+ Chapter 2: Valley Yarns Wachusett, a lovely, soft, round blend of wool and cashmere in worsted weight
+ Chapters 3 and 9: Rowan Alpaca Soft DK, a multi-plied blend of wool and alpaca in a traditional twist
+ Chapters 4 and 5: Brooklyn Tweed Arbor, a DK weight 3-ply of springy American Targhee wool
+ Chapter 6: Kelbourne Woolens Germantown, a revival of a style of yarn first spun in the 1800s, worsted weight and multi-plied
+ Chapter 7: Quince & Co. Chickadee, a 3-ply yarn spun from soft American wool
+ Chapter 8: Brooklyn Tweed Peerie, a fingering-weight 4-ply made with American-grown Merino wool

While choosing yarns for the garments, I widened the field of possibilities and was more adventurous. The chunky-weight single-ply Quince & Co. Puffin, used in Grandpops (page 188), creates large, well-defined twisted stitches, resulting in a pattern of geometric flowers so grand that it boldly sprawls across the surface of the cardigan. Jill Draper Makes Stuff Valkill, used in the Cropped Cardi (page 202), is another single-ply yarn. Valkill is hand dyed in a relatively high-contrast semisolid, with a variety of shades of the same hue. The contrast of dark and light pushed my limits, but I think it works because of the great definition this yarn gives to the pattern stitch. Another semisolid, Neighborhood Fiber Co. Studio DK, knit into the Hat & Mitts (page 212), is more subtle and doesn't interfere with the stitch pattern at all, only enhances it.

I've been mentioning plies a lot, but not all yarns are plied. Rowan Softyak DK is a ribbon, made in a knitted tube, which works up beautifully in the Deep Yoke Pullover (page 177). As far as other color variation goes, there is no need to shy away from tweeds and heathers. As seen in the Infinity Cowl (page 172), the heathered shade of Berroco Ultra Wool adds some interest but doesn't detract from the pattern stitch. While I'd avoid extra texture, a soft halo isn't a quality to be afraid of. Blue Sky Fibers Eco-Cashmere (Michelle Sleeveless, page 198), mYak Baby Yak (Hexagon Pullover, page 242), and Quince & Co. Crane (Romantic Pullover, page 195) all have a soft halo, especially after being washed. The lightly fuzzy surface doesn't interfere with the pattern at all. While I can tell you which yarns I like best and give you a few hints about what qualities to avoid, the best advice I can give is to swatch and swatch some more. Try several yarns, and test out a few needle sizes for each yarn. I've found that with twisted stitches, a firm tension is better than a fabric that is too loose.

Don't skip blocking your swatch. If you think the fabric looks a little loose and open, which can happen with twisted stitches, washing may allow the yarn to bloom and transform your swatch into the fabric you were looking for. Blocking can really improve the look of your finished piece and may change the gauge a bit, depending on your yarn. Remember to block your swatch the way the garment will be treated in use. Most knit garments will be hand washed; some, machine washed. My favorite method of blocking is steaming, using the kind of garment steamer that has a reservoir of water and a stand for the wand. The result is similar to wet blocking for many yarns, but special care needs to be taken when working with superwash and other shrink-resistant yarns, because they will loosen up and stretch when wet, while more rustic fibers will bloom and become more full when wet blocked, neither of which can be duplicated with steaming.

Working Twisted Stitches

Are you a combination knitter or a standard knitter? The instructions for working RT and LT are different depending on how you knit. Some continental knitters (or pickers) purl in a particularly efficient way, resulting in their stitches being seated from back to front after working a purl row. In every Twisted Stitch class I teach, one or two knitters newly discover that they are combination knitters. For our purposes here, we'll call all non-combination knitters *standard knitters*. Are you a combination knitter? If you knit using the English method, also called throwing, you can skip this section. You are not a combination knitter. If you use the continental method, or picking, you may or may not be a combination knitter. To find out, start knitting in Stockinette stitch. Work a purl row, then turn your work over, ready to start your knit row. Are the stitches on your nonworking needle starting in the back right and coming over the needle to the front left? You are a combination knitter. Are the stitches on your nonworking needle starting in the front right and going over the needle to the back left? You are a standard knitter.

RT AND LT INSTRUCTIONS FOR STANDARD KNITTERS

To work a right twist (RT) on right-side rows: K2tog, leaving the original sts on LH needle, then knit the first st only and slip both sts from needle.

To work a left twist (LT) on right-side rows: Slip 1 st knitwise, slip a second st knitwise, slip both sts back to LH needle in their new orientation (just like for the beginning of ssk); knit into the back of the second st (approaching from the back), then knit into the back of both sts together and slip both sts from needle.

I consider working twists on wrong-side rows to be a more advanced technique, but it's really not hard to accomplish; it's just hard to see what you are doing.

RT (WS rows): Purl into the second st, leaving the original sts on LH needle, then purl into the first and second sts together and slip both sts from needle.

LT (WS rows): Slip 1 st knitwise, slip a second st knitwise, slip both sts back to LH needle in their new orientation (just like for the beginning of ssk); purl into the back of both sts together (approaching from the back), then into the back of the first st only and slip both sts from needle.

RT AND LT INSTRUCTIONS FOR COMBINATION KNITTERS

While teaching I discovered that, when it comes to combination knitting, it is confusing, maybe meaningless, to talk about slipping knitwise or purlwise on the knit rows, where the stitches are oriented from back to front. Instead, I refer to changing the orientation of a stitch. For instance, if the stitches on your needle start in the front right and go over the needle to the back, after you reorient them, the stitches will start in the back right and come over the needle to the front.

Combination RT (RS rows): Reverse the orientation of the next 2 sts. K2tog, leaving the original sts on LH needle, then knit the first st only and slip both sts from needle.

Combination LT (RS rows): Knit into the back of the second st (approaching from the back), then knit into

the back of both sts together and slip both sts from needle.

The instructions for working RT and LT on wrong-side rows is the same for combination knitters and standard knitters. I am repeating the definitions here for easy reference.

RT (WS rows): Purl into the second st, leaving the original sts on LH needle, then purl into the first and second sts together and slip both sts from needle.

LT (WS rows): Reverse the orientation of the next 2 sts; purl into the back of both sts together (approaching from the back), then into the back of the first st only and slip both sts from needle.

TROUBLESHOOTING YOUR TWISTS

Before I tell you how to fix problems and mistakes, I'd like to ask you not to be too much of a perfectionist. Look closely and you'll notice that, on all the swatches in this book, most of which were knit by me, the left-slanting lines and the right-slanting lines are not identical. My left slants tend to be smoother than my right slants. On right slants, my stitches tend to alternate larger and smaller, making the right-slanting line bumpier compared with the smoother left-slanting lines. I ignore this. My knitting is good enough. If you examine your work too closely, something will always seem wrong. I prefer enjoying knitting to figuring out the causes of small imperfections.

However, there are a few things to watch out for that can be easily corrected. It's important that the right slants and left slants appear to lift up from the fabric about the same amount. In classes where I'm teaching twisted stitches, I have worked with some knitters whose left twists barely lift from the fabric and are not nearly as evident as their right slants. If this is true for you, try working farther from the tip of your left needle and make larger motions when pulling your yarn through to make a new loop. In some cases, you may want to work the left twist the way I did, quite happily, for twenty years, without reorienting the stitches before working the twist:

Alternate LT for standard knitters (RS rows): Knit into the back of the second st (approaching from the back), then knit into the back of both sts together and slip both sts from needle. Alternate RT for combination knitters (RS rows): K2tog, leaving the original sts on left-hand needle, then knit the first st only and slip both sts from needle.

I had trouble getting my left twist to lift from the surface when I was knitting the swatch for #43, Chevron (see above), and had better results when I used this method. If you look very carefully, you can see that the legs of the stitches on the left slant are crossed over each other (twisted in the other sense) every other row. For combination knitters, this problem is more likely to happen with their right twist, and the solution is the same, omitting the reorientation of the stitches before working the twist.

ABOUT PSS

I wanted there to be a way for knitters to customize the knitting patterns in this book by changing the stitches. This would be fairly easy if all twisted-stitch patterns had the same gauge, but some pull in more than others.

Those with a higher concentration of twists, and the stitches that incorporate a lot of ribbing, pull in the most. Almost all of them have a tighter gauge than Stockinette stitch when knit in the same yarn with the same size needles. I thought a clear way to note the difference in size, regardless of yarn weight, would be to show how big that stitch would be compared with the same number of stitches in Stockinette stitch. First, I determined the Stockinette stitch gauge of yarn used for each chapter knit on the same needles used to knit all the swatches. Then, I measured the pattern portion of each swatch, or a wide pattern repeat within a swatch, and took note of how many stitches made up that width. I calculated how wide that number of Stockinette stitches would be, and I divided the width of the twisted stitches by the width of the Stockinette stitches to see what percentage the twisted stitches pull in.

For example, for Zirconia (#10), 40 stitches = 6.75" (17 cm). My Stockinette gauge with the same yarn and needles is 5.5 stitches to 1" (2.5 cm), so 40 sts = 7.27" in Stockinette stitch. I divided 6.75 by 7.27, which = .92. So, Zirconia pulls in the width of approximately 90 percent of the Stockinette-stitch gauge. I rounded up and down to the closest 5 percent.

You can easily substitute stitches with the same Percentage of Stockinette Stitch (PSS). If the PSS is off by 5, your garment will be off by that 5 percent around the chest, which is close enough for loads of folks, but not for the most exacting personalities. To give you an idea, if the entire surface of a 44" (112 cm)–chest sweater is worked in a twisted-stitch pattern, and the new stitch is 5 percent smaller than the original, the new chest measurement would be about 42" (106.5 cm). If it were 5 percent larger, the new chest measurement would be about 46" (117 cm). To help you make substitutions specific to each garment pattern, you'll find notes about substitution and some suggestions at the end of each pattern.

FIXING MISTAKES

There are several reasons you might want to drop down a row to fix a small mistake. Although I tried to keep it to a minimum, some patterns introduce reverse Stockinette stitch on wrong-side rows. It is very easy to forget to work those stitches, and most often you'll discover the mistake when you get to that spot on the next row. It is definitely worth learning to drop one stitch down a row in order to rework it, and it is still worth it to drop a couple of stitches for a couple of rows. Try it. You have nothing to lose, since the other option is ripping clear back to your mistake.

I don't recommend dropping down to change a large number of twisted stitches to Stockinette or vice versa. The twists take up more yarn than Stockinette stitch does, so if you drop down to change twisted stitches to Stockinette, your stitches will grow sloppy as they take up the extra yarn. If you drop down to change stitches from Stockinette to twist, you won't have enough yarn and the new twists will be tight. I've learned this from experience.

WORKING FROM CHARTS

If you are what I call a spreadsheet thinker, your ideal pattern is written out row by row. When you're done with a row, you cross it off on your pattern. When instructions aren't detailed enough for you, you make a spreadsheet, or even write out each row yourself.

If you are what I call a chart thinker, you like to see a visual representation of what you are creating. Following a symbol that looks like the cable you are knitting is much easier for you than reading words that describe each action.

I almost always prefer to work from charts rather than row-by-row instructions, especially when working twisted stitches or cables. When using a chart, if you put your knitting down and come back later, it is much easier to see where you are in the pattern than if you are following written instructions, because you can compare your knitted fabric with the chart. When following written instructions, you can make a mark on the instructions that tells you where you are leaving off, but, in practice, I have found that many knitters with the best of intentions don't succeed at doing this consistently and then struggle to figure out where they are in the pattern.

Charts make it so much easier than written instructions to figure out if you have made a mistake and how far you have to rip, or drop down, to fix it. Just look at your knitting and compare it with the chart. Since twisted-stitch chart symbols are designed to look like the twisted stitches themselves, once you get used to them, you can decipher them at a glance.

As hard as we might try, designers do make mistakes, and even after the technical editor and proofreader have gone over a pattern with their discerning eyes, sometimes mistakes make it into print. But once you start knitting, if you see the mistake in your knitting, by looking at the chart, you'll likely be able to figure out what to do to correct it because you'll be able to discern what was intended.

Compared with working from written words, it is much easier to understand how to decrease or increase in a twisted-stitch pattern when working from a chart. Whereas written instructions may tell you to "work in pattern" and leave it up to you to understand what that means, charted instructions provide visual clues because you can easily see what came before and what comes after.

Once you understand the basics, reading a chart becomes second nature. Here are some general guidelines:

+ The chart is drawn to represent how your knitting will appear when you're looking at the right side of the fabric, the side that will be on the outside. All of the symbols represent how the stitches look on the right side.

+ One square on a chart represents one stitch.

+ Right-side rows are worked from right to left on the chart. Wrong-side rows are worked from left to right on the chart.

+ The row number is placed on the chart where you will begin the row. Right-side rows have the numbers along the right edge of the chart, and wrong-side rows have the numbers along the left edge of the chart.

+ Imagine labeling everything as if you are seeing it from the right (or public) side of your work. Picture those labels pinned to your knitting. Once the right-side row is complete, you'll need to turn the piece over to work on the wrong side. The yarn is now on the edge you have labeled as the left-hand edge. You are working from your right to your left, as always, but since you are on the back of the knitted piece,

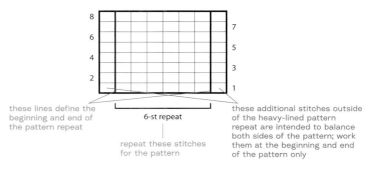

the row is worked from the edge labeled "left" to the edge labeled "right." The chart is also worked the way the piece is labeled, from left to right. If you are having trouble wrapping your mind around this, don't worry. Sometimes a full understanding of the concept comes after you've been knitting for a while.

+ The chart key may give one definition for right-side rows and another for wrong-side rows. Because the symbols on the chart represent how the fabric will appear when looking at the right side, you must do the opposite on a wrong-side row. For instance, a knit stitch is represented as an empty box on the right side. When you see an empty box while working a wrong-side row, you purl it, because when you purl on the wrong side, it will look like a knit on the right side. This is clearly defined in the key as "knit on the RS" and "purl on the WS."

+ If you are working in the round, your round always begins on the right. The charts in this book can all be worked in the round, and the keys have been written with that in mind. (Note that the text has been written for working back and forth in rows, not in the round; if you wish to work in the round, you will need to work from the charts.) If you see a symbol with an explanation for working both on the wrong side and on the right side, but the symbol is placed on a wrong-side row, work that symbol following the directions for working on a right-side row, since if you are working in the round, there are no wrong-side rows.

It's fine to make a photocopy of the chart you are working on for your personal use (but not for distribution).

+ Enlarge the chart when you photocopy it if your vision isn't great. Sometimes it is necessary to photocopy the chart in two pieces if it is long; just make sure that you don't leave out any rows when you do so. For a chart that is really wide, it might help to photocopy each half of the chart, then cut and paste the halves into one full chart so that you can read across the rows without having to consult two separate sheets; again, be sure you're not missing any stitches in the center.

+ A magnet board, highlighter tape, washi tape, or a large sticky note placed above the row you're working on brings your eye right where you want it to be and makes referencing the chart much easier. However, if placing it below works better for you, that's fine, too. The one disadvantage to placing it below your current row is that you'll be obscuring the previous row, which you may need to refer to while you are working. Place a photocopy of the chart in a plastic sleeve if you plan to use any kind of adhesive tape as a row marker. That way you won't risk marring the original printed page.

SYMBOLS

The symbols in this book were designed to tell you as much as possible at a glance about the twisted stitches, fills, and background textures that you are about to work. They are based on standard symbols generally used within the knitting community. To help guide your eye, the symbols have been color-coded. This key contains all the symbols used in this book. Refer back to this key for every chart.

Knit on RS, purl on WS.

Purl on RS, knit on WS.

K1-tbl on RS, p1-tbl on WS.

MB: (K1, k1-tbl, k1, k1-tbl, k1) into one st, slip the 5 sts back to left-hand needle; k5, slip the 5 sts back to left-hand needle; k5, slip the right-most 4 sts over the left-most st.

Yarnover

K2tog on RS, p2tog on WS.

Ssk on RS, ssp on WS.

P2tog on RS, k2tog on WS.

P3tog on RS, k3tog on WS.

RT (RS rows): K2tog leaving the original sts on LH needle, then knit the first st only and slip both sts from needle. (See pages 10–11 for combination knitters.)

RT (WS rows): Purl into the second st leaving the original sts on LH needle, then purl into the first and second sts together and slip both sts from needle. (See pages 10–11 for combination knitters.)

LT (RS rows): Slip 1 st knitwise, slip a second st knitwise, slip both sts back to LH needle in their new orientation (just like for the beginning of ssk); knit into the back of the second st (approaching from the back), then knit into the back of both sts together and slip both sts from needle. (See pages 10–11 for combination knitters.)

LT (WS rows): Slip 1 st knitwise, slip a second st knitwise, slip both sts back to LH needle in their new orientation (just like for the beginning of ssk); purl into the back of both sts together (approaching from the back), then into the back of the first st only and slip both sts from needle. (See pages 10–11 for combination knitters.)

EDGES AND DECREASING IN PATTERN

When knitting flat, I like to have at least one Stockinette stitch at the edge, making sewing pieces together much neater and easier. If you find yourself decreasing into the pattern stitch, keep the edge stitch in Stockinette, and when you can't work a whole twist, work the remaining stitch as knit.

WORKING IN THE ROUND

With the exception of the charts in chapter 9, which are intended to be worked in the round, almost all the charts in this book are written to be worked flat. They are easy to work in the round as well, if there are no stitches before and after the repeating stitches. Here is an example:

If there are stitches before and after the repeating stitches, omit those stitches outside of the repeat, and work only those within the repeat. In the example, Plaid Small, to knit in the round, cast on a multiple of 12 stitches, start knitting with the second stitch, and keep knitting the 12-stitch repeat, never working that first stitch that's outside of the repeat.

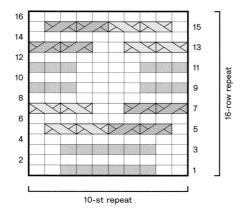

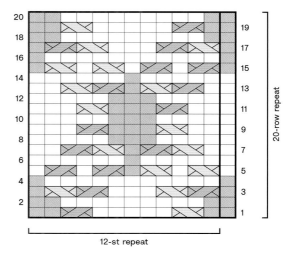

PART I

STITCHES

This is the core of this book: 126 twisted-stitch patterns, organized into eight chapters, opening with stitch designs made solely with diagonal lines, increasing in complexity with the addition of horizontal elements and then verticals before combining them all. The subsequent chapters explore further, using lace stitches in tandem with twists and then, breaking new territory for me, twists worked every row. The final chapter sees a return to my long-standing love of the kaleidoscopic magic made by placing patterns into hexagons.

Diagonal

In this chapter, I begin to explore the variety of forms possible using the diagonal lines created with right and left twists. Slashes, triangles, pyramids, and diamonds are refined, expanded upon, and sometimes combined. Many more stitch patterns explore the illusion of weaving created by alternating right- and left-leaning forms with many variations. It's amazing how much a diagonal line can do.

① Diamond

This solitary diamond motif can be placed strategically, strewn randomly, or repeated in a grid, as you like. See Chapter 11, Lesson 8, page 267, for some pattern placement ideas.

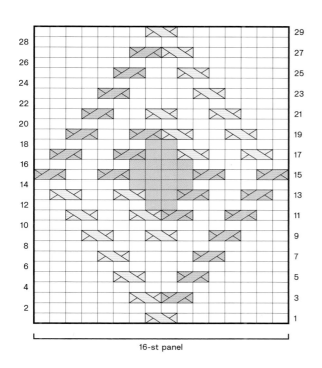

16-st panel

(16-st panel; 29 rows)

PSS: 90

ROW 1 (RS): K7, LT, k7.

ROWS 2, 4, 6, 8, AND 10: Purl.

ROW 3: K6, RT, LT, k6.

ROW 5: K5, RT, k2, LT, k5.

ROW 7: K4, RT, k4, LT, k4.

ROW 9: K3, RT, [k2, LT] twice, k3.

ROW 11: [K2, RT] twice, [LT, k2] twice.

ROW 12: P7, k2, p7.

ROW 13: K1, RT, k2, RT, p2, LT, k2, LT, k1.

ROW 14: P6, k4, p6.

ROW 15: RT, k2, RT, p4, RT, k2, RT.

ROW 16: Repeat Row 14.

ROW 17: K1, LT, k2, LT, p2, RT, k2, RT, k1.

ROW 18: Repeat Row 12.

ROW 19: [K2, LT] twice, [RT, k2] twice.

ROWS 20, 22, 24, 26, AND 28: Purl.

ROW 21: K3, [LT, k2] twice, RT, k3.

ROW 23: K4, LT, k4, RT, k4.

ROW 25: K5, LT, k2, RT, k5.

ROW 27: K6, LT, RT, k6.

ROW 29: Repeat Row 1.

② Diamond Filled

This motif starts out identical to the previous pattern, Diamond (#1). Perfect two-stitch spacing between the lines allows room for filling the void with one more twist. In this case, the fill twists are worked perpendicular to the lines of the diamond, leaving a mini diamond in each corner.

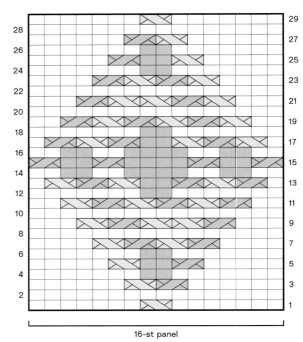

16-st panel

(16-st panel; 29 rows)

PSS: 80

ROW 1 (RS): K7, LT, k7.

ROW 2: Purl.

ROW 3: K6, RT, LT, k6.

ROW 4: P7, k2, p7.

ROW 5: K5, RT, p2, LT, k5.

ROW 6: Repeat Row 4.

ROW 7: K4, [RT, LT] twice, k4.

ROW 8: Purl.

ROW 9: K3, RT, LT twice, RT, LT, k3.

ROW 10: Purl.

ROW 11: K2, [RT, LT] 3 times, k2.

ROW 12: Repeat Row 4.

ROW 13: K1, RT, LT, RT, p2, LT, RT, LT, k1.

ROW 14: P2, k2, p2, k4, p2, k2, p2.

ROW 15: RT, p2, RT, p4, RT, p2, RT.

ROW 16: Repeat Row 14.

ROW 17: K1, LT, RT, LT, p2, RT, LT, RT, k1.

ROW 18: Repeat Row 4.

ROW 19: K2, [LT, RT] 3 times, k2.

ROW 20: Purl.

ROW 21: K3, LT, RT, LT twice, RT, k3.

ROW 22: Purl.

ROW 23: K4, [LT, RT] twice, k4.

ROW 24: Repeat Row 4.

ROW 25: K5, LT, p2, RT, k5.

ROW 26: Repeat Row 4.

ROW 27: K6, LT, RT, k6.

ROW 28: Purl.

ROW 29: Repeat Row 1.

③ Double Diamond

Two diamonds are stacked, overlapping, on top of each other, the second one beginning before the first has ended. Work the chart as shown in the swatch or repeat the center section to add more diamonds between the points.

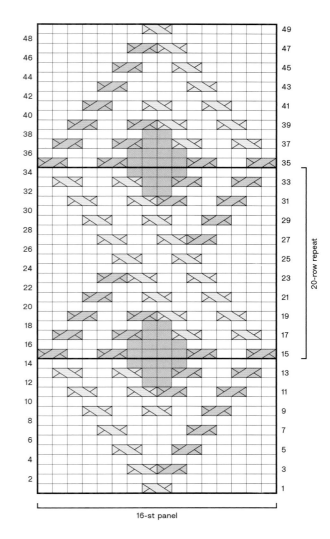

16-st panel

(16-st panel; 20-row repeat)

PSS: 90

ROW 1 (RS): K7, LT, k7.

ROW 2 AND ALL WS ROWS THROUGH ROW 10: Purl.

ROW 3: K6, RT, LT, k6.

ROW 5: K5, RT, k2, LT, k5.

ROW 7: K4, RT, k4, LT, k4.

ROW 9: K3, RT, [k2, LT] twice, k3.

ROW 11: [K2, RT] twice, [LT, k2] twice.

ROW 12: P7, k2, p7.

ROW 13: K1, RT, k2, RT, p2, LT, k2, LT, k1.

ROW 14: P6, k4, p6.

ROW 15: RT, k2, RT, p4, RT, k2, RT.

ROW 16: P6, k4, p6.

ROW 17: K1, LT, k2, LT, p2, RT, k2, RT, k1.

ROW 18: P7, k2, p7.

ROW 19: [K2, LT] twice, [RT, k2] twice.

ROWS 20, 22, 24, 26, 28, AND 30: Purl.

ROW 21: K3, [LT, k2] twice, RT, k3.

ROW 23: K4, LT, k2, LT, RT, k4.

ROW 25: K5, LT, k2, LT, k5.

ROW 27: K4, RT, LT, k2, LT, k4.

ROW 29: K3, RT, [k2, LT] twice, k3.

ROW 31: [K2, RT] twice, [LT, k2] twice.

ROW 32: Repeat Row 18.

ROW 33: K1, RT, k2, RT, p2, LT, k2, LT, k1.

ROW 34: Repeat Row 16.

Repeat Rows 15–34 as desired.

ROWS 35–42: Repeat Rows 15–22.

ROW 43: K4, LT, k4, RT, k4.

ROW 44: Purl.

ROW 45: K5, LT, k2, RT, k5.

ROW 46: Purl.

ROW 47: K6, LT, RT, k6.

ROW 48: Purl.

ROW 49: K7, LT, k7.

④ Double Diamond Filled

Fill the previous pattern stitch, Double Diamond (#3), with perpendicular twists to form a more ornate motif. You can work the chart as shown in the swatch, or repeat the center section to add more diamonds between the points.

(16-st panel; 20-row repeat)

PSS: 80

ROW 1 (RS): K7, LT, k7.

ROW 2: Purl.

ROW 3: K6, RT, LT, k6.

ROW 4: P7, k2, p7.

ROW 5: K5, RT, p2, LT, k5.

ROW 6: Repeat Row 4.

ROW 7: K4, [RT, LT] twice, k4.

ROW 8: Purl.

ROW 9: K3, RT, LT twice, RT, LT, k3.

ROW 10: Purl.

ROW 11: K2, [RT, LT] 3 times, k2.

ROW 12: Repeat Row 4.

ROW 13: K1, RT, LT, RT, p2, LT, RT, LT, k1.

ROW 14: P2, k2, p2, k4, p2, k2, p2.

ROW 15: RT, p2, RT, p4, RT, p2, RT.

ROW 16: P2, k2, p2, k4, p2, k2, p2.

ROW 17: K1, LT, RT, LT, p2, RT, LT, RT, k1.

ROW 18: P7, k2, p7.

ROW 19: K2, [LT, RT] 3 times, k2.

ROW 20: Purl.

ROW 21: K3, LT, RT, LT twice, RT, k3.

ROW 22: Purl.

ROW 23: K4, [LT, RT] twice, k4.

ROW 24: Repeat Row 18.

ROW 25: K5, LT, p2, LT, k5.

ROW 26: Repeat Row 18.

ROW 27: K4, [RT, LT] twice, k4.

ROW 28: Purl.

ROW 29: K3, RT, LT twice, RT, LT, k3.

ROW 30: Purl.

ROW 31: K2, [RT, LT] 3 times, k2.

ROW 32: Repeat Row 18.

ROW 33: K1, RT, LT, RT, p2, LT, RT, LT, k1.

ROW 34: Repeat Row 16.

Repeat Rows 15–34 as desired.

ROWS 35–44: Repeat Rows 15–24.

ROW 45: K5, LT, p2, RT, k5.

ROW 46: Repeat Row 18.

ROW 47: K6, LT, RT, k6.

ROW 48: Purl.

ROW 49: K7, LT, k7.

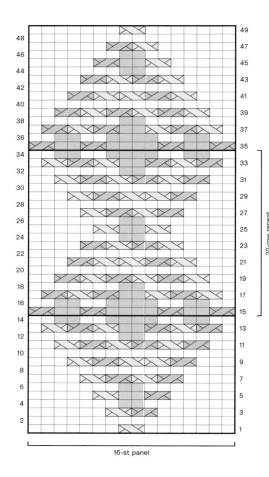

16-st panel

20-row repeat

⑤ Diamonds Allover

An allover variation of Double Diamond (#3) made into columns nestled together. The space between the columns is filled with perpendicular twists, solidifying the pattern and making it easier to pick out the diamonds with your eye.

(multiple of 26 sts + 2; 20-row repeat)

PSS: 85

ROW 1 (RS): K1, *LT, k2, LT, RT, LT, k2, LT, k2, RT, LT, RT, k2, RT; repeat from * to last st, k1.

ROW 2: K2, *p24, k2; repeat from * to end.

ROW 3: P2, *LT, k2, LT, RT, LT, k2, [LT, RT] twice, k2, RT, p2; repeat from * to end.

ROW 4: K3, p22, *k4, p22; repeat from * to last 3 sts, k3.

ROW 5: *P3, RT, k2, RT, LT twice, k2, LT 3 times, k2, RT, p1; repeat from * to last 2 sts, p2.

ROW 6: Repeat Row 4.

ROW 7: P2, *RT, k2, [RT, LT] twice, k2, LT, RT, LT, k2, LT, p2; repeat from * to end.

ROW 8: Repeat Row 2.

ROW 9: K1, *RT, k2, RT, LT, RT, [k2, LT] twice, RT, LT, k2, LT; repeat from * to last st, k1.

ROW 10: Purl.

ROW 11: LT; *k2, RT, LT, RT, k2, RT, LT, k2, LT, RT, LT, k2, LT; repeat from * to end.

ROW 12: P13, k2, *p24, k2; repeat from * to last 13 sts, purl to end.

ROW 13: K1, *[LT, RT] twice, k2, RT, p2, LT, k2, LT, RT, LT, k2; repeat from * to last st, k1.

ROW 14: P12, k4, *p22, k4; repeat from * to last 12 sts, purl to end.

ROW 15: K2, *LT 3 times, k2, LT, p4, RT, k2, RT, LT twice, k2; repeat from * to end.

ROW 16: Repeat Row 14.

ROW 17: K1, *k2, LT, RT, LT, k2, LT, p2, RT, k2, [RT, LT] twice; repeat from * to last st, k1.

ROW 18: Repeat Row 12.

ROW 19: LT, *k2, LT, RT, LT, k2, LT, RT, k2, RT, LT, RT, k2, LT; repeat from * to end.

ROW 20: Purl.

Repeat Rows 1–20 for pattern.

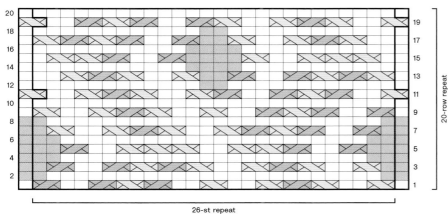

26-st repeat

20-row repeat

⑥ Stack

This elongated motif gives the appearance of three diamonds stacked on top of one another. Reverse Stockinette is introduced in the background and center, bringing some extra clarity to the details.

(14-st panel; 39 rows)

PSS: 95

ROW 1 (RS): K6, RT, k6.

ROW 2 AND ALL WS ROWS THROUGH ROW 10: Purl.

ROW 3: K5, RT, LT, k5.

ROW 5: K4, RT, k2, LT, k4.

ROW 7: K3, [RT, k1] twice, LT, k3.

ROW 9: K2, RT, k1, RT, LT, k1, LT, k2.

ROW 11: P1, RT, k1, RT, k2, LT, k1, LT, p1.

ROW 12: Knit the knit sts and purl the purl sts as they face you.

ROW 13: P1, LT, [RT, k1] twice, LT, RT, p1.

ROW 14: K2, p10, k2.

ROW 15: P2, RT, k1, RT, LT, k1, LT, p2.

ROW 16: Repeat Row 12.

ROW 17: P1, RT, k1, RT, p2, LT, k1, LT, p1.

ROW 18: Repeat Row 12.

ROW 19: RT, k1, RT, p4, LT, k1, LT.

ROW 20: P4, k6, p4.

ROW 21: LT, k1, LT, p4, RT, k1, RT.

ROW 22: Repeat Row 12.

ROW 23: P1, LT, k1, LT, p2, RT, k1, RT, p1.

ROW 24: Repeat Row 14.

ROW 25: P2, LT, k1, LT, RT, k1, RT, p2.

ROW 26: Repeat Row 12.

ROW 27: P1, RT, LT, [k1, RT] twice, LT, p1.

ROW 28: Repeat Row 12.

ROW 29: [K1, LT] twice, k2, [RT, k1] twice.

ROWS 30, 32, 34, 36, AND 38: Purl.

ROW 31: K2, LT, k1, LT, RT, k1, RT, k2.

ROW 33: K3, LT, [k1, RT] twice, k3.

ROW 35: K4, LT, k2, RT, k4.

ROW 37: K5, LT, RT, k5.

ROW 39: K6, RT, k6.

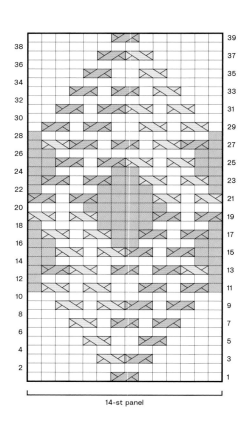

14-st panel

(7) Pyramids Overlap

Pyramids composed of ever-increasing diagonal lines are placed in a compressed checkerboard formation. See Chapter 11, Lesson 9, page 268, for an illustration and discussion of the thought process behind bringing the motifs closer together, rather than leaving them placed farther apart.

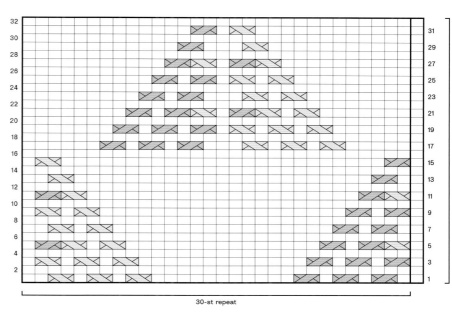

30-st repeat

32-row repeat

(multiple of 30 sts + 1; 32-row repeat)

PSS: 90

ROW 1 (RS): K1, *[k1, RT] 3 times, k11, LT, [k1, LT] twice, k2; repeat from * to end.

ROW 2 AND ALL WS ROWS: Purl.

ROW 3: K1, *RT, [k1, RT] twice, k13, [LT, k1] 3 times; repeat from * to end.

ROW 5: K1, *LT, RT, k1, RT, k15, LT, k1, LT, RT, k1; repeat from * to end.

ROW 7: K1, *[k1, RT] twice, k17, LT, k1, LT, k2; repeat from * to end.

ROW 9: K1, *RT, k1, RT, k19, [LT, k1] twice; repeat from * to end.

ROW 11: K1, *LT, RT, k21, LT, RT, k1; repeat from * to end.

ROW 13: K1, *k1, RT, k23, LT, k2; repeat from * to end.

ROW 15: K1, *RT, k25, LT, k1; repeat from * to end.

ROW 17: K6, LT, [k1, LT] twice, k3, RT, [k1, RT] twice, *k11, LT, [k1, LT] twice, k3, RT, [k1, RT] twice; repeat from * to last 6 sts, knit to end.

ROW 19: K7, LT, [k1, LT] twice, [k1, RT] 3 times, *k13, LT, [k1, LT] twice, [k1, RT] 3 times; repeat from * to last 7 sts, knit to end.

ROW 21: K8, LT, k1, LT, RT, k1, LT, RT, k1, RT, *k15, LT, k1, LT, RT, k1, LT, RT, k1, RT; repeat from * to last 8 sts, knit to end.

ROW 23: K9, LT, k1, LT, k3, RT, k1, RT, *k17, LT, k1, LT, k3, RT, k1, RT; repeat from * to last 9 sts, knit to end.

ROW 25: K10, [LT, k1] twice, RT, k1, RT, *k19, [LT, k1] twice, RT, k1, RT; repeat from * to last 10 sts, knit to end.

ROW 27: K11, LT, RT, k1, LT, RT, *k21, LT, RT, k1, LT, RT; repeat from * to last 11 sts, knit to end.

ROW 29: K12, LT, k3, RT, *k23, LT, k3, RT; repeat from * to last 12 sts, knit to end.

ROW 31: K13, LT, k1, RT, *k25, LT, k1, RT; repeat from * to last 13 sts, knit to end.

ROW 32: Purl.

Repeat Rows 1–32 for pattern.

(8) Pyramid Columns

Repeating this 16-row pattern forms a column you can use alone or in multiples. As charted, one stitch separates the pyramid columns, forming a pleasing allover pattern.

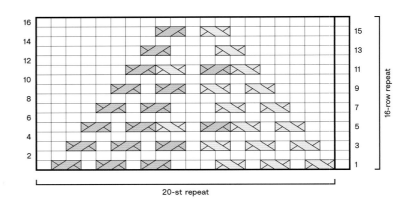

(multiple of 20 sts + 1; 16-row repeat)

PSS: 90

ROW 1 (RS): K1, *LT, [k1, LT] twice, k3, [RT, k1] 3 times; repeat from * to end.

ROW 2 AND ALL WS ROWS: Purl.

ROW 3: K2, LT, [k1, LT] twice, [k1, RT] 3 times, *k3, LT, [k1, LT] twice, [k1, RT] 3 times; repeat from * to last 2 sts, k2.

ROW 5: K3, LT, k1, [LT, RT, k1] twice, RT, *k5, LT, k1, [LT, RT, k1] twice, RT; repeat from * to last 3 sts, k3.

ROW 7: K4, LT, k1, LT, k3, RT, k1, RT, *k7, LT, k1, LT, k3, RT, k1, RT; repeat from * to last 4 sts, knit to end.

ROW 9: K5, LT, k1, LT, [k1, RT] twice, *k9, LT, k1, LT, [k1, RT] twice; repeat from * to last 5 sts, knit to end.

ROW 11: K6, LT, RT, k1, LT, RT, *k11, LT, RT, k1, LT, RT; repeat from * to last 6 sts, knit to end.

ROW 13: K7, LT, k3, RT, *k13, LT, k3, RT; repeat from * to last 7 sts, knit to end.

ROW 15: K8, LT, k1, RT, *k15, LT, k1, RT; repeat from * to last 8 sts, knit to end.

ROW 16: Purl.

Repeat Rows 1–16 for pattern.

⑨ Pyramid Half Drop

Rearrange pattern #8, Pyramid Columns, by moving every other column down half a repeat and you've got this pattern, Pyramid Half Drop. The columns are still separate, and they still have the one stitch between them, but they visually appear to nestle together and fit into each other.

(multiple of 40 sts + 1; 16-row repeat)

PSS: 90

ROW 1 (RS): K1, *k4, LT, k1, LT, [k1, RT] twice, k5, LT, [k1, LT] twice, k3, [RT, k1] 3 times; repeat from * to end.

ROW 2 AND ALL WS ROWS: Purl.

ROW 3: K1, *k5, LT, RT, k1, LT, RT, k7, LT, [k1, LT] twice, [k1, RT] 3 times, k2; repeat from * to end.

ROW 5: K1, *k6, LT, k3, RT, k9, LT, k1, LT, RT, k1, LT, RT, k1, RT, k3; repeat from * to end.

ROW 7: K1, *k7, LT, k1, RT, k11, LT, k1, LT, k3, RT, k1, RT, k4; repeat from * to end.

ROW 9: K1, *LT, [k1, LT] twice, k3, RT, [k1, RT] twice, k5, LT, k1, LT, [k1, RT] twice, k5; repeat from * to end.

ROW 11: K1, *k1, LT, [k1, LT] twice, [k1, RT] 3 times, k7, LT, RT, k1, LT, RT, k6; repeat from * to end.

ROW 13: K1, *k2, LT, k1, [LT, RT, k1] twice, RT, k9, LT, k3, RT, k7; repeat from * to end.

ROW 15: K1, *k3, LT, k1, LT, k3, RT, k1, RT, k11, LT, k1, RT, k8; repeat from * to end.

ROW 16: Purl.

Repeat Rows 1–16 for pattern.

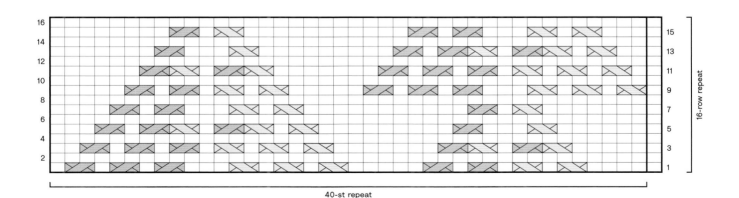

40-st repeat

16-row repeat

⑩ Zirconia

Can you see the two Pyramids in each Zirconia? Pyramids mirrored along a horizontal are transformed into large diamond shapes, playfully named Zirconia. Lesson 8, page 267, in Chapter 11 delves into how to make new multiple patterns out of a single element and its variations.

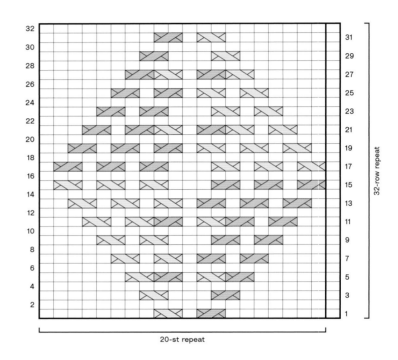

(multiple of 20 sts + 1; 32-row repeat)

PSS: 90

ROW 1 (RS): K1, *k7, RT, k1, LT, k8; repeat from * to end.

ROW 2 AND ALL WS ROWS: Purl.

ROW 3: K1, *k6, RT, k3, LT, k7; repeat from * to end.

ROW 5: K1, *k5, RT, LT, k1, RT, LT, k6; repeat from * to end.

ROW 7: K1, *k4, RT, k1, RT, [k1, LT] twice, k5; repeat from * to end.

ROW 9: K1, *k3, RT, k1, RT, k3, LT, k1, LT, k4; repeat from * to end.

ROW 11: K1, *k2, RT, k1, RT, LT, k1, RT, LT, k1, LT, k3; repeat from * to end.

ROW 13: K1, *k1, RT, [k1, RT] twice, [k1, LT] 3 times, k2; repeat from * to end.

ROW 15: K1, *RT, [k1, RT] twice, k3, [LT, k1] 3 times; repeat from * to end.

ROW 17: K1, *LT, [k1, LT] twice, k3, [RT, k1] 3 times; repeat from * to end.

ROW 19: K1, *k1, LT, [k1, LT] twice, [k1, RT] 3 times, k2; repeat from * to end.

ROW 21: K1, *k2, LT, k1, LT, RT, k1, LT, RT, k1, RT, k3; repeat from * to end.

ROW 23: K1, *k3, LT, k1, LT, k3, RT, k1, RT, k4; repeat from * to end.

ROW 25: K1, *k4, LT, k1, LT, [k1, RT] twice, k5; repeat from * to end.

ROW 27: K1, *k5, LT, RT, k1, LT, RT, k6; repeat from * to end.

ROW 29: K1, *k6, LT, k3, RT, k7; repeat from * to end.

ROW 31: K1, *k7, LT, k1, RT, k8; repeat from * to end.

ROW 32: Purl.

Repeat Rows 1–20 for pattern.

(11) Pyramid Split

The center of Pyramid Split is the column from #8, Pyramid Columns. The Pyramid motif can be easily divided into two halves, since the triangles making the sides do not intertwine. Repeat the right-hand triangle as many times as you like and do the same with the left triangle.

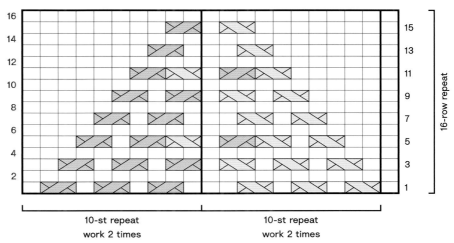

10-st repeat
work 2 times

10-st repeat
work 2 times

16-row repeat

(multiple of 10 sts in 2 separate repeats + 1; 16-row repeat)

PSS: 90

ROW 1 (RS): K1, *LT, [k1, LT] twice, k2; repeat from * once, **k1, [RT, k1] 3 times; repeat from ** once.

ROW 2 AND ALL WS ROWS: Purl.

ROW 3: K1, *k1, [LT, k1] 3 times; repeat from * once, **RT, [k1, RT] twice, k2; repeat from ** once.

ROW 5: K1, *k2, LT, k1, LT, RT, k1; repeat from * once, **LT, RT, k1, RT, k3; repeat from ** once.

ROW 7: K1, *k3, LT, k1, LT, k2; repeat from * once, **[k1, RT] twice, k4; repeat from ** once.

ROW 9: K1, *k4, [LT, k1] twice; repeat from * once, **RT, k1, RT, k5; repeat from ** once.

ROW 11: K1, *k5, LT, RT, k1; repeat from * once, **LT, RT, k6; repeat from ** once.

ROW 13: K1, *k6, LT, k2; repeat from * once, **k1, RT, k7; repeat from ** once.

ROW 15: K1, *k7, LT, k1; repeat from * once, **RT, k8; repeat from ** once.

ROW 16: Purl.

Repeat Rows 1–16 for pattern.

12) Triangle Half Drop

Splitting the Pyramid motif into two triangles opens up a whole new avenue of exploration. Stack these smaller triangles in columns and alternate with a column dropped by half a repeat to make this asymmetrical allover pattern.

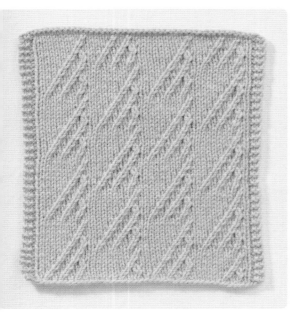

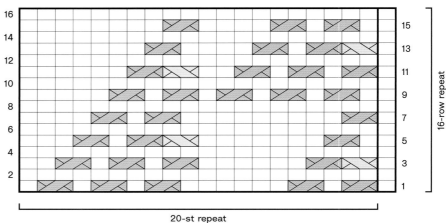

(multiple of 20 sts + 1; 16-row repeat)

PSS: 90

ROW 1 (RS): K1, *RT, k1, RT, k6, [RT, k1] 3 times; repeat from * to end.

ROW 2 AND ALL WS ROWS: Purl.

ROW 3: K1, *LT, RT, k6, RT, [k1, RT] twice, k2; repeat from * to end.

ROW 5: K2, RT, k7, LT, RT, k1, RT, *k4, RT, k7, LT, RT, k1, RT; repeat from * to last 3 sts, k3.

ROW 7: K1, *RT, k9, RT, k1, RT, k4; repeat from * to end.

ROW 9: K2, RT, [k1, RT] 4 times, *k6, RT, [k1, RT] 4 times; repeat from * to last 5 sts, knit to end.

ROW 11: K1, *RT, [k1, RT] twice, k2, LT, RT, k6; repeat from * to end.

ROW 13: K1, *RT, k1, RT, k4, RT, k7; repeat from * to end.

ROW 15: K2, RT, k1, RT, k4, RT, *k9, RT, k1, RT, k4, RT; repeat from * to last 8 sts, knit to end.

ROW 16: Purl.

Repeat Rows 1–16 for pattern.

(13) Triangle Shift

Gazing at the previous pattern, Triangle Half Drop (#12), I began to wonder what would happen if the triangles lined up, with all the longest lines forming one diagonal. The result was very pleasing, but the new pattern repeated every 80 rows, which was rather ungainly. Adding stitches between the new diagonals reduced the row repeat to a manageable 48 rows. (See Chapter 11, Lesson 10, page 269.)

(multiple of 12 sts + 3; 48-row repeat)

PSS: 95

ROW 1 (RS): *K4, RT, [k1, RT] twice; repeat from * to last 3 sts, k3.

ROW 2 AND ALL WS ROWS: Purl.

ROW 3: K3, *RT, [k1, RT] twice, k4; repeat from * to end.

ROW 5: K3, *LT, RT, k1, RT, k5; repeat from * to end.

ROW 7: K4, RT, k1, RT, *k7, RT, k1, RT; repeat from * to last 6 sts, knit to end.

ROW 9: K3, *RT, k1, RT, k7; repeat from * to end.

ROW 11: K3, *LT, RT, k8; repeat from * to end.

ROW 13: K4, RT, *k10, RT; repeat from * to last 9 sts, knit to end.

ROW 15: K3, *RT, k10; repeat from * to end.

ROW 17: K2, RT, k4, *RT, [k1, RT] twice, k4; repeat from * to last 7 sts, RT, k1, RT, k2.

ROW 19: K1, RT, *k4, RT, [k1, RT] twice; repeat from * to end.

ROW 21: RT, *k5, LT, RT, k1, RT; repeat from * to last st, k1.

ROW 23: K8, RT, k1, RT, *k7, RT, k1, RT; repeat from * to last 2 sts, k2.

ROW 25: *K7, RT, k1, RT; repeat from * to last 3 sts, k3.

ROW 27: K7, LT, RT, *k8, LT, RT; repeat from * to last 4 sts, knit to end.

ROW 29: K8, RT, *k10, RT; repeat from * to last 5 sts, knit to end.

ROW 31: K7, RT, *k10, RT; repeat from * to last 6 sts, knit to end.

ROW 33: *RT, [k1, RT] twice, k4; repeat from * to last 3 sts, RT, k1.

ROW 35: K2, RT, k1, RT, k4, *RT, [k1, RT] twice, k4; repeat from * to last 4 sts, RT, k2.

ROW 37: [K1, RT] twice, k5, *LT, RT, k1, RT, k5; repeat from * to last 4 sts, LT, RT.

ROW 39: *RT, k1, RT, k7; repeat from * to last 3 sts, RT, k1.

ROW 41: K2, RT, k7, *RT, k1, RT, k7; repeat from * to last 4 sts, RT, k2.

ROW 43: K1, RT, *k8, LT, RT; repeat from * to end.

ROW 45: RT, *k10, RT; repeat from * to last st, k1.

ROW 47: K11, RT, *k10, RT; repeat from * to last 2 sts, k2.

ROW 48: Purl.

Repeat Rows 1–48 for pattern.

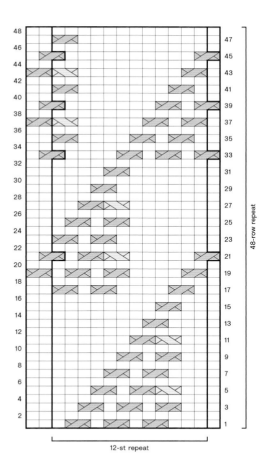

48-row repeat

12-st repeat

(14) Slash

Continuing on the theme of variations, two triangles join forces to make a long slash. Play with the ideas in Chapter 11, Lesson 8, page 267, to see how many new patterns you can make using Slash. See Eyelet Zigzag (#102) for a variation that includes the addition of eyelets.

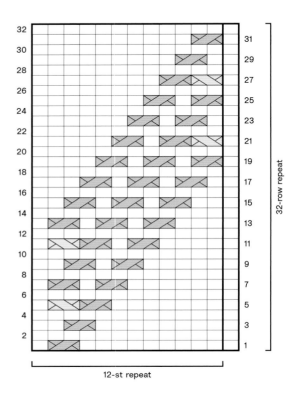

(multiple of 12 sts + 1; 32-row repeat)

PSS: 95

ROW 1 (RS): *K10, RT; repeat from * to last st, k1.

ROW 2 AND ALL WS ROWS: Purl.

ROW 3: K9, RT, *k10, RT; repeat from * to last 2 sts, k2.

ROW 5: *K8, RT, LT; repeat from * to last stitch, k1.

ROW 7: *K7, RT, k1, RT; repeat from * to last st, k1.

ROW 9: K6, RT, k1, RT, *k7, RT, k1, RT; repeat from * to last 2 sts, k2.

ROW 11: *K5, RT, k1, RT, LT; repeat from * to last st, k1.

ROW 13: *K4, RT, [k1, RT] twice; repeat from * to last st, k1.

ROW 15: K3, RT, [k1, RT] twice, *k4, RT, [k1, RT] twice; repeat from * to last 2 sts, k2.

ROW 17: K2, RT, [k1, RT] twice, *k4, RT, [k1, RT] twice; repeat from * to last 3 sts, k3.

ROW 19: K1, *RT, [k1, RT] twice, k4; repeat from * to end.

ROW 21: K1, *LT, RT, k1, RT, k5; repeat from * to end.

ROW 23: K2, RT, k1, RT, *k7, RT, k1, RT; repeat from * to last 6 sts, knit to end.

ROW 25: K1, *RT, k1, RT, k7; repeat from * to end.

ROW 27: K1, *LT, RT, k8; repeat from * to end.

ROW 29: K2, RT, *k10, RT; repeat from * to last 9 sts, knit to end.

ROW 31: K1, *RT, k10; repeat from * to end.

ROW 32: Purl.

Repeat Rows 1–32 for pattern.

(15) Plaid Vast

I didn't realize it at first, but the diagonal elements of Plaid Vast could have evolved from the previous pattern, Slash (#14). In truth, Plaid Vast came first, but the relationship is undeniable.

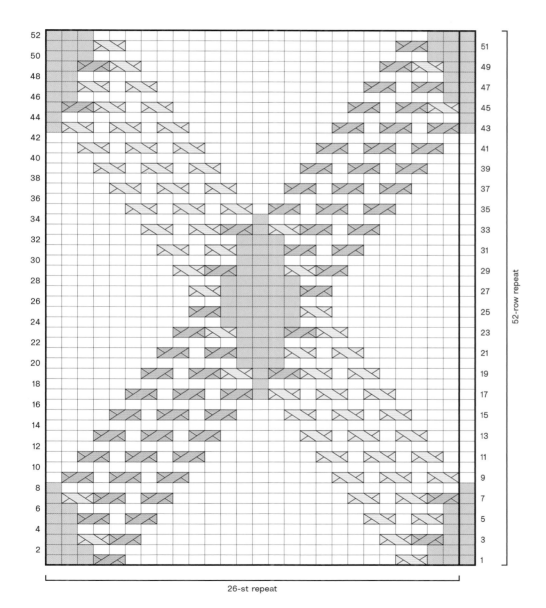

52-row repeat

26-st repeat

(16) Plaid Medium

The smaller cousin to Plaid Vast (#17) has the same carved center, but shorter legs, allowing its stitch repeat to be eight stitches smaller and altering the proportion of Stockinette stitch to twisted stitches. You find the smallest version, Plaid Small (#52), in Chapter 3, on page 70.

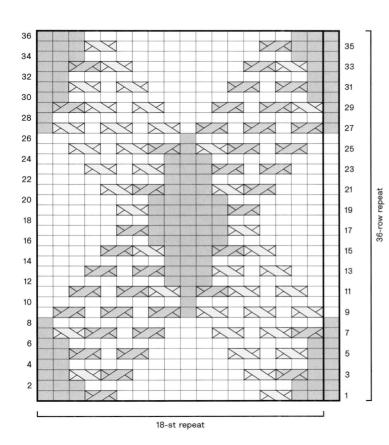

(multiple of 18 sts + 1; 36-row repeat)

PSS: 85

ROW 1 (RS): P3, LT, k9, RT, *p5, LT, k9, RT; repeat from * to last 3 sts, p3.

ROW 2: K3, p13, *k5, p13; repeat from * to last 3 sts, k3.

ROW 3: P2, RT, LT, k7, RT, LT, *p3, RT, LT, k7, RT, LT; repeat from * to last 2 sts, p2.

ROW 4: Knit the knit sts and purl the purl sts as they face you.

ROW 5: P2, LT, k1, LT, k5, RT, k1, RT, *p3, LT, k1, LT, k5, RT, k1, RT; repeat from * to last 2 sts, p2.

ROW 6: Repeat Row 4.

ROW 7: P1, *RT, LT, k1, LT, k3, RT, k1, RT, LT, p1; repeat from * to end.

ROW 8: Repeat Row 4.

ROW 9: K1, *LT, [k1, LT] twice, p1, [RT, k1] 3 times; repeat from * to end.

ROW 10: Repeat Row 4.

ROW 11: K2, LT, k1, LT, RT, p1, LT, RT, k1, RT, *k3, LT, k1, LT, RT, p1, LT, RT, k1, RT; repeat from * to last 2 sts, k2.

ROW 12: P8, k3, *p15, k3; repeat from * to last 8 sts, purl to end.

ROW 13: K3, LT, k1, LT, p3, RT, k1, RT, *k5, LT, k1, LT, p3, RT, k1, RT; repeat from * to last 3 sts, k3.

ROW 14: Repeat Row 4.

ROW 15: K4, LT, RT, p3, LT, RT, *k7, LT, RT, p3, LT, RT; repeat from * to last 4 sts, knit to end.

ROW 16: P7, k5, *p13, k5; repeat from * to last 7 sts, purl to end.

ROW 17: K5, LT, p5, RT, *k9, LT, p5, RT; repeat from * to last 5 sts, knit to end.

ROWS 18, 20, 22, 24, 26, 28, 30, AND 32: Repeat Row 4.

ROW 19: K5, RT, p5, LT, *k9, RT, p5, LT; repeat from * to last 5 sts, knit to end.

ROW 21: K4, RT, LT, p3, RT, LT, *k7, RT, LT, p3, RT, LT; repeat from * to last 4 sts, knit to end.

ROW 22: Repeat Row 4.

ROW 23: K3, RT, k1, RT, p3, LT, k1, LT, *k5, RT, k1, RT, p3, LT, k1, LT; repeat from * to last 3 sts, k3.

ROW 25: K2, RT, k1, RT, LT, p1, RT, LT, k1, LT, *k3, RT, k1, RT, LT, p1, RT, LT, k1, LT; repeat from * to last 2 sts, k2.

ROW 27: P1, *RT, [k1, RT] twice, [k1, LT] 3 times, p1; repeat from * to end.

ROW 29: P1, *LT, RT, k1, RT, k3, LT, k1, LT, RT, p1; repeat from * to end.

ROW 31: P2, RT, k1, RT, k5, LT, k1, LT, *p3, RT, k1, RT, k5, LT, k1, LT; repeat from * to last 2 sts, p2.

ROW 33: P2, LT, RT, k7, LT, RT, *p3, LT, RT, k7, LT, RT; repeat from * to last 2 sts, p2.

ROW 34: Repeat Row 2.

ROW 35: P3, RT, k9, LT, *p5, RT, k9, LT; repeat from * to last 3 sts, p3.

ROW 36: Repeat Row 4.

Repeat Rows 1–36 for pattern.

⑰ Bricks

Inspired by bricks laid in a herringbone pattern, the diagonals formed by right and left twists draw out the edges of the bricks as well as the small spaces left where the bricks don't quite meet.

(multiple of 8 sts + 5; 12-row repeat)

PSS: 90

ROW 1 (RS): K1, *LT, RT, LT, k2; repeat from * to last 4 sts, LT twice.

ROW 2 AND ALL WS ROWS: Purl.

ROW 3: K2, *LT, RT, LT, k2; repeat from * to last 3 sts, LT, k1.

ROW 5: K3, RT, *k2, LT, k2, RT; repeat from * to end.

ROW 7: LT, RT, *k2, RT, LT, RT; repeat from * to last st, k1.

ROW 9: K1, RT, k2; *RT, LT, RT, k2; repeat from * to end.

ROW 11: LT, k2, *RT, k2, LT, k2; repeat from * to last st, k1.

ROW 12: Purl.

Repeat Rows 1–12 for pattern.

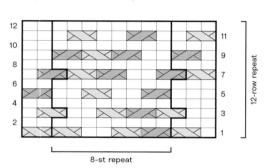

18 Bricks Alternate

Filling the right-leaning brick shapes with parallel lines and leaving the left-leaning shapes plain makes it seem as if two different textures are interweaving.

(multiple of 8 sts + 5; 12-row repeat)

PSS: 90

ROW 1 (RS): K1, *LT, RT, LT, k2; repeat from * to last 4 sts, LT twice.

ROW 2 AND ALL WS ROWS: Purl.

ROW 3: K2, *LT, RT, LT, k2; repeat from * to last 3 sts, LT, k1.

ROW 5: K3, *RT twice, LT, k2; repeat from * to last 2 sts, RT.

ROW 7: LT, *RT 3 times, LT; repeat from * to last 3 sts, RT, k1.

ROW 9: K1, *RT 3 times, LT; repeat from * to last 4 sts, RT twice.

ROW 11: *LT, RT twice, k2; repeat from * to last 5 sts, LT, RT, k1.

ROW 12: Purl.

Repeat Rows 1–12 for pattern.

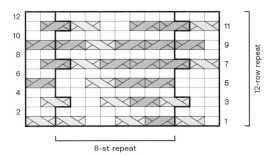

8-st repeat

12-row repeat

19 Brick Lines

Fill in all the open spaces with parallel lines for the most condensed and complex version of the Bricks series (#17–19).

(multiple of 8 sts + 5; 12-row repeat)

PSS: 90

ROW 1 (RS): K1, LT, *RT, LT 3 times; repeat from * to last 2 sts, LT.

ROW 2 AND ALL WS ROWS: Purl.

ROW 3: LT twice, *RT, LT 3 times; repeat from * to last st, k1.

ROW 5: K1, LT, *RT twice, LT twice; repeat from * to last 2 sts, RT.

ROW 7: LT, *RT 3 times, LT; repeat from * to last 3 sts, RT, k1.

ROW 9: K1, *RT 3 times, LT; repeat from * to last 4 sts, RT twice.

ROW 11: LT, *RT twice, LT twice; repeat from * to last 3 sts, RT, k1.

ROW 12: Purl.

Repeat Rows 1–12 for pattern.

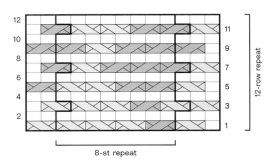

8-st repeat

12-row repeat

(20) Woven

This pattern and the next three are not only related to each other, but, as you can see, also related to the three Brick patterns (#19–21). Woven has more breathing room, as the diagonal elements spread farther apart and the background appears deeper with the addition of reverse Stockinette stitch.

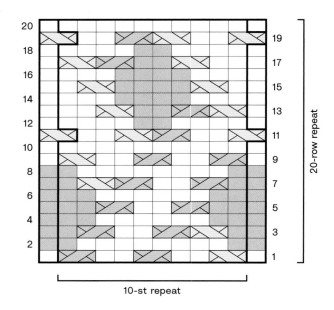

10-st repeat

20-row repeat

(multiple of 10 sts + 2; 20-row repeat)

PSS: 85

ROW 1 (RS): K1, *LT, [k2, RT] twice; repeat from * to last st, k1.

ROW 2: K2, *p8, k2; repeat from * to end.

ROW 3: P2, *LT, RT, k2, RT, p2; repeat from * to end.

ROW 4: K3, p6, *k4, p6; repeat from * to last 3 sts, k3.

ROW 5: P3, RT, k2, RT, *p4, RT, k2, RT; repeat from * to last 3 sts, p3.

ROW 6: Knit the knit sts and purl the purl sts as they face you.

ROW 7: P2, *RT, k2, RT, LT, p2; repeat from * to end.

ROW 8: Repeat Row 6.

ROW 9: K1, *[RT, k2] twice, LT; repeat from * to last st, k1.

ROW 10: Purl.

ROW 11: LT, *k2, RT, LT, k2, LT; repeat from * to end.

ROW 12: P5, k2, *p8, k2; repeat from * to last 5 sts, purl to end.

ROW 13: K1, *LT, RT, p2, LT, k2; repeat from * to last st, k1.

ROW 14: P4, k4, *p6, k4; repeat from * to last 4 sts, purl to end.

ROW 15: K2, *LT, p4, LT, k2; repeat from * to end.

ROW 16: Repeat Row 6.

ROW 17: K3, LT, p2, RT, LT, *k2, LT, p2, RT, LT; repeat from * to last st, k1.

ROW 18: Repeat Row 6.

ROW 19: LT, *k2, LT, RT, k2, LT; repeat from * to end.

ROW 20: Purl.

Repeat Rows 1–20 for pattern.

(21) Woven Alternate

A variation of Woven (#20), enriched by adding a fill of parallel lines in the once-empty right-slanting sections. The juxtaposition of empty centers with filled centers suggests the interweaving of two different colors.

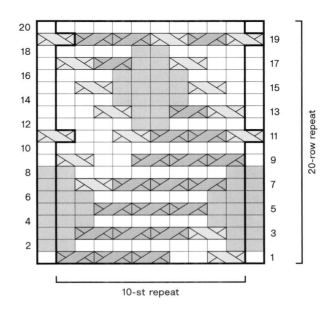

10-st repeat

20-row repeat

(multiple of 10 sts + 2; 20-row repeat)

PSS: 85

ROW 1 (RS): K1, *LT, k2, RT 3 times; repeat from * to last st, k1.

ROW 2: K2, *p8, k2; repeat from * to end.

ROW 3: P2, *LT, RT 3 times, p2; repeat from * to end.

ROW 4: K3, p6, *k4, p6; repeat from * to last 3 sts, k3.

ROW 5: P3, RT 3 times, *p4, RT 3 times; repeat from * to last 3 sts, p3.

ROW 6: Knit the knit sts and purl the purl sts as they face you.

ROW 7: P2, *RT 3 times, LT, p2; repeat from * to end.

ROW 8: Repeat Row 6.

ROW 9: K1, *RT 3 times, k2, LT; repeat from * to last st, k1.

ROW 10: Purl.

ROW 11: LT, *RT twice, LT, k2, LT; repeat from * to end.

ROW 12: P5, k2, *p8, k2; repeat from * to last 5 sts, purl to end.

ROW 13: K1, *LT, RT, p2, LT, k2; repeat from * to last st, k1.

ROW 14: P4, k4, *p6, k4; repeat from * to last 4 sts, purl to end.

ROW 15: K2, *LT, p4, LT, k2; repeat from * to end.

ROW 16: Repeat Row 6.

ROW 17: K3, LT, p2, RT, LT, *k2, LT, p2, RT, LT; repeat from * to last st, k1.

ROW 18: Repeat Row 6.

ROW 19: *LT, RT, LT, RT twice; repeat from * to last 2 sts, LT.

ROW 20: Purl.

Repeat Rows 1–20 for pattern.

(22) Woven Lines

This pattern takes the transition from Woven (#20) to Woven Alternate (#21) one step further by filling in the previously empty left-slanting sections along with the right-slanting sections.

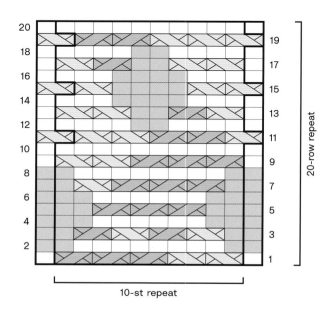

10-st repeat

20-row repeat

(multiple of 10 sts + 2; 20-row repeat)

PSS: 80

ROW 1 (RS): K1, *LT twice, RT 3 times; repeat from * to last st, k1.

ROW 2: K2, *p8, k2; repeat from * to end.

ROW 3: P2, *[LT, RT] twice, p2; repeat from * to end.

ROW 4: K3, p6, *k4, p6; repeat from * to last 3 sts, k3.

ROW 5: P3, RT 3 times, *p4, RT 3 times; repeat from * to last 3 sts, p3.

ROW 6: Knit the knit sts and purl the purl sts as they face you.

ROW 7: P2, *RT 3 times, LT, p2; repeat from * to end.

ROW 8: Repeat Row 6.

ROW 9: K1, *RT 3 times, LT twice; repeat from * to last st, k1.

ROW 10: Purl.

ROW 11: LT, *RT twice, LT 3 times; repeat from * to end.

ROW 12: P5, k2, *p8, k2; repeat from * to last 5 sts, purl to end.

ROW 13: K1, *LT, RT, p2, LT twice; repeat from * to last st, k1.

ROW 14: P4, k4, *p6, k4; repeat from * to last 4 sts, purl to end.

ROW 15: *LT twice, p4, LT; repeat from * to last 2 sts, LT.

ROW 16: Repeat Row 6.

ROW 17: K1, *LT twice, p2, RT, LT; repeat from * to last st, k1.

ROW 18: Repeat Row 6.

ROW 19: *LT 3 times, RT twice; repeat from * to last 2 sts, LT.

ROW 20: Purl.

Repeat Rows 1–20 for pattern.

(23) Woven Filled

The fourth variation of Woven (#20) has the once-open spaces filled with perpendicularly oriented twists. Compare this pattern stitch with Woven Lines (#22) to see how much the look changes simply by changing the direction of the fill twists.

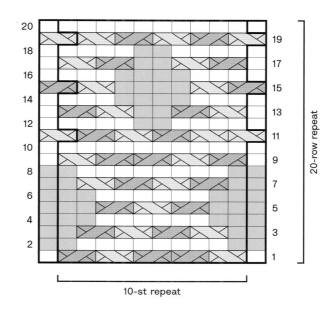

10-st repeat

20-row repeat

(multiple of 10 sts + 2; 20-row repeat)

PSS: 80

ROW 1 (RS): K1, *LT, RT twice, LT, RT; repeat from * to last st, k1.

ROW 2: K2, *p8, k2; repeat from * to end.

ROW 3: P2, *[LT, RT] twice, p2; repeat from * to end.

ROW 4: K3, p6, *k4, p6; repeat from * to last 3 sts, k3.

ROW 5: P3, RT, LT, RT, *p4, RT, LT, RT; repeat from * to last 3 sts, p3.

ROW 6: Knit the knit sts and purl the purl sts as they face you.

ROW 7: P2, *[RT, LT] twice, p2; repeat from * to end.

ROW 8: Repeat Row 6.

ROW 9: K1, *RT, LT, RT twice, LT; repeat from * to last st, k1.

ROW 10: Purl.

ROW 11: *LT twice, RT, LT, RT; repeat from * to last 2 sts, LT.

ROW 12: P5, k2, *p8, k2; repeat from * to last 5 sts, purl to end.

ROW 13: K1, *LT, RT, p2, LT, RT; repeat from * to last st, k1.

ROW 14: P4, k4, *p6, k4; repeat from * to last 4 sts, purl to end.

ROW 15: RT, *LT, p4, LT, RT; repeat from * to end.

ROW 16: Repeat Row 6.

ROW 17: K1, *LT, RT, p2, RT, LT; repeat from * to last st, k1.

ROW 18: Repeat Row 6.

ROW 19: *LT, [RT, LT] twice; repeat from * to last 2 sts, LT.

ROW 20: Purl.

Repeat Rows 1–20 for pattern.

㉔ Triplet Weave

Sets of three parallel lines, set on a Stockinette stitch background, give the suggestion of weaving over and under one another, though the illusion is not as strong as in the Woven series (#20–23).

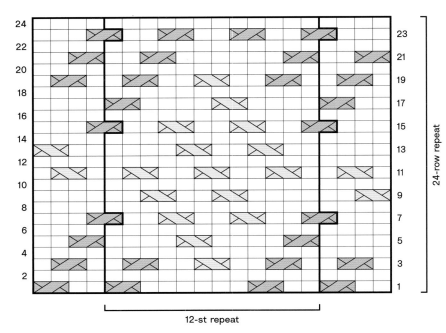

24-row repeat

12-st repeat

(multiple of 12 sts + 8; 24-row repeat)

PSS: 90

ROW 1 (RS): [K2, RT] twice, *k6, RT, k2, RT; repeat from * to end.

ROW 2 AND ALL WS ROWS: Purl.

ROW 3: K1, RT, k2, RT, *k2, LT, [k2, RT] twice; repeat from * to last st, k1.

ROW 5: K4, RT, *k4, LT, k4, RT; repeat from * to last 2 sts, k2.

ROW 7: K3, RT, *k2, [LT, k2] twice, RT; repeat from * to last 3 sts, k3.

ROW 9: LT, k6, *LT, k2, LT, k6; repeat from * to end.

ROW 11: K1, LT, *k2, LT; repeat from * to last st, k1.

ROW 13: K6, LT, *k2, LT, k6, LT; repeat from * to end.

ROW 15: Repeat Row 7.

ROW 17: K2, RT, k4, *LT, k4, RT, k4; repeat from * to end.

ROW 19: K1, RT, k2, RT, *k2, LT, [k2, RT] twice; repeat from * to last st, k1.

ROW 21: RT, k2, RT, *k6, RT, k2, RT; repeat from * to last 2 sts, k2.

ROW 23: K3, RT, *k2, RT; repeat from * to last 3 sts, k3.

ROW 24: Purl.

Repeat Rows 1–24 for pattern.

(25) Triplet Weave Garter

Adding texture to Triplet Weave (#24) by working Garter stitches in the spaces between the parallel lines, this stitch is easy to knit, because the Garter stitch is worked as purl every row, rather than knit every row, leaving the wrong-side row a true resting row.

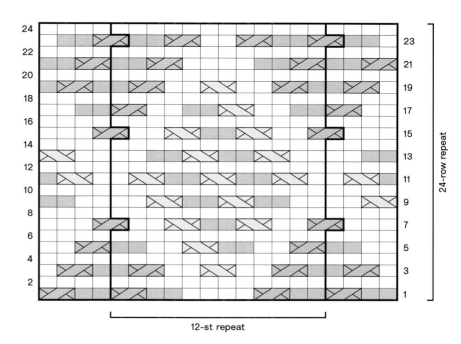

12-st repeat

24-row repeat

(multiple of 12 sts + 8; 24-row repeat)

PSS: 90

ROW 1 (RS): [P2, RT] twice, *k4, [p2, RT] twice; repeat from * to end.

ROW 2 AND ALL WS ROWS: Purl.

ROW 3: K1, RT, p2, RT, *k2, LT, k2, RT, p2, RT; repeat from * to last st, k1.

ROW 5: K2, p2, RT, *k2, p2, LT, k2, p2, RT; repeat from * to last 2 sts, k2.

ROW 7: K3, RT, *k2, LT, p2, LT, k2, RT; repeat from * to last 3 sts, k3.

ROW 9: LT, k4, *[p2, LT] twice, k4; repeat from * to last 2 sts, p2.

ROW 11: P1, LT, k2, *LT, [p2, LT] twice, k2, LT; repeat from * to last st, p1.

ROW 13: P2, k4, *[LT, p2] twice, k4; repeat from * to last 2 sts, LT.

ROW 15: Repeat Row 7.

ROW 17: K2, RT, p2, k2, *LT, p2, k2, RT, p2, k2; repeat from * to end.

ROW 19: Repeat Row 3.

ROW 21: [RT, p2] twice, *k4, [RT, k2] twice; repeat from * to end.

ROW 23: K1, [p2, RT] twice, k2, *RT, [p2, RT] twice, k2; repeat from * to last 9 sts, [RT, p2] twice, k1.

ROW 24: Purl.

Repeat Rows 1–24 for pattern.

㉖ Triplet Weave Filled

In another variation of Triplet Weave (#24), this time opposing twists are added between the parallel lines. Each triplet becomes more solid in appearance, and the illusion of weaving diminishes with this evolutionary step.

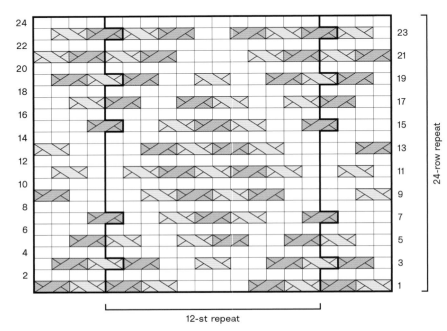

(multiple of 12 sts + 8; 24-row repeat)

PSS: 85

ROW 1 (RS): [LT, RT] twice, *k4, [LT, RT] twice; repeat from * to end.

ROW 2 AND ALL WS ROWS: Purl.

ROW 3: K1, RT, LT, RT, *k2, LT, k2, RT, LT, RT; repeat from * to last st, k1.

ROW 5: K2, LT, RT, k2, *RT, LT, k2, LT, RT, k2; repeat from * to end.

ROW 7: K3, RT, *k2, LT, RT, LT, k2, RT; repeat from * to last 3 sts, k3.

ROW 9: LT, k4, *[RT, LT] twice, k4; repeat from * to last 2 sts, RT.

ROW 11: K1, LT, k2, *LT, [RT, LT] twice, k2; repeat from * to last 3 sts, LT, k1.

ROW 13: RT, k4, *[LT, RT] twice, k4; repeat from * to last 2 sts, LT.

ROW 15: Repeat Row 7.

ROW 17: K2, RT, LT, k2, *LT, RT, k2, RT, LT, k2; repeat from * to end.

ROW 19: K1, RT, LT, RT, *k2, LT, k2, RT, LT, RT; repeat from * to last st, k1.

ROW 21: [RT, LT] twice, *k4, [RT, LT] twice; repeat from * to end.

ROW 23: K1, [LT, RT] twice, k2, *RT, [LT, RT] twice, k2; repeat from * to last 9 sts, [RT, LT] twice, k1.

ROW 24: Purl.

Repeat Rows 1–24 for pattern.

(27) Triplet Weave Filled Carved

The twisted part of this pattern is exactly like Triplet Weave Filled (#26). Here, however, the background has been changed to reverse Stockinette stitch, lifting the twists more from the surface and deepening the ground, so it looks as if it has been carved out with a chisel. Adding the reverse Stockinette stitch ground makes this version more difficult to knit. You have to count on the WS rows.

ROW 7: P3, RT, *p2, LT, RT, LT, p2, RT; repeat from * to last 3 sts, p3.

ROW 8: K7, p6, *k6, p6; repeat from * to last 7 sts, knit to end.

ROW 9: LT, p4, *[RT, LT] twice, p4; repeat from * to last 2 sts, RT.

ROW 10: P2, k4, *p8, k4; repeat from * to last 2 sts, p2.

ROW 11: K1, LT, p2, *LT, [RT, LT] twice, p2; repeat from * to last 3 sts, LT, k1.

ROW 12: Repeat Eow 10.

ROW 13: RT, p4, *[LT, RT] twice, p4; repeat from * to last 2 sts, LT.

ROW 14: Repeat Row 8.

ROW 15: Repeat Row 7.

ROW 16: Repeat Row 6.

ROW 17: P2, RT, LT, p2, *LT, RT, p2, RT, LT, p2; repeat from * to end.

ROW 18: Repeat Row 4.

ROW 19: Repeat Row 3.

ROW 20: Repeat Row 2.

ROW 21: [RT, LT] twice, *p4, [RT, LT] twice; repeat from * to end.

ROW 22: P8, *k4, p8; repeat from * to end.

ROW 23: K1, [LT, RT] twice, p2, *RT, [LT, RT] twice, p2; repeat from * to last 9 sts, [RT, LT] twice, k1.

ROW 24: Repeat Row 22.

Repeat Rows 1–24 for pattern.

(multiple of 12 sts + 8; 24-row repeat)

PSS: 85

ROW 1 (RS): [LT, RT] twice, *p4, [LT, RT] twice; repeat from * to end.

ROW 2: K1, p6, *k6, p6; repeat from * to last st, k1.

ROW 3: P1, RT, LT, RT, *p2, LT, p2, RT, LT, RT; repeat from * to last st, p1.

ROW 4: K2, p4, *k3, p2, k3, p4; repeat from * to last 2 sts, k2.

ROW 5: P2, LT, RT, p2, *RT, LT, p2, LT, RT, p2; repeat from * to end.

ROW 6: K3, p2, k3, *p4, k3, p2, k3; repeat from * to end.

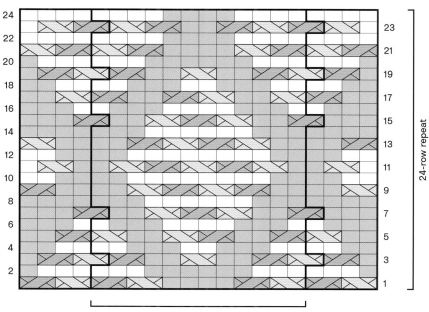

12-st repeat

24-row repeat

㉘ Wonky Weave

A subtle shift of position makes the difference between the triplet weaves in the last four examples and this pattern. The parallel lines of twisted stitches are pushed closer together, one stitch apart rather than two. This leaves more irregular spaces between the sets of lines. The overall pattern is less restful and more interesting.

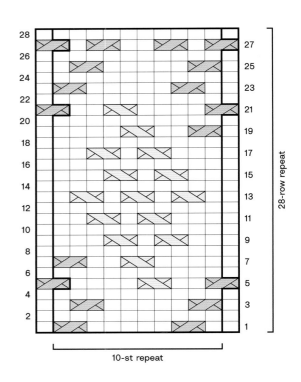

10-st repeat

28-row repeat

(multiple of 10 sts + 2; 28-row repeat)

PSS: 90

ROW 1 (RS): K2, *RT, k5, RT, k1; repeat from * to end.

ROW 2 AND ALL WS ROWS: Purl.

ROW 3: K1, *RT, k5, RT, k1; repeat from * to last st, k1.

ROW 5: RT, *k2, LT, k4, RT; repeat from * to end.

ROW 7: K5, LT, k2, RT, *k4, LT, k2, RT; repeat from * to last st, k1.

ROW 9: K3, LT, k1, LT, *k5, LT, k1, LT; repeat from * to last 4 sts, knit to end.

ROW 11: K4, LT, k1, LT, *k5, LT, k1, LT; repeat from * to last 3 sts, k3.

ROW 13: K2, *LT, [k1, LT] twice, k2; repeat from * to end.

ROW 15: Repeat Row 9.

ROW 17: Repeat Row 11.

ROW 19: K1, *RT, k2, LT, k4; repeat from * to last st, k1.

ROW 21: RT, *k4, LT, k2, RT; repeat from * to end.

ROW 23: K2, *RT, k5, RT, k1; repeat from * to end.

ROW 25: Repeat Row 3.

ROW 27: RT, *k1, RT, k2, RT, k1, RT; repeat from * to end.

ROW 28: Purl.

Repeat Rows 1–28 for pattern.

㉙ Wonky Weave Carved

Carving out background stitches between the sets of three lines significantly changes the character of Wonky Weave (#28) by creating S and Z curves of Stockinette stitch.

ROW 8: *K2, p8; repeat from * to last 2 sts, k1, p1.

ROW 9: P2, *[k1, LT] twice, k2, p2; repeat from * to end.

ROWS 10, 12, 14, 16, AND 18: Repeat Row 2.

ROW 11: P2, *k2, [LT, k1] twice, p2; repeat from * to end.

ROW 13: P2, *LT, [k1, LT] twice, p2; repeat from * to end.

ROW 15: Repeat Row 9.

ROW 17: Repeat Row 11.

ROW 19: P1, *RT, k2, LT, k3, p1; repeat from * to last st, k1.

ROW 20: P1, k1, *p4, k1; repeat from * to end.

ROW 21: RT, *k3, p1, LT, k2, RT; repeat from * to end.

ROW 22: P5, k2, *p8, k2; repeat from * to last 5 sts, knit to end.

ROW 23: Repeat Row 1.

ROW 24: Repeat Row 2.

ROW 25: Repeat Row 3.

ROW 26: Repeat Row 2.

ROW 27: RT, *k1, RT, p2, RT, k1, RT; repeat from * to end.

ROW 28: Repeat Row 2.

Repeat Rows 1–28 for pattern.

(multiple of 10 sts + 2; 28-row repeat)

PSS: 85

ROW 1 (RS): K2, *RT, k1, p2, k2, RT, k1; repeat from * to end.

ROW 2: Knit the knit sts and purl the purl sts as they face you.

ROW 3: K1, *RT, k2, p2, k1, RT, k1; repeat from * to last st, k1.

ROW 4: Repeat Row 2.

ROW 5: RT, *k2, LT, p1, k3, RT; repeat from * to end.

ROW 6: K1, *p4, k1; repeat from * to last st, p1.

ROW 7: K1, p1, *k3, LT, k2, RT, p1; repeat from * to end.

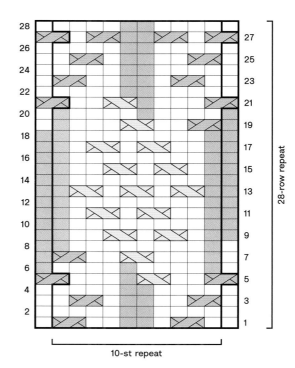

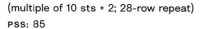

10-st repeat

28-row repeat

Pine Cone Shadow

30

This abstract representation of a conifer cone has right- and left-leaning lines overlapping like the scales of a pine cone. A shadow of reverse Stockinette stitch separates the cone from the moss stitch background.

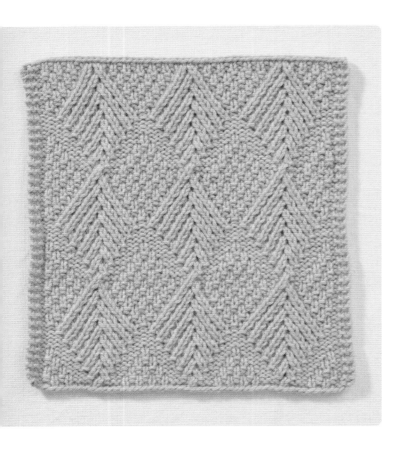

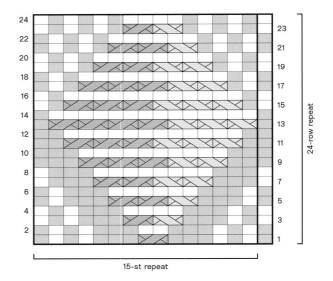

15-st repeat

24-row repeat

(multiple of 15 sts + 1; 24-row repeat)

PSS: 90

ROW 1 (RS): [P1, k1] twice, p3, RT, p3, *k1, [p1, k1] 3 times, p3, RT, p3; repeat from * to last 4 sts, [k1 p1] twice.

ROW 2: [K1, p1] twice, k3, p2, k3, *p1, [k1, p1] 3 times, k3, p2, k3; repeat from * to last 4 sts, [p1, k1] twice.

ROW 3: K1, p1, k1, p3, LT, RT, p3, *k1, [p1, k1] twice, p3, LT, RT, p3; repeat from * to last 3 sts, k1, p1, k1.

ROW 4: P1, k1, p1, k3, p4, k3, *p1, [k1, p1] twice, k3, p4, k3; repeat from * to last 3 sts, p1, k1, p1.

ROW 5: P1, k1, p3, LT, RT twice, p3, *k1, p1, k1, p3, LT, RT twice, p3; repeat from * to last 2 sts, k1, p1.

ROW 6: K1, p1, k3, p6, k3, *p1, k1, p1, k3, p6, k3; repeat from * to last 2 sts, p1, k1.

ROW 7: K1, *p3, LT twice, RT twice, p3, k1; repeat from * to end.

ROW 8: P1, *k3, p8, k3, p1; repeat from * to end.

ROW 9: P3, LT twice, RT 3 times, *p5, LT twice, RT 3 times; repeat from * to last 3 sts, p3.

ROW 10: K3, p10, *k5, p10; repeat from * to last 3 sts, k3.

ROW 11: P2, LT 3 times, RT 3 times, *p3, LT 3 times, RT 3 times; repeat from * to last 2 sts, p2.

Pine Cone Outline

31

The pine cone idea introduced in Pine Cone Shadow (#30) is here outlined with more twisted stitches, lifting it further from the moss stitch background.

ROW 12: K2, p12, *k3, p12; repeat from * to last 2 sts, k2.

ROW 13: P1, *LT 3 times, RT 4 times, p1; repeat from * to end.

ROW 14: K1, *p14, k1; repeat from * to end.

ROW 15: K1, p1, LT 3 times, RT 3 times, *p1, k1, p1, LT 3 times, RT 3 times; repeat from * to last 2 sts, p1, k1.

ROW 16: P1, k1, p12, *k1, p1, k1, p12; repeat from * to last 2 sts, k1, p1.

ROW 17: P1, k1, p1, LT twice, RT 3 times, *p1, [k1, p1] twice, LT twice, RT 3 times; repeat from * to last 3 sts, p1, k1, p1.

ROW 18: K1, p1, k1, p10, *k1, [p1, k1] twice, p10; repeat from * to last 3 sts, k1, p1, k1.

ROW 19: [K1, p1] twice, LT twice, RT twice, *p1, [k1, p1] 3 times, LT twice, RT twice; repeat from * to last 4 sts, [p1, k1] twice.

ROW 20: [P1, k1] twice, p8, *k1, [p1, k1] 3 times, p8; repeat from * to last 4 sts, [k1, p1] twice.

ROW 21: P1, [k1, p1] twice, LT, RT twice, *p1, [k1, p1] 4 times, LT, RT twice; repeat from * to last 5 sts, p1, [k1 p1] twice.

ROW 22: K1, [p1, k1] twice, p6, *k1, [p1, k1] 4 times, p6; repeat from * to last 5 sts, k1, [p1, k1] twice.

ROW 23: [K1, p1] 3 times, LT, RT, *p1, [k1, p1] 5 times, LT, RT; repeat from * to last 6 sts, [p1, k1] 3 times.

ROW 24: [P1, k1] 3 times, p4, *k1, [p1, k1] 5 times, p4; repeat from * to last 6 sts, [p1, k1] 3 times.

Repeat Rows 1–24 for pattern.

(multiple of 15 sts + 1; 24-row repeat)

PSS: 90

ROW 1 (RS): P1, [k1, p1] twice, RT twice, LT, *p1, [k1, p1] 4 times, RT twice, LT; repeat from * to last 5 sts, p1, [k1, p1] twice.

ROW 2: K1, [p1, k1] twice, p6, *k1, [p1, k1] 4 times, p6; repeat from * to last 5 sts, k1, [p1, k1] twice.

ROW 3: [K1, p1] twice, [RT, LT] twice, *p1, [k1, p1] 3 times, [RT, LT] twice; repeat from * to last 4 sts, [p1, k1] twice.

ROW 4: [P1, k1] twice, p8, *k1, [p1, k1] 3 times, p8; repeat from * to last 4 sts, [k1, p1] twice.

ROW 5: P1, k1, p1, RT, LT, RT twice, LT, *p1, [k1, p1] twice, RT, LT, RT twice, LT; repeat from * to last 3 sts, p1, k1, p1.

ROW 6: K1, p1, k1, p10, *k1, [p1, k1] twice, p10; repeat from * to last 3 sts, k1, p1, k1.

ROW 7: K1, p1, RT, LT twice, RT twice, LT, *p1, k1, p1, RT, LT twice, RT twice, LT; repeat from * to last 2 sts, p1, k1.

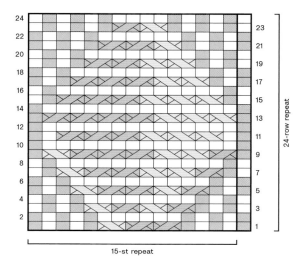

15-st repeat

24-row repeat

ROW 8: P1, k1, p12, *k1, p1, k1, p12; repeat from * to last 2 sts, k1, p1.

ROW 9: P1, *RT, LT twice, RT 3 times, LT, p1; repeat from * to end.

ROW 10: K1, *p14, k1; repeat from * to end.

ROW 11: P1, k1, LT 3 times, RT 3 times, *k1, p1, k1, LT 3 times, RT 3 times; repeat from * to last 2 sts, k1, p1.

ROW 12: Repeat Row 10.

ROW 13: P1, *LT 3 times, RT 4 times, p1; repeat from * to end.

ROW 14: Repeat Row 10.

ROW 15: K1, p1, LT 3 times, RT 3 times, *p1, k1, p1, LT 3 times, RT 3 times; repeat from * to last 2 sts, p1, k1.

ROW 16: Repeat Row 8.

ROW 17: P1, k1, p1, LT twice, RT 3 times, *p1, [k1, p1] twice, LT twice, RT 3 times; repeat from * to last 3 sts, p1, k1, p1.

ROW 18: Repeat Row 6.

ROW 19: [K1, p1] twice, LT twice, RT twice, *p1, [k1, p1] 3 times, LT twice, RT twice; repeat from * to last 4 sts, [p1, k1] twice.

ROW 20: Repeat Row 4.

ROW 21: P1, [k1, p1] twice, LT, RT twice, *p1, [k1, p1] 4 times, LT, RT twice; repeat from * to last 5 sts, p1, [k1, p1] twice.

ROW 22: Repeat Row 2.

ROW 23: [K1, p1] 3 times, LT, RT, *p1, [k1, p1] 5 times, LT, RT; repeat from * to last 6 sts, [p1, k1] 3 times.

ROW 24: [P1, k1] 3 times, *p4, k1, [p1, k1] 5 times; repeat from * to last 10 sts, [k1, p1] 3 times.

Repeat Rows 1–24 for pattern.

(32) Zigzag Panel

Continuing the theme of working with parallel lines in triplicate, here more widely spaced lines are flanked by closely spaced triplets. I think the end result abstractly resembles a head of wheat.

(27-st panel; 20-row repeat)

PSS: 85

ROW 1 (RS): K6, RT 3 times, [k2, RT] twice, LT 3 times, k1.

ROW 2 AND ALL WS ROWS: Purl.

ROW 3: K5, RT 3 times, LT, [RT, k2] twice, LT 3 times.

ROW 5: K4, RT 3 times, k2, LT, [k2, RT] twice, k5.

ROW 7: K3, RT 3 times, LT, k2, LT, RT, k2, RT, k6.

ROW 9: K2, RT 3 times, k2, [LT, k2] twice, RT, k7.

ROW 11: K1, RT 3 times, [LT, k2] twice, LT 3 times, k6.

ROW 13: RT 3 times, [k2, LT] twice, RT, LT 3 times, k5.

ROW 15: K5, [LT, k2] twice, RT, k2, LT 3 times, k4.

ROW 17: K6, LT, k2, LT, RT, k2, RT, LT 3 times, k3.

ROW 19: K7, LT, k2, [RT, k2] twice, LT 3 times, k2.

ROW 20: Purl.

Repeat Rows 1–20 for pattern.

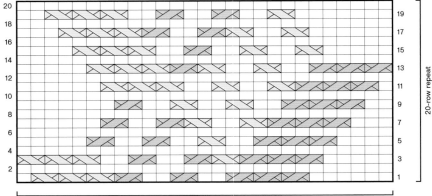

27-st panel

20-row repeat

CHAPTER 3

Small

In this chapter I've grouped small allover patterns, narrow columns, and repeatable chevrons together. All have narrow and short repeats. Use them in concert with larger patterns to outline, fill, or partition. Most of these stitches are made solely from diagonal lines, although an odd horizontal or vertical line slipped in here and there.

�33 Diagonal Columns

Four versions of diagonally striped columns and their mirror images are shown here in the same swatch. These are easy, basic, and useful by themselves or used to visually separate larger patterns. In the smallest variations (A and D, which I refer to as mini cables), one twist is stacked on top of the last in every right-side row.

A B C D E F G H

A
(panel of 2 sts; 2-row repeat)
ROW 1 (RS): RT.
ROW 2: Purl.
Repeat Rows 1 and 2 for pattern.

B
(panel of 3 sts; 4-row repeat)
ROW 1 (RS): K1, RT.
ROW 2: Purl.
ROW 3: RT, k1.
ROW 4: Purl.
Repeat Rows 1–4 for pattern.

C
(panel of 4 sts; 4-row repeat)
ROW 1 (RS): RT twice.
ROW 2: Purl.
ROW 3: K1, RT, k1.
ROW 4: Purl.
Repeat Rows 1–4 for pattern.

D
(panel of 4 sts; 6-row repeat)
ROW 1 (RS): K2, RT.
ROW 2: Purl.
ROW 3: K1, RT, k1.
ROW 4: Purl.
ROW 5: RT, k2.
ROW 6: Purl.
Repeat Rows 1–6 for pattern.

E
(panel of 4 sts; 6-row repeat)
ROW 1 (RS): LT, k2.
ROW 2: Purl.
ROW 3: K1, LT, k1.
ROW 4: Purl.
ROW 5: K2, LT.
ROW 6: Purl.
Repeat Rows 1–6 for pattern.

F
(panel of 4 sts; 4-row repeat)
ROW 1 (RS): LT twice.
ROW 2: Purl.
ROW 3: K1, LT, k1.
ROW 4: Purl.
Repeat Rows 1–4 for pattern.

G
(panel of 3 sts; 4-row repeat)
ROW 1 (RS): LT, k1.
ROW 2: Purl.
ROW 3: K1, LT.
ROW 4: Purl.
Repeat Rows 1–4 for pattern.

H
(panel of 2 sts; 2-row repeat)
ROW 1 (RS): LT.
ROW 2: Purl.
Repeat Rows 1 and 2 for pattern.

A
2-row repeat
2-st panel

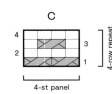

B
4-row repeat
3-st panel

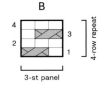

C
4-row repeat
4-st panel

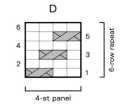

D
6-row repeat
4-st panel

E
6-row repeat
4-st panel

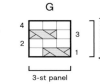

F
4-row repeat
4-st panel

G
4-row repeat
3-st panel

H
2-row repeat
2-st panel

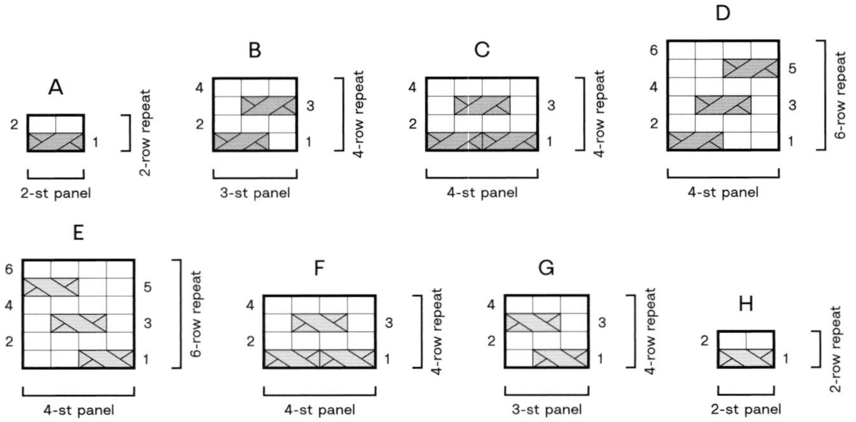

㉞ Braids

Variations on a theme: One idea evolves into the next as these intertwined arrangements get larger, from left to right. Touches of reverse Stockinette stitch help accentuate the structure.

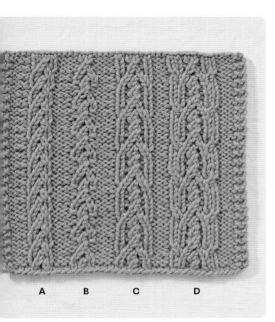

A
(panel of 4 sts; 4-row repeat)
ROW 1 (RS): LT, RT.
ROW 2: Purl.
ROW 3: K1, RT, k1.
ROW 4: Purl.
Repeat Rows 1–4 for pattern.

B
(panel of 4 sts; 6-row repeat)
ROW 1 (RS): K1, RT, k1.
ROW 2: Purl.
ROW 3: LT, RT.
ROW 4: K1, p2, k1.
ROW 5: P1, RT, p1.
ROW 6: Repeat Row 4.
Repeat Rows 1–6 for pattern.

C
(panel of 6 sts; 8-row repeat)
ROW 1 (RS): K1, p1, RT, p1, k1.
ROW 2: P1, k1, p2, k1, p1.
ROW 3: LT, RT twice.
ROW 4: Purl.
ROW 5: K1, LT, RT, k1.
ROW 6: Repeat Row 2.
ROWS 7 AND 8: Repeat Rows 1 and 2.
Repeat Rows 1–8 for pattern.

D
(panel of 8 sts; 8-row repeat)
ROW 1 (RS): K2, p1, RT, p1, k2.
ROW 2: P2, [k1, p2] twice.
ROW 3: K1, LT, RT twice, k1.
ROW 4: Purl.
ROW 5: [RT, LT] twice.
ROW 6: Repeat Row 2.
ROWS 7 AND 8: Repeat Rows 1 and 2.
Repeat Rows 1–8 for pattern.

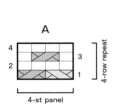

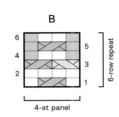

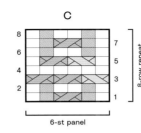

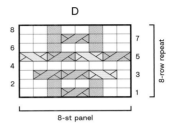

㉟ Mini Os

Riffing on the idea of circles, these four columns become increasingly ornate as you go from left to right. Studying the charts, you can easily see how one idea led to the next.

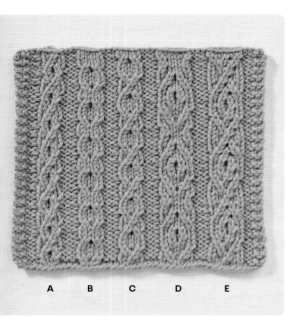

A   B   C   D   E

A
(panel of 4 sts; 6-row repeat)
ROW 1 (RS): RT, LT.
ROW 2 AND ALL WS ROWS: Purl.
ROW 3: LT, RT.
ROW 5: K1, RT, k1.
ROW 6: Purl.
Repeat Rows 1–6 for pattern.

B
(panel of 4 sts; 8-row repeat)
ROW 1 (RS): RT, LT.
ROW 2 AND ALL WS ROWS: Purl.
ROW 3: Knit.
ROW 5: LT, RT.
ROW 7: Knit.
ROW 8: Purl.
Repeat Rows 1–8 for pattern.

C
(panel of 4 sts; 8-row repeat)
ROW 1 (RS): K1, RT, k1.
ROW 2 AND ALL WS ROWS: Purl.
ROW 3: RT, LT.
ROW 5: Knit.
ROW 7: LT, RT.
ROW 8: Purl.
Repeat Rows 1–8 for pattern.

D
(panel of 6 sts; 16-row repeat)
ROW 1 (RS): K1, RT, LT, k1.
ROW 2 AND ALL WS ROWS: Purl.
ROW 3: RT, k2, LT.

ROW 5: Repeat Row 1.
ROW 7: K1, LT, RT, k1.
ROW 9: LT, k2, RT.
ROW 11: Repeat Row 7.
ROW 13: Repeat Row 9.
ROW 15: Repeat Row 3.
ROW 16: Purl.
Repeat Rows 1–16 for pattern.

E
(panel of 6 sts; 14-row repeat)
ROW 1 (RS): K2, RT, k2.
ROW 2 AND ALL WS ROWS: Purl.
ROW 3: K1, RT, LT, k1.
ROW 5: RT twice, LT.
ROW 7: Repeat Row 3.
ROW 9: K1, LT, RT, k1.
ROW 11: LT, RT twice.
ROW 13: Repeat Row 9.
ROW 14: Purl.
Repeat Rows 1–14 for pattern.

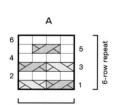

A
6-row repeat
4-st panel

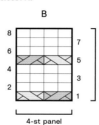

B
8-row repeat
4-st panel

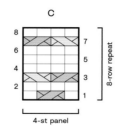

C
8-row repeat
4-st panel

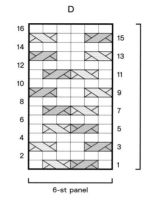

D
16-row repeat
6-st panel

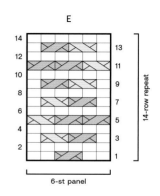

E
14-row repeat
6-st panel

36 Mock Cables

These wider columns expand upon the concept of twisted stitches emulating cables. These columns of twisted stitches not only imitate cables, but are also wide enough that they can be used in their place.

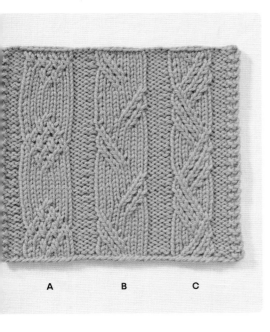

A   B   C

A
(panel of 8 sts; 20-row repeat)
PSS: 95
ROW 1 (RS): K3, RT, k3.
ROW 2 AND ALL WS ROWS: Purl.
ROW 3: K2, LT twice, k2.
ROW 5: K1, RT 3 times, k1.
ROW 7: LT 4 times.
ROW 9: Repeat Row 5.
ROW 11: Repeat Row 3.
ROW 13: Repeat Row 1.
ROWS 15, 17, AND 19: Knit.
ROW 20: Purl.
Repeat Rows 1–20 for pattern.

B
(panel of 8 sts; 20-row repeat)
PSS: 95
ROW 1 (RS): K4, LT, k2.
ROW 2 AND ALL WS ROWS: Purl.
ROW 3: K3, LT twice, k1.
ROW 5: K4, LT twice.
ROW 7: K5, LT, k1.
ROW 9: K6, LT.
ROW 11: K2, RT, k4.
ROW 13: K1, RT twice, k3.
ROW 15: RT twice, k4.
ROW 17: K1, RT, k5.
ROW 19: RT, k6.
ROW 20: Purl.
Repeat Rows 1–20 for pattern.

C
(panel of 7 sts; 20-row repeat)
PSS: 95
ROW 1 (RS): RT 3 times, k1.
ROW 2 AND ALL WS ROWS: Purl.
ROW 3: K1, RT twice, k2.
ROW 5: RT twice, k3.
ROW 7: K1, RT, LT, k2.
ROW 9: RT, LT twice, k1.
ROW 11: K1, LT 3 times.
ROW 13: K2, LT twice, k1.
ROW 15: K3, LT twice.
ROW 17: K2, RT, LT, k1.
ROW 19: K1, RT twice, LT.
ROW 20: Purl.
Repeat Rows 1–20 for pattern.

A
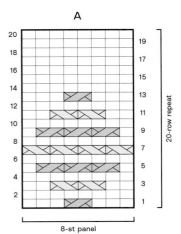
8-st panel

B
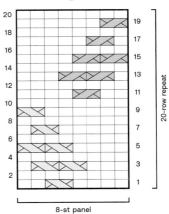
8-st panel

C
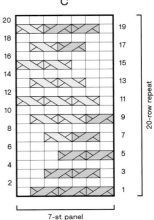
7-st panel

(37) Hilary

This pattern is made by tilting H-shaped motifs both to the right and to the left, then scattering them across fabric with an airy amount of open space between.

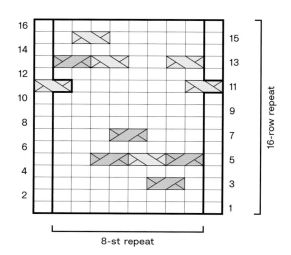

(multiple of 8 sts + 2; 16-row repeat)

PSS: 95

ROW 1 (RS): Knit.

ROW 2 AND ALL WS ROWS: Purl.

ROW 3: K2, *RT, k6; repeat from * to end.

ROW 5: K1, *RT, LT, RT, k2; repeat from * to last st, k1.

ROW 7: K4, RT, *k6, RT; repeat from * to last 4 sts, knit to end.

ROW 9: Knit.

ROW 11: LT, *k6, LT; repeat from * to end.

ROW 13: K1, *LT, k2, LT, RT; repeat from * to last st, k1.

ROW 15: *K6, LT; repeat from * to last 2 sts, k2.

ROW 16: Purl.

Repeat Rows 1–16 for pattern.

(38) Houndstooth

Four short lines intersect in a mini pinwheel to make the houndstooth motif. Each motif is separated from the others with several stitches and rows of Stockinette stitch to make a good overall pattern.

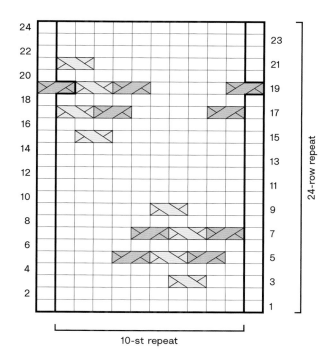

(multiple of 10 sts + 2; 24-row repeat)

PSS: 95

ROW 1 (RS): Knit.

ROW 2 AND ALL WS ROWS: Purl.

ROW 3: K3, LT, *k8, LT; repeat from * to last 7 sts, knit to end.

ROW 5: K2, *RT, LT, RT, k4; repeat from * to end.

ROW 7: K1, *RT, LT, RT, k4; repeat from * to last st, k1.

ROW 9: K4, LT, *k8, LT; repeat from * to last 6 sts, knit to end.

ROWS 11 AND 13: Knit.

ROW 15: *K8, LT; repeat from * to last 2 sts, k2.

ROW 17: K1, *RT, k4, RT, LT; repeat from * to last st, k1.

ROW 19: RT, *k4, RT, LT, RT; repeat from * to end.

ROW 21: K9, LT, *k8, LT; repeat from * to last st, k1.

ROW 23: Knit.

ROW 24: Purl.

Repeat Rows 1–24 for pattern.

③⑨ Rhinestones

Sparkling rhinestones spaced evenly across a background of Stockinette stitch can be used as an allover pattern or in a central panel.

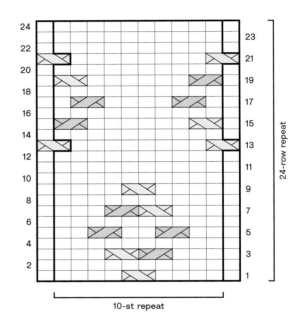

(multiple of 10 sts + 2; 24-row repeat)

PSS: 95

ROW 1 (RS): K5, LT, *k8, LT; repeat from * to last 5 sts, knit to end.

ROW 2 AND ALL WS ROWS: Purl.

ROW 3: K4, RT, LT, *k6, RT, LT; repeat from * to last 4 sts, knit to end.

ROW 5: K3, RT, k2, RT, *k4, RT, k2, RT; repeat from * to last 3 sts, k3.

ROW 7: K4, LT, RT, *k6, LT, RT; repeat from * to last 4 sts, knit to end.

ROW 9: Repeat Row 1.

ROW 11: Knit.

ROW 13: LT, *k8, LT; repeat from * to end.

ROW 15: K1, *LT, k6, RT; repeat from * to last st, k1.

ROW 17: K2, *RT, k4, RT, k2; repeat from * to end.

ROW 19: K1, *RT, k6, LT; repeat from * to last st, k1.

ROW 21: Repeat Row 13.

ROW 23: Knit.

ROW 24: Purl.

Repeat Rows 1–24 for pattern.

⑩ Rune

Extend all the lines of Rhinestones (#39) beyond the diamond shape, and you have Rune, which looks like a symbol from an ancient alphabet.

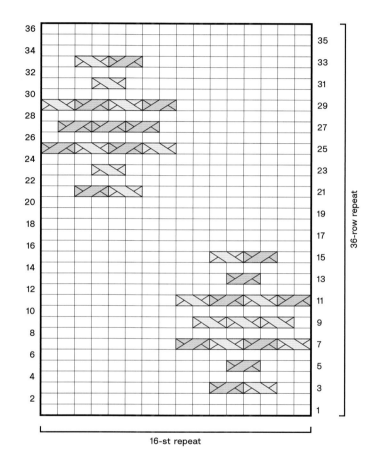

(multiple of 16 sts; 36-row repeat)

PSS: 95

ROW 1 (RS): Knit.

ROW 2 AND ALL WS ROWS: Purl.

ROW 3: K2, LT, RT, *k12, LT, RT; repeat from * to last 10 sts, knit to end.

ROW 5: K3, RT, *k14, RT; repeat from * to last 11 sts, knit to end.

ROW 7: *[LT, RT] twice, k8; repeat from * to end.

ROW 9: K1, LT 3 times, *k10, LT 3 times; repeat from * to last 9 sts, knit to end.

ROW 11: *[RT, LT] twice, k8; repeat from * to end.

ROW 13: Repeat Row 5.

ROW 15: K2, RT, LT, *k12, RT, LT; repeat from * to last 10 sts, knit to end.

ROWS 17 AND 19: Knit.

ROW 21: K10, LT, RT, *k12, LT, RT; repeat from * to last 2 sts, k2.

ROW 23: K11, LT, *k14, LT; repeat from * to last 3 sts, k3.

ROW 25: *K8, [LT, RT] twice; repeat from * to end.

ROW 27: K9, RT 3 times, *k10, RT 3 times; repeat from * to last 1 st, k1.

ROW 29: *K8, [RT, LT] twice; repeat from * to end.

ROW 31: Repeat Row 23.

ROW 33: K10, RT, LT, *k12, RT, LT; repeat from * to last 2 sts, k2.

ROW 35: Knit.

ROW 36: Purl.

Repeat Rows 1–36 for pattern.

⓸① Chevron

This pattern and the three variations that follow can each be worked in several ways. Knit all three portions of the chart as shown in the swatch or use the repeat for the left- or right-leaning slants alone. Here, two opposite-leaning lines meet in the center before the right crosses over the left to cap off the chevron.

(multiple of 6 sts in 2 separate repeats + 12; 12-row repeat)

PSS: 95

NOTE: Place a marker on either side of center 6 sts.

ROW 1 (RS): K3, *LT, k4; repeat from * to marker; sm, k1, LT, RT, k1, sm; **k4, RT; repeat from ** to last 3 sts, k3.

ROW 2 AND ALL WS ROWS: Purl.

ROW 3: K3, *k1, LT, k3; repeat from * to marker; sm, k2, LT, k2, sm; **k3, RT, k1; repeat from ** to last 3 sts, k3.

ROW 5: K3, *k2, LT, k2; repeat from * to marker; sm, k6, sm; **k2, RT, k2; repeat from ** to last 3 sts, k3.

ROW 7: LT, k1, *k3, LT, k1; repeat from * to marker; sm, k6, sm; **k1, RT, k3; repeat from ** to last 3 sts, k1, RT.

ROW 9: K1, LT, *k4, LT; repeat from * to marker; sm, k6, sm; **RT, k4; repeat from ** to last 3 sts, RT, k1.

ROW 11: K2, *LT, k4; repeat from * to 1 st before marker, LT (replacing marker at center of LT), k4, RT (replacing marker at center of RT), **k4, RT; repeat from ** to last 2 sts, k2.

ROW 12: Purl.

Repeat Rows 1–12 for pattern.

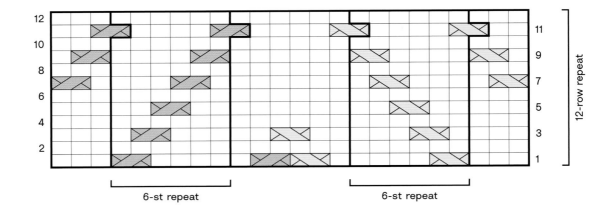

42 Interrupted

The opposing lines of Chevron (#41) don't meet in this version; they are interrupted by a free-standing braid. Knit all three sections of the chart, as shown in the swatch, or use the repeat for the left- or right-leaning slants alone.

(multiple of 6 sts in 2 separate repeats + 13; 12-row repeat)

PSS: 90

NOTE: Place a marker on either side of center 9 sts.

ROW 1 (RS): K2, *LT, k4; repeat from * to marker; sm, LT, p1, k1, RT, p1, RT, sm; **k4, RT; repeat from ** to last 2 sts, k2.

ROW 2 AND ALL WS ROWS: Knit the knit sts and purl the purl sts as they face you.

ROW 3: K2, *k1, LT, k3; repeat from * to marker; sm, k2, p1, LT, k1, p1, k2, sm; **k3, RT, k1; repeat from ** to last 2 sts, k2.

ROW 5: K2, *k2, LT, k2; repeat from * to marker; sm, k2, p1, k1, RT, p1, k2, sm; **k2, RT, k2; repeat from ** to last 2 sts, k2.

ROW 7: K2, *k3, LT, k1; repeat from * to marker; sm, k2, p1, LT, k1, p1, k2, sm; **k1, RT, k3; repeat from ** to last 2 sts, k2.

ROW 9: LT, *k4, LT; repeat from * to marker; sm, k2, p1, k1, RT, p1, k2, sm; **RT, k4; repeat from ** to last 2 sts, RT.

ROW 11: K1, *LT, k4; repeat from * to 1 st before marker, LT (replacing marker at center of LT), k1, p1, LT, k1, p1, k1, RT (replacing marker at center of RT), **k4, RT; repeat from ** to last st, k1.

ROW 12: Repeat Row 2.

Repeat Rows 1–12 for pattern.

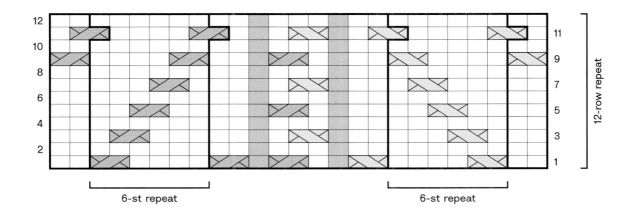

6-st repeat   6-st repeat

12-row repeat

(43) Sprouts

The fanciest of the four chevrons in patterns #41–44, Sprouts starts as two widespread parallel lines and is then embellished with mini cables whose ends emerge from the center like sprouts and roots.

(multiple of 12 sts in 2 separate repeats + 12; 24-row repeat)

PSS: 90

NOTE: Place a marker on either side of center 4 sts.

ROW 1 (RS): LT, RT, *p1, LT, k5, LT, RT; repeat from * to marker; sm, p1, LT, p1, sm; **LT, RT, k5, RT, p1; repeat from ** to last 4 sts, LT, RT.

ROW 2: Knit the knit sts and purl the purl sts as they face you.

ROW 3: K1, RT, k1, *p1, k1, RT, k5, RT, k1; repeat from * to marker; sm, p1, LT, p1, sm; **k1, LT, k5, LT, k1, p1; repeat from ** to last 4 sts, k1, LT, k1.

ROW 4: Repeat Row 2.

ROW 5: K2, LT, *P1, RT, LT, k5, LT; repeat from * to marker; sm, p1, LT, p1, sm; **RT, k5, RT, LT, p1; repeat from ** to last 4 sts, RT, k2.

ROW 6: P4, *k1, p2, k1, p8; repeat from * to marker; sm, k1, p2, k1, sm; **p8, k1, p2, k1; repeat from ** to last 4 sts, p4.

ROW 7: K3, *LT, RT, p1, LT, k5; repeat from * to 1 st before marker; LT (replacing marker at center of LT), LT, RT (replacing marker at center of RT); **k5, RT, p1, LT, RT; repeat from ** to last 3 sts, k3.

ROW 8: Repeat Row 2.

ROW 9: K4, *RT, k1, p1, k1, RT, k5; repeat from * to marker; sm, RT, LT, sm; **k5, LT, k1, p1, k1, LT; repeat from ** to last 4 sts, knit to end.

ROW 10: Repeat Row 2.

ROW 11: K4, *k1, LT, p1, RT, LT, k4; repeat from * to marker; sm, k1, LT, k1, sm; **k4, RT, LT, p1, RT, k1; repeat from ** to last 4 sts, knit to end.

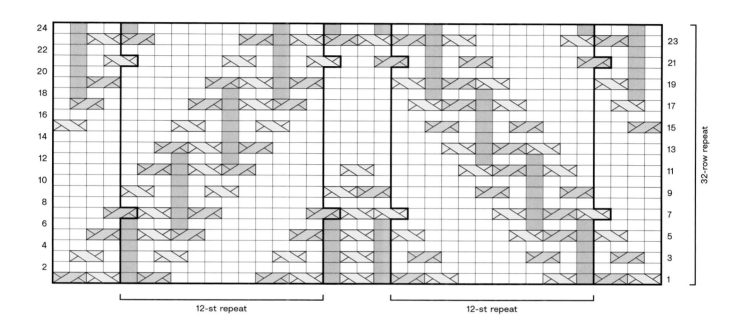

ROW 12: P4, *p3, k1, p2, k1, p5; repeat from * to marker; sm, p4, sm; **p5, k1, p2, k1, p3; repeat from ** to last 4 sts, p4.

ROW 13: K4, *k2, LT, RT, p1, LT, k3; repeat from * to marker; sm, k4, sm; **k3, RT, p1, LT, RT, k2; repeat from ** to last 4 sts, knit to end.

ROW 14: Repeat Row 2.

ROW 15: RT, k2, *k3, RT, k1, p1, k1, RT, k2; repeat from * to marker; sm, k4, sm; **k2, LT, k1, p1, k1, LT, k3; repeat from ** to last 4 sts, k2, LT.

ROW 16: Repeat Row 2.

ROW 17: K1, LT, k1, *k4, LT, p1, RT, LT, k1; repeat from * to marker; sm, k4, sm; **k1, RT, LT, p1, RT, k4; repeat from ** to last 4 sts, K1, RT, k1.

ROW 18: P1, k1, p2, *p6, [k1, p2] twice; repeat from * to marker; sm, p4, sm; **[p2, k1] twice, p6; repeat from ** to last 4 sts, p2, k1, p1.

ROW 19: K1, p1, LT, *k5, LT, RT, p1, LT; repeat from * to marker; sm, k4, sm; **RT, p1, LT, RT, k5; repeat from ** to last 4 sts, RT, p1, k1.

ROW 20: Repeat Row 2.

ROW 21: K1, p1, k1, *RT, k5, RT, k1, p1, k1; repeat from * to 1 st before marker; RT (replacing marker at center of RT), k2, LT (replacing marker at center of LT); **k1, p1, k1, LT, k5, LT; repeat from ** to last 3 sts, k1, p1, k1.

ROW 22: Repeat Row 2.

ROW 23: K1, p1, RT, *LT, k5, LT, p1, RT; repeat from * to marker; sm, LT, RT, sm; **LT, p1, RT, k5, RT; repeat from ** to last 4 sts, LT, p1, k1.

ROW 24: P1, k1, p2, *k1, p8, k1, p2; repeat from * to marker; sm, k1, p2, k1; **p2, k1, p8, k1; repeat from ** to last 4 sts, p2, k1, p1.

Repeat Rows 1–24 for pattern.

Perpendicular

This more ornate chevron is first constructed of diagonal lines, then crowned with opposite twists. All meet and cross in the center. Knit all three sections of the chart, as shown in the swatch, or use the repeat for the left- or right-leaning slants alone.

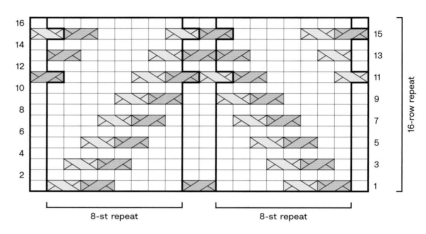

(multiple of 8 sts in 2 separate repeats + 4; 16-row repeat)

PSS: 90

NOTE: Place a marker on either side of center 2 sts.

ROW 1 (RS): K1, *RT, LT, k4; repeat from * to marker; sm, RT, sm; **k4, RT, LT; repeat from ** to last st, k1.

ROW 2 AND ALL WS ROWS: Purl.

ROW 3: K1, *k1, RT, LT, k3; repeat from * to marker; sm, k2, sm; **k3, RT, LT, k1; repeat from ** to last st, k1.

ROW 5: K1, *K2, RT, LT, k2; repeat from * to marker; sm, k2, sm; **k2, RT, LT, k2; repeat from ** to last st, k1.

ROW 7: K1, *k3, RT, LT, k1; repeat from * to marker; sm, k2, sm; **k1, RT, LT, k3; repeat from ** to last st, k1.

ROW 9: K1, *k4, RT, LT; repeat from * to marker; sm, k2, sm; **RT, LT, k4; repeat from ** to last st, k1.

ROW 11: *LT, k4, RT; repeat from * to 1 st before marker; LT (replacing marker at center of LT), RT (replacing marker at center of RT); **LT, k4, RT; repeat from ** to end.

ROW 13: K1, *LT, k4, RT; repeat from * to marker; sm, RT, sm; **LT, k4, RT; repeat from ** to last st, k1.

ROW 15: RT, LT, *k4, RT, LT; repeat from * to end, replacing markers at center of RT and LT.

ROW 16: Purl.

Repeat Rows 1–16 for pattern.

45 Carp

This allover pattern appears to be curved and stacked like the scales of a carp.

(multiple of 8 sts; 8-row repeat)

PSS: 95

ROW 1 (RS): K1, RT, k2, LT, *k2, RT, k2, LT; repeat from * to last st, k1.

ROW 2 AND ALL WS ROWS: Purl.

ROW 3: *RT, k4, LT; repeat from * to end.

ROW 5: K1, LT, k2, RT, *k2, LT, k2, RT; repeat from * to last st, k1.

ROW 7: K2, LT, RT, *k4, LT, RT; repeat from * to last 2 sts, k2.

ROW 8: Purl.

Repeat Rows 1–8 for pattern.

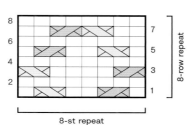

46 Carp Rib

Adding ribs to Carp (#45) highlights the diagonals while creating a central rib. If choosing between this pattern and Carp, know that the wrong side of this one is a bit harder to knit, because of the ribs.

(multiple of 8 sts; 8-row repeat)

PSS: 90

ROW 1 (RS): K1, RT, k2, LT, *k2, RT, k2, LT; repeat from * to last st, k1.

ROW 2: [P2, k1] twice, *p4, k1, p2, k1; repeat from * to last 2 sts, p2.

ROW 3: *RT, p1, k2, p1, LT; repeat from * to end.

ROW 4: Repeat Row 2.

ROW 5: K1, LT, k2, RT, *k2, LT, k2, RT; repeat from * to last st, k1.

ROW 6: P1, k1, p4, k1, *p2, k1, p4, k1; repeat from * to last st, p1.

ROW 7: K1, p1, LT, RT, p1, *k2, p1, LT, RT, p1; repeat from * to last st, k1.

ROW 8: Repeat Row 6.

Repeat Rows 1–8 for pattern.

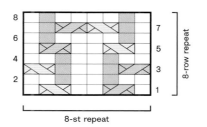

(47) Lizard

Foreshadowing the next chapter, horizontal dashes of Garter stitch overlap the crisscrossed diagonal lines. The result brings to mind the skin of an iguana.

(multiple of 6 sts; 12-row repeat)

PSS: 90

ROW 1 (RS): K1, p4, *k2, p4; repeat from * to last st, k1.

ROW 2 AND ALL WS ROWS: Purl.

ROW 3: K1, RT, LT, *k2, RT, LT; repeat from * to last st, k1.

ROW 5: *RT, k2, LT; repeat from * to end.

ROW 7: P2, k2, *p4, k2; repeat from * to last 2 sts, p2.

ROW 9: *LT, k2, RT; repeat from * to end.

ROW 11: K1, LT, RT, *k2, LT, RT; repeat from * to last st, k1.

ROW 12: Purl.

Repeat Rows 1–12 for pattern.

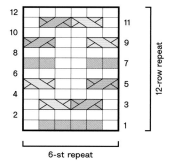

(48) Lattice

Single lines weave over and under each other, making a basic lattice pattern. The Stockinette stitch ground means it is easy to knit.

(multiple of 8 sts + 2; 8-row repeat)

PSS: 90

ROW 1 (RS): K2, *RT, k2; repeat from * to end.

ROW 2 AND ALL WS ROWS: Purl.

ROW 3: K1, *RT, LT; repeat from * to last st, k1.

ROW 5: LT, *k2, LT; repeat from * to end.

ROW 7: K1, *LT, RT; repeat from * to last st, k1.

ROW 8: Purl.

Repeat Rows 1–8 for pattern.

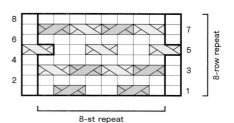

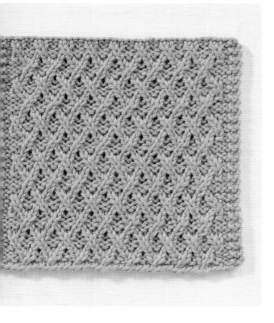

(49) Carved Lattice

Replacing the Stockinette stitch background of Lattice (#48) with reverse Stockinette allows the lattice to pop off of the surface more dramatically, as if the spaces had been carved out. Beware, though—this version is more difficult to knit on the wrong-side rows.

(multiple of 8 sts + 2; 8-row repeat)

PSS: 85

ROW 1 (RS): P2, *RT, p2; repeat from * to end.

ROW 2: K2, *p2, k2; repeat from * to end.

ROW 3: K1, *RT, LT; repeat from * to last st, k1.

ROW 4: P2, *k2, p2; repeat from * to end.

ROW 5: LT, *p2, LT; repeat from * to end.

ROW 6: Repeat Row 4.

ROW 7: K1, *LT, RT; repeat from * to last st, k1.

ROW 8: Repeat Row 2.

Repeat Rows 1–8 for pattern.

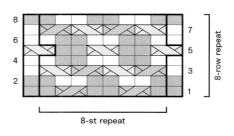

⑤⓪ Crossed

Another variation of Lattice (#48), this version allows more space between each pair of diagonal lines. In addition, the smaller central diamonds are filled with a single twist to create this more ornate and larger lattice.

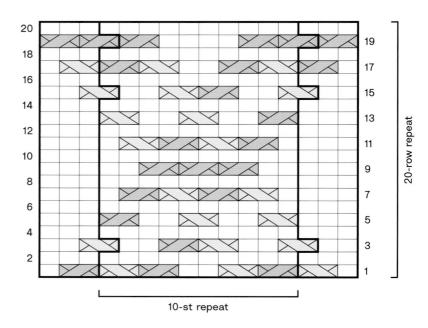

10-st repeat

20-row repeat

(multiple of 10 sts + 6; 20-row repeat)

PSS: 90

ROW 1 (RS): K1, LT, *RT, LT, k2, RT, LT; repeat from * to last 3 sts, RT, k1.

ROW 2 AND ALL WS ROWS: Purl.

ROW 3: K2, *LT, k2, LT, RT, k2; repeat from * to last 4 sts, LT, k2.

ROW 5: K3, *[LT, k2] twice, RT; repeat from * to last 3 sts, k3.

ROW 7: K4, *[LT, RT] twice, k2; repeat from * to last 2 sts, k2.

ROW 9: K5, *RT 3 times, k4; repeat from * to last st, k1.

ROW 11: K4, *[RT, LT] twice, k2; repeat from * to last 2 sts, k2.

ROW 13: K3, *RT, [k2, LT] twice; repeat from * to last 3 sts, k3.

ROW 15: K2, LT, k2, *RT, LT, k2, LT, k2; repeat from * to end.

ROW 17: K1, RT, LT, *RT, k2, LT, RT, LT; repeat from * to last st, k1.

ROW 19: RT 3 times, *k4, RT 3 times; repeat from * to end.

ROW 20: Purl.

Repeat Rows 1–20 for pattern.

(51) Plaid Small Garter

Parallelograms flow together to form Xs with a diamond-shaped background between them. While not strictly a lattice, it's the abstraction of plaid. The small Garter stitch center is purled every row, instead of knitting every row, leaving very easy wrong-side rows.

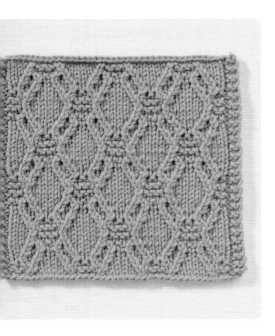

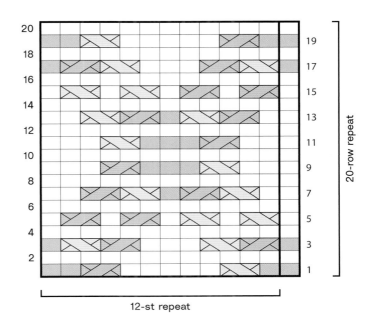

(multiple of 12 sts + 1; 20-row repeat)

PSS: 90

ROW 1 (RS): P2, LT, k5, RT, *p3, LT, k5, RT; repeat from * to last 2 sts, p2.

ROW 2 AND ALL WS ROWS: Purl.

ROW 3: P1, *RT, LT, k3, RT, LT, p1; repeat from * to end.

ROW 5: K1, *[LT, k1] twice, [RT, k1] twice; repeat from * to end.

ROW 7: K2, LT, RT, p1, LT, RT, *k3, LT, RT, p1, LT, RT; repeat from * to last 2 sts, k2.

ROW 9: K3, LT, p3, RT, *k5, LT, p3, RT; repeat from * to last 3 sts, k3.

ROW 11: K3, RT, p3, LT, *k5, RT, p3, LT; repeat from * to last 3 sts, k3.

ROW 13: K2, RT, LT, p1, RT, LT, *k3, RT, LT, p1, RT, LT; repeat from * to last 2 sts, k2.

ROW 15: K1, *[RT, k1] twice, [LT, k1] twice; repeat from * to end.

ROW 17: P1, *LT, RT, k3, LT, RT, p1; repeat from * to end.

ROW 19: P2, RT, k5, LT, *p3, RT, k5, LT; repeat from * to last 2 sts, p2.

ROW 20: Purl.

Repeat Rows 1–20 for pattern.

(52) Plaid Small

Replace the Garter stitch centers of Plaid Small Garter (#51) with reverse Stockinette stitch to make this stitch. More difficult to knit on the wrong-side rows, this variation requires counting, as it's hard to read your knitting.

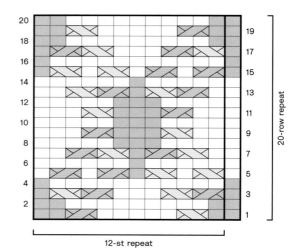

12-st repeat

20-row repeat

(multiple of 12 sts + 1; 20-row repeat)

PSS: 90

ROW 1 (RS): P2, LT, k5, RT, *p3, LT, k5, RT; repeat from * to last 2 sts, p2.

ROW 2: Knit the knit sts and purl the purl sts as they face you.

ROW 3: P1, *RT, LT, k3, RT, LT, p1; repeat from * to end.

ROW 4: Repeat Row 2.

ROW 5: K1, *LT, k1, LT, p1, [RT, k1] twice; repeat from * to end.

ROW 6: Repeat Row 2.

ROW 7: K2, LT, RT, p1, LT, RT, *k3, LT, RT, p1, LT, RT; repeat from * to last 2 sts, k2.

ROW 8: P5, k3, *p9, k3; repeat from * to last 5 sts, p5.

ROW 9: K3, LT, p3, RT, *k5, LT, p3, RT; repeat from * to last 3 sts, k3.

ROW 10: Repeat Row 2.

ROW 11: K3, RT, p3, LT, *k5, RT, p3, LT; repeat from * to last 3 sts, k3.

ROW 12: Repeat Row 2.

ROW 13: K2, RT, LT, p1, RT, LT, *k3, RT, LT, p1, RT, LT; repeat from * to last 2 sts, k2.

ROW 14: Repeat Row 2.

ROW 15: P1, *[RT, k1] twice, LT, k1, LT, p1; repeat from * to end.

ROW 16: Repeat Row 2.

ROW 17: P1, *LT, RT, k3, LT, RT, p1; repeat from * to end.

ROW 18: K2, p9, *k3, p9; repeat from * to last 2 sts, k2.

ROW 19: P2, RT, k5, LT, *p3, RT, k5, LT; repeat from * to last 2 sts, p2.

ROW 20: Repeat Row 2.

Repeat Rows 1–20 for pattern.

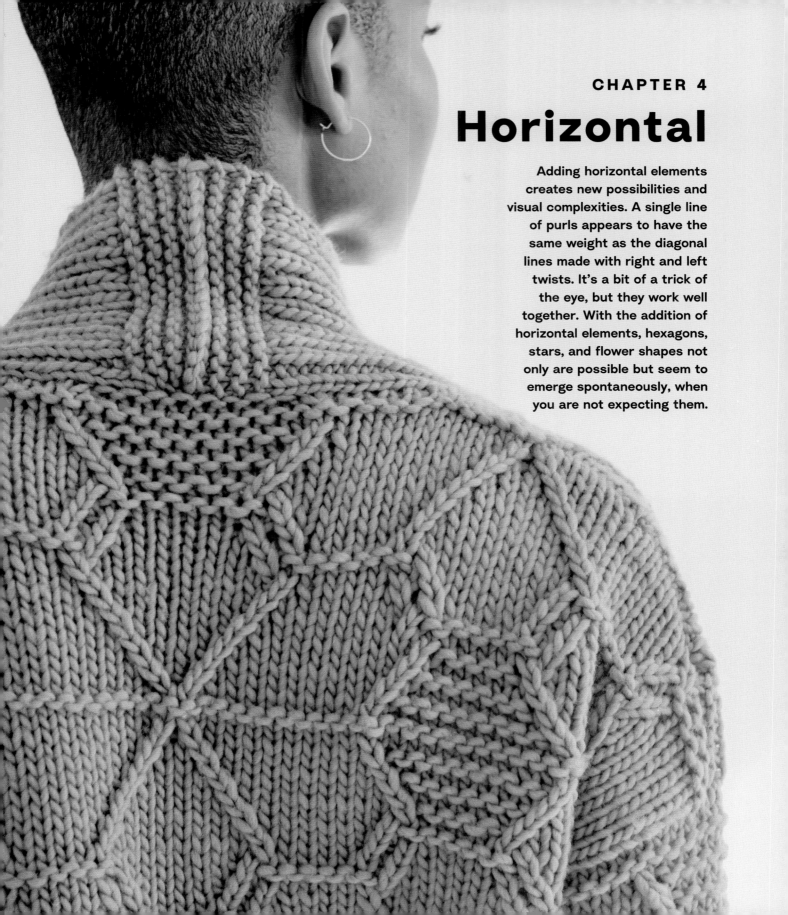

CHAPTER 4
Horizontal

Adding horizontal elements creates new possibilities and visual complexities. A single line of purls appears to have the same weight as the diagonal lines made with right and left twists. It's a bit of a trick of the eye, but they work well together. With the addition of horizontal elements, hexagons, stars, and flower shapes not only are possible but seem to emerge spontaneously, when you are not expecting them.

53 Tri

Opposing diagonals underlined with the horizontal lines of Garter stitch form a matrix of small triangles.

(multiple of 6 sts; 12-row repeat)

PSS: 85

ROW 1 (RS): Purl.

ROW 2 AND ALL WS ROWS: Purl.

ROW 3: K1, RT, LT, *k2, RT, LT; repeat from * to last st, k1.

ROW 5: *RT, k2, LT; repeat from * to end.

ROW 7: Purl.

ROW 9: *LT, k2, RT; repeat from * to end.

ROW 11: K1, LT, RT, *k2, LT, RT; repeat from * to last st, k1.

ROW 12: Purl.

Repeat Rows 1–12 for pattern.

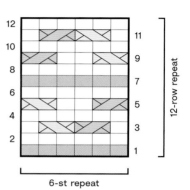

54 Random Tris

Expanding the size of Tri (#53) by one more twist on each diagonal makes the triangles a little larger. Garter stitch fills in the centers of a few of these triangles in an arrangement that appears to be random, but the pattern is actually repeatable.

(multiple of 30 sts; 60-row repeat)

PSS: 90

ROW 1 (RS): Purl.

ROW 2 AND ALL WS ROWS: Purl.

ROW 3: *K3, RT, LT, k3; repeat from * to end.

ROW 5: *K2, [RT, k2, LT, k4] twice, RT, p2, LT, k2; repeat from * to end.

ROW 7: *K1, [RT, k4, LT, k2] twice, RT, p4, LT, k1; repeat from * to end.

ROW 9: *[LT, k6, RT] twice, LT, p6, RT; repeat from * to end.

ROW 11: Purl.

ROW 13: *[LT, k6, RT] 3 times; repeat from * to end.

ROW 15: *K1, LT, k4, RT, k1; repeat from * to end.

ROW 17: *K2, LT, k2, RT, k2; repeat from * to end.

ROW 19: *K3, LT, RT, k3; repeat from * to end.

ROW 21: Purl.

ROW 23: *K3, RT, LT, p6, RT, LT, k6, RT, LT, k3; repeat from * to end.

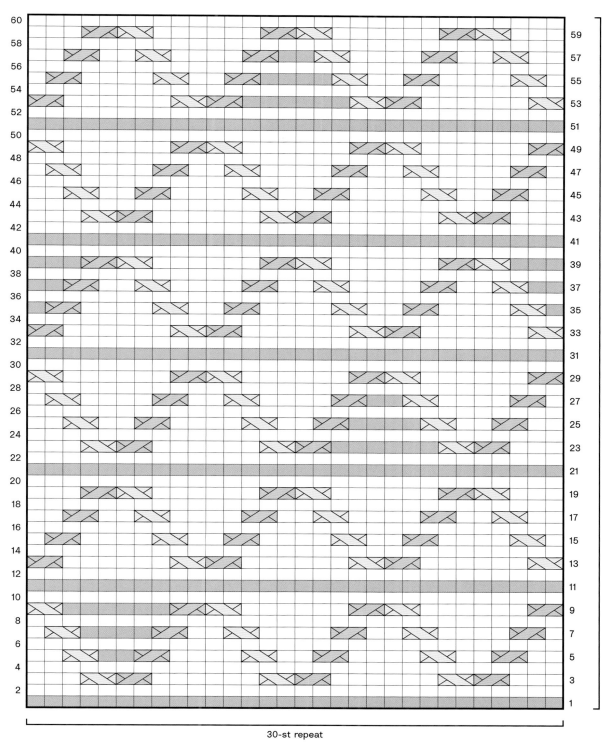

60-row repeat

30-st repeat

ROW 25: *K2, RT, k2, LT, p4, RT, k2, LT, k4, RT, k2, LT, k2; repeat from * to end.

ROW 27: *K1, RT, k4, LT, p2, RT, k4, LT, k2, RT, k4, LT, k1; repeat from * to end.

ROW 29: *RT, k6, LT; repeat from * to end.

ROW 31: Purl.

ROW 33: Repeat Row 13.

ROW 35: *P1, LT, k4, RT, [k2, LT, k4, RT] twice, p1; repeat from * to end.

ROW 37: *P2, LT, k2, RT, [k4, LT, k2, RT] twice, p2; repeat from * to end.

ROW 39: *P3, LT, RT, [k6, LT, RT] twice, p3; repeat from * to end.

ROW 41: Purl.

ROW 43: Repeat Row 3.

ROW 45: *K2, RT, k2, LT, k2; repeat from * to end.

ROW 47: *K1, RT, k4, LT, k1; repeat from * to end.

ROW 49: Repeat Row 29.

ROW 51: Purl.

ROW 53: *LT, k6, RT, LT, p6, RT, LT, k6, RT; repeat from * to end.

ROW 55: *K1, LT, k4, RT, k2, LT, p4, RT, k2, LT, k4, RT, k1; repeat from * to end.

ROW 57: *K2, LT, k2, RT, k4, LT, p2, RT, k4, LT, k2, RT, k2; repeat from * to end.

ROW 59: Repeat Row 19.

ROW 60: Purl.

Repeat Rows 1–60 for pattern.

(55) Multiple Tris

Three sizes of triangles are mixed together in this collage-like arrangement. Mathematical relationships are at play here. Four of the smallest triangles add up to the same width as three of the middle-sized triangles, which also equals the width of two of the largest triangles.

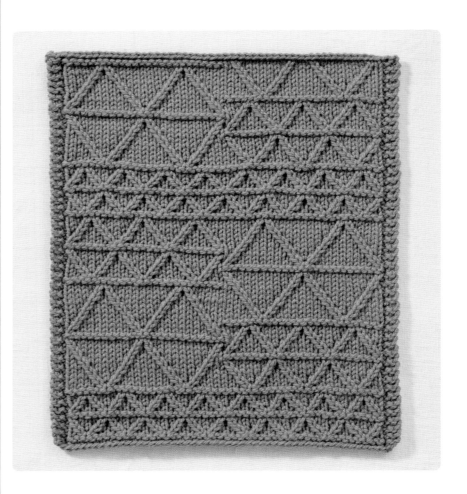

(multiple of 48 sts; 52-row repeat)

PSS: 90

ROW 1 (RS): Purl.

ROW 2 AND ALL WS ROWS: Purl.

ROW 3: *K1, RT, LT, k1; repeat from * to end.

ROW 5: *RT, k2, LT; repeat from * to end.

ROW 7: Purl.

ROW 9: *LT, k2, RT; repeat from * to end.

ROW 11: *K1, LT, RT, k1; repeat from * to end.

ROW 13: Purl.

ROW 15: *[K2, RT, LT, k2] 3 times, [k4, RT, LT, k4] twice; repeat from * to end.

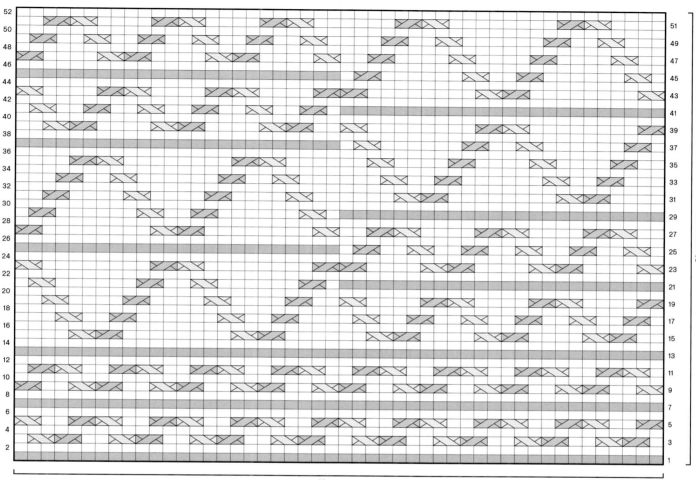

ROW 17: *[K1, RT, k2, LT, k1] 3 times, [k3, RT, k2, LT, k] twice; repeat from * to end.

ROW 19: *[RT, k4, LT] 3 times, [k2, RT, k4, LT, k2] twice; repeat from * to end.

ROW 21: *P24, [k1, RT, k6, LT, k1] twice; repeat from * to end.

ROW 23: *[LT, k4, RT] 3 times, [RT, k8, LT] twice; repeat from * to end.

ROW 25: *[K1, LT, k2, RT, k1] 3 times, p24; repeat from * to end.

ROW 27: *[K2, LT, RT, k2] 3 times, [LT, k8, RT] twice; repeat from * to end.

ROW 29: *P24, [k1, LT, k6, RT, k1] twice; repeat from * to end.

ROW 31: *[K4, RT, LT, k4] twice, [k2, LT, k4, RT, k2] twice; repeat from * to end.

ROW 33: *[K3, RT, k2, LT, k3] twice, [k3, LT, k2, RT, k3] twice; repeat from * to end.

ROW 35: *K2, RT, k4, LT, k4, RT, k4, LT, k6, LT, RT, k8, LT, RT, k4; repeat from * to end.

ROW 37: *K1, RT, k6, LT, k2, RT, k6, LT, k1, p24; repeat from * to end.

ROW 39: *[RT, k8, LT] twice, k2, RT, LT, [k4, RT, LT] twice, k2; repeat from * to end.

ROW 41: *P24, k1, RT, k2, LT, [k2, RT, k2, LT] twice, k1; repeat from * to end.

ROW 43: *[LT, k8, RT] twice, [RT, k4, LT] 3 times; repeat from * to end.

ROW 45: *K1, LT, k6, RT, k2, LT, k6, RT, k1, p24; repeat from * to end.

ROW 47: *K2, LT, k4, RT, k4, LT, k4, RT, k2, [LT, k4, RT] 3 times; repeat from * to end.

ROW 49: *K3, LT, k2, RT, k6, LT, k2, RT, k4, LT, k2, RT, [k2, LT, k2, RT] twice, k1; repeat from * to end.

ROW 51: *K4, LT, RT, k8, LT, RT, k6, LT, RT, [k4, LT, RT] twice, k2; repeat from * to end.

ROW 52: Purl.

Repeat Rows 1–52 for pattern.

56 Flowers Allover

Giant geometric blooms join forces, and the spaces between them are hexagons, which are highlighted with a Garter stitch fill.

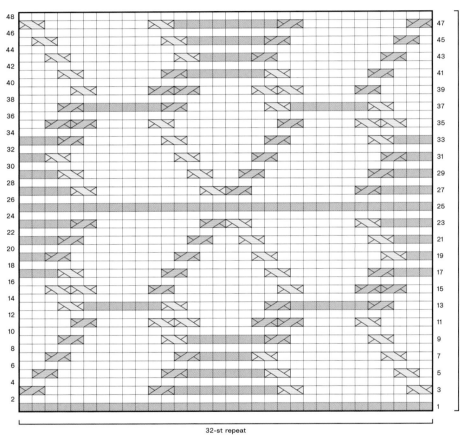

32-st repeat

48-row repeat

(57) Single Flowers

Four separate flowers are shown here in one swatch. Both large and small, with single diagonals and double, these flowers can be placed as you like. Use them alone, combined in a grid, or strewn in a more haphazard arrangement.

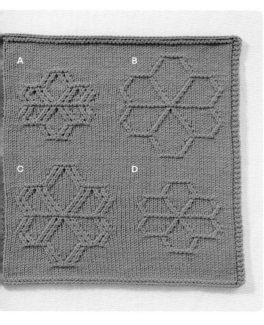

A
(panel of 22 sts; 29 rows)
PSS: 85
ROW 1 (RS): K8, p6, k8.
ROW 2 AND ALL WS ROWS: Purl.
ROW 3: K7, RT twice, LT twice, k7.
ROW 5: K6, RT twice, k2, LT twice, k6.
ROW 7: K2 p6, k6, p6, k2.
ROW 9: K1, RT twice, LT twice, k4, RT twice, LT twice, k1.
ROW 11: [LT twice, k2] twice, RT twice, k2, RT twice.
ROW 13: K1, LT twice, k2, LT twice, RT twice, k2, RT twice, k1.
ROW 15: K2, p18, k2.

ROW 17: K1, RT twice, k2, RT twice, LT twice, k2, LT twice, k1.
ROW 19: [RT twice, k2] twice, LT twice, k2, LT twice.
ROW 21: K1, LT twice, RT twice, k4, LT twice, RT twice, k1.
ROW 23: Repeat Row 7.
ROW 25: K6, LT twice, k2, RT twice, k6.
ROW 27: K7, LT twice, RT twice, k7.
ROW 29: Repeat Row 1.

B
(panel of 28 sts; 41 rows)
PSS: 85
ROW 1 (RS): K11, p6, k11.
ROW 2 AND ALL WS ROWS: Purl.
ROW 3: K10, RT, k4, LT, k10.
ROW 5: K9, RT, k6, LT, k9.
ROW 7: K8, RT, k8, LT, k8.
ROW 9: K3, p6, k10, p6, k3.
ROW 11: K2, RT, k4, LT, k8, RT, k4, LT, k2.
ROW 13: K1, RT, k6, LT, k6, RT, k6, LT, k1.
ROW 15: LT, k8, LT, k4, RT, k8, RT.
ROW 17: K1, LT, k8, LT, k2, RT, k8, RT, k1.
ROW 19: K2, LT, k8, LT, RT, k8, RT, k2.
ROW 21: K3, p22, k3.
ROW 23: K2, RT, k8, RT, LT, k8, LT, k2.
ROW 25: K1, RT, k8, RT, k2, LT, k8, LT, k1.
ROW 27: RT, k8, RT, k4, LT, k8, LT.
ROW 29: K1, LT, k6, RT, k6, LT, k6, LT, k1.
ROW 31: K2, LT, k4, RT, k8, LT, k4, RT, k2.
ROW 33: Repeat Row 9.
ROW 35: K8, LT, k8, RT, k8.
ROW 37: K9, LT, k6, RT, k9.
ROW 39: K10, LT, k4, RT, k10
ROW 41: Repeat Row 1.

C
(panel of 28 sts; 41 rows)
PSS: 85
ROW 1 (RS): K11, p6, k11.
ROW 2 AND ALL WS ROWS: Purl.
ROW 3: K10, RT twice, LT twice, k10.
ROW 5: K9, RT twice, k2, LT twice, k9.
ROW 7: K8, RT twice, k4, LT twice, k8.
ROW 9: K3, p6, RT, k6, LT, p6, k3.
ROW 11: K2, RT twice, LT twice, k8, RT twice, LT twice, k2.
ROW 13: K1, RT twice, k2, LT twice, k6, RT twice, k2, LT twice, k1.
ROW 15: [LT twice, k4] twice, RT twice, k4, RT twice.
ROW 17: K1, LT twice, k4, LT twice, k2, RT twice, k4, RT twice, k1.
ROW 19: K2, LT twice, k4, LT twice, RT twice, k4, RT twice, k2.
ROW 21: K3, p22, k3.
ROW 23: K2, RT twice, k4, RT twice, LT twice, k4, LT twice, k2.
ROW 25: K1, RT twice, k4, RT twice, k2, LT twice, k4, LT twice, k1.
ROW 27: [RT twice, k4] twice, LT twice, k4, LT twice.
ROW 29: K1, LT twice, k2, RT twice, k6, LT twice, k2, RT twice, k1.
ROW 31: K2, LT twice, RT twice, k8, LT twice, RT twice, k2.
ROW 33: K3, p6, LT, k6, RT, p6, k3.
ROW 35: K8, LT twice, k4, RT twice, k8.
ROW 37: K9, LT twice, k2, RT twice, k9.
ROW 39: K10, LT twice, RT twice, k10.
ROW 41: Repeat Row 1.

A

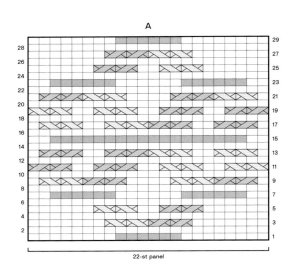

22-st panel

B

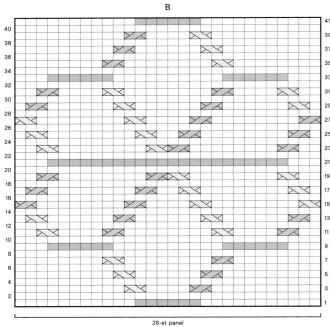

28-st panel

C

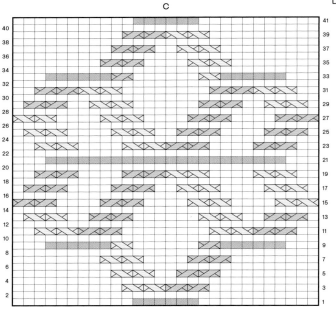

28-st panel

D

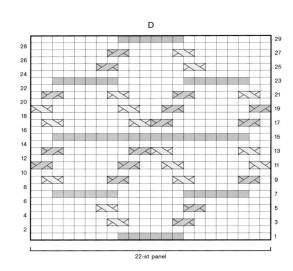

22-st panel

D

(panel of 22 sts; 29 rows)

PSS: 85

ROW 1 (RS): K8, p6, k8.

ROW 2 AND ALL WS ROWS: Purl.

ROW 3: K7, RT, k4, LT, k7.

ROW 5: K6, RT, k6, LT, k6.

ROW 7: K2, p6, k6, p6, k2.

ROW 9: K1, RT, k4, LT, k4, RT, k4, LT, k1.

ROW 11: LT, k6, LT, k2, RT, k6, RT.

ROW 13: K1, LT, k6, LT, RT, k6, RT, k1.

ROW 15: K2, p18, k2.

ROW 17: K1, RT, k6, RT, LT, k6, LT, k1.

ROW 19: RT, k6, RT, k2, LT, k6, LT.

ROW 21: K1, LT, k4, RT, k4, LT, k4, RT, k1.

ROW 23: Repeat Row 7.

ROW 25: K6, LT, k6, RT, k6.

ROW 27: K7, LT, k4, RT, k7.

ROW 29: Repeat Row 1.

(58) Nested Vortex

Truncated diamonds have small diamond centers with their diagonals extended. I see an angular version of the symbol for a hurricane.

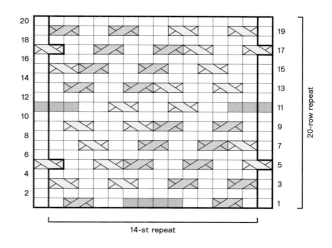

(multiple of 14 sts + 2; 20-row repeat)

PSS: 85

ROW 1 (RS): K2, *RT, k2, p4, k2, RT, k2; repeat from * to end.

ROW 2 AND ALL WS ROWS: Purl.

ROW 3: K1, *[RT, k2] twice, LT, k2, LT; repeat from * to last st, k1.

ROW 5: LT, *[k2, RT] twice, LT, k2, LT; repeat from * to end.

ROW 7: K1, *LT, [RT, k2] twice, LT, k2; repeat from * to last st, k1.

ROW 9: K2, *RT, k2, RT, [LT, k2] twice; repeat from * to end.

ROW 11: P3, k2, [LT, k2] twice, *p4, k2, [LT, k2] twice; repeat from * to last 3 sts, p3.

ROW 13: K2, *LT, k2, LT, [RT, k2] twice; repeat from * to end.

ROW 15: K1, *k2, LT, [k2, RT] twice, LT; repeat from * to last st, k1.

ROW 17: LT, *k2, LT, [RT, k2] twice, LT; repeat from * to end.

ROW 19: K1, *LT, k2, LT, [k2, RT] twice; repeat from * to last st, k1.

ROW 20: Purl.

Repeat Rows 1–20 for pattern.

⑤⑨ X & O Lattice

The well-known symbols for hugs and kisses, Xs and Os, are nestled in a diagonal lattice and boxed in by horizontal lines. The idea started with a row of Xs and Os and became more ornate and intertwined from there.

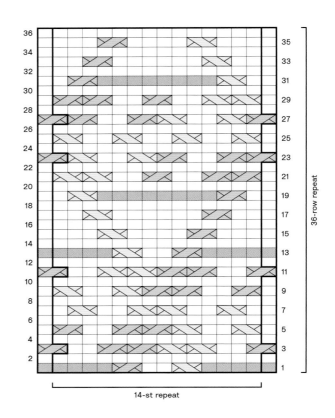

(multiple of 14 sts + 2; 36-row repeat)

PSS: 80

ROW 1 (RS): P5, LT, k2, RT, *p8, LT, k2, RT; repeat from * to last 5 sts, purl to end.

ROW 2 AND ALL WS ROWS: Purl.

ROW 3: RT, *k2, LT twice, RT twice, k2, RT; repeat from * to end.

ROW 5: K1, *LT, k2, LT, RT twice, k2, RT; repeat from * to last st, k1.

ROW 7: K2, *LT, k2, LT twice, k2, LT, k2; repeat from * to end.

ROW 9: K1, *RT, k2, RT twice, LT, k2, LT; repeat from * to last st, k1.

ROW 11: RT, *k2, RT twice, LT twice, k2, RT; repeat from * to end.

ROW 13: P5, RT, k2, LT, *p8, RT, k2, LT; repeat from * to last 5 sts, purl to end.

ROW 15: K4, RT, k4, LT, *k6, RT, k4, LT; repeat from * to last 4 sts, knit to end.

ROW 17: K3, RT, k6, LT, *k4, RT, k6, LT; repeat from * to last 3 sts, k3.

ROW 19: K2, *RT, p8, LT, k2; repeat from * to end.

ROW 21: K1, *RT twice, k2, RT, k2, LT twice; repeat from * to last st, k1.

ROW 23: *RT twice, k2, RT, LT, k2, LT; repeat from * to last 2 sts, RT.

ROW 25: K1, *LT, [k2, LT] 3 times; repeat from * to last st, k1.

ROW 27: RT, *LT, k2, LT, RT, k2, RT twice; repeat from * to end.

ROW 29: K1, *LT twice, k2, RT, k2, RT twice; repeat from * to last st, k1.

ROW 31: K2, *LT, p8, RT, k2; repeat from * to end.

ROW 33: K3, LT, k6, RT, *k4, LT, k6, RT; repeat from * to last 3 sts, k3.

ROW 35: K4, LT, k4, RT, *k6, LT, k4, RT; repeat from * to last 4 sts, knit to end.

ROW 36: Purl.

Repeat Rows 1–36 for pattern.

(60) Rattan

Double diagonal and horizontal lines interlace to form hexagonal centers.
These interweaving forms are reminiscent of rattan chair caning.

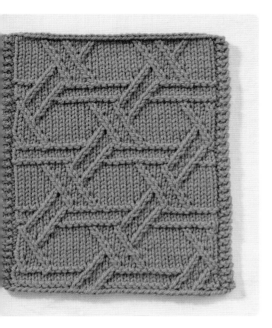

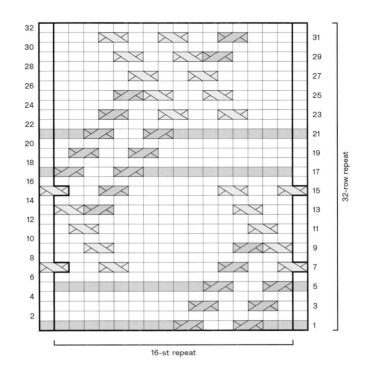

(multiple of 16 sts + 2; 32-row repeat)

PSS: 90

ROW 1 (RS): P3, RT, k2, RT, *p10, RT, k2, RT; repeat from * to last 9 sts, purl to end.

ROW 2 AND ALL WS ROWS: Purl.

ROW 3: K2, *RT, k2, RT, k10; repeat from * to end.

ROW 5: P1 *RT, k2, RT, p10; repeat from * to last st, k1.

ROW 7: LT, *k2, RT, k6, LT, k2, LT; repeat from * to end.

ROW 9: K1, *LT, RT, k8, LT, k2; repeat from * to last st, k1.

ROW 11: K2, *LT, k10, LT, k2; repeat from * to end.

ROW 13: K1, *k2, LT, k8, RT, LT; repeat from * to last st, k1.

ROW 15: LT, *k2, LT, k6, RT, k2, LT; repeat from * to end.

ROW 17: K1, *p10, RT, k2, RT; repeat from * to last st, p1.

ROW 19: *K10, LT, k2, LT; repeat from * to last 2 sts, k2.

ROW 21: P9, RT, k2, RT, *p10, RT, k2, RT; repeat from * to last 3 sts, p3.

ROW 23: K4, [LT, k2] twice, RT, *k6, [LT, k2] twice, RT; repeat from * to last 4 sts, knit to end.

ROW 25: K5, LT, k2, LT, RT, *k8, LT, k2, LT, RT, repeat from * to last 5 sts, knit to end.

ROW 27: K6, LT, k2, LT, *k10, LT, k2, LT; repeat from * to last 6 sts, knit to end.

ROW 29: K5, RT, LT, k2, LT, *k8, RT, LT, k2, LT; repeat from * to last 5 sts, knit to end.

ROW 31: K4, RT, [k2, LT] twice, *k6, RT, [k2, LT] twice; repeat from * to last 4 sts, knit to end.

ROW 32: Purl.

Repeat Rows 1–32 for pattern.

(61) Rattan Filled

Fill the double lines of Rattan (#60) for more ornate and substantial lines. Note that the diagonal twists are two stitches apart before filling and the horizontal lines had three plain rows between them, laying the perfect groundwork for the addition of more twists.

(multiple of 16 sts + 2; 32-row repeat)

PSS: 85

ROW 1 (RS): P3, RT, LT, RT, *p10, RT, LT, RT; repeat from * to last 9 sts, purl to end.

ROW 2 AND ALL WS ROWS: Purl.

ROW 3: *RT twice, LT, RT 5 times; repeat from * to last 2 sts, RT.

ROW 5: P1, *RT, LT, RT, p10; repeat from * to last st, k1.

ROW 7: *LT twice, RT, k6, LT, RT; repeat from * to last 2 sts, LT.

ROW 9: K1, *LT, RT, k8, LT, RT; repeat from * to last st, k1.

ROW 11: RT, *LT, k10, LT, RT; repeat from * to end.

ROW 13: K1, *RT, LT, k8, RT, LT; repeat from * to last st, k1.

ROW 15: LT, *RT, LT, k6, RT, LT twice; repeat from * to end.

ROW 17: K1, *p10, RT, LT, RT; repeat from * to last st, p1.

ROW 19: *RT 6 times, LT, RT; repeat from * to last 2 sts, RT.

ROW 21: P9, RT, LT, RT, *p10, RT, LT, RT; repeat from * to last 3 sts, p3.

ROW 23: K4, LT, RT, LT twice, RT, *k6, LT, RT, LT twice, RT; repeat from * to last 4 sts, knit to end.

ROW 25: K5, [LT, RT] twice, *k8, [LT, RT] twice, repeat from * to last 5 sts, knit to end.

ROW 27: K6, LT, RT, LT, *k10, LT, RT, LT; repeat from * to last 6 sts, knit to end.

ROW 29: K5, [RT, LT] twice, *k8, [RT, LT] twice; repeat from * to last 5 sts, knit to end.

ROW 31: K4, RT, LT twice, RT, LT, *k6, RT, LT twice, RT, LT; repeat from * to last 4 sts, knit to end.

ROW 32: Purl.

Repeat Rows 1–32 for pattern.

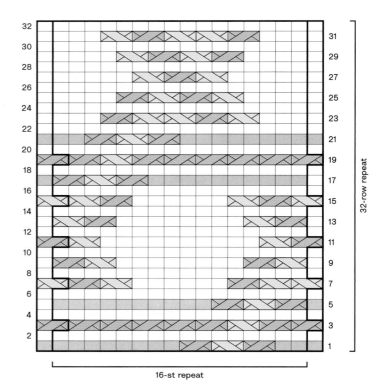

16-st repeat

32-row repeat

(62) Stars Abound

Each single star is made with a simple outline. When they're stacked together, celestial points just touching, a shimmering illusion appears. Which did you see first, the angular clover leaves or the stars?

(multiple of 20 sts + 2; 40-row repeat)

PSS: 90

ROW 1 (RS): K2, *p5, RT, k4, LT, p5, k2; repeat from * to end.

ROW 2 AND ALL WS ROWS: Purl.

ROW 3: K2, *LT, k14, RT, k2; repeat from * to end.

ROW 5: K3, LT, k12, LT, *k4, LT, k12, RT; repeat from * to last 3 sts, k3.

ROW 7: K4, RT, k10, RT, *k6, RT, k10, RT; repeat from * to last 4 sts, knit to end.

ROW 9: K3, RT, k12, LT, *k4, RT, k12, LT; repeat from * to last 3 sts, k3.

ROW 11: K2, *RT, k14, LT, k2; repeat from * to end.

ROW 13: K2, *p5, LT, k4, RT, p5, k2; repeat from * to end.

ROW 15: LT, *k6, LT, k2, RT, k6, LT; repeat from * to end.

ROW 17: K1, *LT, k6, LT, RT, k6, RT; repeat from * to last st, k1.

ROW 19: K2, *[LT, k6] twice, RT, k2; repeat from * to end.

ROW 21: K3, LT, p5, k2, p5, RT, *k4, LT, p5, k2, p5, RT; repeat from * to last 3 sts, k3.

ROW 23: K8, RT, k2, LT, *k14, RT, k2, LT; repeat from * to last 8 sts, knit to end.

ROW 25: K7, RT, k4, LT, *k12, RT, k4, LT; repeat from * to last 7 sts, knit to end.

ROW 27: [K6, RT] twice, *k10, RT, k6, RT; repeat from * to last 6 sts, knit to end.

ROW 29: K7, LT, k4, RT, *k12, LT, k4, RT; repeat from * to last 7 sts, knit to end.

ROW 31: K8, LT, k2, RT, *k14, LT, k2, RT; repeat from * to last 8 sts, knit to end.

ROW 33: K3, RT, p5, k2, p5, LT, *k4, RT, p5, k2, p5, LT; repeat from * to last 3 sts, k3.

ROW 35: K2, *RT, [k6, LT] twice, k2; repeat from * to end.

ROW 37: K1, *RT, k6, RT, LT, k6, LT; repeat from * to last st, k1.

ROW 39: LT, *k6, RT, k2, LT, k6, LT; repeat from * to end.

ROW 40: Purl.

Repeat Rows 1–40 for pattern.

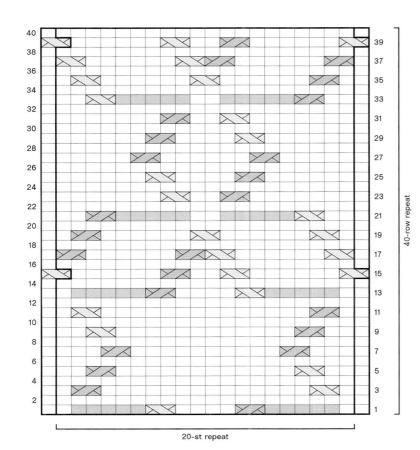

20-st repeat

40-row repeat

(63) Diamond Star

Six-pointed stars come together effortlessly with the combination of diagonal and horizontal lines. Look carefully and you will see two triangles intertwining with each other. Doubling the diagonals adds strength and interest and an opportunity for weaving at the intersections.

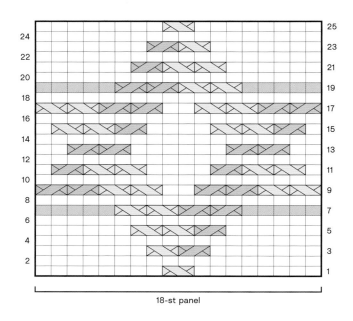

18-st panel

(panel of 18 sts; 25 rows)

PSS: 90

ROW 1 (RS): K8, LT, k8.

ROW 2 AND ALL WS ROWS: Purl.

ROW 3: K7, RT, LT, k7.

ROW 5: K6, RT, LT twice, k6.

ROW 7: P5, RT twice, LT twice, p5.

ROW 9: LT twice, RT twice, k2, LT twice, RT twice.

ROW 11: K1, LT twice, RT, k4, LT twice, RT, k1.

ROW 13: K2, RT twice, k6, RT twice, k2.

ROW 15: K1, RT, LT twice, k4, RT, LT twice, k1.

ROW 17: RT twice, LT twice, k2, RT twice, LT twice.

ROW 19: P5, LT twice, RT twice, p5.

ROW 21: K6, LT twice, RT, k6.

ROW 23: K7, LT, RT, k7.

ROW 25: K8, LT, k8.

(64) Smocking

While this swatch actually came first, take a look at #47, Lizard, and you'll see that Smocking is an extension of Lizard with every line, both diagonal and horizontal, worked twice.

(multiple of 10 sts; 16-row repeat)

PSS: 90

ROW 1 (RS): K2, p6, *k4, p6; repeat from * to last 2 sts, k2.

ROW 2 AND ALL WS ROWS: Purl.

ROW 3: Repeat Row 1.

ROW 5: K1, RT twice, LT twice, *k2, RT twice, LT twice; repeat from * to last st, k1.

ROW 7: *RT twice, k2, LT twice; repeat from * to end.

ROW 9: *P3, k4, p3; repeat from * to end.

ROW 11: Repeat Row 9.

ROW 13: *LT twice, k2, RT twice; repeat from * to end.

ROW 15: K1, LT twice, RT twice, *k2, LT twice, RT twice; repeat from * to last st, k1.

ROW 16: Purl.

Repeat Rows 1–16 for pattern.

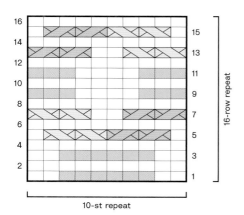

10-st repeat · 16-row repeat

(65) Smocking Half Step

Moving the diamond and Garter motif over five stitches every eight rows creates a smooth transition from plain Stockinette stitch into the allover pattern.

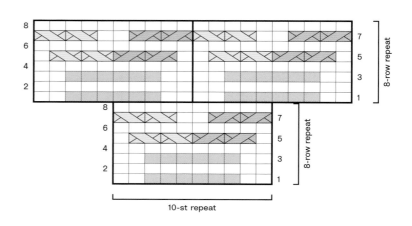

10-st repeat

(panel of 10 sts; one 10-st panel added to pattern every 8 rows; 8-row repeat)

PSS: 90

NOTE: Place a marker on either side of 10 sts to mark first 10-st panel; you will work Rows 1–8 of pattern between these markers.

ROW 1 (RS): K2, p6, k2.

ROW 2 AND ALL WS ROWS: Purl.

ROW 3: Repeat Row 1.

ROW 5: K1, RT twice, LT twice, k1.

ROW 7: RT twice, k2, LT twice.

ROW 8: Purl.

NEXT 8 ROWS: Add a marker 5 sts before first marker and 5 sts after last marker; remove markers from previous repeat of Rows 1–8. Add markers every 10 sts between new outside markers. Repeat Rows 1–8 between each set of markers.

Continue as established, adding one new 10-st panel every 8 rows as desired.

CHART NOTES

Place a marker on either side of 10 sts to mark first 10-st panel; you will work Rows 1–8 of pattern between these markers.

After working Rows 1–8 for the first time, add a marker 5 sts before first marker and 5 sts after last marker; remove markers from previous repeat of Rows 1–8. Add markers every 10 sts between new outside markers. Repeat Rows 1–8 between each set of markers.

Continue as established, adding one new 10-st panel every 8 rows as desired.

(66) Smocking Grow

Expanded by a full repeat each side every 16 rows, this pattern actually grows at the same rate as Smocking Half Step (#65), but with a more jagged edge.

[panel of 10 sts at beginning; one 10-st panel added to either side of pattern every 16 rows; 16-row repeat]

NOTE: Place a marker on either side of 10 sts to mark first 10-st panel; you will work Rows 1–16 of pattern between these markers.

PSS: 90

ROW 1 (RS): K2, p6, k2.

ROW 2 AND ALL WS ROWS: Purl.

ROW 3: Repeat Row 1.

ROW 5: K1, RT twice, LT twice, k1.

ROW 7: RT twice, k2, LT twice.

ROW 9: P3, k4, p3.

ROW 11: Repeat Row 9.

ROW 13: LT twice, k2, RT twice.

ROW 15: K1, LT twice, RT twice, k1.

ROW 16: Purl.

NEXT 16 ROWS: Add a marker 10 sts before first marker and 10 sts after last marker; repeat Rows 1–16 between each set of markers.

Continue as established, adding one 10-st panel to each side every 16 rows as desired.

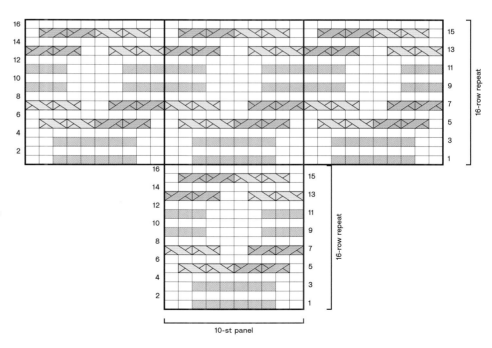

⑥⑦ Smocking Fancy

Leaving a few stitches out of the interior of Smocking Grow (#66) gives it a lace-like and more baroque quality.

(panel of 50 sts; 32-row repeat + 32 rows)

PSS: 90

ROW 1 (RS): K22, p6, k22.

ROW 2 AND ALL WS ROWS: Purl.

ROW 3: Repeat Row 1.

ROW 5: K21, RT twice, LT twice, k21.

ROW 7: K20, RT twice, k2, LT twice, k20.

ROW 9: K20, p3, k4, p3, k20.

ROW 11: Repeat Row 9.

ROW 13: K20, LT twice, k2, RT twice, k20.

ROW 15: K21, LT twice, RT twice, k21.

ROW 17: K12, p6, [k4, p6] twice, k12.

ROW 19: Repeat Row 17.

ROW 21: K11, RT twice, LT twice, [k2, RT twice, LT twice] twice, k11.

ROW 23: K10, [RT twice, k2, LT twice] 3 times, k10.

ROW 25: K10, p3, k4, [p6, k4] twice, p3, k10.

ROW 27: Repeat Row 25.

ROW 29: K10, LT twice, k2, RT twice, k10, LT twice, k2, RT twice, k10.

ROW 31: K11, LT twice, RT twice, k12, LT twice, RT twice, k11.

ROW 33: K2, p6, k4, p6, k14, p6, k4, p6, k2.

ROW 35: Repeat Row 33.

ROW 37: K1, RT twice, LT twice, k2, RT twice, LT twice, k12, RT twice, LT twice, k2, RT twice, LT twice, k1.

ROW 39: [RT twice, k2, LT twice] twice, k10, [RT twice, k2, LT twice] twice.

ROW 41: P3, k4, [p6, k4] 4 times, p3.

ROW 43: Repeat Row 41.

ROW 45: LT twice, k2, RT twice, [k10, LT twice, k2, RT twice] twice.

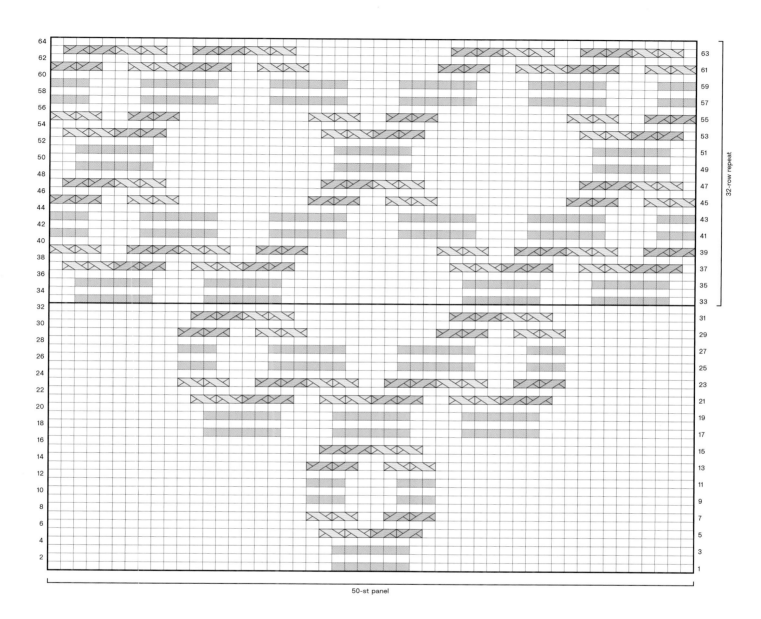

64
63
62
61
60
59
58
57
56
55
54
53
52
51
50
49
48
47
46
45
44
43
42
41
40
39
38
37
36
35
34
33
32
31
30
29
28
27
26
25
24
23
22
21
20
19
18
17
16
15
14
13
12
11
10
9
8
7
6
5
4
3
2
1

32-row repeat

50-st panel

ROW 47: K1, LT twice, RT twice, [k12, LT twice, RT twice] twice, k1.

ROW 49: K2, p6, [k14, p6] twice, k2.

ROW 51: Repeat Row 51.

ROW 53: K1, RT twice, LT twice, [k12, RT twice, LT twice] twice, k1.

ROW 55: RT twice, k2, LT twice, [k10, RT twice, k2, LT twice] twice.

ROW 57: Repeat Row 41.

ROW 59: Repeat Row 41.

ROW 61: [LT twice, k2, RT twice] twice, k10, [LT twice, k2, RT twice] twice.

ROW 63: K1, LT twice, RT twice, k2, LT twice, RT twice, k12, LT twice, RT twice, k2, LT twice, RT twice, k1.

ROW 64: Purl.

Repeat Rows 33–64 for pattern.

(68) Twirl

The combination of diagonal and horizontal lines forms three different parallelograms, which are placed together in a whirligig formation. The star center came as a surprise.

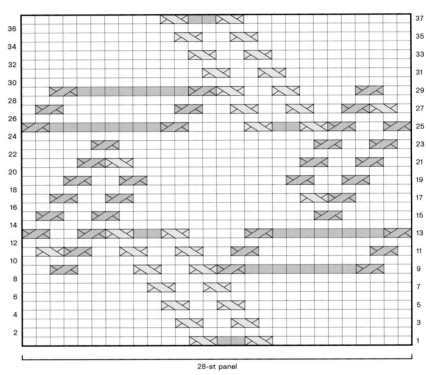

28-st panel

(28-st panel; 37 rows)

PSS: 90

ROW 1 (RS): K10, LT, p2, LT, k12.

ROW 2 AND ALL WS ROWS: Purl.

ROW 3: K11, LT, k2, LT, k11.

ROW 5: K12, LT, k2, LT, k10.

ROW 7: K13, LT, k2, LT, k9.

ROW 9: K2, RT, p8, RT, LT, k2, LT, k4, RT, k2.

ROW 11: K1, RT, k8, RT, k2, [LT, k2] twice, RT, LT, k1.

ROW 13: RT, p8, RT, k4, LT, p2, LT, RT, k2, RT.

ROW 15: K5, RT, k14, RT, k2, RT, k1.

ROW 17: K4, RT, LT, k12, [RT, k2] twice.

ROW 19: K3, RT, k2, RT, k10, RT, k2, RT, k3.

ROW 21: [K2, RT] twice, k12, LT, RT, k4.

ROW 23: K1, RT, k2, RT, k14, RT k5.

ROW 25: RT, k2, RT, LT, p2, LT, k4, RT, p8, RT.

ROW 27: K1, LT, RT, k2, [LT, k2] twice, RT, k8, RT, k1.

ROW 29: K2, RT, k4, LT, k2, LT, RT, p8, RT, k2.

ROW 31: K9, LT, k2, LT, k13.

ROW 33: K10, LT, k2, LT, k12.

ROW 35: K11, LT, k2, LT, k11.

ROW 37: K12, LT, p2, LT, k10.

⑥⑨ Twirl Allover

Repeating the whirligigs of Twirl (#68) makes an interesting allover pattern.

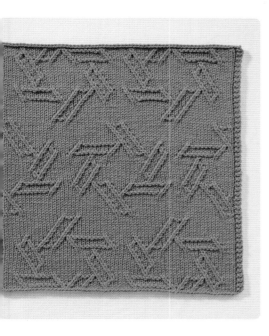

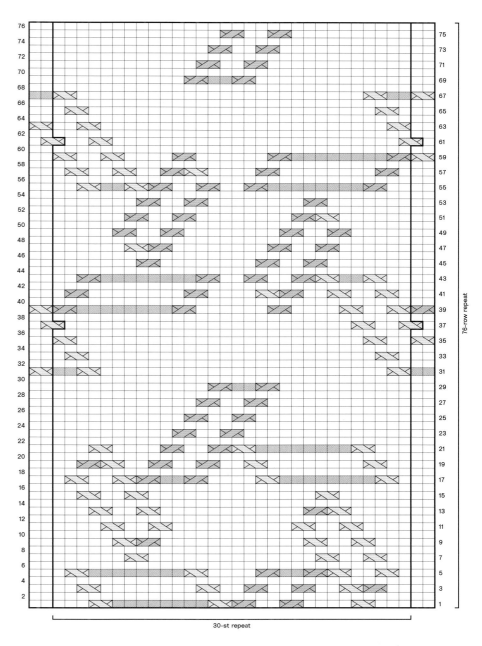

76-row repeat

30-st repeat

⑦⓪ Arrows

Two of the three parallelograms from Twirl (#68) are rearranged to form a large arrow, which is then alternated with its own mirror image.

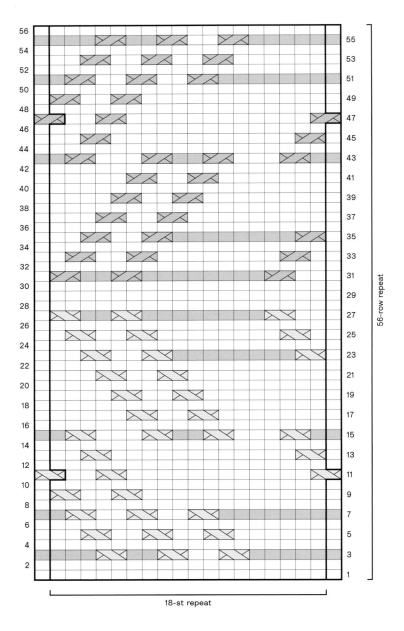

18-st repeat

56-row repeat

(71) Blanket Star

Although not obvious at first glance, Blanket Star was constructed using two elements from Twirl (#68) and their mirror images.

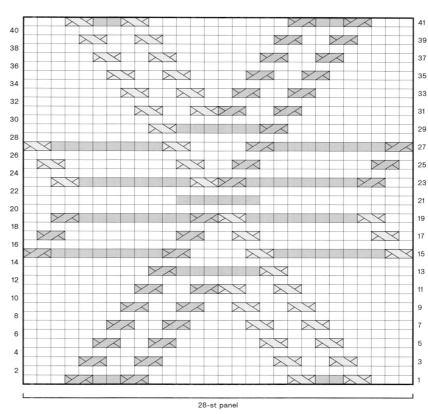

28-st panel

(panel of 28 sts; 41 rows)

PSS: 90

ROW 1 (RS): K3, LT, p2, LT, k10, RT, p2, RT, k3.

ROW 2 AND ALL WS ROWS: Purl.

ROW 3: K4, LT, k2, LT, k8, RT, k2, RT, k4.

ROW 5: K5, LT, k2, LT, k6, RT, k2, RT, k5.

ROW 7: K6, LT, k2, LT, k4, RT, k2, RT, k6.

ROW 9: K7, [LT, k2] twice, RT, k2, RT, k7.

ROW 11: K8, LT, k2, LT, RT, k2, RT, k8.

ROW 13: K9, LT, p6, RT, k9.

ROW 15: LT, p8, LT, k4, RT, p8, RT.

ROW 17: K1, LT, k8, LT, k2, RT, k8, RT, k1.

ROW 19: K2, LT, p8, LT, RT, p8, RT, k2.

ROW 21: K11, p6, k11.

ROW 23: K2, RT, p8, RT, LT, p8, LT, k2.

ROW 25: K1, RT, k8, RT, k2, LT, k8, LT, k1.

ROW 27: RT, p8, RT, k4, LT, p8, LT.

ROW 29: K9, RT, p6, LT, k9.

ROW 31: K8, RT, k2, RT, LT, k2, LT, k8.

ROW 33: K7, [RT, k2] twice, LT, k2, LT, k7.

ROW 35: K6, RT, k2, RT, k4, LT, k2, LT, k6.

ROW 37: K5, RT, k2, RT, k6, LT, k2, LT, k5.

ROW 39: K4, RT, k2, RT, k8, LT, k2, LT, k4.

ROW 41: K3, RT, p2, RT, k10, LT, p2, LT, k3.

(72) Big Star

Big Star is a further evolution of Blanket Star (#71), with some elements shortened and diamonds added.

(panel of 36 sts; 51 rows)

PSS: 90

ROW 1 (RS): K17, RT, k17.

ROW 2 AND ALL WS ROWS THROUGH ROW 24: Purl.

ROW 3: K16, RT, LT, k16.

ROW 5: K15, RT, k2, LT, k15.

ROW 7: K14, RT, k4, LT, k14.

ROW 9: K13, RT, k6, LT, k13.

ROW 11: K6, LT, p2, LT, k2, LT, k4, RT, k2, RT, p2, RT, k6.

ROW 13: K7, [LT, k2] 3 times, RT, [k2, RT] twice, k7.

ROW 15: K8, LT, [k2, LT] twice, RT, [k2, RT] twice, k8.

ROW 17: K9, [LT, k2] twice, RT, [k2, RT] twice, k9.

ROW 19: LT, p5, LT, k1, LT, k2, LT, k4, RT, k2, RT, k1, RT, p5, RT.

ROW 21: K1, LT, k5, LT, k1, [LT, k2] twice, RT, k2, RT, k1, RT, k5, RT, k1.

ROW 23: K2, LT, p5, LT, k1, LT, p2, LT, RT, p2, RT, k1, RT, p5, RT, k2.

ROW 25: Knit.

ROW 26: P3, k30, p3.

ROW 27: Knit.

ROW 28 AND ALL WS ROWS THROUGH ROW 50: Purl.

ROW 29: K2, RT, p5, RT, k1, RT, p2, RT, LT, p2, LT, k1, LT, p5, LT, k2.

ROW 31: K1, RT, k5, RT, k1, [RT, k2] twice, LT, k2, LT, k1, LT, k5, LT, k1.

ROW 33: RT, p5, RT, k1, RT, k2, RT, k4, LT, k2, LT, k1, LT, p5, LT.

ROW 35: K9, [RT, k2] 3 times, LT, k2, LT, k9.

ROW 37: K8, RT, [k2, RT] twice, LT, [k2, LT] twice, k8.

ROW 39: K7, [RT, k2] 3 times, LT, [k2, LT] twice, k7.

ROW 41: K6, RT, p2, RT, k2, RT, k4, LT, k2, LT, p2, LT, k6.

ROW 43: K13, LT, k6, RT, k13.

ROW 45: K14, LT, k4, RT, k14.

ROW 47: K15, LT, k2, RT, k15.

ROW 49: K16, LT, RT, k16.

ROW 51: K17, RT, k17.

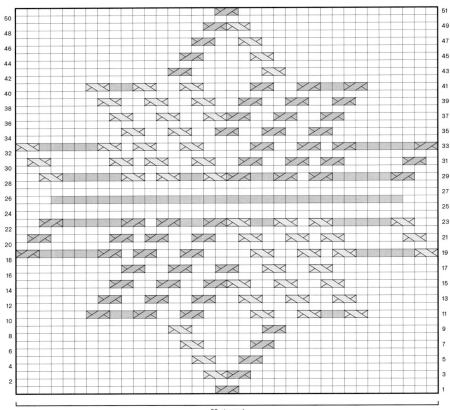

36-st panel

CHAPTER 5

Vertical

In this chapter, vertical and diagonal lines coexist. A variety of techniques are used to bring in upright elements. The simp lest is the transition from knit to purl, seen in Pleated (#79) and Quiver (#80). Ribs and twisted ribs make crisp vertical lines, while mini cables make more textured, wider lines. With the addition of vertical lines comes the ability to simulate curves and round things out, illustrated best in Droplets (#87).

(73) Starburst

While swatching another pattern, now forgotten to me, I envisioned this arrangement of diagonals and mini cables. The strong vertical elements are twists stacked on top of each other to make mini cables, while a few columns of reverse Stockinette stitch add vertical reinforcement.

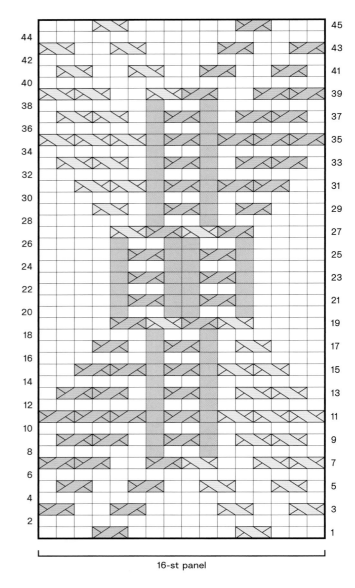

16-st panel

(16-st panel; 45 rows)

PSS: 85

ROW 1 (RS): K3, LT, k6, RT, k3.

ROW 2: Purl.

ROW 3: LT, k2, LT, k4, RT, k2, RT.

ROW 4: Purl.

ROW 5: K1, [LT, k2] twice, RT, k2, RT, k1.

ROW 6: Purl.

ROW 7: LT twice, k2, LT, RT, k2, RT twice.

ROW 8: P6, k1, p2, k1, p6.

ROW 9: K1, LT twice, k1, p1, RT, p1, k1, RT twice, k1.

ROW 10 AND ALL WS ROWS THROUGH ROW 18: Knit the knit sts and purl the purl sts as they face you.

ROW 11: LT 3 times, p1, RT, p1, RT 3 times.

ROW 13: Repeat Row 9.

ROW 15: K2, LT twice, p1, RT, p1, RT twice, k2.

ROW 17: K3, LT, k1, p1, RT, p1, k1, RT, k3.

ROW 19: K4, [LT, RT] twice, k4.

ROW 20: P4, k1, p2, k2, p2, k1, p4.

ROW 21: K4, p1, RT, p2, RT, p1, k4.

ROWS 22-25: Repeat Rows 20 and 21 twice.

ROW 26: Repeat Row 20.

ROW 27: K4, [RT, LT] twice, k4.

ROW 28: P6, k1, p2, k1, p6.

ROW 29: K3, RT, k1, p1, RT, p1, k1, LT, k3.

ROW 30 AND ALL WS ROWS THROUGH ROW 38: Repeat Row 10.

ROW 31: K2, RT twice, p1, RT, p1, LT twice, k2.

ROW 33: K1, RT twice, k1, p1, RT, p1, k1, LT twice, k1.

ROW 35: RT 3 times, p1, RT, p1, LT 3 times.

ROW 37: Repeat Row 33.

ROW 39: RT twice, k2, RT, LT, k2, LT twice.

ROW 40: Purl.

ROW 41: K1, [RT, k2] twice, LT, k2, LT, k1.

ROW 42: Purl.

ROW 43: RT, k2, RT, k4, LT, k2, LT.

ROW 44: Purl.

ROW 45: K3, RT, k6, LT, k3.

Spruce

This column of twists and texture can be worked as a single column or repeated as an allover composition. A twisted knit worked through the back loop on every row forms the crisp central vertical line.

(multiple of 16 sts + 1; 6-row repeat)

PSS: 80

ROW 1 (RS): P1, *k2, RT, k1, p1, [k1-tbl, p1] twice, k1, LT, k2, p1; repeat from * to end.

ROW 2: K1, *p6, p1-tbl, k1, p1-tbl, p6, k1; repeat from * to end.

ROW 3: P1, *k1, RT, k2, p1, [k1-tbl, p1] twice, k2, LT, k1, p1; repeat from * to end.

ROW 4: Repeat Row 2.

ROW 5: P1, *RT, k1, RT, p1, [k1-tbl, p1] twice, LT, k1, LT, p1; repeat from * to end.

ROW 6: Repeat Row 2.

Repeat Rows 1–6 for pattern.

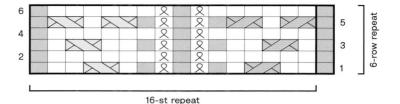

16-st repeat

6-row repeat

(75) Spire

A subtle vertical mini cable adds a spine to this arrangement of expanding, then diminishing, chevrons.

(multiple of 14 sts; 63 rows)

PSS: 80

ROW 1 (RS): K6, RT, *k12, RT; repeat from * to last 6 sts, knit to end.

ROW 2 AND ALL WS ROWS: Purl.

ROW 3: K5, RT, LT, *k10, RT, LT; repeat from * to last 5 sts, knit to end.

ROW 5: Repeat Row 1.

ROW 7: Repeat Row 3

ROW 9: K4, RT twice, LT, *k8, RT twice, LT; repeat from * to last 4 sts, knit to end.

ROW 11: Repeat Row 3.

ROW 13: Repeat Row 9.

ROW 15: K3, [RT, k1] twice, LT, *k6, [RT, k1] twice, LT; repeat from * to last 3 sts, k3.

ROW 17: Repeat Row 3.

ROW 19: Repeat Row 9.

ROW 21: Repeat Row 15.

ROW 23: K2, RT, k1, RT, LT, k1, LT, *k4, RT, k1, RT, LT, k1, LT; repeat from * to last 2 sts, k2.

ROW 25: Repeat Row 9.

ROW 27: Repeat Row 15.

ROW 29: *LT, [RT, k2] twice, LT, RT; repeat from * to end.

ROW 31: K1, [RT, k3] twice, LT, *k2, [RT, k3] twice, LT; repeat from * to last st, k1.

ROW 33: K1, LT, [k3, RT] twice, *k2, LT, [k3, RT] twice; repeat from * to last st, k1.

ROW 35: *RT, LT, [k2, RT] twice, LT; repeat from * to end.

ROW 37: K3, *LT, [k1, RT] twice, *k6, LT, [k1, RT] twice; repeat from * to last 3 sts, k3.

ROW 39: K4, LT, RT twice, *k8, LT, RT twice; repeat from * to last 4 sts, knit to end.

ROW 41: K2, LT, k1, LT, RT, k1, RT, *k4, LT, k1, LT, RT, k1, RT; repeat from * to last 2 sts, k2.

ROW 43: Repeat Row 37.

ROW 45: Repeat Row 39.

ROW 47: K5, LT, RT, *k10, LT, RT; repeat from * to last 5 sts, knit to end.

ROW 49: Repeat Row 37.

ROW 51: Repeat Row 39.

ROW 53: Repeat Row 47.

ROW 55: Repeat Row 39

ROW 57: Repeat Row 47.

ROW 59: K6, RT, *k12, RT; repeat from * to last 6 sts, knit to end.

ROW 61: Repeat Row 47.

ROW 63: Repeat Row 59.

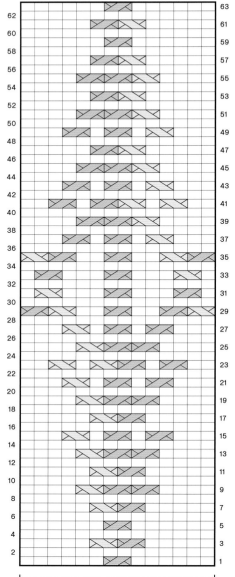

14-st repeat

(76) Deco Dragon Left

I see these pointed triangles as an abstraction of dragon scales. The spaces between the twisted-stitch half diamonds are filled with 1×1 rib, which provides the vertical element. Plain 1×1 rib, as charted, works fine for some yarns, while others benefit from knitting some of the rib through the back loop. See the half-twisted rib variation used for the Cropped Cardi on page 202.

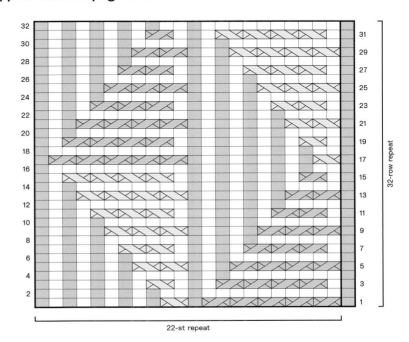

22-st repeat

32-row repeat

(multiple of 22 sts + 1; 32-row repeat)

PSS: 80

ROW 1 (RS): P1, *RT 5 times, p1, LT, p1, [k1, p1] 4 times; repeat from * to end.

ROW 2: Knit the knit sts and purl the purl sts as they face you.

ROW 3: P1, *k1, RT 4 times, k1, p1, k1, LT, [k1, p1] 4 times; repeat from * to end.

ROW 4: K1, *[p1, k1] 3 times, p4, k1, p1, k1, p8, k1; repeat from * to end.

ROW 5: P1, *RT 4 times, p1, k1, p1, LT twice, p1, [k1, p1] 3 times; repeat from * to end.

ROW 6: Repeat Row 2.

ROW 7: P1, *k1, RT 3 times, k1, [p1, k1] twice, LT twice, [k1, p1] 3 times; repeat from * to end.

ROW 8: K1, *[p1, k1] twice, p6, k1, [p1, k1] twice, p6, k1; repeat from * to end.

ROW 9: P1, *RT 3 times, p1, [k1, p1] twice, LT 3 times, p1, [k1, p1] twice; repeat from * to end.

ROW 10: Repeat Row 2.

ROW 11: P1, *k1, RT twice, k1, [k1, p1] 3 times, LT 3 times, [k1, p1] twice; repeat from * to end.

ROW 12: K1, *p1, k1, p8, k1, [p1, k1] 3 times, p4, k1; repeat from * to end.

ROW 13: P1, *RT twice, p1, [k1, p1] 3 times, LT 4 times, p1, k1, p1; repeat from * to end.

ROW 14: Repeat Row 2.

ROW 15: P1, *k1, RT, k1, [p1, k1] 4 times, LT 4 times, k1, p1; repeat from * to end.

ROW 16: K1, *p10, k1, [p1, k1] 4 times, p2, k1; repeat from * to end.

ROW 17: P1, *LT, p1, [k1, p1] 4 times, RT 5 times, p1; repeat from * to end.

ROW 18: Repeat Row 2.

ROW 19: P1, *k1, LT, k1, [k1, p1] 4 times, RT 4 times, k1, p1; repeat from * to end.

ROW 20: K1, *p1, k1, p8, k1, [p1, k1] 3 times, p4, k1; repeat from * to end.

ROW 21: P1, *LT twice, p1, [k1, p1] 3 times, RT 4 times, p1, k1, p1; repeat from * to end.

ROW 22: Repeat Row 2.

ROW 23: P1, *k1, LT twice, k1, [p1, k1] 3 times, RT 3 times, [k1, p1] twice; repeat from * to end.

ROW 24: K1, *[p1, k1] twice, p6, k1, [p1, k1] twice, p6, k1; repeat from * to end.

ROW 25: P1, *LT 3 times, p1, [k1, p1] twice, RT 3 times, p1, [k1, p1] twice; repeat from * to end.

ROW 26: Repeat Row 2.

ROW 27: P1, *k1, LT 3 times, k1, [k1, p1] twice, RT twice, [k1, p1] 3 times; repeat from * to end.

ROW 28: K1, *[p1, k1] 3 times, p4, k1, p1, k1, p8, k1; repeat from * to end.

ROW 29: P1, *LT 4 times, p1, k1, p1, RT twice, p1, [k1, p1] 3 times; repeat from * to end.

ROW 30: Repeat Row 2.

ROW 31: P1, *k1, LT 4 times, k1, p1, k1, RT, [k1, p1] 4 times; repeat from * to end.

ROW 32: K1, *[p1, k1] 4 times, p2, k1, p10, k1; repeat from * to end.

Repeat Rows 1–32 for pattern.

(77) Seahook

The first few rows of this versatile zigzag can be repeated for ribbing that is then topped with peaks. Stockinette stitch gives some visual rest before the next peaks and valleys begin. I borrowed this formation from a sweater I designed many years ago. There are so many variations waiting to be explored.

(multiple of 12 sts + 4; 2 separate repeats of 2 rows and 34 rows)

PSS: 95

ROW 1 (RS): P1, RT, p1, *k2, p1, LT, p1, k2, p1, RT, p1; repeat from * to end.

ROW 2: Knit the knit sts and purl the purl sts as they face you.

Repeat Rows 1–2 as desired, for ribbing.

ROWS 3–6: Repeat Rows 1 and 2.

ROW 7: P1, RT, p1, *k2, RT, LT, k2, p1, RT, p1; repeat from * to end.

ROW 9: P1, RT, p1, *k1, RT, LT twice, k1, p1, RT, p1; repeat from * to end.

ROWS 8, 10, AND 12: Repeat Row 2.

ROW 11: P1, RT, p1, *RT twice, LT twice, p1, RT, p1; repeat from * to end.

ROW 13: K1, RT 3 times, k2, LT twice, *RT 3 times, k2, LT twice; repeat from * to last 3 sts, RT, k1.

ROW 14 AND ALL WS ROWS THROUGH ROW 22: Purl.

ROW 15: LT, *RT twice, k4, LT twice; repeat from * to last 2 sts, RT.

ROW 17: K1, RT, *RT, k6, LT twice; repeat from * to last st, k1.

ROW 19: LT, RT, *k8, LT, RT; repeat from * to end.

ROW 21: K1, RT, *k10, RT; repeat from * to last st, k1.

ROW 23: K7, LT, *k10, LT; repeat from * to last 7 sts, knit to end.

ROW 24 AND ALL WS ROWS THROUGH ROW 30: Purl.

ROW 25: K6, RT, LT, *k8, RT, LT; repeat from * to last 6 sts, knit to end.

ROW 27: K5, RT, LT twice, *k6, RT, LT twice; repeat from * to last 5 sts, knit to end.

ROW 29: K4, *RT twice, LT twice, k4; repeat from * to end.

ROW 31: K3, *RT twice, LT 3 times, k2; repeat from * to last st, k1.

ROW 32: P6, k1, p2, k1, *p8, k1, p2, k1; repeat from * to last 6 sts, purl to end.

ROW 33: LT, *RT twice, p1, LT, p1, LT twice; repeat from * to last 2 sts, RT.

ROW 34: Repeat Row 2.

ROW 35: K1, *RT twice, k1, p1, LT, p1, k1, LT; repeat from * to last 3 sts, RT, k1.

ROW 36: Repeat Row 2.

ROW 37: LT, RT, *k2, p1, LT, p1, k2, LT, RT; repeat from * to end.

ROW 38: K1, *p2, k1; repeat from * to end.

ROW 39: P1, RT, p1, *k2, p1, LT, p1, k2, p1, RT, p1; repeat from * to end.

ROW 40: Repeat Row 2.

ROW 41: P1, RT, p1, *k2, RT, LT, k2, p1, RT, p1; repeat from * to end.

ROW 42: K1, p2, k1, *p8, k1, p2, k1; repeat from * to end.

ROW 43: P1, RT, p1, *k1, RT, LT twice, k1, p1, RT, p1; repeat from * to end.

ROW 44: Repeat Row 2.

ROW 45: P1, RT, p1, *RT twice, LT twice, p1, RT, p1; repeat from * to end.

ROW 46: Repeat Row 2.

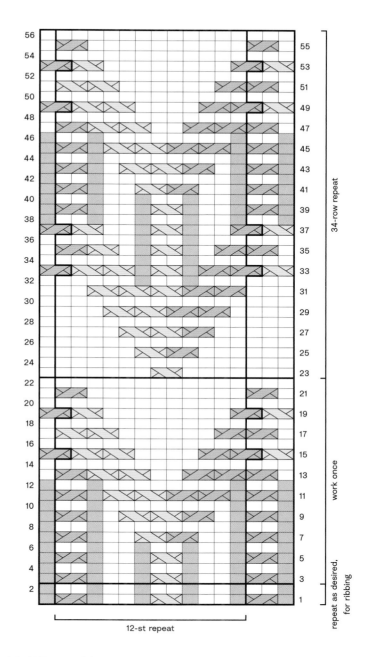

12-st repeat

34-row repeat

work once

repeat as desired, for ribbing

ROW 47: K3, *RT twice, k2, LT twice, k2; repeat from * to last st, k1.

ROW 48 AND ALL WS ROWS THROUGH ROW 54: Purl.

ROW 49: LT, *RT twice, k4, LT twice; repeat from * to last 2 sts, RT.

ROW 51: K1, *RT twice, k6, LT; repeat from * to last 3 sts, RT, k1.

ROW 53: LT, RT, *k8, LT, RT; repeat from * to end.

ROW 55: K1, RT, *k10, RT; repeat from * to last st, k1.

ROW 56: Purl.

Repeat Rows 23–56 for pattern.

78 Deco Dragon Right

The mirror image of Deco Dragon Left (#76) is very useful for cardigans. Plain 1×1 rib, as charted, works fine for some yarns, while others benefit from knitting some of the rib through the back loop. See the half-twisted rib variation used for the Cropped Cardi on page 202.

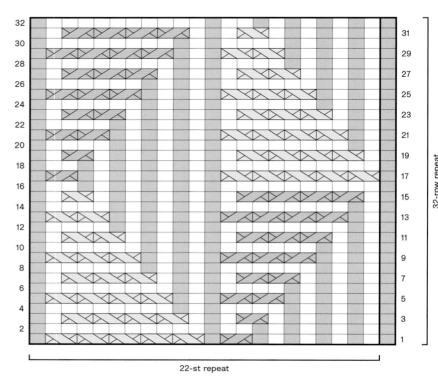

22-st repeat

32-row repeat

(multiple of 22 sts + 1; 32-row repeat)

PSS: 80

ROW 1 (RS): P1, *[k1, p1] 4 times, RT, p1, LT 5 times, p1; repeat from * to end.

ROW 2: Knit the knit sts and purl the purl sts as they face you.

ROW 3: P1, *k1, [p1, k1] 3 times, RT, k1, p1, k1, LT 4 times, k1, p1; repeat from * to end.

ROW 4: K1, *p8, k1, p1, k1, p4, k1, [p1, k1] 3 times; repeat from * to end.

ROW 5: P1, *[k1, p1] 3 times, RT twice, p1, k1, p1, LT 4 times, p1; repeat from * to end.

ROW 6: Repeat Row 2.

ROW 7: P1, *k1, [p1, k1] twice, RT twice, k1, [p1, k1] twice, LT 3 times, k1, p1; repeat from * to end.

ROW 8: K1, *p6, k1, [p1, k1] twice, p6, k1, [p1, k1] twice; repeat from * to end.

ROW 9: P1, *[k1, p1] twice, RT 3 times, p1, [k1, p1] twice, LT 3 times, p1; repeat from * to end.

ROW 10: Repeat Row 2.

ROW 11: P1, *k1, p1, k1, RT 3 times, k1, [p1, k1] 3 times, LT twice, k1, p1; repeat from * to end.

ROW 12: K1, *p4, k1, [p1, k1] 3 times, p8, k1, p1, k1; repeat from * to end.

ROW 13: P1, *k1, p1, RT 4 times, p1, [k1, p1] 3 times, LT twice, p1; repeat from * to end.

ROW 14: Repeat Row 2.

ROW 15: P1, *k1, RT 4 times, k1, [p1, k1] 4 times, LT, k1, p1; repeat from * to end.

79 Pleated

Composed mostly of 4×2 ribbing, this pattern contains a few carefully placed twisted stitches that provide the transition from one wide rib to the next. If not a convincing illusion of pleats, it's at least an abstraction of them.

ROW 16: K1, *p2, k1, [p1, k1] 4 times, p10, k1; repeat from * to end.

ROW 17: P1, *LT 5 times, p1, [k1, p1] 4 times, RT, p1; repeat from * to end.

ROW 18: Repeat Row 2.

ROW 19: P1, *k1, LT 4 times, k1, [p1, k1] 4 times, RT, k1, p1; repeat from * to end.

ROW 20: K1, *p4, k1, [p1, k1] 3 times, p8, k1, p1, k1; repeat from * to end.

ROW 21: P1, *k1, p1, LT 4 times, p1, [k1, p1] 3 times, RT twice, p1; repeat from * to end.

ROW 22: Repeat Row 2.

ROW 23: P1, *k1, p1, k1, LT 3 times, k1, [p1, k1] 3 times, RT twice, k1, p1; repeat from * to end.

ROW 24: K1, *p6, k1, [p1, k1] twice, p6, k1, [p1, k1] twice; repeat from * to end.

ROW 25: P1, *[k1, p1] twice, LT 3 times, p1, [k1, p1] twice, RT 3 times, p1; repeat from * to end.

ROW 26: Repeat Row 2.

ROW 27: P1, *k1, [p1, k1] twice, LT twice, k1, [p1, k1] twice, RT 3 times, k1, p1; repeat from * to end.

ROW 28: K1, *p8, k1, p1, k1, p4, k1, [p1, k1] 3 times; repeat from * to end.

ROW 29: P1, *[k1, p1] 3 times, LT twice, p1, k1, p1, RT 4 times, p1; repeat from * to end.

ROW 30: Repeat Row 2.

ROW 31: P1, *k1, [p1, k1] 3 times, LT, k1, p1, k1, RT 4 times, k1, p1; repeat from * to end.

ROW 32: K1, *p10, k1, p2, k1, [p1, k1] 4 times; repeat from * to end.

Repeat Rows 1–32 for pattern.

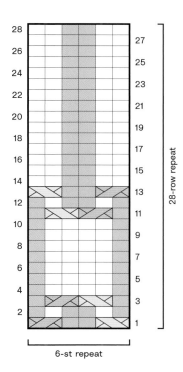

(multiple of 6 sts; 28-row repeat)

PSS: 85

ROW 1 (RS): *LT, p2, RT; repeat from * to end.

ROW 2: K1, p1, *k2, p1; repeat from * to end.

ROW 3: *P1, LT, RT, p1; repeat from * to end.

ROWS 4–10: Knit the knit sts and purl the purl sts as they face you.

ROW 11: P1, RT, LT, *p2, LT, RT; repeat from * to last st, p1.

ROW 12: Repeat Row 2.

ROW 13: *RT, p2, LT; repeat from * to end.

ROWS 14–28: Repeat Row 4.

Repeat Rows 1–28 for pattern.

80 Quiver

Starting out as an expanded version of Pleated (#79), the larger version allows room for strong vertical center rib worked through the back loop on every row and a more ornate arrangement of diagonal arrows nestled together as if in a quiver.

(multiple of 24 sts + 15; 48-row repeat)

PSS: 85

ROW 1 (RS): K2, p5, k1-tbl, p5, *k5, p3, k5, p5, k1-tbl, p5; repeat from * to last 2 sts, k2.

ROW 2: P2, k5, p1-tbl, k5, *p5, k3, p5, k5, p1-tbl, k5; repeat from * to last 2 sts, p2.

ROW 3: RT, p5, k1-tbl, p5, *LT, k3, p3, k3, RT, p5, k1-tbl, p5; repeat from * to last 2 sts, RT.

ROW 4: Repeat Row 2.

ROW 5: K1, LT, p4, k1-tbl, p4, RT, *LT, k2, p3, k2, RT, LT, p4, k1-tbl, p4, RT; repeat from * to last st, k1.

ROW 6: P3, k4, p1-tbl, k4, *p6, k3, p6, k4, p1-tbl, k4; repeat from * to last 3 sts, p3.

ROW 7: RT, LT, p3, k1-tbl, p3, RT, *LT twice, k1, p3, k1, RT twice, LT, p3, k1-tbl, p3, RT; repeat from * to last 2 sts, LT.

ROW 8: P4, k3, p1-tbl, k3, *[p7, k3] twice, p1-tbl, k3; repeat from * to last 4 sts, knit to end.

ROW 9: K3, LT, p2, k1-tbl, p2, RT, k2, *LT twice, p3, RT twice, k2, LT, p2, k1-tbl, p2, RT, k2; repeat from * to last st, k1.

ROW 10: P5, k2, p1-tbl, k2, p4, *k1, p3, k3, p3, k1, p4, k2, p1-tbl, k2, p4; repeat from * to last st, p1.

ROW 11: K4, LT, p1, k1-tbl, p1, RT, k3, *p1, LT twice, p1, RT twice, p1, k3, LT, p1, k1-tbl, p1, RT, k3; repeat from * to last st, k1.

ROW 12: P6, k1, p1-tbl, k1, p5, *k2, p3, k1, p3, k2, p5, k1, p1-tbl, k1, p5; repeat from * to last st, p1.

ROW 13: K5, LT, k1-tbl, RT, k4, *p2, LT, k1, p1, k1, RT, p2, k4, LT, k1-tbl, RT, k4; repeat from * to last st, k1.

ROW 14: P14, *k3, p2, k1, p2, k3, p13; repeat from * to last st, p1.

ROW 15: K6, p3, k5, *p3, LT, k1-tbl, RT, [p3, k5] twice; repeat from * to last st, k1.

ROW 16: P6, k3, p5, *k4, p1, p1-tbl, p1, k4, p5, k3, p5; repeat from * to last st, p1.

ROW 17: K6, p3, k5, *p5, k1-tbl, p5, k5, p3, k5; repeat from * to last st, k1.

ROW 18: P6, k3, p5, *k5, p1-tbl, k5, p5, k3, p5; repeat from * to last st, p1.

ROWS 19–26: Repeat Rows 17 and 18 four times.

ROW 27: K1, LT, k3, p3, k3, RT, *p5, k1-tbl, p5, LT, k3, p3, k3, RT; repeat from * to last st, k1.

ROW 28: Repeat Row 18.

ROW 29: RT, LT, k2, p3, k2, RT, LT, *p4, k1-tbl, p4, RT, LT, k2, p3, k2, RT, LT; repeat from * to end.

ROW 30: P6, k3, p6, *k4, p1-tbl, k4, p6, k3, p6; repeat from * to end.

ROW 31: K1, LT twice, k1, p3, k1, RT twice, *LT, p3, k1-tbl, p3, RT, LT twice, k1, p3, k1, RT twice; repeat from * to last st, k1.

ROW 32: P6, k3, *p7, k3, p1-tbl, k3, p7, k3; repeat from * to last 6 sts, purl to end.

ROW 33: K2, LT twice, p3, RT twice, k2, *LT, p2, k1-tbl, p2, RT, k2, LT twice, p3, RT twice, k2; repeat from * to end.

ROW 34: P2, k1, p3, k3, p3, k1, *p4, k2, p1-tbl, k2, p4, k1, p3, k3, p3, k1; repeat from * to last 2 sts, p2.

ROW 35: K2, p1, LT twice, p1, RT twice, p1, *k3, LT, p1, k1-tbl, p1, RT, k3, p1, LT twice, p1, RT twice, p1; repeat from * to last 2 sts, k2.

ROW 36: P2, k2, p3, k1, p3, k2, *p5, k1, p1-tbl, k1, p5, k2, p3, k1, p3, k2; repeat from * to last 2 sts, p2.

ROW 37: K2, p2, LT, k1, p1, k1, RT, p2, *k4, LT, k1-tbl, RT, k4, p2, LT, k1, p1, k1, RT, p2; repeat from * to last 2 sts, k2.

ROW 38: P2, k3, p2, k1, p2, k3, *p13, k3, p2, k1, p2, k3; repeat from * to last 2 sts, p2.

ROW 39: K2, p3, LT, k1-tbl, RT, p3, *[k5, p3] twice, LT, k1-tbl, RT, p3; repeat from * to last 2 sts, k2.

ROW 40: P2, k4, p1, p1-tbl, p1, k4, *p5, k3, p5, k4, p1, p1-tbl, p1, k4; repeat from * to last 2 sts, p2.

ROW 41: K2, p5, k1-tbl, p5, *k5, p3, k5, p5, k1-tbl, p5; repeat from * to last 2 sts, k2.

ROW 42: P2, k5, p1-tbl, k5, *p5, k3, p5, k5, p1-tbl, k5; repeat from * to last 2 sts, p2.

ROWS 43–48: Repeat Rows 41 and 42 three times.

Repeat Rows 1–48 for pattern.

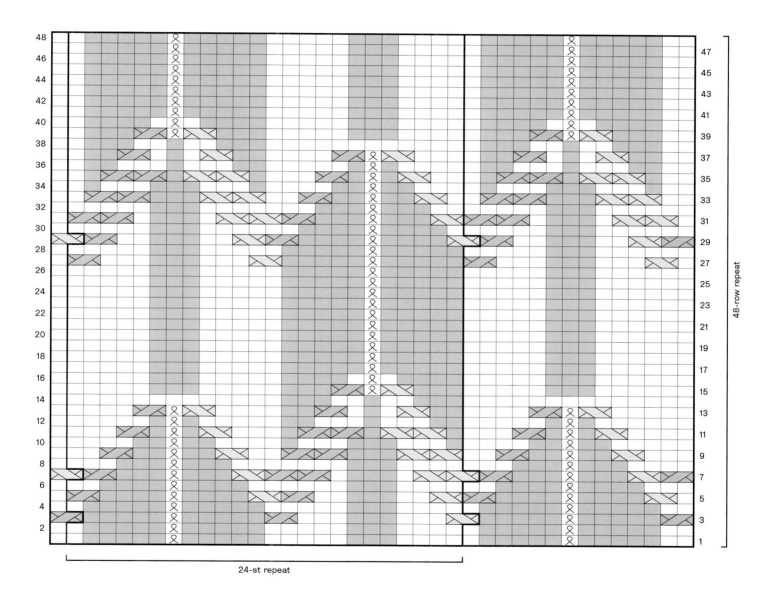

⑧¹ Pine Cone Column

The pine cone motif introduced in Chapter 1, Pine Cone Shadow (#30), is split in two and bisected with a mini cable of right twists. Shown here as a column, the chart can be used to make an allover pattern, spaced as you like on a Stockinette stitch ground.

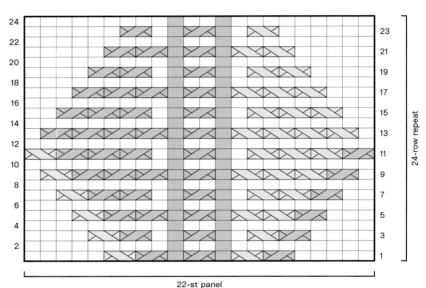

22-st panel

(22-st panel; 24-row repeat)

PSS: 80

ROW 1 (RS): K5, RT, LT, [p1, RT] twice, LT, k5.

ROW 2 AND ALL WS ROWS: Knit the knit sts and purl the purl sts as they face you.

ROW 3: K4, RT, LT, k1, p1, RT, p1, k1, RT, LT, k4.

ROW 5: K3, RT, LT twice, p1, RT, p1, RT twice, LT, k3.

ROW 7: K2, RT, LT twice, k1, p1, RT, p1, k1, RT twice, LT, k2.

ROW 9: K1, RT, LT 3 times, p1, RT, p1, RT 3 times, LT, k1.

ROW 11: RT, LT 3 times, k1, p1, RT, p1, k1, RT 3 times, LT.

ROW 13: K1, LT 4 times, p1, RT, p1, RT 4 times, k1.

ROW 15: K2, LT 3 times, k1, p1, RT, p1, k1, RT 3 times, k2.

ROW 17: K3, LT 3 times, p1, RT, p1, RT 3 times, k3.

ROW 19: K4, LT twice, k1, p1, RT, p1, k1, RT twice, k4.

ROW 21: K5, LT twice, p1, RT, p1, RT twice, k5.

ROW 23: K6, LT, k1, p1, RT, p1, k1, RT, k6.

ROW 24: Repeat Row 2.

Repeat Rows 1–24 for pattern.

(82) Mossy Pine Cone

Add a background of moss stitch and replace the center mini cable with three stitches of rib to make something new out of Pine Cone Column (#81). The swatch shows this column with Stockinette stitch on either side, but you can work it on a moss stitch ground to make an allover pattern.

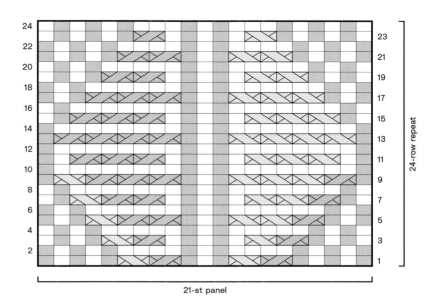

(21-st panel; 24-row repeat)

PSS: 80

ROW 1 (RS): P1, [k1, p1] twice, RT, LT, p1, k1, p1, RT, LT, p1, [k1, p1] twice.

ROW 2 AND ALL WS ROWS: Knit the knit sts and purl the purl sts as they face you.

ROW 3: [K1, p1] twice, RT, LT, k1, [p1, k1] twice, RT, LT, [p1, k1] twice.

ROW 5: P1, k1, p1, RT, LT twice, p1, k1, p1, RT twice, LT, p1, k1, p1.

ROW 7: K1, p1, RT, LT twice, k1, [p1, k1] twice, RT twice, LT, p1, k1.

ROW 9: P1, RT, LT 3 times, p1, k1, p1, RT 3 times, LT, p1.

ROW 11: P1, k1, LT 3 times, k1, [p1, k1] twice, RT 3 times, k1, p1.

ROW 13: P1, LT 4 times, p1, k1, p1, RT 4 times, p1.

ROW 15: K1, p1, LT 3 times, k1, [p1, k1] twice, RT 3 times, p1, k1.

ROW 17: P1, k1, p1, LT 3 times, p1, k1, p1, RT 3 times, p1, k1, p1.

ROW 19: [K1, p1] twice, LT twice, k1, [p1, k1] twice, RT twice, [p1, k1] twice.

ROW 21: P1, [k1, p1] twice, LT twice, p1, k1, p1, RT twice, p1, [k1, p1] twice.

ROW 23: [K1, p1] 3 times, LT, p1, [k1, p1] twice, RT, [p1, k1] 3 times.

ROW 24: Knit the knit sts and purl the purl sts as they face you.

Repeat Rows 1–24 for pattern.

⑧③ Pine Cone Carved

A bed of reverse Stockinette stitch appears to be deeply carved and raises the pinecones from the surface. Compare this with Pine Cone Column (#81), the same pattern on a Stockinette stitch background.

(22-st panel; 24-row repeat)

PSS: 80

ROW 1 (RS): P5, RT, LT, [p1, RT] twice, LT, p5.

ROW 2 AND ALL WS ROWS: Knit the knit sts and purl the purl sts as they face you.

ROW 3: P4, RT, LT, k1, p1, RT, p1, k1, RT, LT, p4.

ROW 5: P3, RT, LT twice, p1, RT, p1, RT twice, LT, p3.

ROW 7: P2, RT, LT twice, k1, p1, RT, p1, k1, RT twice, LT, p2.

ROW 9: P1, RT, LT 3 times, p1, RT, p1, RT 3 times, LT, p1.

ROW 11: P1, k1, LT 3 times, k1, p1, RT, p1, k1, RT 3 times, k1, p1.

ROW 13: P1, LT 4 times, p1, RT, p1, RT 4 times, p1.

ROW 15: P2, LT 3 times, k1, p1, RT, p1, k1, RT 3 times, p2.

ROW 17: P3, LT 3 times, p1, RT, p1, RT 3 times, p3.

ROW 19: P4, LT twice, k1, p1, RT, p1, k1, RT twice, p4.

ROW 21: P5, LT twice, p1, RT, p1, RT twice, p5.

ROW 23: P6, LT, k1, p1, RT, p1, k1, RT, p6.

ROW 24: Repeat Row 2.

Repeat Rows 1–24 for pattern.

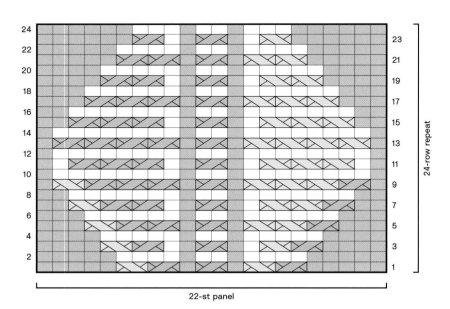

24-row repeat

22-st panel

⟨84⟩ Tafoni

Elongated hexagons quietly inhabit the surface of this allover pattern. The mini cables are flanked by twisted stitches—the kind made by working through the back loop, which highlights the mini cables somewhat, but more subtly than when placed next to reverse Stockinette stitch.

(multiple of 6 sts + 4; 32-row repeat)

PSS: 80

ROW 1 (RS): K1, *LT twice, RT; repeat from * to last 3 sts, LT, k1.

ROW 2: Purl.

ROW 3: RT, LT, *RT twice, LT; repeat from * to end.

ROW 4: P1-tbl, k2, p1-tbl, *p2, p1-tbl, k2, p1-tbl; repeat from * to end.

ROW 5: K1-tbl, p2, k1-tbl, *RT, k1-tbl, p2, k1-tbl; repeat from * to end.

ROWS 6–15: Repeat Rows 4 and 5 five times.

ROW 16: Repeat Row 4.

ROW 17: LT, *RT twice, LT; repeat from * to last 2 sts, RT.

ROW 18: Purl.

ROW 19: K1, LT, *RT, LT twice; repeat from * to last st, k1.

ROW 20: P1-tbl, p2, p1-tbl, *k2, p1-tbl, p2, p1-tbl; repeat from * to end.

ROW 21: K1-tbl, LT, k1-tbl, *p2, k1-tbl, LT, k1-tbl; repeat from * to end.

ROWS 22–31: Repeat Rows 20 and 21 five times.

ROW 32: Repeat Row 20.

Repeat Rows 1–32 for pattern.

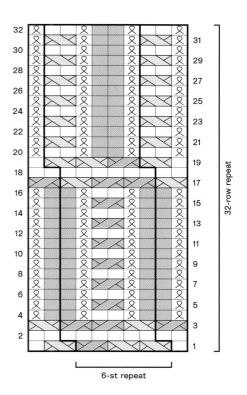

6-st repeat

32-row repeat

⑧⑤ Blackwork

In this pattern inspired by traditional blackwork embroidery, the carefully placed lines of twists along with knit/purl verticals draw out what look to me to be large knit stitches.

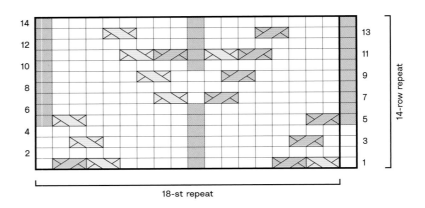

18-st repeat

14-row repeat

(multiple of 18 sts + 1; 14-row repeat)

PSS: 80

ROW 1 (RS): K1, *LT, RT, k4, p1, k4, LT, RT, k1; repeat from * to end.

ROWS 2, 4, 6, AND 8: Knit the knit sts and purl the purl sts as they face you.

ROW 3: K2, RT, k5, p1, k5, LT, *k3, RT, k5, p1, k5, LT; repeat from * to last 2 sts, k2.

ROW 5: P1, *RT, k6, p1, k6, LT, p1; repeat from * to end.

ROW 7: P1, *k6, RT, k1, LT, k6, p1; repeat from * to end.

ROW 9: P1, *k5, RT, k3, LT, k5, p1; repeat from * to end.

ROW 10: K1, *p8, k1; repeat from * to end.

ROW 11: P1, *k4, RT, LT, p1, RT, LT, k4, p1; repeat from * to end.

ROW 12: Repeat Row 2.

ROW 13: P1, *k3, RT, k3, p1, k3, LT, k3, p1; repeat from * to end.

ROW 14: Repeat Row 2.

Repeat Rows 1–14 for pattern.

(86) Wheat

Reverse Stockinette stitch parallelograms appear to curve where the diagonal outline meets the vertical line made by a switch from knit to purl. The resulting shape is evocative of a kernel of wheat.

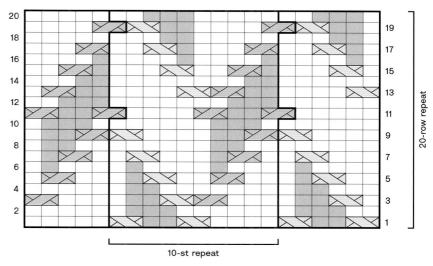

10-st repeat

(multiple of 10 sts + 11; 20-row repeat)

PSS: 80

ROW 1 (RS): *LT, p2, LT, k4; repeat from * to last st, k1.

ROW 2: P6, k3, *p7, k3; repeat from * to last 2 sts, p2.

ROW 3: K1, *LT, p2, k4, RT; repeat from * to end.

ROW 4: P6, k2, *p8, k2; repeat from * to last 3 sts, p3.

ROW 5: *K2, LT, p1, k3, RT; repeat from * to last st, k1.

ROW 6: P1, *k1, p4; repeat from * to end.

ROW 7: *K3, LT, k2, RT, p1; repeat from * to last st, k1.

ROW 8: P1, *k2, p8; repeat from * to end.

ROW 9: *K4, LT, RT, p2; repeat from * to last st, k1.

ROW 10: P1, *k3, p7; repeat from * to end.

ROW 11: K1, *k4, RT, p2, RT; repeat from * to end.

ROW 12: P2, k3, *p7, k3; repeat from * to last 6 sts, knit to end.

ROW 13: *LT, k4, p2, RT; repeat from * to last st, k1.

ROW 14: P3, k2, *p8, k2; repeat from * to last 6 sts, knit to end.

ROW 15: K1, *LT, k3, p1, RT, k2; repeat from * to end.

ROW 16: *P4, k1; repeat from * to last st, p1.

ROW 17: K1, *p1, LT, k2, RT, k3; repeat from * to end.

ROW 18: *P8, k2; repeat from * to last st, p1.

ROW 19: K1, *p2, LT, RT, k4; repeat from * to end.

ROW 20: *P7, k3; repeat from * to last st, p1.

Repeat Rows 1–20 for pattern.

(87) Droplets

Adding a straight section elongates these once-diamond shapes and makes them appear to be rounded droplet shapes that look more intricate than they are.

(multiple of 12 sts + 2; 32-row repeat)

PSS: 80

ROW 1 (RS): P3, k1-tbl, p1, k4, p1, k1-tbl, *p4, k1-tbl, p1, k4, p1, k1-tbl; repeat from * to last 3 sts, k3.

ROW 2: Knit the knit sts and purl the purl sts as they face you.

ROW 3: P2, *RT, k6, LT, p2; repeat from * to end.

ROW 4: Repeat Row 2.

ROW 5: K1, *[RT, k3] twice, LT; repeat from * to last st, k1.

ROW 6: Purl.

ROW 7: RT, *k3, RT, LT, k3, RT; repeat from * to end.

ROW 8: Purl.

ROW 9: K4, RT twice, LT, *k6, RT twice, LT; repeat from * to last 4 sts, knit to end.

ROW 10: Purl.

ROW 11: K3, RT twice, LT twice, *k4, RT twice, LT twice; repeat from * to last 3 sts, k3.

ROW 12: P6, k2, *p10, k2; repeat from * to last 6 sts, knit to end.

ROW 13: P2, *RT twice, p2, LT twice, p2; repeat from * to end.

ROW 14: K2, *p3, k4, p3, k2; repeat from * to end.

ROW 15: P2, *k1, RT, p4, LT, k1, p2; repeat from * to end.

ROW 16: Repeat Row 14.

ROW 17: P2, *k1, LT, p4, RT, k1, p2; repeat from * to end.

ROW 18: Repeat Row 14.

ROW 19: K2, *LT twice, p2, RT twice, k2; repeat from * to end.

ROW 20: Repeat Row 12.

ROW 21: K3, LT twice, RT twice, *k4, LT twice, RT twice; repeat from * to last 3 sts, k3.

ROW 22: Purl.

ROW 23: K4, LT, RT twice, *k6, LT, RT twice; repeat from * to last 4 sts, knit to end.

ROW 24: Purl.

ROW 25: LT, *k3, LT, RT, k3, RT; repeat from * to end.

ROW 26: Purl.

ROW 27: K1, *LT, [k3, RT] twice; repeat from * to last st, k1.

ROW 28: Repeat Row 4.

ROW 29: P2, *LT, p1, k4, p1, RT, p2; repeat from * to end.

ROW 30: Repeat Row 2.

ROWS 31 AND 32: Repeat Rows 1 and 2.

Repeat Rows 1–32 for pattern.

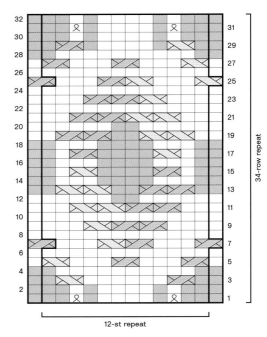

Carpet Allover

Inspired by the figures found in traditional carpets all over the world, this large allover pattern uses long strands of mini cables to connect the large diamond motifs.

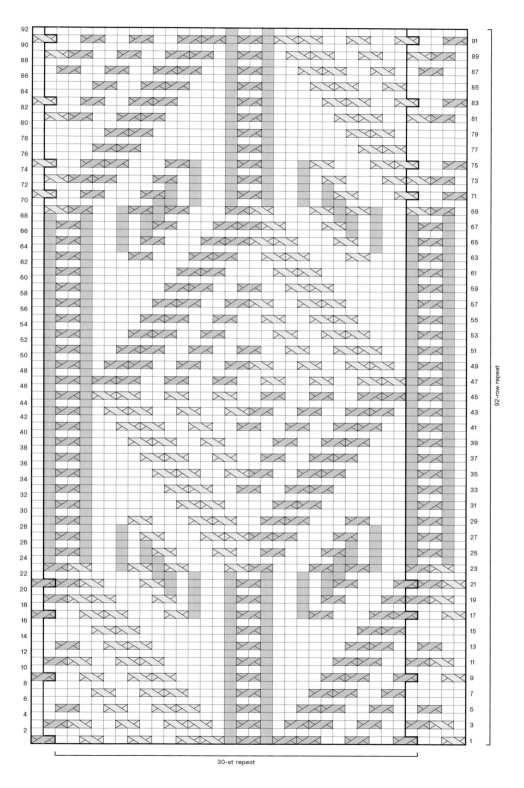

92-row repeat

30-st repeat

Carpet Column

Extracted from the previous pattern, Carpet Allover (#88), these columns can stand alone, while the original is meant to be used in multiples.

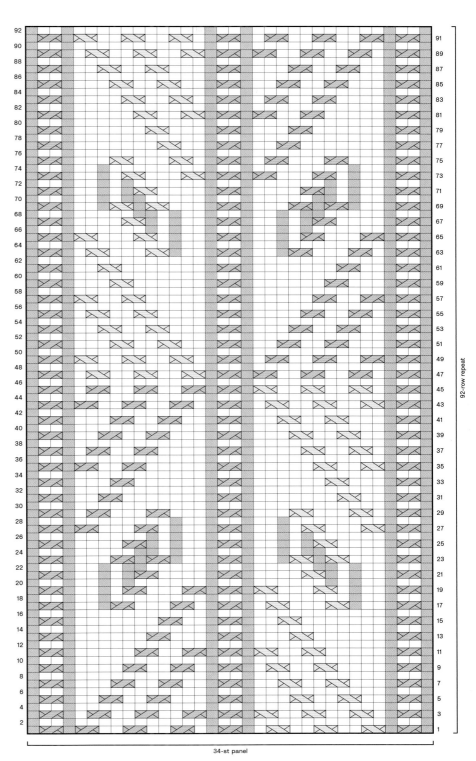

92-row repeat

34-st panel

Barbed

A large diamond is bisected by a rope of mini cables, separating it into two triangles. Use this motif placed where you like on a Stockinette stitch ground, repeated to form a barbed column or alternated like a checkerboard for an allover pattern.

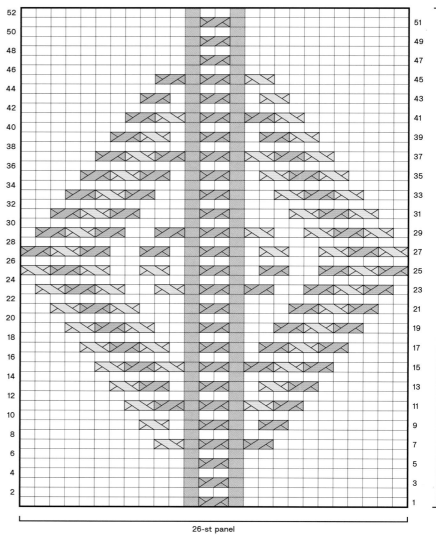

(26-st panel; 52-row repeat)

PSS: 85

ROW 1 (RS): K11, p1, RT, p1, k11.

ROW 2 AND ALL WS ROWS: Knit the knit sts and purl the purl sts as they face you.

ROW 3: Repeat Row 1.

ROW 5: Repeat Row 1.

ROW 7: K9, [RT, p1] twice, LT, k9.

ROW 9: K8, RT, k1, p1, RT, p1, k1, LT, k8.

ROW 11: K7, RT, LT, [p1, RT] twice, LT, k7.

ROW 13: K6, RT, LT, k1, p1, RT, p1, k1, RT, LT, k6.

52-row repeat

26-st panel

ROW 15: K5, RT, LT, [RT, p1] twice, LT, RT, LT, k5.

ROW 17: K4, RT, LT, RT, k1, p1, RT, p1, k1, LT, RT, LT, k4.

ROW 19: K3, RT, LT, RT, k2, p1, RT, p1, k2, LT, RT, LT, k3.

ROW 21: K2, RT, LT, RT, k3, p1, RT, p1, k3, LT, RT, LT, k2.

ROW 23: K1, RT, LT, RT, k2, [RT, p1] twice, LT, k2, LT, RT, LT, p1.

ROW 25: RT, LT, RT, k2, RT, k1, p1, RT, p1, k1, LT, k2, LT, RT, LT.

ROW 27: LT, RT, LT, k2, LT, k1, p1, RT, p1, k1, RT, k2, RT, LT, RT.

ROW 29: K1, LT, RT, LT, k2, LT, [p1, RT] twice, k2, RT, LT, RT, k1.

ROW 31: K2, LT, RT, LT, k3, p1, RT, p1, k3, RT, LT, RT, k2.

ROW 33: K3, LT, RT, LT, k2, p1, RT, p1, k2, RT, LT, RT, k3.

ROW 35: K4, LT, RT, LT, k1, p1, RT, p1, k1, RT, LT, RT, k4.

ROW 37: K5, LT, RT, LT, [p1, RT] twice, LT, RT, k5.

ROW 39: K6, LT, RT, k1, p1, RT, p1, k1, LT, RT, k6.

ROW 41: K7, LT, [RT, p1] twice, LT, RT, k7.

ROW 43: K8, LT, k1, p1, RT, p1, k1, RT, k8.

ROW 45: K9, LT, [p1, RT] twice, k9.

ROW 47: Repeat Row 1.

ROW 49: Repeat Row 1.

ROW 51: Repeat Row 1.

ROW 52: Repeat Row 2.

Repeat Rows 1–52 for pattern.

(91) Cherries

Here a traditional bobble pattern is made with twisted stitches and a twisted-stitch column (the knit-through-the-back-loop kind). Reverse Stockinette stitch ribs on either side of the center rib make it stand out, while the rest of the background is Stockinette stitch, keeping the wrong side easy.

(multiple of 20 sts + 1; 28-row repeat)

PSS: 80

NOTE: MB (make bobble): (K1, k1-tbl, k1, k1-tbl, k1) into one st, slip the 5 sts back to left-hand needle; k5, slip the 5 sts back to left-hand needle; k5, slip the right-most 4 sts over the left-most st.

ROW 1 (RS): K5, LT, k2, p1, k1-tbl, p1, k2, RT, *k9, LT, k2, p1, k1-tbl, p1, k2, RT; repeat from * to last 5 sts, knit to end.

ROW 2: P9, k1, p1-tbl, k1, *p17, k1, p1-tbl, k1; repeat from * to last 9 sts, purl to end.

ROW 3: MB, *p1, k4, LT, k1, p1, k1-tbl, p1, k1, RT, k4, p1, MB; repeat from * to end.

ROW 4: P1-tbl, *k1, p7, k1, p1-tbl, k1, p7, k1, p1-tbl; repeat from * to end.

ROW 5: K1-tbl, *p1, k5, LT, p1, k1-tbl, p1, RT, k5, p1, k1-tbl; repeat from * to end.

ROW 6: Repeat Row 4.

ROW 7: K1-tbl, *p1, k2, MB, k3, LT, k1-tbl, RT, k3, MB, k2, p1, k1-tbl; repeat from * to end.

ROW 8: P1-tbl, *k1, p17, k1, p1-tbl; repeat from * to end.

ROW 9: K1-tbl, *p1, k1, RT, k2, MB, k5, MB, k2, LT, k1, p1, k1-tbl; repeat from * to end.

ROW 10: Repeat Row 8.

ROW 11: K1-tbl, *p1, RT, k2, RT, k5, LT, k2, LT, p1, k1-tbl; repeat from * to end.

ROW 12: Repeat Row 8.

ROW 13: K1-tbl, *RT, k2, RT, k7, LT, k2, LT, k1-tbl; repeat from * to end.

ROW 14: P1-tbl, *p19, p1-tbl; repeat from * to end.

ROW 15: K1-tbl, *p1, k2, RT, k9, LT, k2, p1, k1-tbl; repeat from * to end.

ROW 16: Repeat Row 8.

ROW 17: K1-tbl, *k1, p1, RT, k4, p1, MB, p1, k4, LT, k1, p1, k1-tbl; repeat from * to end.

ROW 18: Repeat Row 4.

ROW 19: K1-tbl, *p1, RT, k5, p1, k1-tbl, p1, k5, LT, p1, k1-tbl; repeat from * to end.

ROW 20: Repeat Row 4.

ROW 21: K1-tbl, *RT, k3, MB, k2, p1, k1-tbl, p1, k2, MB, k3, LT, k1-tbl; repeat from * to end.

ROW 22: Repeat Row 2.

ROW 23: K4, MB, k1, LT, k1, p1, k1-tbl, p1, k1, RT, k1, MB, *k7, MB, k1, LT, k1, p1, k1-tbl, p1, k1, RT, k1, MB; repeat from * to last 4 sts, knit to end.

ROW 24: Repeat Row 2.

ROW 25: K4, LT, k1, LT, p1, k1-tbl, p1, RT, k1, RT, *k7, LT, k1, LT, p1, k1-tbl, p1, RT, k1, RT; repeat from * to last 4 sts, knit to end.

ROW 26: Repeat Row 2.

ROW 27: K5, LT, k1, LT, k1-tbl, RT, k1, RT, *k9, LT, k1, LT, k1-tbl, RT, k1, RT; repeat from * to last 5 sts, knit to end.

ROW 28: P10, p1-tbl, *p19, p1-tbl; repeat from * to last 10 sts, knit to end.

Repeat Rows 1–28 for pattern.

MB: (K1, k1-tbl, k1, k1-tbl, k1) into one st, slip the 5 sts back to left-hand needle; k5, slip the 5 sts back to left-hand needle; k5, slip the right-most 4 sts over the left-most st.

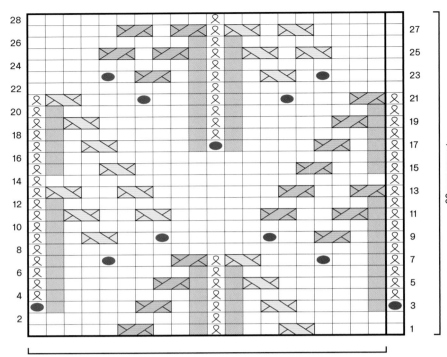

28-row repeat

20-st repeat

(92) Carved Cherries

If you'd like the cherries to stand out from the surface, make them on a bed of reverse Stockinette stitch. This version is more difficult to knit than its sister, Cherries (#91), because you'll need to count on wrong-side rows.

CARVED BOBBLE

(multiple of 20 sts + 1; 28-row repeat)

PSS: 85

NOTE: MB (bobble): (K1, k1-tbl, k1, k1-tbl, k1) into one st, slip the 5 sts back to left-hand needle; k5, slip the 5 sts back to left-hand needle; k5, slip the right-most 4 sts over the left-most st.

ROW 1 (RS): P5, LT, p3, k1-tbl, p3, RT, *p9, LT, p3, k1-tbl, p3, RT; repeat from * to last 5 sts, purl to end.

ROW 2: K6, p1, k3, p1-tbl, k3, p1, *k11, p1, k3, p1-tbl, k3, p1; repeat from * to last 6 sts, knit to end.

ROW 3: MB, *p5, LT, p2, k1-tbl, p2, RT, p5, MB; repeat from * to end.

ROW 4: P1-tbl, *k6, p1, k2, p1-tbl, k2, p1, k6, p1-tbl; repeat from * to end.

ROW 5: K1-tbl, *p6, LT, p1, k1-tbl, p1, RT, p6, k1-tbl; repeat from * to end.

ROW 6: P1-tbl, *k7, p1, k1, p1-tbl, k1, p1, k7, p1-tbl; repeat from * to end.

ROW 7: K1-tbl, *p3, MB, p3, LT, k1-tbl, RT, p3, MB, p3, k1-tbl; repeat from * to end.

ROW 8: P1-tbl, *k3, p1, k4, p1, p1-tbl, p1, k4, p1, k3, p1-tbl; repeat from * to end.

ROW 9: K1-tbl, *p2, RT, p2, MB, p5, MB, p2, LT, p2, k1-tbl; repeat from * to end.

ROW 10: P1-tbl, *k2, p1, k3, p1, k5, p1, k3, p1, k2, p1-tbl; repeat from * to end.

ROW 11: K1-tbl, *p1, RT, p2, RT, p5, LT, p2, LT, p1, k1-tbl; repeat from * to end.

ROW 12: P1-tbl, *k1, p1, k3, p1, k7, p1, k3, p1, k1, p1-tbl; repeat from * to end.

ROW 13: K1-tbl, *RT, p2, RT, p7, LT, p2, LT, k1-tbl; repeat from * to end.

ROW 14: P1-tbl, *p1, k3, p1, k9, p1, k3, p1, p1-tbl; repeat from * to end.

ROW 15: K1-tbl, *p3, RT, p9, LT, p3, k1-tbl; repeat from * to end.

ROW 16: P1-tbl, *k3, p1, k11, p1, k3, p1-tbl; repeat from * to end.

ROW 17: K1-tbl, *p2, RT, p5, MB, p5, LT, p2, k1-tbl; repeat from * to end.

ROW 18: P1-tbl, *k2, p1, k6, p1-tbl, k6, p1, k2, p1-tbl; repeat from * to end.

ROW 19: K1-tbl, *p1, RT, p6, k1-tbl, p6, LT, p1, k1-tbl; repeat from * to end.

ROW 20: P1-tbl, *k1, p1, k7, p1-tbl, k7, p1, k1, p1-tbl; repeat from * to end.

ROW 21: K1-tbl, *RT, p3, MB, p3, k1-tbl, p3, MB, p3, LT, k1-tbl; repeat from * to end.

ROW 22: P1-tbl, *p1, k4, p1, k3, p1-tbl, k3, p1, k4, p1, p1-tbl; repeat from * to end.

ROW 23: P4, MB, p1, LT, p2, k1-tbl, p2, RT, p1, MB, *p7, MB, p1, LT, p2, k1-tbl, p2, RT, p1, MB; repeat from * to last 4 sts, purl to end.

ROW 24: K4, [p1, k2] twice, p1-tbl, [k2, p1] twice, *k7, [p1, k2] twice, p1-tbl, [k2, p1] twice; repeat from * to last 4 sts, knit to end.

ROW 25: P4, [LT, p1] twice, k1-tbl, [p1, RT] twice, *p7, [LT, p1] twice, k1-tbl, [p1, RT] twice; repeat from * to last 4 sts, purl to end.

ROW 26: K5, p1, k2, p1, k1, p1-tbl, k1, p1, k2, p1, *k9, p1, k2, p1, k1, p1-tbl, k1, p1, k2, p1; repeat from * to last 5 sts, knit to end.

ROW 27: P5, LT, p1, LT, k1-tbl, RT, p1, RT, *p9, LT, p1, LT, k1-tbl, RT, p1, RT; repeat from * to last 5 sts, purl to end.

ROW 28: K6, p1, k2, p1, p1-tbl, p1, k2, p1, *k11, p1, k2, p1, p1-tbl, p1, k2, p1; repeat from * to last 6 sts, knit to end.

Repeat Rows 1–28 for pattern.

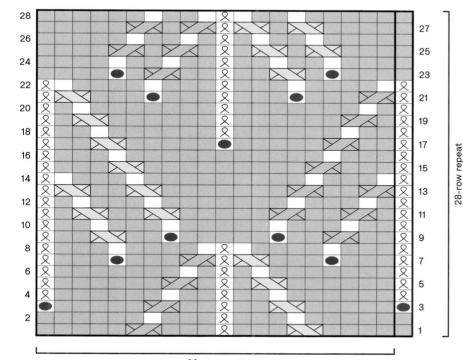

28-row repeat

20-st repeat

MB: (K1, k1-tbl, k1, k1-tbl, k1) into one st, slip the 5 sts back to left-hand needle; k5, slip the 5 sts back to left-hand needle; k5, slip the right-most 4 sts over the left-most st.

CHAPTER 6
Compass

It's time to go in all directions
at once. These pattern stitches
each incorporate diagonals,
horizontals, and verticals all in
one composition. Here we see the
emergence of eight-pointed stars
along with other complexities.

93 Always

This is one of the simplest arrangements of vertical, horizontal, and diagonal lines possible. Stare at this pattern for a while. There is so much to see.

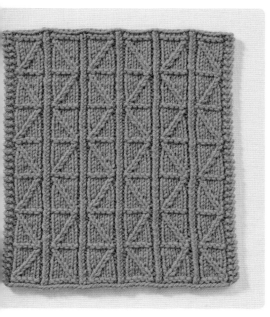

(multiple of 16 sts + 13; 20-row repeat)

PSS: 80

ROW 1 (RS): P6, k1-tbl, *p7, k1-tbl; repeat from * to last 6 sts, purl to end.

ROW 2 AND ALL WS ROWS: P5, *k1, p1-tbl, k1, p5; repeat from * to end.

ROW 3: LT, k3, p1, k1-tbl, p1, k3, RT, *p1, k1-tbl, p1, LT, k3, p1, k1-tbl, p1, k3, RT; repeat from * to end.

ROW 5: K1, LT, k2, p1, k1-tbl, p1, k2, RT, k1, *p1, k1-tbl, p1, k1, LT, k2, p1, k1-tbl, p1, k2, RT, k1; repeat from * to end.

ROW 7: K2, LT, k1, p1, k1-tbl, p1, k1, RT, k2, *p1, k1-tbl, p1, k2, LT, k1, p1, k1-tbl, p1, k1, RT, k2; repeat from * to end.

ROW 9: K3, LT, p1, k1-tbl, p1, RT, k3, *p1, k1-tbl, p1, k3, LT, p1, k1-tbl, p1, RT, k3; repeat from * to end.

ROW 11: Repeat Row 1.

ROW 13: K3, RT, p1, k1-tbl, p1, LT, k3, *p1, k1-tbl, p1, k3, RT, p1, k1-tbl, p1, LT, k3; repeat from * to end.

ROW 15: K2, RT, k1, p1, k1-tbl, p1, k1, LT, k2, *p1, k1-tbl, p1, k2, RT, k1, p1, k1-tbl, p1, k1, LT, k2; repeat from * to end.

ROW 17: K1, RT, k2, p1, k1-tbl, p1, k2, LT, k1, *p1, k1-tbl, p1, k1, RT, k2, p1, k1-tbl, p1, k2, LT, k1; repeat from * to end.

ROW 19: RT, k3, p1, k1-tbl, p1, k3, LT, *p1, k1-tbl, p1, RT, k3, p1, k1-tbl, p1, k3, LT; repeat from * to end.

ROW 20: Repeat Row 2.

Repeat Rows 1–20 for pattern.

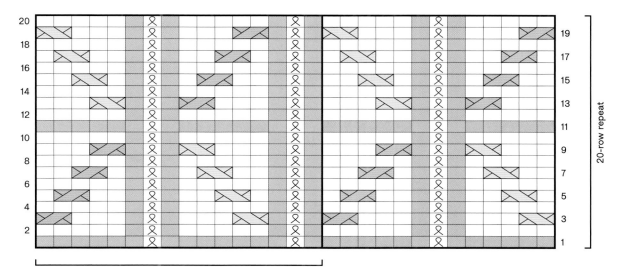

16-st repeat

20-row repeat

94 Pi

Starting out as a representation of the mathematical symbol for pi (π), this pattern was transformed by the addition of a central mini cable and by linking the forms together, creating an allover design. I still see pi in there, but it's obscured by the strong verticals and elongated hexagons that have emerged.

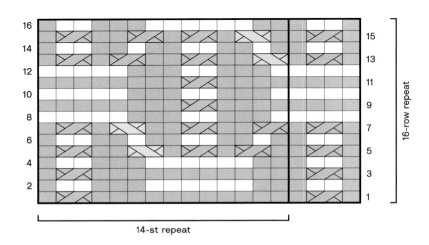

14-st repeat

16-row repeat

(multiple of 14 sts + 4; 16-row repeat)

PSS: 90

ROW 1 (RS): P1, RT, *p12, RT; repeat from * to last st, p1.

ROW 2: K1, p2, *k3, p6, k3, p2; repeat from * to last st, k1.

ROWS 3 AND 4: Repeat Rows 1 and 2.

ROW 5: P1, RT, *p2, [RT, p1] twice, LT, p2, RT; repeat from * to last st, p1.

ROW 6: K1, p2, *k2, p1, k2, p2; repeat from * to last st, k1.

ROW 7: P1, RT, p1, *[RT, p2] twice, LT, p1, RT, p1; repeat from * to end.

ROW 8: P5, k3, p2, k3, *p6, k3, p2, k3; repeat from * to last 5 sts, purl to end.

ROW 9: P8, RT, *p12, RT; repeat from * to last 8 sts, purl to end.

ROWS 10 AND 11: Repeat Rows 8 and 9.

ROW 12: Repeat Row 8.

ROW 13: P1, RT, p1, *LT, [p2, RT] twice, p1, RT, p1; repeat from * to end.

ROW 14: K1, p2, *k2, p1, k2, p2; repeat from * to last st, k1.

ROW 15: P1, RT, *p2, LT, [p1, RT] twice, p2, RT; repeat from * to last st, p1.

ROW 16: Repeat Row 2.

Repeat Rows 1–16 for pattern.

95 Damask

Based on a textile pattern, the interplay of both horizontal and vertical elements, along with diagonals, makes a pattern both elaborate and modern at the same time.

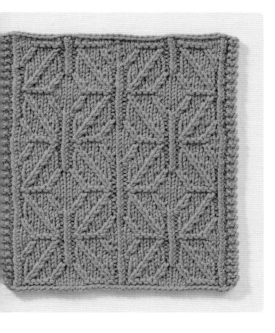

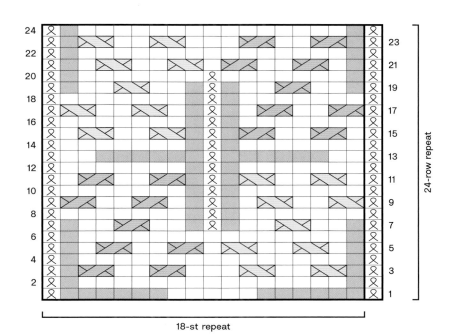

18-st repeat

24-row repeat

(multiple of 18 sts + 1; 24-row repeat)

PSS: 90

ROW 1 (RS): K1-tbl, *p6, k5, p6, k1-tbl; repeat from * to end.

ROWS 2, 4, AND 6: P1-tbl, *k1, p15, k1, p1-tbl; repeat from * to end.

ROW 3: K1-tbl, *p1, LT, k2, LT, k3, RT, k2, RT, p1, k1-tbl; repeat from * to end.

ROW 5: K1-tbl, *p1, k1, LT, k2, LT, k1, RT, k2, RT, k1, p1, k1-tbl; repeat from * to end.

ROW 7: K1-tbl, *p1, k2, LT, k2, p1, k1-tbl, p1, k2, RT, k2, p1, k1-tbl; repeat from * to end.

ROWS 8, 10, 12, 14, 16, AND 18: P1-tbl, *p7, k1, p1-tbl, k1, p7, p1-tbl; repeat from * to end.

ROW 9: K1-tbl, *LT, k2, LT, k1, p1, k1-tbl, p1, k1, RT, k2, RT, k1-tbl; repeat from * to end.

ROW 11: K1-tbl, *k1, LT, k2, LT, p1, k1-tbl, p1, RT, k2, RT, k1, k1-tbl; repeat from * to end.

ROW 13: K1-tbl, *k2, p6, k1-tbl, p6, k2, k1-tbl; repeat from * to end.

ROW 15: K1-tbl, *k1, RT, k2, RT, p1, k1-tbl, p1, LT, k2, LT, k1, k1-tbl; repeat from * to end.

ROW 17: K1-tbl, *RT, k2, RT, k1, p1, k1-tbl, p1, k1, LT, k2, LT, k1-tbl; repeat from * to end.

ROW 19: K1-tbl, *p1, k2, RT, k2, p1, k1-tbl, p1, k2, LT, k2, p1, k1-tbl; repeat from * to end.

ROW 20: P1-tbl, *k1, p7, p1-tbl, p7, k1, p1-tbl; repeat from * to end.

ROW 21: K1-tbl, *p1, k1, RT, k2, RT, k1, LT, k2, LT, k1, p1, k1-tbl; repeat from * to end.

ROW 22: P1-tbl, *k1, p15, k1, p1-tbl; repeat from * to end.

ROW 23: K1-tbl, *p1, RT, k2, RT, k3, LT, k2, LT, p1, k1-tbl; repeat from * to end.

ROW 24: Repeat Row 22.

Repeat Rows 1–24 for pattern.

(96) Hugs & Kisses

A variation on a classic, Xs and Os naturally nestle together. This version has horizontal and vertical elements as well. One repeat fits perfectly on the back of a hand in the Hat & Mitts set on page 212.

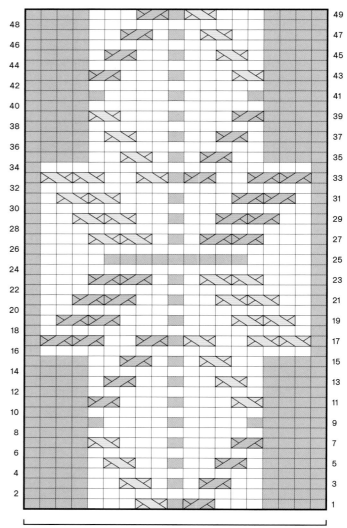

19-st panel

(panel of 19 sts; 49 rows)

PSS: 90

ROW 1 (RS): P4, k3, RT, p1, LT, k3, p4.

ROWS 2, 4, 6, 8, 10, 12, AND 14: K4, p11, k4.

ROW 3: P4, k2, RT, k1, p1, k1, LT, k2, p4.

ROW 5: *P4, k1, RT, k2, p1, k2, LT, k1, p4.

ROW 7: P4, RT, k3, p1, k3, LT, p4.

ROW 9: P5, k4, p1, k4, p5.

ROW 11: P4, LT, k3, p1, k3, RT, p4.

ROW 13: P4, k1, LT, k2, p1, k2, RT, k1, p4.

ROW 15: P4, k2, LT, k1, p1, k1, RT, k2, p4.

ROW 16 AND ALL WS ROWS THROUGH ROW 34: K1, p17, k1.

ROW 17: P1, LT twice, k2, LT, p1, RT, k2, RT twice, p1.

ROW 19: P1, k1, LT twice, k3, p1, k3, RT twice, k1, p1.

ROW 21: P1, k2, LT twice, k2, p1, k2, RT twice, k2, p1.

ROW 23: P1, k3, LT twice, k1, p1, k1, RT twice, k3, p1.

ROW 25: P1, k4, p9, k4, p1.

ROW 27: P1, k3, RT twice, k1, p1, k1, LT twice, k3, p1.

ROW 29: P1, k2, RT twice, k2, p1, k2, LT twice, k2, p1.

ROW 31: P1, k1, RT twice, k3, p1, k3, LT twice, k1, p1.

ROW 33: P1, RT twice, k2, RT, p1, LT, k2, LT twice, p1.

ROWS 35-47: Repeat Rows 3–15.

ROW 48: Repeat Row 2.

ROW 49: *P4, k3, LT, p1, RT, k3, p4; repeat from * to end.

(97) Swedish Star

This eight-pointed star is made possible through the inclusion of rib for the vertical lines and Garter stitch for the short, but crucial, horizontal segments. The crossing of vertical lines forming a center diamond, while not integral to the star, adds visual interest.

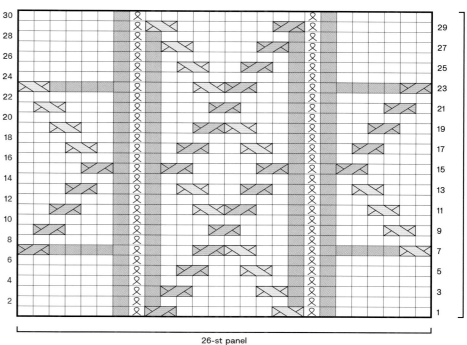

26-st panel

(26-st panel; 30-row repeat)

PSS: 90

ROW 1 (RS): K6, p1, k1-tbl, LT, k6, RT, k1-tbl, p1, k6.

ROW 2 AND ALL WS ROWS THROUGH ROW 28: P6, k1, p1-tbl, k1, p8, k1, p1-tbl, k1, p6.

ROW 3: K6, p1, k1-tbl, p1, LT, k4, RT, p1, k1-tbl, p1, k6.

ROW 5: K6, p1, k1-tbl, p1, k1, LT, k2, RT, k1, p1, k1-tbl, p1, k6.

ROW 7: LT, p5, k1-tbl, p1, k2, LT, RT, k2, p1, k1-tbl, p5, RT.

ROW 9: K1, LT, k3, p1, k1-tbl, p1, k3, RT, k3, p1, k1-tbl, p1, k3, RT, k1.

ROW 11: K2, [LT, k2, p1, k1-tbl, p1, k2, RT] twice, k2.

ROW 13: K3, LT, k1, p1, k1-tbl, p1, k1, RT, k2, LT, k1, p1, k1-tbl, p1, k1, RT, k3.

ROW 15: K4, RT, p1, k1-tbl, p1, RT, k4, RT, p1, k1-tbl, p1, RT, k4.

ROW 17: K3, RT, k1, p1, k1-tbl, p1, k1, LT, k2, RT, k1, p1, k1-tbl, p1, k1, LT, k3.

ROW 19: K2, [RT, k2, p1, k1-tbl, p1, k2, LT] twice, k2.

ROW 21: K1, RT, k3, p1, k1-tbl, p1, k3, RT, k3, p1, k1-tbl, p1, k3, LT, k1.

ROW 23: RT, p5, k1-tbl, p1, k2, RT, LT, k2, p1, k1-tbl, p5, LT.

ROW 25: K6, p1, k1-tbl, p1, k1, RT, k2, LT, k1, p1, k1-tbl, p1, k6.

ROW 27: K6, p1, k1-tbl, p1, RT, k4, LT, p1, k1-tbl, p1, k6.

ROW 29: K6, p1, k1-tbl, RT, k6, LT, k1-tbl, p1, k6.

ROW 30: P6, k1, p1-tbl, p10, p1-tbl, k1, p6.

Repeat Rows 1–30 for pattern.

(98) Swedish Star Allover

Repeating Swedish Star (#97) in an ever-so-slightly overlapping checkerboard formation creates an allover pattern where, depending on how you look at it, sometimes the stars are dominant and sometimes you notice other elements first.

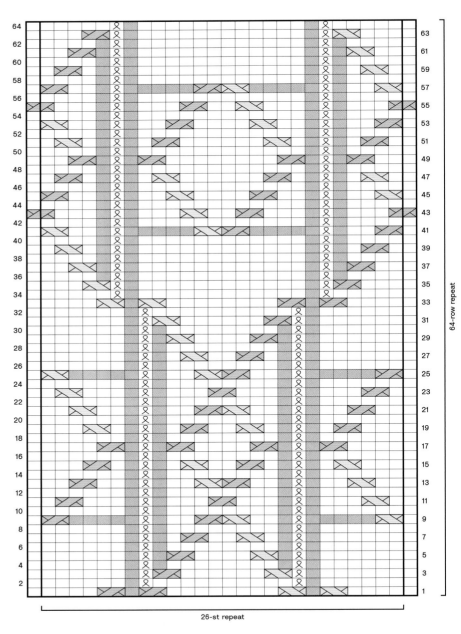

64-row repeat

26-st repeat

(99) Chain Mesh

The combination of diagonals and verticals once again tricks the eye into seeing rounded shapes, as we first saw in Chapter 5. Three ridges of Garter stitch give the centers stability and plumpness where they might otherwise collapse inward.

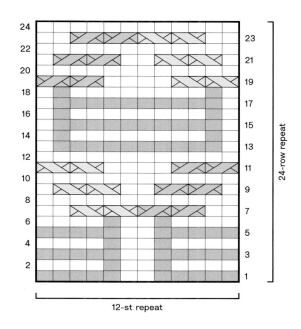

(multiple of 12 sts; 24-row repeat)

PSS: 85

ROW 1 (RS): P5, k2, *p10, k2; repeat from * to last 5 sts, purl to end.

ROW 2: P4, k1, p2, k1, *p8, k1, p2, k1; repeat from * to last 4 sts, purl to end.

ROWS 3–6: Repeat Rows 1 and 2 twice.

ROW 7: K2, RT twice, LT twice, *k4, RT twice, LT twice; repeat from * to last 2 sts, k2.

ROW 8: Purl.

ROW 9: K1, RT twice, k2, LT twice, *k2, RT twice, k2, LT twice; repeat from * to last st, k1.

ROW 10: Purl.

ROW 11: *RT twice, k4, LT twice; repeat from * to end.

ROW 12: Purl.

ROW 13: K1, p10, *k2, p10; repeat from * to last st, k1.

ROW 14: P1, k1, p8, k1, *p2, k2, p8, k1, repeat from * to last st, p1.

ROWS 15–18: Repeat Rows 13 and 14 twice.

ROW 19: *LT twice, k4, RT twice; repeat from * to end.

ROW 20: Purl.

ROW 21: K1, LT twice, k2, RT twice, *k2, LT twice, k2, RT twice; repeat from * to last st, k1.

ROW 22: Purl.

ROW 23: K2, LT twice, RT twice, *k4, LT twice, RT twice; repeat from * to last 2 sts, k2.

ROW 24: Purl.

Repeat Rows 1–24 for pattern.

⑽ Small Mesh

In this smaller version of Chain Mesh (#99), the width has been reduced by only two stitches, but that change and the omission of one Garter ridge reduced the number of rows by a third, altering the scale of the pattern quite a bit.

(multiple of 10 sts; 16-row repeat)

PSS: 85

ROW 1 (RS): P4, k2, *p8, k2; repeat from * to last 4 sts, purl to end.

ROW 2: P3, k1, p2, k1, *p6, k1, p2, k1; repeat from * to last 3 sts, p3.

ROWS 3 AND 4: Repeat Rows 1 and 2.

ROW 5: K1, RT twice, LT twice, *k2, RT twice, LT twice; repeat from * to last st, k1.

ROW 6: Purl.

ROW 7: *RT twice, k2, LT twice; repeat from * to end.

ROW 8: Purl.

ROW 9: K1, p8, *k2, p8; repeat from * to last st, k1.

ROW 10: P1, k1, p6, k1, *p2, k1, p6, k1, repeat from * to last st, p1.

ROWS 11 AND 12: Repeat Rows 9 and 10.

ROW 13: *LT twice, k2, RT twice; repeat from * to end.

ROW 14: Purl.

ROW 15: K1, LT twice, RT twice, *k2, LT twice, RT twice; repeat from * to last st, k1.

ROW 16: Purl.

Repeat Rows 1–16 for pattern.

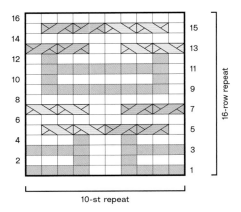

10-st repeat

16-row repeat

⑾ Mesh Columns

This pattern is a bonus, because it can be worked from the same chart as #100, Small Mesh. To make these columns, add two stitches of reverse Stockinette between each repeat. Look at what a difference it makes.

CHAPTER 7
Eyelet

Openwork can coordinate perfectly with twisted stitches. Both tend to move at the same rate, shifting one stitch every right-side row. A diagonal of yarnovers and their paired decreases can replace a diagonal of twisted stitches to transform an existing twisted-stitch pattern. Take care though, as the motions involved in making decreases are almost identical to the motions used to make twisted stitches. It's easy to forget what you are doing and work one when you meant to do the other.

(102) Eyelet Zigzag

Remember the progression of pyramids and triangles that led to Slash (#14) in Chapter 2? Eyelet Zigzag is the natural next step. Mirror image Slash to form a zigzag and replace the top row of twists with a diagonal made from eyelets and decreases.

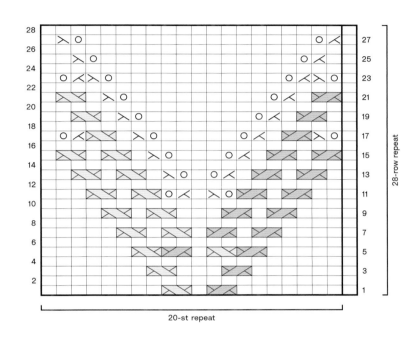

(multiple of 20 sts + 1; 28-row repeat)

PSS: 100

ROW 1 (RS): K8, RT, k1, LT, *k15, RT, k1, LT; repeat from * to last 8 sts, knit to end.

ROW 2 AND ALL WS ROWS: Purl.

ROW 3: K7, RT, k3, LT, *k13, RT, k3, LT; repeat from * to last 7 sts, knit to end.

ROW 5: K6, RT, LT, k1, RT, LT, *k11, RT, LT, k1, RT, LT; repeat from * to last 6 sts, knit to end.

ROW 7: K5, [RT, k1] twice, LT, k1, LT, *k9, [RT, k1] twice, LT, k1, LT; repeat from * to last 5 sts, knit to end.

ROW 9: K4, RT, k1, RT, k3, LT, k1, LT, *k7, RT, k1, RT, k3, LT, k1, LT; repeat from * to last 4 sts, knit to end.

ROW 11: K3, RT, k1, RT, yo, ssk, k1, k2tog, yo, LT, k1, LT, *k5, RT, k1, RT, yo, ssk, k1, k2tog, yo, LT, k1, LT; repeat from * to last 3 sts, k3.

ROW 13: K2, [RT, k1] twice, k2tog, yo, k1, yo, ssk, [k1, LT] twice, *k3, [RT, k1] twice, k2tog, yo, k1, yo, ssk, [k1, LT] twice; repeat from * to last 2 sts, k2.

ROW 15: K1, *[RT, k1] twice, k2tog, yo, k3, yo, ssk, k1, [LT, k1] twice; repeat from * to end.

ROW 17: K1, *yo, ssk, RT, k1, k2tog, yo, k5, yo, ssk, k1, LT, k2tog, yo, k1; repeat from * to end.

ROW 19: K2, RT, k1, k2tog, yo, k7, yo, ssk, k1, LT, *k3, RT, k1, k2tog, yo, k7, yo, ssk, k1, LT; repeat from * to last 2 sts, k2.

ROW 21: K1, *RT, k1, k2tog, yo, k9, yo, ssk, k1, LT, k1; repeat from * to end.

ROW 23: K1, *yo, ssk, k2tog, yo, k11, yo, ssk, k2tog, yo, k1; repeat from * to end.

ROW 25: K2, k2tog, yo, k13, yo, ssk, *k3, k2tog, yo, k13, yo, ssk; repeat from * to last 2 sts, k2.

ROW 27: K1, *k2tog, yo, k15, yo, ssk, k1; repeat from * to end.

ROW 28: Purl.

Repeat Rows 1–28 for pattern.

(103) Open Pyramids

In this sister to Pyramids Overlap (#7), the top row of twists along with a few other key twists are replaced with eyelets and decreases to make Open Pyramids.

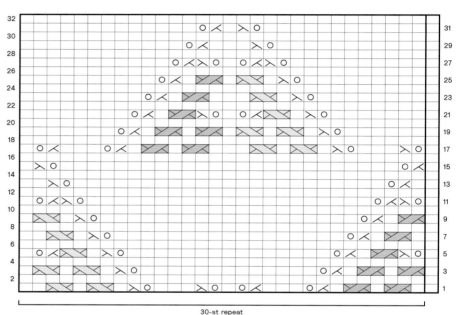

30-st repeat

32-row repeat

(multiple of 30 sts + 1; 32-row repeat)

PSS: 100

ROW 1 (RS): K1, *k1, [RT, k1] twice, k2tog, yo, k3, k2tog, yo, k1, yo, ssk, k3, yo, ssk, [k1, LT] twice, k2; repeat from * to end.

ROW 2 AND ALL WS ROWS: Purl.

ROW 3: K1, *[RT, k1] twice, k2tog, yo, k13, yo, ssk, k1, [LT, k1] twice; repeat from * to end.

ROW 5: K1, *yo, ssk, RT, k1, k2tog, yo, k15, yo, ssk, k1, LT, k2tog, yo, k1; repeat from * to end.

ROW 7: K1, *k1, RT, k1, k2tog, yo, k17, yo, ssk, k1, LT, k2; repeat from * to end.

ROW 9: K1, *RT, k1, k2tog, yo, k19, yo, ssk, k1, LT, k1; repeat from * to end.

ROW 11: K1, *yo, ssk, k2tog, yo, k21, yo, ssk, k2tog, yo, k1; repeat from * to end.

ROW 13: K1, *k1, k2tog, yo, k23, yo, ssk, k2; repeat from * to end.

ROW 15: K1, * k2tog, yo, k25, yo, ssk, k1; repeat from * to end.

ROW 17: K1, *yo, ssk, k3, yo, ssk, [k1, LT] twice, k3, [RT, k1] twice, k2tog, yo, k3, k2tog, yo, k1; repeat from * to end.

ROW 19: K1, *k6, yo, ssk, [k1, LT] twice, k1, [RT, k1] twice, k2tog, yo, k7; repeat from * to end.

ROW 21: K1, *k7, yo, ssk, k1, LT, k2tog, yo, k1, yo, ssk, RT, k1, k2tog, yo, k8; repeat from * to end.

ROW 23: K1, *k8, yo, ssk, k1, LT, k3, RT, k1, k2tog, yo, k9; repeat from * end.

ROW 25: K1, *k9, yo, ssk, k1, LT, k1, RT, k1, k2tog, yo, k10; repeat from * to end.

ROW 27: K1, *k10, yo, ssk, k2tog, yo, k1, yo, ssk, k2tog, yo, k11; repeat from * to to end.

ROW 29: K1, *k11, yo, ssk, k3, k2tog, yo, k12; repeat from * to end.

ROW 31: K1, *k12, yo, ssk, k1, k2tog, yo, k13; repeat from * to end.

ROW 32: Purl.

Repeat Rows 1–32 for pattern.

(104) Alberta

My imagination sees mountains, clouds, and rivers represented in abstract form by this combination of twisted stitches and lace.

(multiple of 12 sts + 2; 28-row repeat)

PSS: 100

ROW 1 (RS): Purl.

ROW 2 AND ALL WS ROWS: Purl.

ROW 3: Purl.

ROW 5: K2, *yo, ssk, RT 3 times, k2tog, yo, k2; repeat from * to end.

ROW 7: K3, yo, ssk, LT twice, k2tog, yo, *k4, yo, ssk, LT twice, k2tog, yo; repeat from * to last 3 sts, k3.

ROW 9: K4, yo, ssk, RT, k2tog, yo, *k6, yo, ssk, RT, k2tog, yo; repeat from * to last 4 sts, knit to end.

ROW 11: K5, yo, ssk, k2tog, yo, *k8, yo, ssk, k2tog, yo; repeat from * to last 5 sts, knit to end.

ROW 13: RT, *k4, k2tog, yo, k4, RT; repeat from * to end.

ROW 15: K1, *LT, k8, RT; repeat from * to last st, k1.

ROW 17: RT, *LT, k6, RT twice; repeat from * to end.

ROW 19: K1, *LT twice, k4, RT twice; repeat from * to last st, k1.

ROW 21: Purl.

ROW 23: Purl.

ROW 25: K1, *k2tog, yo; repeat from * to last st, k1.

ROW 27: K1, *yo, ssk; repeat from * to last st, k1.

ROW 28: Purl.

Repeat Rows 1–28 for pattern.

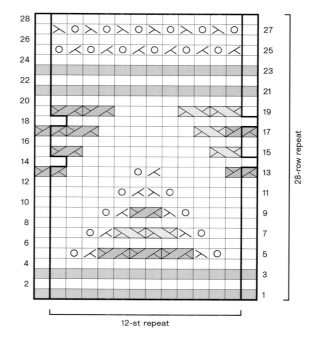

(105) Jagged

The slightly asymmetrical form gives an unusual air and a bit of tension in the form of imbalance to this zigzagging pattern stitch.

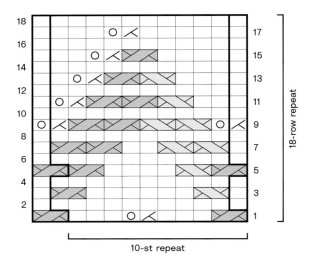

(multiple of 10 sts + 2; 18-row repeat)

PSS: 100

ROW 1 (RS): RT, *k3, k2tog, yo, k3, RT; repeat from * end.

ROW 2 AND ALL WS ROWS: Purl.

ROW 3: K1, *LT, k6, RT; repeat from * to last st, k1.

ROW 5: RT, *LT, k4, RT twice; repeat from * to end.

ROW 7: K1, *LT twice, k2, RT twice; repeat from * to last st, k1.

ROW 9: K2tog, yo, *LT twice, RT twice, k2tog, yo; repeat from * to end.

ROW 11: K1, *k2, LT, RT twice, k2tog, yo; repeat from * to last st, k1.

ROW 13: *K4, LT, RT, k2tog, yo; repeat from * to last 2 sts, k2.

ROW 15: K5, RT, k2tog, yo, *k6, RT, k2tog, yo; repeat from * to last 3 sts, k3.

ROW 17: K6, k2tog, yo, *k8, k2tog, yo; repeat from * to last 4 sts, knit to end.

ROW 18: Purl.

Repeat Rows 1–18 for pattern.

(106) Open Lattice

The simple lattice of Lattice (#47) is punctured by working two yarnovers and their paired decreases on some of the wrong-side rows.

(multiple of 4 sts + 2; 8-row repeat)
PSS: 100

ROW 1 (RS): K1, *RT, LT; repeat from * to last st, k1.

ROW 2: P1, *ssp, yo twice, p2tog; repeat from * to last st, p1.

ROW 3: LT, *(k1, p1) into double yo, LT; repeat from * to end.

ROW 4: Purl.

ROW 5: K1, *LT, RT; repeat from * to last st, k1.

ROW 6: P1, yo, p2tog, ssp, *yo twice, p2tog, ssp; repeat from * to last st, yo, p1.

ROW 7: K1, p1, RT, *(k1, p1) into double yo, RT; repeat from * to last 2 sts, k2.

ROW 8: Purl.

Repeat Rows 1–8 for pattern.

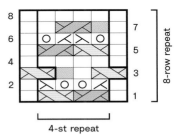

(107) Collision

Flanked by columns of five-stitch braid, lines of openwork begin moving toward each other and, when they collide, become interwoven twisted stitches. The first 46 rows are worked once, then the following 4 rows can be repeated over and over. There is a gauge difference between the bottom and the top of this pattern. You'll want to plan for a slight flare.

(38-st panel; 4-row repeat)
PSS: 100

ROW 1 (RS): LT twice, k1, p1, yo, ssk, k22, k2tog, yo, p1, k1, RT twice.

ROW 2 AND ALL WS ROWS THROUGH ROW 46: Knit the knit sts and purl the purl sts as they face you.

ROW 3: K1, RT twice, p1, k1, yo, ssk, k20, k2tog, yo, k1, p1, LT twice, k1.

ROW 5: LT twice, k1, p1, [yo, ssk] twice, k18, [k2tog, yo] twice, p1, k1, RT twice.

ROW 7: K1, RT twice, p1, k1, [yo, ssk] twice, k16, [k2tog, yo] twice, k1, p1, LT twice, k1.

ROW 9: LT twice, k1, p1, [yo, ssk] 3 times, k14, [k2tog, yo] 3 times, p1, k1, RT twice.

ROW 11: K1, RT twice, p1, k1, [yo, ssk] 3 times, k12, [k2tog, yo] 3 times, k1, p1, LT twice, k1.

ROW 13: LT twice, k1, p1, [yo, ssk] 4 times, k10, [k2tog, yo] 4 times, p1, k1, RT twice.

ROW 15: K1, RT twice, p1, k1, [yo, ssk] 4 times, k8, [k2tog, yo] 4 times, k1, p1, LT twice, k1.

ROW 17: LT twice, k1, p1, [yo, ssk] 5 times, k6, [k2tog, yo] 5 times, p1, k1, RT twice.

ROW 19: K1, RT twice, p1, k1, [yo, ssk] 5 times, k4, [k2tog, yo] 5 times, k1, p1, LT twice, k1.

ROW 21: LT twice, k1, p1, [yo, ssk] 6 times,

k2, [k2tog, yo] 6 times, p1, k1, RT twice.

ROW 23: K1, RT twice, p1, k1, [yo, ssk] 6 times, [k2tog, yo] 6 times, k1, p1, LT twice, k1.

ROW 25: LT twice, k1, p1, [yo, ssk] 6 times, RT, [k2tog, yo] 6 times, p1, k1, RT twice.

ROW 27: K1, RT twice, p1, k1, [yo, ssk] 5 times, LT twice, [k2tog, yo] 5 times, k1, p1, LT twice, k1.

ROW 29: LT twice, k1, p1, [yo, ssk] 5 times, RT 3 times, [k2tog, yo] 5 times, p1, k1, RT twice.

ROW 31: K1, RT twice, p1, k1, [yo, ssk] 4 times, LT 4 times, [k2tog, yo] 4 times, k1, p1, LT twice, k1.

ROW 33: LT twice, k1, p1, [yo, ssk] 4 times, RT 5 times, [k2tog, yo] 4 times, p1, k1, RT twice.

ROW 35: K1, RT twice, p1, k1, [yo, ssk] 3 times, LT 6 times, [k2tog, yo] 3 times, k1, p1, LT twice, k1.

ROW 37: LT twice, k1, p1, [yo, ssk] 3 times, RT 7 times, [k2tog, yo] 3 times, p1, k1, RT twice.

ROW 39: K1, RT twice, p1, k1, [yo, ssk] twice, LT 8 times, [k2tog, yo] twice, k1, p1, LT twice, k1.

ROW 41: LT twice, k1, p1, [yo, ssk] twice, RT 9 times, [k2tog, yo] twice, p1, k1, RT twice.

ROW 43: K1, RT twice, p1, k1, yo, ssk, LT 10 times, k2tog, yo, k1, p1, LT twice, k1.

ROW 45: LT twice, k1, p1, yo, ssk, RT 11 times, k2tog, yo, p1, k1, RT twice.

ROW 47: K1, RT twice, p1, k1, LT 12 times, k1, p1, LT twice, k1.

ROW 48: Repeat Row 2.

ROW 49: LT twice, k1, p1, RT 13 times, p1, k1, RT twice.

ROW 50: Repeat Row 2.

Repeat Rows 47–50 for pattern.

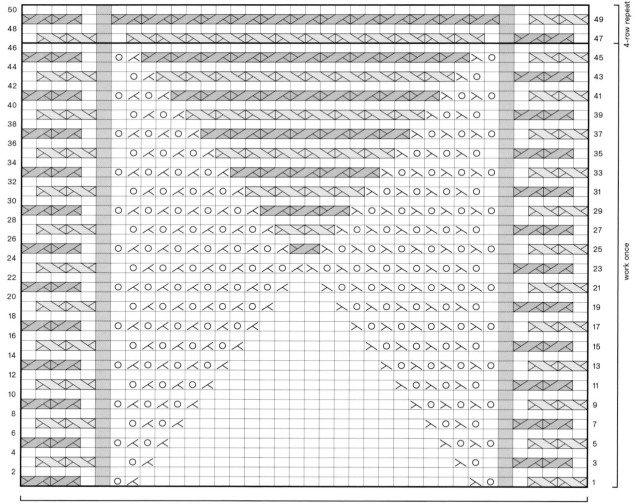

38-st panel

(108) Tents

A string of diamond shapes is nestled in half-drop formation, each diamond perforated with double yarnovers worked on some of the wrong-side rows.

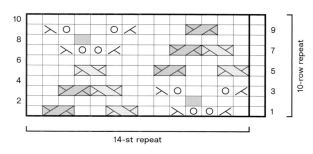

14-st repeat

10-row repeat

(multiple of 14 sts + 1; 10-row repeat)

PSS: 100

ROW 1 (RS): *K2, k2tog, yo twice, ssk, k2, LT, k2, RT; repeat from * to last st, k1.

ROW 2: P10, (k1, p1) into double yo, *p12, (k1, p1) into double yo; repeat from * to last 3 sts, p3.

ROW 3: K1, *k2tog, yo, k2, yo, ssk, k2, LT, RT, k2; repeat from * to end.

ROW 4: Purl.

ROW 5: K1, *LT, k2, RT, k3, LT, k3; repeat from * to end.

ROW 6: Purl.

ROW 7: K2, LT, RT, k3, k2tog, yo twice, ssk, *k3, LT, RT, k3, k2tog, yo twice, ssk; repeat from * to last 2 sts, k2.

ROW 8: P3, (k1, p1) into double yo, *p12, (k1, p1) into double yo; repeat from * to last 10 sts, purl to end.

ROW 9: *K3, RT, k3, k2tog, yo, k2, yo, ssk; repeat from * to last st, k1.

ROW 10: Purl.

Repeat Rows 1–10 for pattern.

Boxes

This elaborate allover pattern has boxes within boxes within boxes. There are even boxes on the corners of some of those boxes. Eyelets add some asymmetry and depth, acting like shadows in the composition.

28-st repeat

56-row repeat

CHAPTER 8
Extreme

For years I avoiding working twisted stitch on wrong-side rows. I thought it couldn't or shouldn't be done. While it is easy to see where to work twists on right-side rows, the same cannot be said for the wrong side. In this chapter I broke my own rule and experimented with twists every row. The new possibilities opened by having lines at two different slopes were too much to resist. I comfort myself with the popularity of circular knitting. Worked in the round, twists every round are no problem at all.

(110) Finger Trap

The sharp angle of the notches at both ends of these Garter stitch bars is only possible by working twists on the wrong side. Originally inspired by motifs incorporated into rugs of the American Southwest, I now see either two-headed fish or finger traps of practical joke fame.

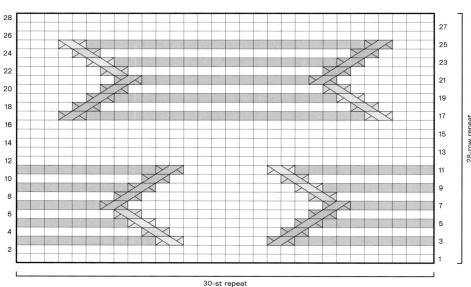

(multiple of 30 sts; 28-row repeat)

PSS: 95

ROW 1 (RS): Knit.

ROW 2: Purl.

ROW 3: *P10, RT, k6, LT, p10; repeat from * to end.

ROW 4: *P9, LT, p8, RT, p9; repeat from * to end.

ROW 5: *P8, RT, k10, LT, p8; repeat from * to end.

ROW 6: *P7, LT, p12, RT, p7; repeat from * to end.

ROW 7: *P6, RT, k14, RT, p6; repeat from * to end.

ROW 8: *P7, RT, p12, LT, p7; repeat from * to end.

ROW 9: *P8, LT, k10, RT, p8; repeat from * to end.

ROW 10: *P9, RT, p8, LT, p9; repeat from * to end.

ROW 11: *P10, LT, k6, RT, p10; repeat from * to end.

ROW 12: Purl.

ROW 13: Knit.

ROW 14: Purl.

ROW 15: Knit.

ROW 16: Purl.

ROW 17: *K3, LT, p20, RT, k3; repeat from * to end.

ROW 18: *P4, RT, p18, LT, p4; repeat from * to end.

ROW 19: *K5, LT, p16, RT, k5; repeat from * to end.

ROW 20: *P6, RT, k14, LT, p6; repeat from * to end.

ROW 21: *K7, RT, p12, RT, k7; repeat from * to end.

ROW 22: *P6, LT, k14, RT, p6; repeat from * to end.

ROW 23: *K5, RT, p16, LT, k5; repeat from * to end.

ROW 24: *P4, LT, p18, RT, p4; repeat from * to end.

ROW 25: *K3, RT, p20, LT, k3; repeat from * to end.

ROW 26: Purl.

ROW 27: Knit.

ROW 28: Purl.

Repeat Rows 1–28 for pattern.

(111) Kilim

I've long admired the jagged motifs often found in traditional woven kilims. The use of acute angles of twists made every row makes this interpretation possible.

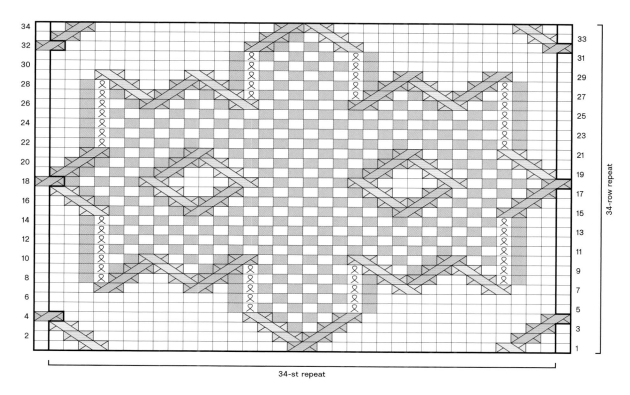

34-st repeat

34-row repeat

(112) Sashiko

In this pattern, named and fashioned after the Japanese art of mending stitches, zigzags and boxes are drawn with twisted stitches worked every row. The pointed bottom and top rows of this pattern are worked only once, while the center can be repeated as many times as you choose.

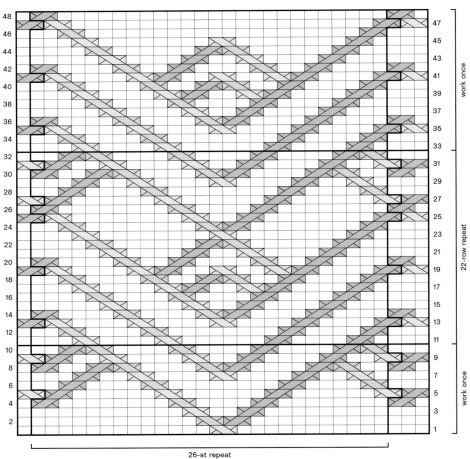

26-st repeat

(113) Sashiko Compact

In this variation of Sashiko (#112), the pattern is compressed, with less space between the zigzags. Again, the pointed bottom and top rows of this pattern are worked only once, while the center can be repeated as many times as you choose.

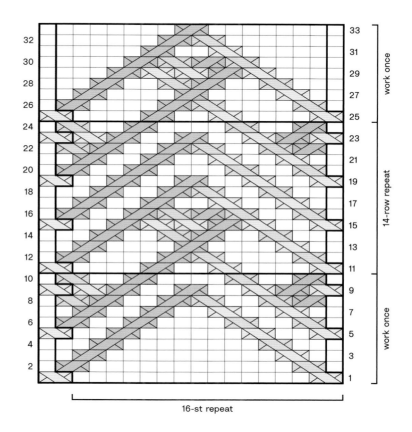

(114) Folded

Emulating the lines left scored into the paper when you unfold a piece of origami, the acute angles are made possible by working twists on wrong-side rows as well as the right side.

(multiple of 22 sts + 1; 48-row repeat)

PSS: 85

ROW 1 (RS): Purl.

ROW 2: Purl.

ROW 3: K1, *k8, RT, k1-tbl, LT, k9; repeat from * to end.

ROW 4: P1, *p7, LT, p1, p1-tbl, p1, RT, p8; repeat from * to end.

ROW 5: K1, *k6, RT twice, k1-tbl, LT twice, k7; repeat from * to end.

ROW 6: P1, *p5, LT, p2, k1, p1-tbl, k1, p2, RT, p6; repeat from * to end.

ROW 7: K1, *k4, RT, k1, RT, p1, k1-tbl, p1, LT, k1, LT, k5; repeat from * to end.

ROW 8: P1, *p3, LT, p4, k1, p1-tbl, k1, p4, RT, p4; repeat from * to end.

ROW 9: K1, *[k2, RT] twice, k1, p1, k1-tbl, p1, k1, LT, k2, LT, k3; repeat from * to end.

ROW 10: P1, *p1, LT, p6, k1, p1-tbl, k1, p6, RT, p2; repeat from * to end.

ROW 11: K1-tbl, *p1, k4, RT, k2, p1, k1-tbl, p1, k2, LT, k4, p1, k1-tbl; repeat from * to end.

ROW 12: P1-tbl, *k1, p8, k1, p1-tbl, k1, p8, k1, p1-tbl; repeat from * to end.

ROW 13: K1-tbl, *p1, k3, RT, k3, p1, k1-tbl, p1, k3, LT, k3, p1, k1-tbl; repeat from * to end.

ROW 14: Repeat Row 12.

ROW 15: K1-tbl, *p1, k2, RT, k4, p1, k1-tbl, p1, k4, LT, k2, p1, k1-tbl; repeat from * to end.

ROW 16: P1-tbl, *k1, p6, LT, p3, RT, p6, k1, p1-tbl; repeat from * to end.

ROW 17: K1-tbl, *p1, k1, RT, k2, RT, k5, LT, k2, LT, k1, p1, k1-tbl; repeat from * to end.

ROW 18: P1-tbl, *k1, p4, LT, p7, RT, p4, k1, p1-tbl; repeat from * to end.

ROW 19: K1-tbl, *p1, RT, k1, RT, k9, LT, k1, LT, p1, k1-tbl; repeat from * to end.

ROW 20: P1-tbl, *k1, p2, LT, p11, RT, p2, k1, p1-tbl; repeat from * to end.

ROW 21: K1-tbl, *RT twice, k13, LT twice, k1-tbl; repeat from * to end.

ROW 22: P1-tbl, *p1, LT, p15, RT, p1, p1-tbl; repeat from * to end.

ROW 23: K1-tbl, *RT, k17, LT, k1-tbl; repeat from * to end.

ROWS 24–26: Purl.

ROW 27: K1-tbl, *LT, k17, RT, k1-tbl; repeat from * to end.

ROW 28: P1-tbl, *p1, RT, p15, LT, p1, p1-tbl; repeat from * to end.

ROW 29: K1-tbl, *LT twice, k13, RT twice, k1-tbl; repeat from * to end.

ROW 30: P1-tbl, *k1, p2, RT, p11, LT, p2, k1, p1-tbl; repeat from * to end.

ROW 31: K1-tbl, *p1, LT, k1, LT, k9, RT, k1, RT, p1, k1-tbl; repeat from * to end.

ROW 32: P1-tbl, *k1, p4, RT, p7, LT, p4, k1, p1-tbl; repeat from * to end.

ROW 33: K1-tbl, *p1, k1, LT, k2, LT, k5, RT, k2, RT, k1, p1, k1-tbl; repeat from * to end.

ROW 34: P1-tbl, *k1, p6, RT, p3, LT, p6, k1, p1-tbl; repeat from * to end.

ROW 35: K1-tbl, *p1, k2, LT, k4, p1, k1-tbl, p1, k4, RT, k2, p1, k1-tbl; repeat from * to end.

ROW 36: Repeat Row 12.

ROW 37: K1-tbl, *p1, k3, LT, k3, p1, k1-tbl, p1, k3, RT, k3, p1, k1-tbl; repeat from * to end.

ROW 38: Repeat Row 12.

ROW 39: K1-tbl, *p1, k4, LT, k2, p1, k1-tbl, p1, k2, RT, k4, p1, k1-tbl; repeat from * to end.

ROW 40: P1, *p1, RT, p6, k1, p1-tbl, k1, p6, LT, p2; repeat from * to end.

ROW 41: K1, *k2, LT, k2, LT, k1, p1, k1-tbl, p1, k1, RT, k2, RT, k3; repeat from * to end.

ROW 42: P1, *p3, RT, p4, k1, p1-tbl, k1, p4, LT, p4; repeat from * to end.

ROW 43: K1, *k4, LT, k1, LT, p1, k1-tbl, p1, RT, k1, RT, k5; repeat from * to end.

ROW 44: P1, *p5, RT, p2, k1, p1-tbl, k1, p2, LT, p6; repeat from * to end.

ROW 45: K1, *k6, LT twice, k1-tbl, RT twice, k7; repeat from * to end.

ROW 46: P1, *p7, RT, p1, p1-tbl, p1, LT, p8; repeat from * to end.

ROW 47: K1, *k8, LT, k1-tbl, RT, k9; repeat from * to end.

ROW 48: Purl.

Repeat Rows 1–48 for pattern.

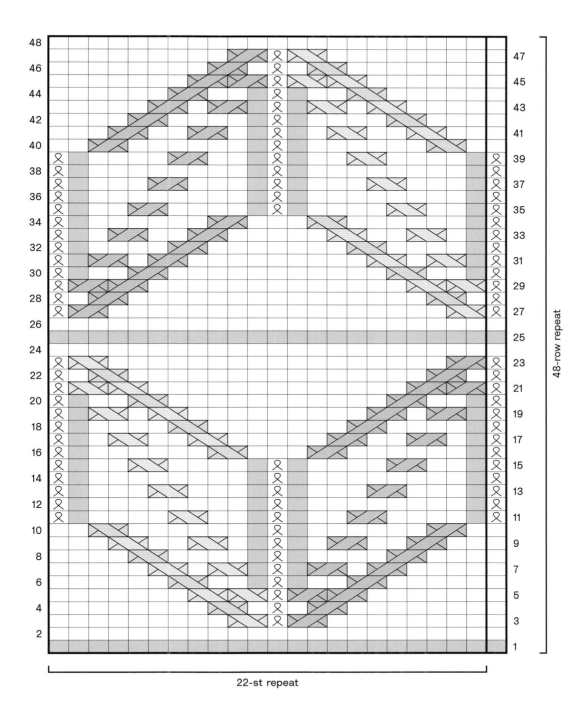

48-row repeat

22-st repeat

(115) Sketch

It's not easy to get the look of randomness in a repeatable pattern. Lines drawn at two angles help achieve an irregular appearance in this medley of scattered shards.

(multiple of 35 sts + 2; 46-row repeat)

PSS: 85

ROW 1 (RS): LT, *k4, RT, k9, LT, [p1, k1] 5 times, RT, k4, LT; repeat from * to end.

ROW 2: P1, *p6, RT, [k1, p1] 4 times, LT, p17; repeat from * to last st, p1.

ROW 3: K1, *LT, k2, RT, k12, LT, [k1, p1] 3 times, RT, k7; repeat from * to last st, k1.

ROW 4: P1, *p8, RT, [p1, k1] twice, LT, p19; repeat from * to last st, p1.

ROW 5: K1, *p1, LT, RT, k12, RT, k1, LT, p1, k1, RT, k7, RT; repeat from * to last st, p1.

ROW 6: K1, *p10, RT, LT, p20, k1; repeat from * to last st, p1.

ROW 7: P1, k1, *p1, LT, k12, RT, k4, RT, LT, k6, RT, p1, k1; repeat from * to end.

ROW 8: P1, k1, *p11, RT, p19, k1, p1, k1; repeat from * to end.

ROW 9: K1, *p1, k1, p1, LT, k10, [RT, k3] twice, LT, k4, RT, p1, k1; repeat from * to last st, p1.

ROW 10: K1, *p1, k1, p12, RT, p16, k1, p1, k1; repeat from * to last st, p1.

ROW 11: P1, *[k1, p1] twice, LT, k8, RT, k2, RT, k6, LT, k2, RT, p1, k1, p1; repeat from * to last st, k1.

ROW 12: P1, *k1, p1, k1, p13, RT, p13, [k1, p1] twice; repeat from * to last st, k1.

ROW 13: K1, *p1, [k1, p1] twice, LT, k6, RT, k1, RT, k9, LT, RT, [p1, k1] twice; repeat from * to last st, p1.

ROW 14: K1, *[p1, k1] twice, p14, RT, p10, k1, [p1, k1] twice; repeat from * to last st, p1.

ROW 15: P1, *[k1, p1] 3 times, LT, k4, RT twice, LT, k10, RT, p1, [k1, p1] twice; repeat from * to last st, k1.

ROW 16: P1, *k1, [p1, k1] twice, p15, RT, p7, [k1, p1] 3 times; repeat from * to last st, k1.

ROW 17: K1, *p1, [k1, p1] 3 times, LT, k3, RT, k3, LT, k8, RT, [p1, k1] 3 times; repeat from * to last st, p1.

ROW 18: K1, *[p1, k1] 3 times, p16, RT, p4, k1, [p1, k1] 3 times; repeat from * to last st, p1.

ROW 19: P1, *[k1, p1] 4 times, LT, RT, k6, LT, k6, RT, p1, [k1, p1] 3 times; repeat from * to last st, k1.

ROW 20: P1, *k1, [p1, k1] 3 times, p17, RT, p1, [k1, p1] 4 times; repeat from * to last st, k1.

ROW 21: K1, *[p1, k1] 4 times, RT, k9, LT, k4, RT, [p1, k1] 4 times; repeat from * to last st, k1.

ROW 22: K1, *[p1, k1] 3 times, p1, LT, p17, RT, k1, [p1, k1] 3 times; repeat from * to last st, p1.

ROW 23: P1, *[k1, p1] 3 times, RT, LT, k10, LT, k2, RT, k1, LT, [k1, p1] 3 times; repeat from * to last st, k1.

ROW 24: P1, *k1, [p1, k1] twice, LT, p21, RT, p1, [k1, p1] twice; repeat from * to last st, k1.

ROW 25: K1, *[p1, k1] twice, RT, k3, LT, k10, LT, RT, k4, LT, [p1, k1] twice; repeat from * to last st, p1.

ROW 26: row 26: K1, *p1, k1, p1, LT, p25, RT, k1, p1, k1; repeat from * to last st, p1.

ROW 27: P1, *k1, p1, RT, k6, LT, k10, RT, LT, k5, LT, k1, p1; repeat from * to last st, k1.

ROW 28: P1, k1, *LT, p29, RT, p1, k1; repeat from * to end.

ROW 29: K1, *RT, k9, LT, k8, RT, p1, k1, LT, k6, LT; repeat from * to last st, p1.

ROW 30: LT, *p10, k1, p22, LT; repeat from * to end.

ROW 31: K1, *LT, k10, LT, k6, RT, [p1, k1] twice, LT, k7; repeat from * to last st, k1.

ROW 32: *P11, k1, p1, k1, p19, LT; repeat from * to last 2 sts, p2.

ROW 33: K1, *RT, LT, k9, LT, k4, RT, [p1, k1] 3 times, LT, k6; repeat from * to last st, k1.

ROW 34: P1, *p9, k1, [p1, k1] twice, p16, LT, p3; repeat from * to last st, p1.

ROW 35: RT, *k3, LT, k8, LT, k2, RT, [p1, k1] 4 times, LT, k4, RT; repeat from * to end.

ROW 36: P1, *p8, k1, [p1, k1] 3 times, p13, LT, p5; repeat from * to last st, p1.

ROW 37: K1, *k6, LT, k7, LT, RT, [p1, k1] 5 times, LT, k2, RT; repeat from * to last st, k1.

ROW 38: P1, *p7, k1, [p1, k1] 4 times, p10, LT, p7; repeat from * to last st, p1.

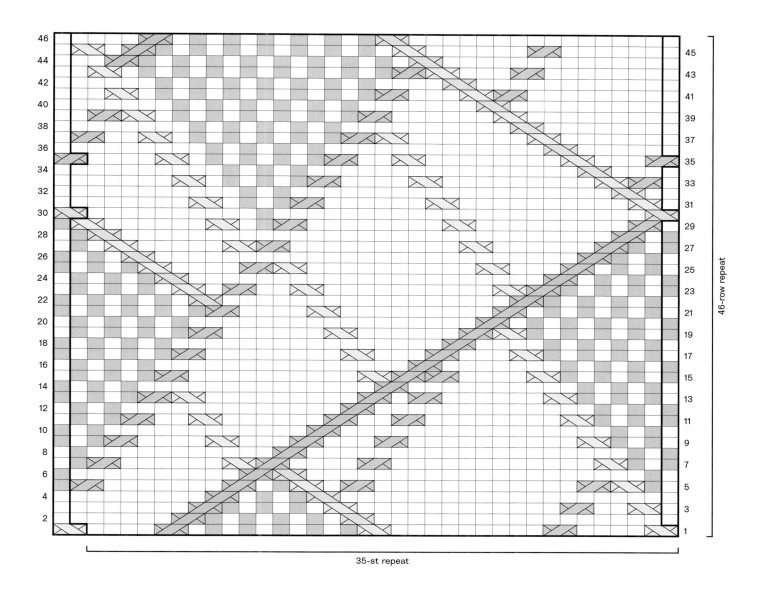

35-st repeat

46-row repeat

ROW 39: *K9, LT, k6, RT, [p1, k1] 6 times, LT, RT; repeat from * to last 2 sts, k2.

ROW 40: P1, *p6, k1, [p1, k1] 5 times, p7, LT, p9; repeat from * to last st, p1.

ROW 41: K1, *k8, RT, LT, k3, RT, [p1, k1] 7 times, LT, k2; repeat from * to last st, k1.

ROW 42: P1, *p5, k1, [p1, k1] 6 times, p4, LT, p11; repeat from * to last st, p1.

ROW 43: *K8, RT, k3, LT, RT, [p1, k1] 8 times, LT; repeat from * to last 2 sts, k2.

ROW 44: P1, *p2, RT, [k1, p1] 8 times, LT, p13; repeat from * to last st, p1.

ROW 45: K1, *k6, RT, k6, LT, [k1, p1] 7 times, RT, k1, LT; repeat from * to last st, k1.

ROW 46: P1, *p4, RT, [p1, k1] 6 times, LT, p15; repeat from * to last st, p1.

Repeat Rows 1–46 for pattern.

Fountain

As we've seen previously, for example in Droplets (#87), verticals and diagonals together form the illusion of curves. Here, twists worked every row are added to further enhance the illusion.

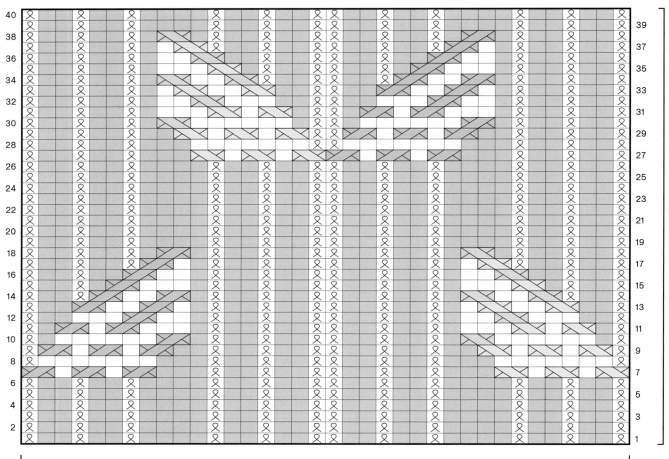

(117) Watch

In this pattern, lines slanting at two different angles are used in combination to form diamonds within diamonds. The resulting shapes are highlighted by the contrast of Stockinette and the carved-out spaces made with reverse Stockinette. I see the abstraction of watching eyes.

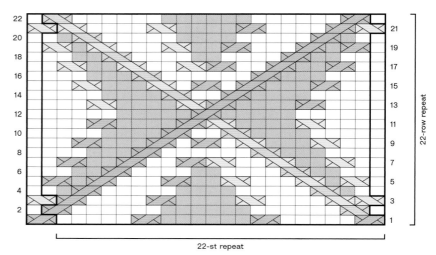

(multiple of 22 sts + 2; 22-row repeat)

PSS: 85

ROW 1 (RS): RT, *k5, RT, p6, RT, k5, RT; repeat from * to end.

ROW 2: P1, *RT, p6, k6, p6, LT; repeat from * to last st, p1.

ROW 3: *LT twice, k4, LT, p4, RT, k4, RT; repeat from * to last 2 sts, LT.

ROW 4: P2, *k1, RT, p5, k4, p5, LT, k1, p2; repeat from * to end.

ROW 5: K1, *LT, p1, LT, k3, LT, p2, RT, k3, RT, p1, RT; repeat from * to last st, k1.

ROW 6: P1, *p2, k2, RT, p4, k2, p4, LT, k2, p2; repeat from * to last st, p1.

ROW 7: K2, *LT, p2, LT, k2, LT, RT, k2, RT, p2, RT, k2; repeat from * to end.

ROW 8: P1, *p3, k3, RT, p6, LT, k3, p3; repeat from * to last st, p1.

ROW 9: K1, *k2, LT, p3, LT, [k1, RT] twice, p3, RT, k2; repeat from * to last st, k1.

ROW 10: P1, *p4, k4, RT, k2, LT, k4, p4; repeat from * to last st, p1.

ROW 11: K1, *k3, LT, p4, LT, RT, p4, RT, k3; repeat from * to last st, k1.

ROW 12: P1, *p5, k5, RT, k5, p5; repeat from * to last st, p1.

ROW 13: K1, *k3, RT, p4, RT, LT, p4, LT, k3; repeat from * to last st, k1.

ROW 14: P1, *p4, k4, LT, k2, RT, k4, p4; repeat from * to last st, p1.

ROW 15: K1, *k2, RT, p3, RT, k1, RT, k1, LT, p3, LT, k2; repeat from * to last st, k1.

ROW 16: P1, *p3, k3, LT, p6, RT, k3, p3; repeat from * to last st, p1.

ROW 17: K2, *RT, p2, RT, k2, RT, LT, k2, LT, p2, LT, k2; repeat from * to end.

ROW 18: P1, *p2, k2, LT, p4, k2, p4, RT, k2, p2; repeat from * to last st, p1.

ROW 19: K1, *RT, p1, RT, k3, RT, p2, LT, k3, LT, p1, LT; repeat from * to last st, k1.

ROW 20: P2, *k1, LT, p5, k4, p5, RT, k1, p2; repeat from * to end.

ROW 21: LT, *RT, k4, RT, p4, LT, k4, LT twice; repeat from * to end.

ROW 22: P1, *LT, p6, k6, p6, RT; repeat from * to last st, p1.

Repeat Rows 1–22 for pattern.

CHAPTER 9

Kaleidoscope

Repeating an equilateral triangle six times around creates an impressive and beautiful hexagon. I like to think of this technique as the knitter's version of a kaleidoscope. Worked in the round, from the outside in, these polygons can be knit onto each other for no-sew construction of sweaters and accessories.

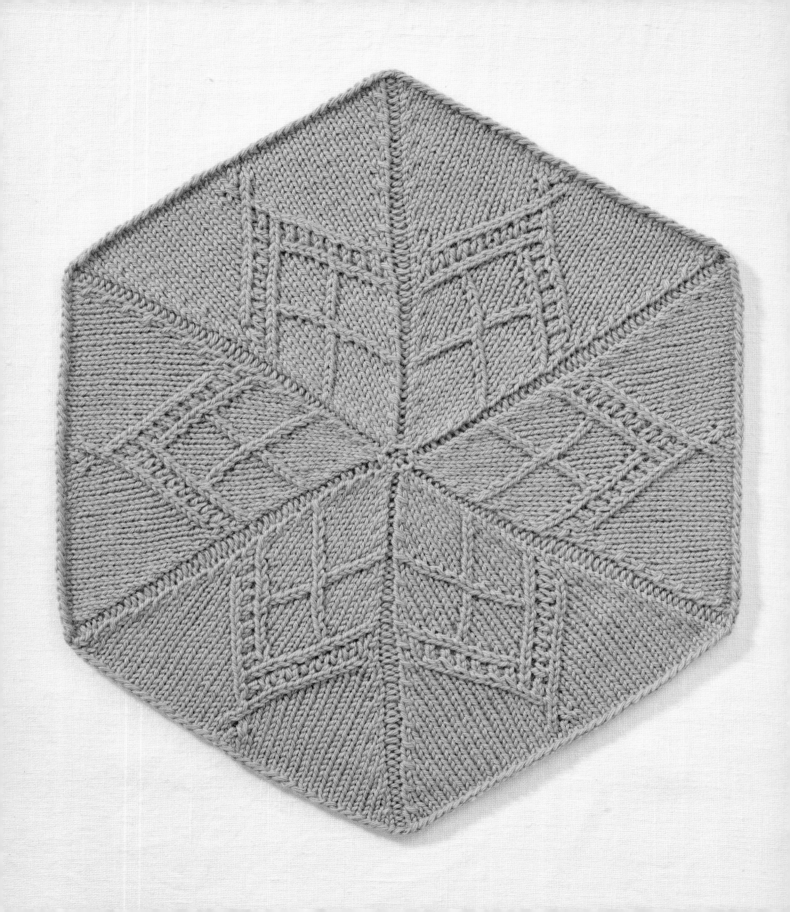

118 Water Lily

A simple composition of thick and thin lines transforms into a flower shape when repeated six times around.

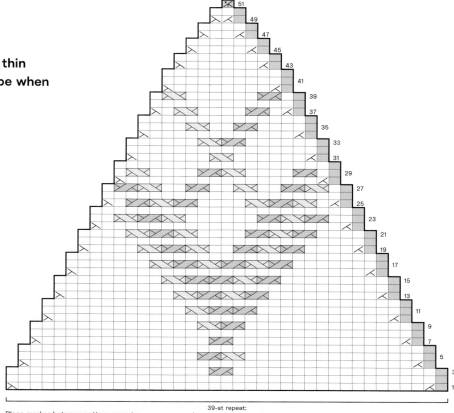

39-st repeat;
decreases to 1-st repeat

Place marker between pattern repeats.

(multiple of 39 sts, decreases to multiple of 1 st; 51 rnds)

Place a marker between pattern repeats.

RND 1: *P1, k2tog, knit to 2 sts before marker, ssk; repeat from * to end–2 sts decreased.

RND 2: *P1, knit to marker; repeat from * to end.

RND 3: *P1, k17, RT, knit to marker; repeat from * to end.

RND 4: Repeat Rnd 1.

RND 5: *P1, k15, LT, RT, knit to marker; repeat from * to end.

RND 6: Repeat Rnd 2.

RND 7: *P1, k2tog, k14, RT, knit to 2 sts before marker, ssk; repeat from * to end–2 sts decreased.

RND 8: Repeat Rnd 2.

RND 9: *P1, k14, RT, LT, knit to marker; repeat from * to end.

RND 10: Repeat Rnd 1.

RND 11: *P1, k12, RT twice, LT, knit to marker; repeat from * to end.

RND 12: Repeat Rnd 2.

RND 13: *P1, k2tog, k9, [RT, LT] twice, knit to 2 sts before marker, ssk; repeat from * to end–2 sts decreased.

RND 14: Repeat Rnd 2.

RND 15: *P1, k9, RT, LT, RT twice, LT, knit to marker; repeat from * to end.

RND 16: Repeat Rnd 1.

RND 17: *P1, k7, [RT, LT] 3 times, knit to marker; repeat from * to end.

RND 18: Repeat Rnd 2.

RND 19: *P1, k2tog, k4, RT, LT, RT, k2, LT, RT, LT, k4, ssk; repeat from * to end–2 sts decreased.

RND 20: Repeat Rnd 2.

RND 21: *P1, k4, RT, LT, RT, k4, RT, LT, k4; repeat from * to end.

RND 22: Repeat Rnd 1.

RND 23: *P1, k2, RT, LT, RT, k6, LT, RT, LT, k2; repeat from * to end.

RND 24: Repeat Rnd 2.

RND 25: *P1, k2tog, k1, LT, RT, LT, k4, RT, LT, RT, k1, ssk; repeat from * to end–2 sts decreased.

RND 26: Repeat Rnd 2.

RND 27: *P1, k1, LT, RT, k2, LT, k2, RT, k2, LT, RT, k1; repeat from * to end.

RND 28: Repeat Rnd 1.

RND 29: *P1, k1, [RT, k4, LT] twice, k1; repeat from * to end.

RND 30: Repeat Rnd 2.

RND 31: *P1, k2tog, k6, LT, knit to 2 sts before marker, ssk; repeat from * to end–2 sts decreased.

RND 32: Repeat Rnd 2.

RND 33: *P1, k6, RT, LT, knit to marker; repeat from * to end.

RND 34: Repeat Rnd 1.

RND 35: *P1, k4, RT, k2, LT, k4; repeat from * to end.

RND 36: Repeat Rnd 2.

RND 37: *P1, k2tog, k1, RT, k4, LT, k1, ssk; repeat from * to end–2 sts decreased.

RND 38: Repeat Rnd 2.

RND 39: *P1, k1, RT, k6, LT, k1; repeat from * to end.

RNDS 40 AND 41: Repeat Rnds 1 and 2.

RND 42: Repeat Rnd 2.

RNDS 43-48: Repeat Rnds 1 and 2 three times.

RND 49: *P1, k2tog, ssk; repeat from * to end–2 sts decreased.

RND 50: *P1, k2; repeat from * to end.

RND 51: *P3tog; repeat from * to end–2 sts decreased.

(119) Whirlwind

An octet of diagonal lines appears to rush across the triangles, each line ending when it hits the other side. The result is the appearance of a whirlwind and, in the center, a slender star.

(multiple of 39 sts, decreases to multiple of 1 st; 51 rnds)

Place a marker between pattern repeats.

RND 1: *P1, k2tog, LT, [k2, LT] 8 times, ssk; repeat from * to end—2 sts decreased.

RND 2: *P1, knit to marker; repeat from * to end.

RND 3: *P1, [k2 LT] 9 times; repeat from * to end.

RND 4: *P1, k2tog, knit to 2 sts before marker, ssk; repeat from * to end—2 sts decreased.

RND 5: *P1, k2, [LT, k2] 8 times; repeat from * to end.

RND 6: Repeat Rnd 2.

RND 7: *P1, k2tog, k1, [LT, k2] 7 times, ssk, k1; repeat from * to end—2 sts decreased.

RND 8: Repeat Rnd 2.

RND 9: *P1, k3, LT, [k2, LT] 6 times, k1, LT; repeat from * to end.

RND 10: Repeat Rnd 4.

RND 11: *P1, k3, LT, [k2 LT] 6 times, k1; repeat from * to end.

RND 12: Repeat Rnd 2.

RND 13: *P1, k2tog, k2, [LT, k2] 6 times, ssk; repeat from * to end—2 sts decreased.

RND 14: Repeat Rnd 2.

RND 15: *P1, k4, [LT, k2] 6 times; repeat from * to end.

RND 16: Repeat Rnd 4.

RND 17: *P1, k4, LT, [k2, LT] 5 times; repeat from * to end.

RND 18: Repeat Rnd 2.

RND 19: *P1, k2tog, k3, LT, [k2, LT] 4 times, k1, ssk; repeat from * to end—2 sts decreased.

RND 20: Repeat Rnd 2.

RND 21: *P1, k5, LT, [k2, LT] 4 times, k1; repeat from * to end.

RND 22: Repeat Rnd 4.

RND 23: *P1, k5, LT, [k2, LT] 3 times, k3; repeat from * to end.

RND 24: Repeat Rnd 2.

RND 25: *P1, k2tog, k4, LT, [k2, LT] 3 times, ssk; repeat from * to end—2 sts decreased.

RND 26: Repeat Rnd 2.

RND 27: *P1, k6, LT, [k2, LT] 3 times; repeat from * to end.

RND 28: Repeat Rnd 4.

RND 29: *P1, k6, [LT, k2] 3 times; repeat from * to end.

RND 30: Repeat Rnd 2.

RND 31: *P1, k2tog, k5, [LT, k2] twice, ssk, k1; repeat from * to end—2 sts decreased.

RND 32: Repeat Rnd 2.

RND 33: *P1, k7, LT, k2, LT, k1, LT; repeat from * to end.

RND 34: Repeat Rnd 4.

RND 35: *P1, k7, LT, k2, LT, k1; repeat from * to end.

RND 36: Repeat Rnd 2.

RND 37: *P1, k2tog, k6, LT, k2, ssk; repeat from * to end—2 sts decreased.

RND 38: Repeat Rnd 2.

RND 39: *P1, k8, LT, k2; repeat from * to end.

RND 40: Repeat Rnd 4.

RND 41: *P1, k8, LT; repeat from * to end.

RNDS 42, 44, 46, AND 48: Repeat Rnd 2.

RNDS 43, 45, AND 47: Repeat Rnd 4.

RND 49: *P1, k2tog, ssk; repeat from * to end—2 sts decreased.

RND 50: *P1, k2; repeat from * to end.

RND 51: *P3tog; repeat from * to end—2 sts decreased.

Place marker between pattern repeats.

39-st repeat; decreases to 1-st repeat

(120) Balsam

The cone motif and reverse Stockinette stitch shadow are borrowed from Pine Cone Shadow (#30). The cones all spring from the center, as the whorled branches of balsam emerge from the trunk.

(multiple of 39 sts, decreases to multiple of 1 st; 51 rnds)

Place a marker between pattern repeats.

RND 1: *P1, k2tog, k16, p2, knit to 2 sts before marker, ssk; repeat from * to end—2 sts decreased.

RND 2: *P1, k17, p2, knit to marker; repeat from * to end.

RND 3: *P1, k16, p4, knit to marker; repeat from * to end.

RND 4: *P1, k2tog, k14, p4, knit to 2 sts before marker, ssk; repeat from * to end—2 sts decreased.

RND 5: *P1, k14, p6, knit to marker; repeat from * to end.

RND 6: Repeat Rnd 5.

RND 7: *P1, k2tog, k11, p3, RT, p3, knit to 2 sts before marker, ssk; repeat from * to end—2 sts decreased.

RND 8: *P1, k12, p3, k2, p3, knit to marker; repeat from * to end.

RND 9: *P1, k11, p3, LT, RT, p3, knit to marker; repeat from * to end.

RND 10: *P1, k2tog, k9, p3, k4, p3, knit to 2 sts before marker, ssk; repeat from * to end—2 sts decreased.

RND 11: *P1, k9, p3, LT, RT twice, p3, knit to marker; repeat from * to end.

RND 12: *P1, k9, p3, k6, p3, knit to marker; repeat from * to end.

RND 13: *P1, k2tog, k6, p3, LT twice, RT twice, p3, knit to 2 sts before marker, ssk; repeat from * to end—2 sts decreased.

RND 14: *P1, k7, p3, k8, p3, knit to marker; repeat from * to end.

RND 15: *P1, k6, p3, LT twice, RT 3 times, p3, knit to marker; repeat from * to end.

RND 16: *P1, k2tog, k4, p3, k10, p3, knit to 2 sts before marker, ssk; repeat from * to end—2 sts decreased.

RND 17: *P1, k4, p3, LT 3 times, RT 3 times, p3, k4; repeat from * to end.

RND 18: *P1, k4, p3, k12, p3, k4; repeat from * to end.

RND 19: *P1, k2tog, k1, p3, LT 3 times, RT 4 times, p3, k1, ssk; repeat from * to end—2 sts decreased.

RND 20: *P1, k2, p3, k14, p3, k2; repeat from * to end.

RND 21: *P1, k2, p2, LT 4 times, RT 4 times, p2, k2; repeat from * to end.

RND 22: *P1, k2tog, p2, k16, p2, ssk; repeat from * to end—2 sts decreased.

RND 23: *P1, k1, p1, LT 4 times, RT 5 times, p1, k1; repeat from * to end.

RND 24: *P1, k1, p1, k18, p1, k1; repeat from * to end.

RND 25: *P1, k2tog, p1, LT 4 times, RT 4 times, p1, ssk; repeat from * to end—2 sts decreased.

RND 26: *P1, k1, p1, k16, p1, k1; repeat from * to end.

RND 27: *P1, k2, p1, LT 3 times, RT 4 times, p1, k2; repeat from * to end.

RND 28: *P1, k2tog, p1, k14, p1, ssk; repeat from * to end—2 sts decreased.

RND 29: *P1, k2, p1, LT 3 times, RT 3 times, p1, k2; repeat from * to end.

RND 30: *P1, k2, p1, k12, p1, k2; repeat from * to end.

RND 31: *P1, k2tog, k1, p1, LT twice, RT 3 times, p1, k1, ssk; repeat from * to end—2 sts decreased.

RND 32: *P1, k2, p1, k10, p1, k2; repeat from * to end.

RND 33: *P1, k3, p1, LT twice, RT twice, p1, k3; repeat from * to end.

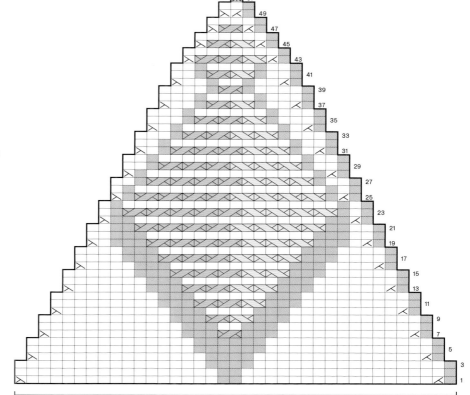

Place marker between pattern repeats.

39-st repeat;
decreases to 1-st repeat

RND 34: *P1, k2tog, k1, p1, k8, p1, k1, ssk; repeat from * to end—2 sts decreased.

RND 35: *P1, k3, p1, LT, RT twice, p1, k3; repeat from * to end.

RND 36: *P1, k3, p1, k6, p1, k3; repeat from * to end.

RND 37: *P1, k2tog, k2, p1, LT, RT, p1, k2, ssk; repeat from * to end—2 sts decreased.

RND 38: *P1, k3, p1, k4, p1, k3; repeat from * to end.

RND 39: *P1, k4, p1, RT, p1, k4; repeat from * to end.

RND 40: *P1, k2tog, k2, [p1, k2] twice, ssk; repeat from * to end—2 sts decreased.

RND 41: *P1, k2, p1, LT, RT, p1, k2; repeat from * to end.

RND 42: *P1, k2, p1, k4, p1, k2; repeat from * to end.

RND 43: *P1, k2tog, LT, RT twice, ssk; repeat from * to end—2 sts decreased.

RND 44: *P1, knit to marker; repeat from * to end.

RND 45: *P1, k2tog, LT, RT, ssk; repeat from * to end—2 sts decreased.

RND 46: Repeat Rnd 44.

RND 47: *P1, k2tog, RT, ssk; repeat from * to end—2 sts decreased.

RND 48: Repeat Rnd 44.

RND 49: *P1, k2tog, ssk; repeat from * to end—2 sts decreased.

RND 50: *P1, k2; repeat from * to end.

RND 51: *P3tog; repeat from * to end—2 sts decreased.

(121) Wheel Folds

One repeat of Woven Lines (#22) is centered in each of the six segments. It was easy, and seemed natural, to pare the center of the pattern into a point, which then fits snugly into the decreasing point of the triangle.

(multiple of 39 sts, decreases to multiple of 1 st; 51 rnds)

Place a marker between pattern repeats.

RND 1: *P1, k2tog, k15, RT twice, knit to 2 sts before marker, ssk; repeat from * to end—2 sts decreased.

RND 2: *P1, knit to marker; repeat from * to end.

RND 3: *P1, k15, RT 3 times, knit to marker; repeat from * to end.

RND 4: *P1, k2tog, knit to 2 sts before marker, ssk; repeat from * to end—2 sts decreased.

RND 5: *P1, k13, RT 3 times, LT, knit to marker; repeat from * to end.

RND 6: Repeat Rnd 2.

RND 7: *P1, k2tog, k10, RT 3 times, LT twice, knit to 2 sts before marker, ssk; repeat from * to end—2 sts decreased.

RND 8: Repeat Rnd 2.

RND 9: *P1, k9, p1, LT, RT twice, LT 3 times, p1, knit to marker; repeat from * to end.

RND 10: *P1, k2tog, k7, p1, k5, p2, k5, p1, knit to 2 sts before marker, ssk; repeat from * to end—2 sts decreased.

RND 11: *P1, k8, p1, k1, LT, RT, p2, LT twice, k1, p1, knit to marker; repeat from * to end.

RND 12: *P1, k8, p1, k4, p4, k4, p1, knit to marker; repeat from * to end.

RND 13: *P1, k2tog, k6, p1, LT twice, p4, LT twice, p1, knit to 2 sts before marker, ssk; repeat from * to end—2 sts decreased.

RND 14: *P1, k7, p1, k4, p4, k4, p1, knit to marker; repeat from * to end.

RND 15: *P1, k7, p1, k1, LT twice, p2, RT, LT, k1, p1, knit to marker; repeat from * to end.

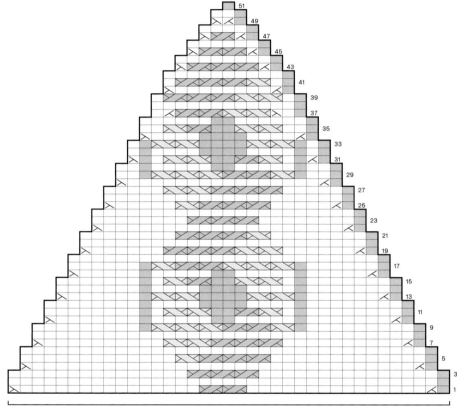

Place marker between pattern repeats.

39-st repeat;
decreases to 1-st repeat

RND 16: *P1, k2tog, k5, p1, k5, p2, k5, p1, knit to 2 sts before marker, ssk; repeat from * to end—2 sts decreased.

RND 17: *P1, k6, p1, LT 3 times, RT twice, LT, p1, knit to marker; repeat from * to end.

RND 18: Repeat Rnd 2.

RND 19: *P1, k2tog, k6, LT twice, RT 3 times, knit to 2 sts before marker, ssk; repeat from * to end—2 sts decreased.

RND 20: Repeat Rnd 2.

RND 21: *P1, k8, LT, RT 3 times, knit to marker; repeat from * to end.

RND 22: Repeat Rnd 4.

RND 23: *P1, k8, RT 3 times, knit to marker; repeat from * to end.

RND 24: Repeat Rnd 2.

RND 25: *P1, k2tog, k5, RT 3 times, LT, knit to 2 sts before marker, ssk; repeat from * to end—2 sts decreased.

RND 26: Repeat Rnd 2.

RND 27: *P1, k5, RT 3 times, LT twice, knit to marker; repeat from * to end.

RND 28: Repeat Rnd 4.

RND 29: *P1, k2, p1, LT, RT twice, LT 3 times, p1, k2; repeat from * to end.

RND 30: *P1, k2, p1, k5, p2, k5, p1, k2; repeat from * to end.

RND 31: *P1, k2tog, p1, k1, LT, RT, p2, LT twice, k1, p1, ssk; repeat from * to end—2 sts decreased.

RND 32: *P1, k1, p1, k4, p4, k4, p1, k1; repeat from * to end.

RND 33: *P1, k1, p1, LT twice, p4, LT twice, p1, k1; repeat from * to end.

RND 34: *P1, k2tog, k4, p4, k4, ssk; repeat from * to end—2 sts decreased.

RND 35: *P1, k2, LT twice, p2, RT, LT, k2; repeat from * to end.

RND 36: *P1, k6, p2, k6; repeat from * to end.

RND 37: *P1, k1, ssk, LT twice, RT twice, k2tog, k1; repeat from * to end—2 sts decreased.

RND 38: Repeat Rnd 2.

RND 39: *P1, k1, LT twice, RT 3 times, k1; repeat from * to end.

RND 40: Repeat Rnd 4.

RND 41: *P1, k1, LT, RT 3 times, k1; repeat from * to end.

RNDS 42, 44, 46, AND 48: Repeat Rnd 2.

RND 43: *P1, k2tog, RT 3 times, ssk; repeat from * to end—2 sts decreased.

RND 45: *P1, k2tog, RT twice, ssk; repeat from * to end—2 sts decreased.

RND 47: *P1, k2tog, RT, ssk; repeat from * to end—2 sts decreased.

RND 49: *P1, k2tog, ssk; repeat from * to end—2 sts decreased.

RND 50: *P1, k2; repeat from * to end.

RND 51: *P3tog; repeat from * to end—2 sts decreased.

(122) Droid

Originally inspired by a Celtic knot pattern, this composition of interlacing lines snuggles neatly into the equilateral triangles that make up a hexagon. I was able to use only about three-quarters of the original length, since it was important to me to keep all of the hexagon charts the same size, so the pattern was truncated, leaving the knot unfinished.

(multiple of 39 sts, decreases to a multiple of 1 st; 51 rnds)

Place a marker between pattern repeats.

RND 1: *P1, k2tog, k7, LT, k16, RT, knit to 2 sts before marker, ssk; repeat from * to end−2 sts decreased.

RND 2: *P1, knit to marker; repeat from * to end.

RND 3: *P1, k9, LT, k2, RT, k6, LT, k2, RT, knit to marker; repeat from * to end.

RND 4: *P1, k2tog, knit to 2 sts before marker, ssk; repeat from * to end−2 sts decreased.

RND 5: *P1, k9, LT, RT, LT k4, RT, LT, RT, knit to marker; repeat from * to end.

RND 6: *P1, k12, p2, k6, p2, knit to marker; repeat from * to end.

RND 7: *P1, k2tog, k8, LT, p2, LT, k2, RT, p2, RT, knit to 2 sts before marker, ssk; repeat from * to end−2 sts decreased.

RND 8: *P1, k11, p3, k4, p3, knit to marker; repeat from * to end.

RND 9: *P1, k8, RT, LT, p2, LT, RT, p2, RT, LT, knit to marker; repeat from * to end.

RND 10: *P1, k2tog, k10, p3, k2, p3, knit to 2 sts before marker, ssk; repeat from * to end−2 sts decreased.

RND 11: *P1, k6, RT, k2, [LT, p2] twice, RT, k2, LT, knit to marker; repeat from * to end.

RND 12: *P1, k12, p2, k2, p2, knit to marker; repeat from * to end.

RND 13: *P1, k2tog, k3, RT, k4, [LT, RT] twice, k4, LT, k3, ssk, repeat from * to end−2 sts decreased.

RND 14: *P1, k13, p2, knit to marker; repeat from * to end.

RND 15: *P1, k3, RT, [k2, RT] twice, p2, RT, [k2, LT] twice, k3; repeat from * to end.

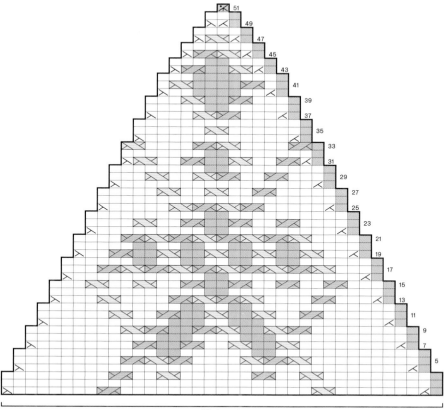

Place marker between pattern repeats.

39-st repeat;
decreases to 1-st repeat

RND 16: *P1, k2tog, k11, p2, knit to 2 sts before marker, ssk; repeat from * to end—2 sts decreased.

RND 17: *P1, k3, [LT, RT] 5 times, k3; repeat from * to end.

RND 18: *P1, k6, p2, [k2, p2] 3 times, knit to marker; repeat from * to end.

RND 19: *P1, k2tog, k2, [LT, p2] 4 times, RT, k2, ssk; repeat from * to end—2 sts decreased.

RND 20: *P1, k5, p2, [k2, p2] 3 times, knit to marker; repeat from * to end.

RND 21: *P1, k4, [LT, RT] 4 times, k4; repeat from * to end.

RND 22: *P1, k2tog, k9, p2, knit to 2 sts before marker, ssk; repeat from * to end—2 sts decreased.

RND 23: *P1, k4, RT, k2, RT, p2, RT, k2, LT, k4; repeat from * to end.

RND 24: *P1, k10, p2, knit to marker; repeat from * to end.

RND 25: *P1, k2tog, k5, [RT, LT] twice, knit to 2 sts before marker, ssk; repeat from * to end—2 sts decreased.

RND 26: Repeat Rnd 2.

RND 27: *P1, k5, RT, [k2, LT] twice, knit to marker; repeat from * to end.

RND 28: Repeat Rnd 4.

RND 29: *P1, k3, RT, k2, RT, LT, k2, LT, k3; repeat from * to end.

RND 30: *P1, k8, p2, knit to marker; repeat from * to end.

RND 31: *P1, k2tog, RT, k2, LT, p2, RT, k2, LT, ssk; repeat from * to end—2 sts decreased.

RND 32: *P1, k7, p2, knit to marker; repeat from * to end.

RND 33: *P1, [RT, k4, LT] twice; repeat from * to end.

RND 34: Repeat Rnd 4.

RND 35: *P1, k6, LT, knit to marker; repeat from * to end.

RND 36: Repeat Rnd 2.

RND 37: *P1, k2tog, k3, RT, LT, k3, ssk; repeat from * to end—2 sts decreased.

RND 38: *P1, k5, p2, knit to marker; repeat from * to end.

RND 39: *P1, k3, RT, p2, LT, k3; repeat from * to end.

RND 40: *P1, k2tog, k2, p4, k2, ssk, repeat from * to end—2 sts decreased.

RND 41: *P1, k1, RT, p4, LT, k1; repeat from * to end.

RND 42: *P1, k3, p4, k3; repeat from * to end.

RND 43: *P1, k2tog, LT, p2, RT, ssk; repeat from * to end—2 sts decreased.

RND 44: *P1, k3, p2, k3; repeat from * to end.

RND 45: *P1, k2tog, LT, RT, ssk; repeat from * to end—2 sts decreased.

RND 46: Repeat Rnd 2.

RND 47: *P1, k2tog, LT, ssk; repeat from * to end—2 sts decreased.

RND 48: Repeat Rnd 2.

RND 49: *P1, k2tog, ssk, repeat from * to end—2 sts decreased.

RND 50: *P1, k2; repeat from * to end.

RND 51: *P3tog; repeat from * to end—2 sts decreased.

(123) Prism Plaid

One repeat of Plaid Medium (#16) reveals a surprisingly pleasing pattern when repeated six times around. Read about making your own hexagon pattern using parts of existing patterns in Chapter 11, Ten Lessons, on page 260.

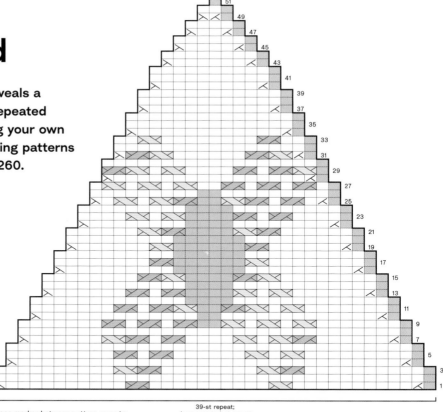

Place marker between pattern repeats.

39-st repeat;
decreases to 1-st repeat

(multiple of 39 sts, decreases to multiple of 1 st; 51 rnds)

Place a marker between pattern repeats.

RND 1: *P1, k2tog, k10, LT, k10, RT, knit to 2 sts before marker, ssk; repeat from * to end−2 sts decreased.

RND 2: *P1, knit to marker; repeat from * to end.

RND 3: *P1, k10, RT, LT, k8, RT, LT, knit to marker; repeat from * to end.

RND 4: *P1, k2tog, knit to 2 sts before marker, ssk; repeat from * to end−2 sts decreased.

RND 5: *P1, k9, LT, k1, LT, k6, RT, k1, RT, knit to marker; repeat from * to end.

RND 6: Repeat Rnd 2.

RND 7: *P1, k2tog, k6, RT, LT, k1, LT, k4, RT, k1, RT, LT, knit to 2 sts before marker, ssk; repeat from * to end−2 sts decreased.

RND 8: Repeat Rnd 2.

RND 9: *P1, k7, LT, [k1, LT] twice, p2, RT, [k1, RT] twice, knit to marker; repeat from * to end.

RND 10: Repeat Rnd 4.

RND 11: *P1, k7, LT, k1, LT, RT, p2, LT, RT, k1, RT, knit to marker; repeat from * to end.

RND 12: *P1, k13, p4, knit to marker; repeat from * to end.

RND 13: *P1, k2tog, k6, LT, k1, LT, p4, RT, k1, RT, knit to 2 sts before marker, ssk; repeat from * to end−2 sts decreased.

RND 14: *P1, k12, p4, knit to marker; repeat from * to end.

RND 15: *P1, k8, LT, RT, p4, LT, RT, knit to marker; repeat from * to end.

RND 16: *P1, k2tog, k9, p6, knit to 2 sts before marker, ssk; repeat from * to end−2 sts decreased.

RND 17: *P1, k8, LT, p6, RT, knit to marker; repeat from * to end.

RND 18: *P1, k10, p6, knit to marker; repeat from * to end.

RND 19: *P1, k2tog, k6, RT, p6, LT, knit to 2 sts before marker, ssk; repeat from * to end−2 sts decreased.

RND 20: *P1, k9, p6, knit to marker; repeat from * to end.

RND 21: *P1, k6, RT, LT, p4, RT, LT, knit to marker; repeat from * to end.

RND 22: *P1, k2tog, k8, p4, knit to 2 sts before marker, ssk; repeat from * to end−2 sts decreased.

RND 23: *P1, k4, RT, k1, RT, p4, LT, k1, LT, knit to marker; repeat from * to end.

RND 24: *P1, k9, p4, knit to marker; repeat from * to end.

RND 25: *P1, k2tog, [k1, RT] twice, LT, p2, RT, [LT, k1] twice, ssk; repeat from * to end−2 sts decreased.

RND 26: *P1, k9, p2, knit to marker; repeat from * to end.

RND 27: *P1, [k1, RT] 3 times, k2, [LT, k1] 3 times; repeat from * to end.

RND 28: Repeat Rnd 4.

RND 29: *P1, LT, RT, k1, RT, k4, LT, k1, LT, RT; repeat from * to end.

RND 30: Repeat Rnd 2.

RND 31: *P1, k2tog, LT, RT, k6, LT, RT, ssk; repeat from * to end−2 sts decreased.

RND 32: Repeat Rnd 2.

RND 33: *P1, k2, RT, k8, LT, k2; repeat from * to end.

RND 34: Repeat Rnd 4.

RNDS 35, 36, 38, 39, 41, 42, 44, 46, AND 48: Repeat Rnd 2.

RNDS 37, 40, 43, 45, AND 47: Repeat Rnd 4.

RND 49: *P1, k2tog, ssk; repeat from * to end−2 sts decreased.

RND 50: *P1, k2; repeat from * to end.

RND 51: *P3tog; repeat from * to end−2 sts decreased.

(124) Spiderweb

The largest braided column from Braids (#34) is extended by letting its outward-facing twists escape from the boundaries of the original column until they meet the edges of the triangle here. The result is reminiscent of a spider's masterwork.

(multiple of 39 sts, decreases to a multiple of 1 st; 51 rnds)

Place a marker between pattern repeats.

RND 1: *P1, k2tog, k14, LT, RT twice, knit to 2 sts before marker, ssk; repeat from * to end—2 sts decreased.

RND 2: *P1, knit to marker; repeat from * to end.

RND 3: *P1, k14, [RT, LT] twice, knit to marker; repeat from * to end.

RND 4: *P1, k2tog, k14, p1, k2, p1, knit to 2 sts before marker, ssk; repeat from * to end—2 sts decreased.

RND 5: *P1, k12, RT, k1, p1, RT, p1, k1, LT, knit to marker; repeat from * to end.

RND 6: *P1, k15, p1, k2, p1, knit to marker; repeat from * to end.

RND 7: *P1, k2tog, k9, RT, k2, p1, RT, p1, k2, LT, knit to 2 sts before marker, ssk; repeat from * to end—2 sts decreased.

RND 8: *P1, k14, p1, k2, p1, knit to marker; repeat from * to end.

RND 9: *P1, k9, RT, k2, LT, RT twice, k2, LT, knit to marker; repeat from * to end.

RND 10: *P1, k2tog, knit to 2 sts before marker, ssk; repeat from * to end—2 sts decreased.

RND 11: *P1, k7, RT, k2, [RT, LT] twice, k2, LT, knit to marker; repeat from * to end.

RND 12: *P1, k13, p1, k2, p1, knit to marker; repeat from * to end.

RND 13: *P1, k2tog, k4, RT, k2, RT, k1, p1, RT, p1, k1, LT, k2, LT, k4, ssk, repeat from * to end—2 sts decreased.

RND 14: *P1, k12, p1, k2, p1, knit to marker; repeat from * to end.

RND 15: *P1, k4, [RT, k2] twice, p1, RT, p1, [k2, LT] twice, k4; repeat from * to end.

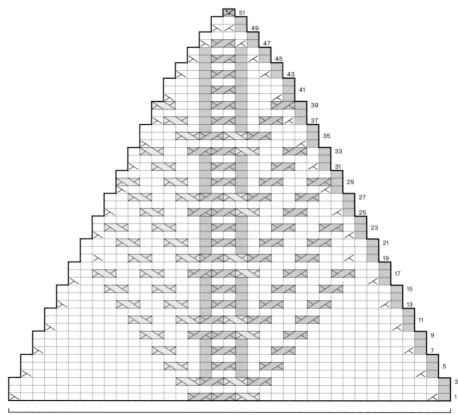

39-st repeat;
decreases to 1-st repeat

Place marker between pattern repeats.

RND 16: *P1, k2tog, k10, p1, k2, p1, knit to 2 sts before marker, ssk; repeat from * to end—2 sts decreased.

RND 17: *P1, k2, [RT, k2] twice, LT, RT twice, k2, [LT, k2] twice; repeat from * to end.

RND 18: Repeat Rnd 2.

RND 19: *P1, k1, k2tog, [k2, RT] twice, LT, RT, [LT, k2] twice, ssk, k1; repeat from * to end—2 sts decreased.

RND 20: *P1, k10, p1, k2, p1, knit to marker; repeat from * to end.

RND 21: *P1, k3, RT, k2, RT, k1, p1, RT, p1, k1, LT, k2, LT, k3; repeat from * to end.

RND 22: *P1, k2tog, k8, p1, k2, p1, knit to 2 sts before marker, ssk; repeat from * to end—2 sts decreased.

RND 23: *P1, k1, [RT, k2] twice, p1, RT, p1, [k2, LT] twice, k1; repeat from * to end.

RND 24: *P1, k9, p1, k2, p1, knit to marker; repeat from * to end.

RND 25: *P1, k2tog, k2, RT, k2, LT, RT twice, k2, LT, k2, ssk; repeat from * to end−2 sts decreased.

RND 26: Repeat Rnd 2.

RND 27: *P1, [k2, RT] twice, LT, RT, [LT, k2] twice; repeat from * to end.

RND 28: *P1, k2tog, k6, p1, k2, p1, knit to 2 sts before marker, ssk, repeat from * to end−2 sts decreased.

RND 29: *P1, RT, k2, RT, k1, p1, RT, p1, k1, LT, k2, LT; repeat from * to end.

RND 30: *P1, k7, p1, k2, p1, knit to marker; repeat from * to end.

RND 31: *P1, k2tog, k1, RT, k2, p1, RT, p1, k2, LT, k1, ssk; repeat from * to end−2 sts decreased.

RND 32: *P1, k6, p1, k2, p1, knit to marker; repeat from * to end.

RND 33: *P1, k1, RT, k2, LT, RT twice, k2, LT, k1; repeat from * to end.

RND 34: Repeat Rnd 10.

RND 35: *P1, k3, [RT, LT] twice, k3; repeat from * to end.

RND 36: *P1, k5, p1, k2, p1, knit to marker; repeat from * to end.

RND 37: *P1, k2tog, RT, k1, p1, RT, p1, k1, LT, ssk; repeat from * to end−2 sts decreased.

RND 38: *P1, k4, p1, k2, p1, k4; repeat from * to end.

RND 39: *P1, RT, k2, p1, RT, p1, k2, LT; repeat from * to end.

RND 40: *P1, k2tog, k2, [p1, k2] twice, ssk, repeat from * to end−2 sts decreased.

RND 41: *P1, k3, p1, RT, p1, k3; repeat from * to end.

RND 42: *P1, k3, p1, k2, p1, k3; repeat from * to end.

RND 43: *P1, k2tog, k1, p1, RT, p1, k1, ssk; repeat from * to end−2 sts decreased.

RND 44: *[P1, k2] 3 times; repeat from * to end.

RND 45: *P1, k2tog, p1, RT, p1, ssk; repeat from * to end−2 sts decreased.

RND 46: *P1, k1, p1, k2, p1, k1; repeat from * to end.

RND 47: *P1, k2tog, RT, ssk; repeat from * to end−2 sts decreased.

RND 48: Repeat Rnd 2.

RND 49: *P1, k2tog, ssk, repeat from * to end−2 sts decreased.

RND 50: *P1, k2; repeat from * to end.

RND 51: *P3tog; repeat from * to end−2 sts decreased.

(125) Snowflake

The pattern filling the center of each triangle began as Spire (#75). After the point was laid into the center, about three-quarters of the original pattern fit into the appointed length, and that's when improvisation took over.

(multiple of 39 sts, decreases to multiple of 1 st; 51 rnds)

Place a marker between pattern repeats.

RND 1: *P1, k2tog, k16, RT, knit to 2 sts before marker, ssk; repeat from * to end—2 sts decreased.

RND 2: *P1, knit to marker; repeat from * to end.

RND 3: *P1, k16, RT, LT, knit to marker; repeat from * to end.

RND 4: *P1, k2tog, knit to 2 sts before marker, ssk; repeat from * to end—2 sts decreased.

RND 5: *P1, k14, RT twice, LT, knit to marker; repeat from * to end.

RND 6: Repeat Rnd 2.

RND 7: *P1, k2tog, k11, [RT, k1] twice, LT, knit to 2 sts before marker, ssk; repeat from * to end—2 sts decreased.

RND 8: Repeat Rnd 2.

RND 9: *P1, k11, RT, k1, RT, LT, k1, LT, knit to marker; repeat from * to end.

RND 10: Repeat Rnd 4.

RND 11: *P1, k9, RT, k1, RT twice, LT, k1, LT, knit to marker; repeat from * to end.

RND 12: *P1, k13, p1, k2, p1, knit to marker; repeat from * to end.

RND 13: *P1, k2tog, k6, RT, k1, [RT, p1] twice, LT, k1, LT, knit to 2 sts before marker, ssk; repeat from * to end—2 sts decreased.

RND 14: *P1, k11, p2, k2, p2, knit to marker; repeat from * to end.

RND 15: *P1, k7, LT, [RT, p2] twice, LT, RT, knit to marker; repeat from * to end.

RND 16: *P1, k2tog, k5, p1, k2, [p3, k2] twice, p1, knit to 2 sts before marker, ssk; repeat from * to end—2 sts decreased.

RND 17: *P1, k6, p1, RT, [p3, RT] twice, p1, knit to marker; repeat from * to end.

RND 18: *P1, k6, p1, k2, [p3, k2] twice, p1, knit to marker; repeat from * to end.

RND 19: *P1, k2tog, k4, p1, LT, [p3, RT] twice, p1, k4, ssk; repeat from * to end—2 sts decreased.

RND 20: *P1, k5, p1, k2, [p3, k2] twice, p1, knit to marker; repeat from * to end.

RND 21: *P1, k5, RT, LT, [p2, RT] twice, LT, knit to marker; repeat from * to end.

RND 22: *P1, k2tog, k5, p1, k1, p2, k2, p2, k1, p1, knit to 2 sts before marker, ssk; repeat from * to end—2 sts decreased.

RND 23: *P1, k3, RT, k1, p1, LT, p1, [RT, p1] twice, k1, LT, k3; repeat from * to end.

RND 24: *P1, k6, p1, [k2, p1] 3 times, knit to marker; repeat from * to end.

RND 25: *P1, k2tog, RT, k2, RT, LT, RT twice, LT, k2, LT, ssk; repeat from * to end—2 sts decreased.

RND 26: *P1, k7, p1, k4, p1, knit to marker; repeat from * to end.

RND 27: *P1, RT, k3, LT, p1, LT, RT, p1, RT, k3, LT; repeat from * to end.

RND 28: *P1, k2tog, k5, p2, k2, p2, knit to 2 sts before marker, ssk; repeat from * to end—2 sts decreased.

RND 29: *P1, k3, RT, LT, [p1, RT] twice, LT, k3; repeat from * to end.

RND 30: *P1, k7, p1, k2, p1, knit to marker; repeat from * to end.

RND 31: *P1, k2tog, RT, k2, LT, RT twice, k2, LT, ssk; repeat from * to end—2 sts decreased.

RND 32: Repeat Rnd 2.

RND 33: *P1, [RT, k4, LT] twice; repeat from * to end.

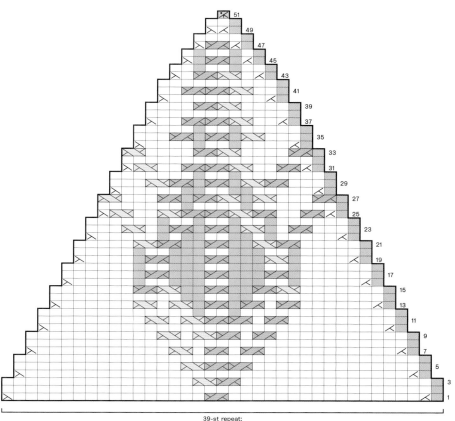

Place marker between pattern repeats.

39-st repeat;
decreases to 1-st repeat

RND 34: *P1, k2tog, k4, p1, k2, p1, k4, ssk; repeat from * to end—2 sts decreased.

RND 35: *P1, k3, LT, [p1, RT] twice, k3; repeat from * to end.

RND 36: *P1, k5, p1, k2, p1, knit to marker; repeat from * to end.

RND 37: *P1, k2tog, k2, LT, RT twice, k2, ssk; repeat from * to end—2 sts decreased.

RND 38: Repeat Rnd 2.

RND 39: *P1, k4, LT, RT, k4; repeat from * to end.

RND 40: Repeat Rnd 4.

RND 41: *P1, k2, LT, RT twice, k2; repeat from * to end.

RND 42: Repeat Rnd 2.

RND 43: *P1, k2tog, k1, LT, RT, k1, ssk; repeat from * to end—2 sts decreased.

RND 44: *P1, k2; repeat from * to end.

RND 45: *P1, k2tog, p1, RT, p1, ssk; repeat from * to end—2 sts decreased.

RND 46: *P1, k1, p1, k2, p1, k1; repeat from * to end.

RND 47: *P1, k2tog, RT, ssk; repeat from * to end—2 sts decreased.

RND 48: *P1, k4; repeat from * to end.

RND 49: *P1, k2tog, ssk; repeat from * to end—2 sts decreased.

RND 50: *P1, k2; repeat from * to end.

RND 51: *P3tog; repeat from * to end—2 sts decreased.

126 Lotus

Inspired by a Japanese Sashiko embroidery pattern, a single ornate triangle is repeated six times to create a lotus flower. Lotus is a variation of Sashiko (#112), which had to be pared down and simplified to work here.

(multiple of 39 sts, decreases to multiple of 1 st; 51 rnds)

Place a marker between pattern repeats.

RND 1: *P1, k2tog, k16, LT, knit to 2 sts before marker, ssk; repeat from * to end—2 sts decreased.

RND 2: *P1, k16, RT, LT, knit to marker; repeat from * to end.

RND 3: *P1, k15, RT, k2, LT, knit to marker; repeat from * to end.

RND 4: *P1, k2tog, k12, RT, k4, LT, knit to 2 sts before marker, ssk; repeat from * to end—2 sts decreased.

RND 5: *P1, k12, RT, k6, LT, knit to marker; repeat from * to end.

RND 6: *P1, k11, RT, k8, LT, knit to marker; repeat from * to end.

RND 7: *P1, k2tog, k8, RT, [k4, LT] twice, knit to 2 sts before marker, ssk; repeat from * to end—2 sts decreased.

RND 8: *P1, k8, RT, k4, RT, LT, k4, LT, knit to marker; repeat from * to end.

RND 9: *P1, k7, RT, k4, RT, k2, LT, k4, LT, knit to marker; repeat from * to end.

RND 10: *P1, k2tog, k4, [RT, k4] twice, [LT, k4] twice, ssk; repeat from * to end—2 sts decreased.

RND 11: *P1, [k4, RT] twice, LT, k2, RT, [LT, k4] twice; repeat from * to end.

RND 12: *P1, k3, RT, k4, [RT, k2, LT] twice, k4, LT, k3; repeat from * to end.

RND 13: *P1, k2tog, RT, k4, RT, [LT, k2] twice, RT, LT, k4, LT, ssk; repeat from * to end—2 sts decreased.

RND 14: *P1, RT, k4, RT, k2, LT, k4, RT, k2, LT, k4, LT; repeat from * to end.

RND 15: *P1, k5, RT, k4, LT, k2, RT, k4, LT, k5; repeat from * to end.

RND 16: *P1, k2tog, k2, [RT, k6, LT] twice, k2, ssk; repeat from * to end—2 sts decreased.

RND 17: *P1, k2, RT, k8, LT, k8, LT, k2; repeat from * to end.

RND 18: *P1, k1, RT, k8, RT, LT, k8, LT, k1; repeat from * to end.

RND 19: *P1, k2tog, k8, RT, k2, LT, k8, ssk; repeat from * to end—2 sts decreased.

RND 20: *P1, k8, RT, k4, LT, k8; repeat from * to end.

RND 21: *P1, k7, RT, k6, LT, k7; repeat from * to end.

RND 22: *P1, k2tog, k4, RT, k8, LT, k4, ssk; repeat from * to end—2 sts decreased.

RND 23: *P1, k4, RT, k4, [LT, k4] twice; repeat from * to end.

RND 24: *P1, k3, RT, k4, RT, LT, k4, LT, k3; repeat from * to end.

RND 25: *P1, k2tog, RT, k4, RT, k2, LT, k4, LT, ssk; repeat from * to end—2 sts decreased.

RND 26: *P1, RT, k4, RT, [k4, LT] twice; repeat from * to end.

RND 27: *P1, k5, RT, k6, LT, k5; repeat from * to end.

RND 28: *P1, k2tog, k2, RT, k8, LT, k2, ssk; repeat from * to end—2 sts decreased.

RND 29: *P1, k2, RT, [k4, LT] twice, k2; repeat from * to end.

RND 30: *P1, k1, RT, k4, RT, LT, k4, LT, k1; repeat from * to end.

RND 31: *P1, k2tog, k4, RT, k2, LT, k4, ssk; repeat from * to end—2 sts decreased.

RND 32: *P1, k4, RT, k4, LT, k4; repeat from * to end.

RND 33: *P1, k3, RT, LT, k2, RT, LT, k3; repeat from * to end.

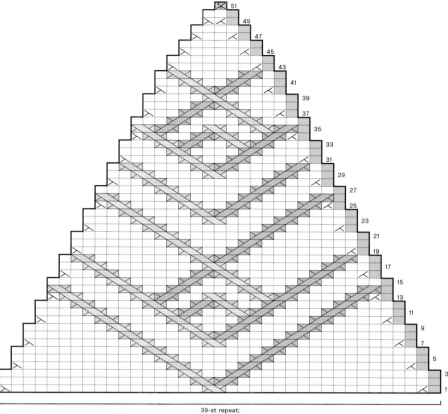

Place marker between pattern repeats.

39-st repeat;
decreases to 1-st repeat

NOTE Chart is worked in the rnd, so all RTs and LTs are worked as if for RS rows. Symbols are given for RTs and LTs on WS rows for those who might wish to work this chart in rows rather than in rnds.

RND 34: *P1, k2tog, [RT, k2, LT] twice, ssk; repeat from * to end—2 sts decreased.

RND 35: *P1, RT, [LT, k2] twice, RT, LT; repeat from * to end.

RND 36: *P1, k3, LT, k4, RT, k3; repeat from * to end

RND 37: *P1, k2tog, k2, LT, k2, RT, k2, ssk; repeat from * to end—2 sts decreased.

RND 38: *P1, k4, LT, RT, k4; repeat from * to end.

RND 39: *P1, k5, LT, k5; repeat from * to end.

RND 40: *P1, k2tog, k2, RT, LT, k2, ssk; repeat from * to end—2 sts decreased.

RND 41: *P1, k2, RT, k2, LT, k2; repeat from * to end.

RND 42: *P1, k1, RT, k4, LT, k1; repeat from * to end.

RND 43: *P1, k2tog, knit to 2 sts before marker, ssk; repeat from * to end—2 sts decreased.

RND 44: *P1, knit to marker; repeat from * to end.

RNDS 45-48: Repeat Rnd 43 and 44 twice.

RND 49: *P1, k2tog, ssk; repeat from * to end—2 sts decreased.

RND 50: *P1, k2; repeat from * to end.

RND 51: *P3tog; repeat from * to end—2 sts decreased.

PART II

GARMENTS

Oversized or fitted, knit in the round or worked flat and seamed, cropped or long, classic or more avant-garde—every knitter has their favorite kind of sweater and their most-loved working method. No matter your preference, there should be something for you in this collection. The fifteen patterns are designed to showcase stitches from all nine stitch chapters. Many of these garment patterns can easily be personalized by switching in your choice of pattern stitch. Look toward the end of each garment's instructions for thoughts and tips on substituting pattern stitches for that garment.

Infinity Cowl

This five-foot-long loop is designed either to be worn wrapped twice around the neck for the ultimate warmth or to hang in a single relaxed loop when you need more air. Knit in the round as a tube, the finished cowl is round and substantial, with no wrong side emerging no matter how you find yourself wanting to wrap it. If you'd like to substitute stitches, here is a great opportunity to try out a stitch that may be more difficult to knit flat, with either purls or twists on the wrong-side row.

FINISHED MEASUREMENTS
Approximately 68½" (174 cm) circumference × 9¼" (23.5 cm) width

YARN
Berroco Ultra Wool [100% superwash wool; 219 yards (200 meters)/3½ ounces (100 grams)]: 5 balls #33123 Iris

NEEDLES
One 16" (40 cm) long circular needle size 6 (4 mm)

Change needle size if necessary to obtain correct gauge.

NOTIONS
Stitch marker

GAUGE
24 sts and 28 rows = 4" (10 cm) in Wonky Weave Carved

NOTE: Steam or wet block your swatch for an accurate gauge. Superwash yarn will relax when blocked.

STITCH PATTERN
WONKY WEAVE CARVED (#29)
(multiple of 10 sts; 28-rnd repeat)

RND 1: *K1, RT, k1, p2, k2, RT; repeat from * to end.

RND 2: Knit the knit sts and purl the purl sts as they face you.

RND 3: *RT, k2, p2, k1, RT, k1; repeat from * to end.

RND 4: Knit the knit sts and purl the purl sts as they face you to last st; the last st will be worked with the first st of the next rnd.

RND 5: *RT (removing beginning-of-rnd marker on first repeat and replacing it at center of RT), k2, LT, p1, k3; repeat from * to last st, k1.

RND 6: *P1, k4; repeat from * to end.

RND 7: *P1, k3, LT, k2, RT; repeat from * to end.

RND 8: P1, k8, *p2, k8; repeat from * to last st, p1.

RND 9: P1, [k1, LT] twice, k2, *p2, [k1, LT] twice, k2; repeat from * to last st, p1.

RNDS 10, 12, 14, 16, AND 18: Repeat Rnd 2.

RND 11: P1, k2, [LT, k1] twice, *p2, k2, [LT, k1] twice; repeat from * to last st, p1.

RND 13: P1, LT, [k1, LT] twice, *p2, LT, [k1, LT] twice; repeat from * to last st, p1.

RND 15: Repeat Rnd 9.

RND 17: Repeat Rnd 11.

RND 19: *RT, k2, LT, k3, p1; repeat from * to end.

RND 20: *K4, p1; repeat from * to last 5 sts, k4; the last st will be worked with the first st of Rnd 21.

RND 21: *RT (removing beginning-of-rnd marker on first repeat and replacing it at center of RT), k3, p1, LT, k2; repeat from * to last st, k1.

RND 22: Repeat Rnd 2.

RNDS 23–26: Repeat Rnds 1–4.

RND 27: *RT (removing beginning-of-rnd marker on first repeat and replacing it at center of RT), k1, RT, p2, RT, k1; repeat from * to last st, k1.

RND 28: Repeat Rnd 2.

Repeat Rnds 1–28 for pattern.

SPECIAL TECHNIQUE
GRAFTING LIVE STITCHES TO A CAST-ON EDGE
Using a blunt tapestry needle, thread a length of yarn approximately 4 times the length of the section to be joined. Because this piece was worked in the round, there is a front and back to both the live stitches and the cast-on edge. The front is the side closest to you and the back is the side furthest from you. Hold the live stitches in front with the needle tips pointing to the right; you will begin grafting the live stitches with the stitches on the front needle. Bring the cast-on edge up behind the live stitches, being careful not to twist the piece. You will begin grafting the cast-on stitches with the back side of the cast-on edge. Working from right to left, insert the tapestry needle into the first stitch on the front needle as if to purl, pull the yarn through, leaving the stitch on the needle; insert the tapestry

needle purlwise under both legs of the first cast-on stitch on the back side of the cast-on edge, pull the yarn through; *insert the tapestry needle into the first stitch on the front needle as if to knit, pull the yarn through, remove the stitch from the needle; insert the tapestry needle into the next stitch on the front needle as if to purl, pull the yarn through, leave the stitch on the needle; insert the tapestry needle under both legs of the next cast-on stitch on the back side of the cast-on edge as if to purl, pull the yarn through. Repeat from *, working 3 or 4 stitches at a time, then go back and adjust the tension to match the pieces being joined. When 1 live stitch remains, cut yarn and pass through the last live stitch and cast-on stitch to fasten off.

PATTERN NOTES
The cowl is worked in the round in a long tube, then the ends of the tube are grafted together, grafting cast-on stitches to live stitches. If you prefer, you may use a provisional cast-on, then graft the provisional stitches to the live stitches; or you may bind off the stitches, then sew the two ends together.

Cowl
Using the Long-Tail Cast-On (see Special Techniques, page 270), CO 110 sts. Join for working in the rnd, being careful not to twist sts; pm for beginning of rnd.
Knit 1 round.
Begin Wonky Weave Carved; work Rnds 1–28 fourteen times, then work Rnds 1–27 once more. Cut yarn, leaving a tail 4 times the circumference of the piece for grafting. If you prefer, you may bind off sts.

FINISHING
Graft live sts to CO edge.
Block as desired.

Substitute almost any chart from Chapters 2–8. The Percentage of Stockinette Stitch (PSS) is not important here, since a variance in the circumference of the cowl isn't a problem. Adjust the number of stitches cast on to match the repeat of your chosen pattern (omitting any extra edge stitches, since this piece is worked in the round), while aiming for approximately the same number of stitches called for. Remember, if you are using more stitches, you may need more yarn.*

WONKY WEAVE CARVED

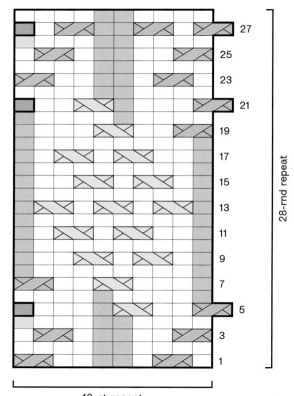

28-rnd repeat

10-st repeat

On last repeat of rnd only, do not work this st; it will be worked with the first st of the following rnd. On all preceding repeats, knit this st.

On last repeat of rnd only, knit this st. On all preceding repeats, omit this st.

On last repeat of rnd only, do not work this st; it will be worked with the first st of the following rnd. On all preceding repeats, purl this st.

Deep Yoke Pullover

A cross between a poncho and a more traditional yoked pullover, the Deep Yoke Pullover begins its unusual construction with a long, narrow band, turned sideways. Stitches picked up on one edge are worked upward to the neck, with decreases in concentric circles culminating in a shaped neckline. Stitches picked up on the other edge of the center band are worked downward and split into abbreviated sleeves and a wide body ribbing.

SIZES
To fit bust 30 (34, 38, 42, 46) (50, 54, 58, 62)" [76 (86.5, 96.5, 106.5, 117) (127, 137, 147.5, 157.5) cm]

FINISHED MEASUREMENTS
33 (37¾, 40¾, 45, 49½) (51, 58¼, 62½, 65½)" [85 (96, 103.5, 114.5, 125.5) (129.5, 148, 159, 166.5) cm] bust

YARN
Rowan Softyak DK [76% cotton/15% yak/9% nylon; 148 yards (135 meters)/50 grams]: 6 (7, 8, 9, 9) (10, 11, 12, 13) balls #246 Lantana

NEEDLES
One pair straight needles, size 6 (4 mm)

One 16" (40 cm)-long circular needle, size 4 (3.5 mm)

One 32" (80 cm)-long or longer circular needle, size 4 (3.5 mm)

One 32" (80 cm)-long or longer circular needle, size 6 (4 mm)

Needle(s) in preferred style for small circumference circular knitting in the rnd, size US 4 (3.5 mm)

Needle(s) in preferred style for small circumference circular knitting in the rnd, size US 6 (4 mm)

NOTIONS
Stitch markers; removable stitch markers; stitch holders or waste yarn

GAUGES
22 sts and 32 rows = 4" (10 cm) in St st, using larger needles

14-st Stack panel measures 2½" (6.5 cm) wide, using larger needles

27-st Zigzag Panel measures 4¼" (11 cm) wide, using larger needles

STITCH PATTERNS
2×2 RIB
(multiple of 4 sts + 2; 2-row repeat)
ALL RNDS: K2, *p2, k2; repeat from * to end.

ZIGZAG PANEL (#32)
(27-st panel; 20-row repeat)
ROW 1 (RS): K6, RT 3 times, [k2, RT] twice, LT 3 times, k1.
ROW 2 AND ALL WS ROWS: Purl.
ROW 3: K5, RT 3 times, LT, [RT, k2] twice, LT 3 times.
ROW 5: K4, RT 3 times, k2, LT, [k2, RT] twice, k5.
ROW 7: K3, RT 3 times, LT, k2, LT, RT, k2, RT, k6.
ROW 9: K2, RT 3 times, k2, [LT, k2] twice, RT, k7.
ROW 11: K1, RT 3 times, [LT, k2] twice, LT 3 times, k6.
ROW 13: RT 3 times, [k2, LT] twice, RT, LT 3 times, k5.

ROW 15: K5, [LT, k2] twice, RT, k2, LT 3 times, k4.
ROW 17: K6, LT, k2, LT, RT, k2, RT, LT 3 times, k3.
ROW 19: K7, LT, k2, [RT, k2] twice, LT 3 times, k2.
ROW 20: Purl.
Repeat Rows 1–20 for pattern.

STACK
(14-st panel; 39 rnds)
RND 1 (RS): K6, RT, k6.
RND 2 AND ALL WS RNDS THROUGH RND 10: Knit.
RND 3: K5, RT, LT, k5.
RND 5: K4, RT, k2, LT, k4.
RND 7: K3, [RT, k1] twice, LT, k3.
RND 9: K2, RT, k1, RT, LT, k1, LT, k2.
RND 11: P1, RT, k1, RT, k2, LT, k1, LT, p1.
RND 12: Knit the knit sts and purl the purl sts as they face you.
RND 13: P1, LT, [RT, k1] twice, LT, RT, p1.
RND 14: P2, k10, p2.
RND 15: P2, RT, k1, RT, LT, k1, LT, p2.
RND 16: Repeat Rnd 12.
RND 17: P1, RT, k1, RT, p2, LT, k1, LT, p1.
RND 18: Repeat Rnd 12.
RND 19: RT, k1, RT, p4, LT, k1, LT.
RND 20: K4, p6, k4.
RND 21: LT, k1, LT, p4, RT, k1, RT.
RND 22: Repeat Rnd 12.
RND 23: P1, LT, k1, LT, p2, RT, k1, RT, p1.
RND 24: Repeat Rnd 14.
RND 25: P2, LT, k1, LT, RT, k1, RT, p2.
RND 26: Repeat Rnd 12.

RND 27: P1, RT, LT, [k1, RT] twice, LT, p1.

RND 28: Repeat Rnd 12.

RND 29: [K1, LT] twice, k2, [RT, k1] twice.

RNDS 30, 32, 34, 36, AND 38: Knit.

RND 31: K2, LT, k1, LT, RT, k1, RT, k2.

RND 33: K3, LT, [k1, RT] twice, k3.

RND 35: K4, LT, k2, RT, k4.

RND 37: K5, LT, RT, k5.

RND 39: K6, RT, k6.

HILARY

(multiple of 8 sts + 2; 16-row repeat)

ROW 1 (RS): Knit.

ROW 2 AND ALL WS ROWS: Purl.

ROW 3: K2, *RT, k6; repeat from * to end.

ROW 5: K1, *RT, LT, RT, k2; repeat from * to last st, k1.

ROW 7: K4, RT, *k6, RT; repeat from * to last 4 sts, knit to end.

ROW 9: Knit.

ROW 11: LT, *k6, LT; repeat from * to end.

ROW 13: K1, *LT, k2, LT, RT; repeat from * to last st, k1.

ROW 15: *K6, LT; repeat from * to last 2 sts, k2.

ROW 16: Purl.

Repeat Rows 1–16 for pattern.

SPECIAL TECHNIQUE
GRAFTING LIVE STITCHES
TO A CAST-ON EDGE

Using a blunt tapestry needle, thread a length of yarn approximately 4 times the length of the section to be joined. Because this piece was worked in the round, there is a front and back to both the live stitches and the cast-on edge. The front is the side closest to you and the back is the side furthest from you. Hold the live stitches in front with the needle tips pointing to the right; you will begin grafting the live stitches with the stitches on the front needle. Bring the cast-on edge up behind the live stitches, being careful not to twist the piece. You will begin grafting the cast-on stitches with the back side of the cast-on edge. Working from right to left, insert the tapestry needle into the first stitch on the front needle as if to

ZIGZAG PANEL

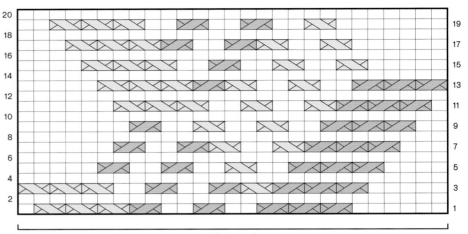

27-st panel

HILARY

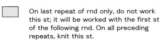

16-rnd repeat

8-st repeat

On last repeat of rnd only, do not work this st; it will be worked with the first st of the following rnd. On all preceding repeats, knit this st.

On last repeat of rnd only, knit this st; on all preceding repeats, omit this st.

On first repeat of rnd only, after working LT, replace beginning-of-rnd marker in center of LT. On all following repeats, work as LT.

STACK

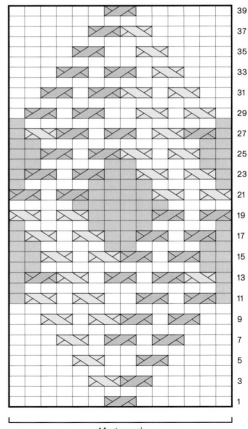

14-st panel

purl, pull the yarn through, leaving the stitch on the needle; insert the tapestry needle purlwise under both legs of the first cast-on stitch on the back side of the cast-on edge, pull the yarn through; *insert the tapestry needle into the first stitch on the front needle as if to knit, pull the yarn through, remove the stitch from the needle; insert the tapestry needle into the next stitch on the front needle as if to purl, pull the yarn through, leave the stitch on the needle; insert the tapestry needle under both legs of the next cast-on stitch on the back side of the cast-on edge as if to purl, pull the yarn through. Repeat from *, working 3 or 4 stitches at a time, then go back and adjust the tension to match the pieces being joined. When 1 live stitch remains, cut yarn and pass through the last live stitch and cast-on stitch to fasten off.

PATTERN NOTES

This pullover begins with the center panel of the yoke, which is worked in one long piece, then the ends are grafted together, grafting cast-on stitches to live stitches. If you prefer, you may use a provisional cast-on, then graft the provisional stitches to the live stitches; or you may bind off the stitches, then sew the two ends together. Stitches for the upper yoke are picked up from one edge and worked to the neck. Stitches for the lower yoke are picked up from the remaining edge of the center panel, then worked to the underarms. The body and sleeves are divided and worked separately in the round to the bottom edge.

Center Yoke Panel

Using larger straight needles and Long-Tail Cast-On (see Special Techniques, page 270), CO 29 sts.
Purl 1 row.
SET-UP ROW (RS): K1 (edge st; keep in St st), work Zigzag Panel to last st, k1 (edge st; keep in St st).
Work even until you have completed Rows 1–20 of Zigzag Panel a total of 21 (23, 25, 27, 29) (30, 33, 34, 36) times. Cut yarn, leaving a tail 4 times the width of the

piece for grafting. If you prefer, you may bind off sts. Graft live sts to CO edge.

Upper Yoke

With RS of center yoke panel facing, using larger 32" (80 cm) circular needle and beginning at seam, pick up and knit 272 (306, 323, 340, 374) (391, 425, 442, 459) sts evenly around right-hand edge of center yoke panel (picking up approximately 12–13 sts for every vertical repeat of Zigzag Panel). Join for working in the rnd; pm for beginning of rnd.
SET-UP RND: *K3, work Stack across 14 sts; repeat from * to end.
Work even through Rnd 39 of Stack. Knit 1 rnd.

SIZES 33, 37¾, 40¾, 45, 58¼, AND 62½" (85, 96, 103.5, 114.5, 148, AND 159 CM) ONLY:
NEXT RND: [K2 (2, 2, 2, –) (–, 3, 3, –), k2tog] 32 (37, 38, 38, –) (–, 40, 41, –) times, k8 (4, 10, 18, –) (–, 10, 16, 5), [k2 (2, 2, 2, –) (–, 5, 5, –), k2tog] 32 (37, 37, 38, –) (–, 41, 41, –) times, knit to end—208 (232, 248, 264, –) (–, 344, 360, –) sts remain.

SIZE 49½" (125.5 CM) ONLY:
NEXT RND: [K2, k2tog, k3, k2tog] 20 times, k10, [k2, k2tog, k3, k2tog] 19 times, knit to end—296 sts remain.

SIZE 51" (129.5 CM) ONLY:
NEXT RND: *K3, k2tog, k4, k2tog; repeat from * to last 6 sts, k4, k2tog—320 sts remain.

SIZE 65½" (166.5 CM) ONLY:
NEXT RND: [(K3, k2tog) twice, k4, k2tog] 27 times, k5, [k4, k2tog] twice, k10—376 sts remain.

ALL SIZES:
Begin Hilary pattern; work 7 (7, 7, 15, 15) (15, 23, 23, 23) rnds even.
Knit 1 rnd.
NEXT RND: *K1, k2tog; repeat from * to last 4 (4, 8, 0, 8) (8, 8, 0, 4) sts, knit to end—140 (156, 168, 176, 200) (216, 232, 240, 252) sts remain.
Lay piece flat with beginning of rnd approximately where a back left raglan

would be. Choose one diamond motif from the Hilary pattern to be at the center front. Place a removable marker on the needle directly above the center of this motif. Place 2 more removable markers on the needle, each 9 (9, 9, 11, 11) (11, 13, 13, 13) sts to either side of the center marker, then remove center marker; you should now have 18 (18, 18, 22, 22) (22, 26, 26, 26) sts between markers.
Place an additional 2 removable markers on the needle for shoulders, each 26 (30, 33, 33, 39) (43, 45, 47, 50) sts to either side of center sts.

Shape Neck

RND 1: Knit to second marker, BO center 18 (18, 18, 22, 22) (22, 26, 26, 26) sts, knit to end—122 (138, 150, 154, 178) (194, 206, 214, 226) sts remain.
Change to working back and forth.
ROW 2 (WS): BO 4 sts, purl to end.
ROW 3: BO 4 sts, [knit to 4 sts before marker, ssk, k2, sm, k2, k2tog] twice, knit to end—110 (126, 138, 142, 166) (182, 194, 202, 214) sts remain.
ROW 4: BO 3 sts, purl to end.
ROW 5: BO 3 sts, [knit to 4 sts before marker, ssk, k2, sm, k2, k2tog] knit to end—100 (116, 128, 132, 156) (172, 184, 192, 204) sts remain.
Repeat Rows 4 and 5 zero (0, 0, 1, 1) (1, 1, 1, 2) more time(s)—100 (116, 128, 122, 146) (162, 174, 182, 184) sts remain.
ROW 6: BO 2 sts, purl to end.
ROW 7: BO 2 sts, [knit to 4 sts before marker, ssk, k2, sm, k2, k2tog] knit to end—92 (108, 120, 114, 138) (154, 166, 174, 176) sts remain.
Repeat Rows 6 and 7 one (2, 3, 2, 3) (3, 3, 3, 4) more times—84 (92, 96, 98, 114) (130, 142, 150, 144) sts remain.

SIZES 49½, 51, 58¼, 62½, AND 65½" (125.5, 129.5, 148, 159, AND 166.5 CM) ONLY:
ROW 8: Purl.
ROW 9: K1, sssk, k4, k2tog, knit to 4 sts before marker, ssk, k2, sm, k2, k3tog, knit to 4 sts before marker, sssk, k2, sm, k2, k2tog, knit to last 10 sts, ssk, k4, k3tog, k1—12 sts decreased.

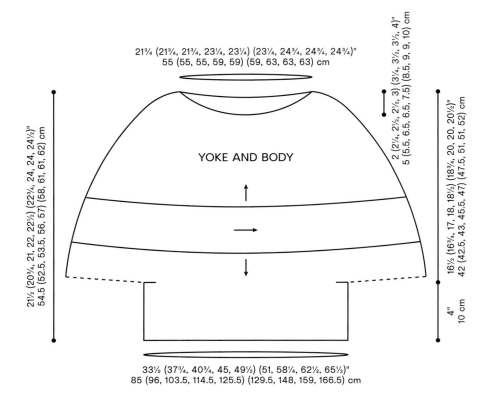

21¾ (21¾, 21¾, 23¼, 23¼) (23¼, 24¾, 24¾, 24¾)"
55 (55, 55, 59, 59) (59, 63, 63, 63) cm

2 (2¼, 2¼, 2½, 3) (3¼, 3½, 3½, 4)"
5 (5.5, 6.5, 6.5, 7.5) (8.5, 9, 9, 10) cm

YOKE AND BODY

21½ (20¾, 21, 22, 22½) (22¾, 24, 24, 24½)"
54.5 (52.5, 53.5, 56, 57) (58, 61, 61, 62) cm

16½ (16¾, 17, 18, 18½) (18¾, 20, 20, 20½)"
42 (42.5, 43, 45.5, 47) (47.5, 51, 51, 52) cm

4"
10 cm

33½ (37¾, 40¾, 45, 49½) (51, 58¼, 62½, 65½)"
85 (96, 103.5, 114.5, 125.5) (129.5, 148, 159, 166.5) cm

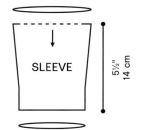

13 (13, 13, 14¼, 14¼) (14¼, 15¼, 15¼, 15¼)"
33 (33, 33, 36, 36) (36, 38.5, 38.5, 38.5) cm

SLEEVE

5½"
14 cm

10¼ (10¼, 10¼, 11, 11) (11, 12¼, 12¼, 12¼)"
26 (26, 26, 28, 28) (28, 31, 31, 31) cm

Repeat Rows 8 and 9 – (–, –, –, 0) (1, 1, 2, 1) more time(s)– – (–, –, –, 102) (106, 118, 114, 120) sts remain.

ALL SIZES:
Purl 1 row, removing all markers.
DECREASE ROW (RS): K1, sssk, k4, k2tog, knit to last 10 sts, ssk, k4, k3tog, k1–6 sts decreased.
Repeat last 2 rows 1 (2, 2, 2, 2) (2, 3, 2, 3) more time(s)–72 (74, 78, 80, 84) (88, 94, 96, 96) sts remain.
Purl 1 row.
NEXT ROW: K5 (2, 7, 1, 7) (3, 3, 1, 1), *k2tog, k2 (2, 1, 2, 1) (1, 1, 1, 1); repeat from * to last 7 (4, 8, 6, 3) (4, 4, 2, 2) sts, k2tog, knit to end–56 (56, 56, 60, 60) (60, 64, 64, 64) sts remain.
Change to 16" (40 cm) circular needle. With RS still facing, pm for beginning of rnd, pick up and knit 64 (64, 64, 68, 68) (68, 72, 72, 72) sts along neck edge (picking up 1 full st in from edge–120 (120, 120, 128, 128) (128, 136, 136, 136) sts. Join for working in the rnd. Work in 2x2 Rib for ¾" (2 cm). BO all sts in pattern.

Lower Yoke
With RS facing, using larger 32" (80 cm) circular needle, pick up and knit 296 (320, 336, 368, 392) (400, 440, 464, 480) sts around remaining edge of Zigzag Panel (picking up approximately 13-14 sts for every vertical repeat of Zigzag Panel pattern). Join for working in the rnd; pm for beginning of rnd.
Begin Hilary pattern; work even until chart is complete.
Change to St st; work even until piece measures 3" (7.5 cm) from pick-up rnd.

Divide for Body and Sleeves
Lay piece flat. Using the center diamond motif at the front neck edge as a guide, place a marker on the needle between the center 2 sts.
Place 2 more removable markers on the needle, each 42 (48, 52, 58, 64) (66, 74, 80, 84) sts to either side of the center marker, then remove center marker; you should now have 84 (96, 104, 116, 128) (132, 148, 160, 168) sts between markers for front.

Place an additional 2 removable markers on the needle for sleeves, each 64 (64, 64, 68, 68) (68, 72, 72, 72) sts to either side of front sts; you should have 84 (96, 104, 116, 128) (132, 148, 160, 168) sts between these markers for back.
DIVIDING RND: [Knit to marker, transfer next 64 (64, 64, 68, 68) (68, 72, 72, 72) sts to st holder or waste yarn for sleeve (removing markers), using Cable Cast-On (see Special Techniques, page 270), CO 8 (8, 8, 8, 8) (8, 12, 12, 12) sts for underarm] twice, knit to end–184 (208, 224, 248, 272) (280, 320, 344, 360) sts.

Body
Knit 5 rnds.
Change to smaller 32" (80 cm) long or longer circular needle.
Knit 1 rnd.
Work in 2×2 Rib for 4" (10 cm). BO all sts in pattern.

Sleeves
Using needle(s) in preferred style for small circumference knitting in the rnd,

and beginning at center of CO underarm sts, pick up and knit 4 (4, 4, 5, 5) (5, 6, 6, 6) sts, knit across 64 (64, 64, 68, 68) (68, 72, 72, 72) sts from holder, pick up and knit 4 (4, 4, 5, 5) (5, 6, 6, 6) sts to center of underarm—72 (72, 72, 78, 78) (78, 84, 84, 84) sts. Join for working in the rnd; pm for beginning of rnd.
Knit 5 rnds.

SHAPE SLEEVE
DECREASE RND: K1, k2tog, knit to last 3 sts, ssk, k1—2 sts decreased.
Repeat Decrease Rnd every 5 (5, 5, 4, 4) (4, 5, 5, 5) rnds 7 (7, 7, 8, 8) (8, 7, 7, 7) more times—56 (56, 56, 60, 60) (60, 68, 68, 68) sts remain.
Work even in St st until piece measures 5½" (14 cm) from pick-up rnd.
Change to smaller needle(s).
Knit 1 rnd.
Work in 2×2 Rib for 2" (5 cm). BO all sts in pattern.
Sew underarm seams.

FINISHING
Block as desired.

You can easily substitute the center band pattern, Zigzag Panel (#32), with another column or insert that has a similar number of stitches. Look for a stitch with a PSS within 5 of the original PSS of 85; for instance, Blanket Star (#71), Barbed (#90), or Always (#93). Your chosen pattern may not end at a perfect repeat, but that's okay, the seam lands, inconspicuously, on the back left shoulder. The first pattern in the yoke, Stack (#6), may also be substituted. Look for an insert near 14 stitches wide, or look for something to fit the number of stitches picked up above the central band, remembering to look for similar PSS. You can adjust the number of stitches picked up to match the repeat of your chosen pattern, but only by a few. Think about how your new pattern will look when worked for thirty-nine rows.

Island Pullover

Each of the three twisted-stitch patterns visually imitates patterns you might find in a traditional Irish knit. Setting the wide center panel and flanking side "cables" in a moss stitch background supports the illusion. Wear this simple drop-shoulder pullover anywhere from 4–12" (10–30.5 cm) oversized. You can compare the look of the same sweater shown on Lilly, opposite, with about 6" (15 cm) of ease, page 248, and on Jordan, page 248, with an ease of about 12" (30.5 cm).

SIZES
To fit bust 30 (34, 38, 42, 46) (50, 54, 58, 62)" [76 (86.5, 96.5, 106.5, 117) (127, 137, 147.5, 157.5) cm]

FINISHED MEASUREMENTS
43 (46½, 50½, 55, 59) (62, 66½, 70½, 73½)" [109 (118, 128.5, 139.5, 150) (157.5, 169, 179, 186.5) cm] bust

YARN
Brooklyn Tweed Peerie [100% American merino wool; 210 yards (192 meters)/50 grams]: 7 (8, 8, 9, 10) (10, 11, 12, 12) skeins Aurora

NEEDLES
One pair straight needles, size US 2 (2.75 mm)

One 16" (40 cm) long circular needle, size US 2 (2.75 mm)

One pair straight needles, size US 3 (3.25 mm)

Change needle size if necessary to obtain correct gauge.

NOTIONS
Stitch markers; stitch holders or waste yarn

GAUGES
29 sts and 44 rows = 4" (10 cm) in Seed Stitch, using larger needles

34 sts and 44 rows = 4" (10 cm) in Plaid Garter Small, using larger needles

24-st panel from Three Columns pattern measures 2½" (6.5 cm), using larger needles

STITCH PATTERNS

FLAT 2×2 RIB
(multiple of 4 sts + 2; 2-row repeat)
ROW 1 (RS): K2, *p2, k2; repeat from * to end.
ROW 2: P2, *k2, p2; repeat from * to end.
Repeat Rows 1 and 2 for pattern.

CIRCULAR 2×2 RIB
(multiple of 4 sts; 1-rnd repeat)
ALL RNDS: K1, p2, *k2, p2; repeat from * to last st, k1.

HALF TWISTED RIB
(odd number of sts; 2-row repeat)
ROW 1 (RS): K1-tbl, *p1, k1-tbl; repeat from * to end.
ROW 2: P1, *k1-tbl, p1; repeat from * to end.
Repeat Rows 1 and 2 for pattern.

**SEED STITCH
(BEGINNING WITH A PURL)**
(even number of sts; 1-row repeat)
ALL ROWS: *P1, k1; repeat from * to end.

**SEED STITCH
(BEGINNING WITH A KNIT)**
(even number of sts; 1-row repeat)
ALL ROWS: *K1, p1; repeat from * to end.

PLAID SMALL GARTER (#51)
(multiple of 12 sts + 1; 20-row repeat)
ROW 1 (RS): P2, LT, k5, RT, *p3, LT, k5, RT; repeat from * to last 2 sts, p2.
ROW 2 AND ALL WS ROWS: Purl.
ROW 3: P1, *RT, LT, k3, RT, LT, p1; repeat from * to end.
ROW 5: K1, *[LT, k1] twice, [RT, k1] twice; repeat from * to end.
ROW 7: K2, LT, RT, p1, LT, RT, *k3, LT, RT, p1, LT, RT; repeat from * to last 2 sts, k2.
ROW 9: K3, LT, p3, RT, *k5, LT, p3, RT; repeat from * to last 3 sts, k3.
ROW 11: K3, RT, p3, LT, *k5, RT, p3, LT; repeat from * to last 3 sts, k3.
ROW 13: K2, RT, LT, p1, RT, LT, *k3, RT, LT, p1, RT, LT; repeat from * to last 2 sts, k2.
ROW 15: K1, *[RT, k1] twice, [LT, k1] twice; repeat from * to end.
ROW 17: P1, *LT, RT, k3, LT, RT, p1; repeat from * to end.
ROW 19: P2, RT, k5, LT, *p3, RT, k5, LT; repeat from * to last 2 sts, p2.
ROW 20: Purl.
Repeat Rows 1–20 for pattern.

THREE COLUMNS
(panel of 24 sts; 8-row repeat)
ROW 1 (RS): P2, LT, RT, p2, k2, p1, RT, p1, k2, p2, LT, RT, p2.

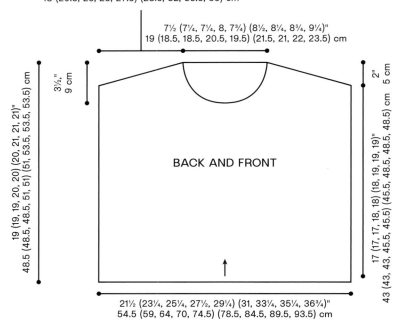

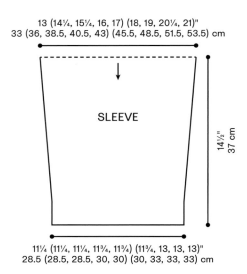

ROW 2: Knit the knit sts and purl the purl sts as they face you.

ROW 3: P2, k1, RT, k1, p2, k1, LT, RT twice, k1, p2, k1, RT, k1, p2.

ROW 4: Repeat Row 2.

ROW 5: P2, LT, RT, p2, [RT, LT] twice, p2, LT, RT, p2.

ROW 6: K2, p4, k2, p2, [k1, p2] twice, k2, p4, k2.

ROW 7: P2, k1, RT, k1, p2, k2, p1, RT, p1, k2, p2, k1, RT, k1, p2.

ROW 8: Repeat Row 2.

Repeat Rows 1–8 for pattern.

PATTERN NOTES

The back and front of this pullover are worked from the bottom up in pieces, with short-row shaping to shape the shoulders, which are then joined using 3-Needle Bind-Off. The sleeves are picked up from the armhole edges and worked back and forth in rows to the cuffs.

When working neck shaping, if there are not enough stitches to work a full twisted stitch, work the affected stitch in Stockinette stitch instead.

Back

Using larger needles and Long-Tail Cast-On (see Special Techniques, page 270), CO 185 (201, 213, 237, 257) (265, 281, 301, 309) sts.

SET-UP ROW (WS): Work Flat 2×2 Rib over 38 (46, 46, 58, 62) (66, 74, 78, 82) sts, pm, work Three-Columns pattern over 24 sts, pm, work Half Twisted Rib over 61 (61, 73, 73, 85) (85, 85, 97, 97) sts, pm, work Three Columns pattern over 24 sts, pm, work Flat 2×2 Rib over 38 (46, 46, 58, 62) (66, 74, 78, 82) sts.

Work even until piece measures 2" (5 cm) from the beginning, ending with a RS row. Change to larger needles.

NEXT ROW (WS): P3 (2, 4, 4, 3) (4, 5, 2, 5), [p2tog, k8 (6, 10, 5, 4) (6, 7, 6, 8)] 3 (5, 3, 7, 9) (7, 7, 9, 7) times, p2tog, purl to marker, sm, work as established to

marker, sm, purl to marker, sm, work as established to marker, sm, p3 (2, 4, 4, 3) (4, 5, 2, 5), [p2tog, p8 (6, 10, 5, 4) (6, 7, 6, 8)] 3 (5, 3, 7, 9) (7, 7, 9, 7) times, p2tog, purl to end—177 (189, 205, 221, 237) (249, 265, 281, 293) sts remain.

SET-UP ROW: K2 (edge sts; keep in St st), work Seed Stitch (beginning with a purl) to marker, sm, work as established to marker, sm, work Plaid Small Garter to marker, sm, work as established to marker, sm, work Seed Stitch (beginning with a knit) to last 2 sts, k2 (edge sts; keep in St st).

Work even until piece measures 17 (17, 17, 18, 18) (18, 19, 19, 19)" [43 (43, 43, 45.5, 45.5) (45.5, 48.5, 48.5, 48.5) cm], ending with a WS row.

SHAPE SHOULDERS

NOTE: Shoulders are shaped using German Short Rows (see Special Techniques, page 270).

SHORT ROW 1 (RS): Work to last 5 (5, 5, 7,

7) (8, 8, 9, 9) sts, turn.

SHORT ROW 2: DS, work to last 5 (5, 5, 7, 7) (8, 8, 9, 9) sts, turn.

SHORT ROW 3: DS, work to 4 (4, 5, 6, 7) (7, 8, 9, 9) sts before DS from previous RS row, turn.

SHORT ROW 4: DS, work to 4 (4, 5, 6, 7) (7, 8, 9, 9) sts before DS from previous WS row, turn.

Repeat Short Rows 3 and 4 eight (1, 2, 8, 4) (8, 3, 0, 6) more time(s).

SIZES 46½, 50½, 59, 66½, 70½, AND 73½" [118, 128.5, 150, 169, 179, AND 186.5 CM] ONLY:

SHORT ROW 5: DS, work to – (5, 6, –, 6) (–, 7, 8, 8) sts before DS from previous RS row, turn.

SHORT ROW 6: DS, work to – (5, 6, –, 6) (–, 7, 8, 8) sts before DS from previous WS row, turn.

Repeat Short Rows 5 and 6 – (14, 12, –, 8) (–, 10, 16, 4) more times.

ALL SIZES:

SHORT ROW 7: Work to end, closing each DS as you come to it.

Purl 1 row, closing each remaining DS as you come to it. Cut yarn, leaving a tail 3 times the width of your piece, place sts on a st holder or waste yarn.

Front

Work as for back until piece measures 15½ (15½, 15½, 16½, 16½) (16½, 17½, 17½, 17½)" [39 (39, 39, 42, 42) (42, 44.5, 44.5, 44.5) cm] from the beginning, ending with a WS row—177 (189, 205, 221, 237) (249, 265, 281, 293) sts remain.

SHAPE NECK AND SHOULDERS

NOTE: Neck and shoulder shaping are worked at the same time, beginning with neck shaping; please read entire section through before beginning.

NEXT ROW (RS): Work 77 (83, 91, 97, 105) (109, 117, 123, 127) sts, join a second ball of yarn, BO center 23 (23, 23, 27, 27) (31, 31, 35, 39) sts, work to end.

Working both sides at once, BO 4 sts at each neck edge once, 3 sts twice, 2 sts 3 times, then 1 st 4 times. AT THE SAME

TIME, when piece measures 17 (17, 17, 18, 18) (18, 19, 19, 19)" [43 (43, 43, 45.5, 45.5) (45.5, 48.5, 48.5, 48.5) cm], ending with a WS row, begin shoulder shaping as follows:

SHORT ROW 1 (RS): Work to last 5 (5, 5, 7, 7) (8, 8, 9, 9) sts, turn.

SHORT ROW 2: DS, work to last 5 (5, 5, 7, 7) (8, 8, 9, 9) sts, turn.

SHORT ROW 3: DS, work to 4 (4, 5, 6, 7) (7, 8, 9, 9) sts before DS from previous RS row, turn.

SHORT ROW 4: DS, work to 4 (4, 5, 6, 7) (7, 8, 9, 9) sts before DS from previous WS row, turn.

Repeat Short Rows 3 and 4 eight (1, 2, 8, 4) (8, 3, 0, 6) more time(s).

SIZES 46½, 50½, 59, 66½, 70½, AND 73½" [118, 128.5, 150, 169, 179, AND 186.5 CM] ONLY:

SHORT ROW 5: DS, work to – (5, 6, –, 6) (–, 7, 8, 8) sts before DS from previous RS row, turn.

SHORT ROW 6: DS, work to – (5, 6, –, 6) (–, 7, 8, 8) sts before DS from previous WS row, turn.

Repeat Short Rows 5 and 6 – (14, 12, –, 8) (–, 10, 16, 4) more times.

ALL SIZES:

SHORT ROW 7: Work to end, closing each DS as you come to it.

NEXT ROW: Purl to neck edge; cut yarn, leaving a 6" (15 cm) tail and leaving sts on the needle; purl to end, closing each

PLAID SMALL GARTER

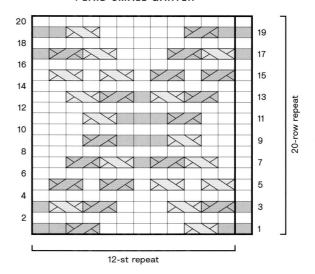

12-st repeat

THREE COLUMNS

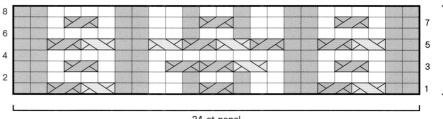

24-st panel

remaining DS as you come to it; cut yarn, leaving a 6" (15 cm) tail.

With WSs of front and back together (seam will be on the RS), and with back facing you, using yarn attached to back, join shoulders using 3-Needle Bind-off (see Special Techniques, page 270.

Sleeves

Place removable markers 7 (7½, 8, 8½, 9) (9½, 10, 10½, 11)" [18 (19, 20.5, 21.5, 23) (24, 25.5, 26.5, 28) cm] down from each shoulder seam on front and back. NOTE: The distance between the markers is approximately 1" (2.5 cm) wider than the top of the sleeve. This makes the sleeve lie flat and keeps it from bulging at the top.

With RS facing, using larger needles, pick up and knit 94 (104, 110, 116, 124) (130, 138, 146, 152) sts between markers. Do not join; work back and forth in rows. Purl 1 row.

SET-UP ROW (RS): K2 (edge sts; keep in St st), work in Seed Stitch (beginning with a purl) to last 2 sts, k2 (edge sts; keep in St st). p2.

Work 8 rows even.

SHAPE SLEEVE

DECREASE ROW (RS): K1, ssk, work to last 3 sts, k2tog, k1—2 sts decreased.

Repeat Decrease Row every 20 (10, 8, 8, 6) (6, 6, 4, 4) rows 5 (10, 11, 8, 14) (8, 8, 25, 23) more times, then every 0 (0, 6, 6, 4) (4, 4, 0, 2) rows 0 (0, 2, 6, 4) (13, 13, 0, 5) times—82 (82, 82, 86, 86) (86, 94, 94, 94) sts remain.

Work even until piece measures 11½" (29 cm) from pick-up row, ending with a RS row.

Change to smaller needles.

NEXT ROW (WS): P6 (6, 6, 5, 5) (5, 5, 5, 5), [M1P, p10 (10, 10, 11, 11) (11, 12, 12, 12)] 7 times, M1P, purl to end—90 (90, 90, 94, 94) (94, 102, 102, 102) sts.

Work in Flat 2×2 Rib for 3" (7.5 cm).

BO all sts in pattern.

FINISHING

Block as desired.

NECKBAND

Using circular needle, beginning at center back neck, pick up and knit 152 (160, 168, 176, 184) (192, 200, 208, 216) sts evenly around neck opening. Join for working in the rnd; pm for beginning of rnd. Work in Circular 2×2 Rib for 1" (2.5 cm). BO all sts in pattern.

Substitute charts from other chapters for the center panel, as long as their PSS is close to 90, keeping approximately the same number of stitches for the panel. Take a look at Triplet Weave Garter (#25), Smocking (#64), or Pi (#94). Any of the three would work well as a center panel, but they are certainly not the only possibilities. If you'd like to pick up your own side panels, the stitches in Chapter 3 would be best suited for this.

Grandpops

Twisted stitches take on a hyper dimension when knit in a bulky yarn. Giant styled flowers fill the simple silhouette of this drop-shouldered cardigan, while narrow sleeves offset the roominess of the length and width. If you prefer a looser sleeve, or if you are a man, or knitting this for a man, pick up and knit the sleeve in a larger size. A high collar hugs the neck in a clean, simple modification of a shawl collar, which is not meant to fold over.

SIZES
To fit bust 30 (34, 38, 42, 46) (50, 54, 58, 62)" [76 (86.5, 96.5, 106.5, 117) (127, 137, 147, 157.5) cm]

FINISHED MEASUREMENTS
40 (44½, 48½, 50¼, 55¼) (60½, 64, 68, 72½)" [101.5 (113, 123, 127.5, 140.5) (153.5, 162.5, 172.5, 184) cm] bust, buttoned

YARN
Quince & Co. Puffin [100% American wool; 112 yards (102 meters)/100 grams]: 9 (9, 10, 11, 12) (13, 14, 15, 16) skeins Bird's Egg

NEEDLES
One pair straight needles, size 9 (5.5 mm)

One pair straight needles, size 10½ (6.5 mm)

One spare needle in any style, size 9 (5.5 mm), for 3-Needle Bind-Off

Change needle size if necessary to obtain correct gauge.

NOTIONS
Stitch markers; removable stitch markers; row counter (optional); stitch holder or waste yarn; five 1" (25 mm) buttons

GAUGE
12 sts and 19 rows = 4" (10 cm) in Flowers Allover, using larger needles

STITCH PATTERNS

1×1 RIB
(even number of sts; 1-row repeat)
ALL ROWS: *K1, p1; repeat from * to end.

FLOWERS ALLOVER (#56)
Note: Pattern is worked from chart only; work swatch from Flowers Allover, page 76.

PATTERN NOTES
The back and fronts of this cardigan are worked from the bottom up in pieces, then the shoulders are sewn together. The sleeves are picked up from the armholes and worked back and forth in rows to the cuffs. The front bands/collars are worked separately from the bottom up, sewn in place, then joined at the center back neck using 3-Needle Bind-Off.

When working neck shaping, if there are not enough stitches to work a full twisted stitch, work the affected stitch in Stockinette stitch instead.

The front bands/collar are worked to the same number of rows as the fronts; you may wish to use a row counter to keep track of the rows as you work the fronts.

Back
Using smaller needles and Long-Tail Cast-On (see Special Techniques, page 270), CO 62 (68, 78, 80, 86) (94, 102, 108, 114) sts.
Begin 1×1 Rib; work 8 rows even.
Change to larger needles.
NEXT ROW (WS): P8 (8, 6, 8, 11) (11, 10, 8, 11), *p2tog, p7 (8, 7, 7, 7) (8, 7, 8, 8); repeat from * to last 0 (0, 0, 0, 3) (3, 2, 0, 3) sts, purl to end—56 (62, 70, 72, 78) (86, 92, 98, 104) sts remain.
SET-UP ROW: K1 (edge st; keep in St st), work Flowers Allover Chart (beginning and ending as indicated in chart for your size), to last st, k1 (edge st; keep in St st). Work even until piece measures 26½ (26½, 27, 27, 27½) (27½, 28, 28, 28½)" [67.5 (67.5, 68.5, 68.5, 70) (70, 71, 71, 72.5) cm] from the beginning, ending with a WS row.

SHAPE SHOULDERS
BO 4 (5, 6, 6, 7) (7, 8, 9, 9) sts at beginning of next 4 (6, 8, 6, 8) (2, 4, 8, 2) rows, then 5 (6, 0, 7, 0) (8, 9, 0, 10) sts at beginning of next 4 (2, 0, 2, 0) (6, 4, 0, 6) rows.
BO remaining 20 (20, 22, 22, 22) (24, 24, 26, 26) sts.

Left Front
Using smaller needles and Long-Tail CO, CO 32 (36, 40, 42, 46) (50, 52, 56, 60) sts.
Begin 1×1 Rib; work 8 rows even.
Change to larger needles.
NEXT ROW (WS): P5 (6, 5, 7, 6) (5, 7, 8, 6), *p2tog, p7 (8, 5, 5, 6) (7, 7, 6, 7); repeat from * to end—29 (33, 35, 37, 41) (45, 47, 50, 54) sts remain.
SET-UP ROW: K1 (edge st; keep in St st), work Flowers Allover Chart (beginning and ending as indicated in chart for your size), to last st, k1 (edge st; keep in St st). Work even until piece measures 16½ (16½, 17, 17, 17½) (17½, 18, 18, 18½)" [42 (42, 43, 43, 44.5) (44.5, 45.5, 45.5, 47) cm] from the beginning, ending with a WS row.

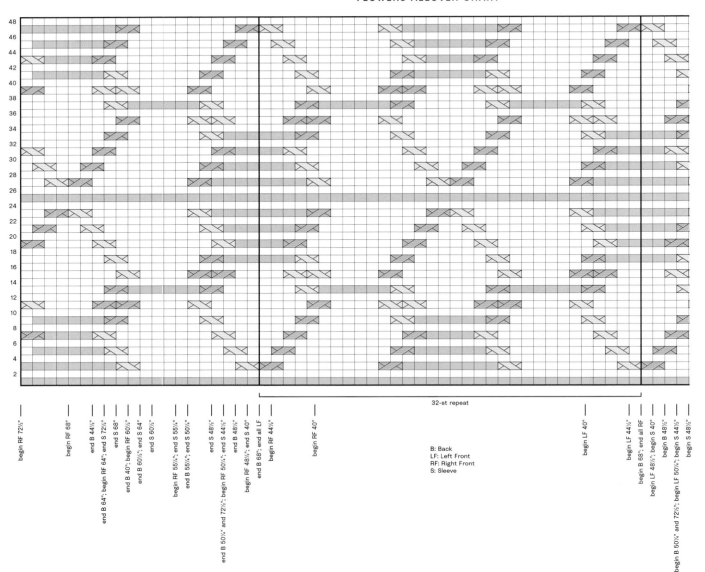

32-st repeat

B: Back
LF: Left Front
RF: Right Front
S: Sleeve

Labels (left to right along bottom):
begin RF 72½" · begin RF 68" · end B 44½" · end B 64"; begin RF 64"; end S 72½" · end S 68" · end B 40"; begin RF 60½" · end B 60½"; end S 64" · end S 60½" · begin RF 55¼"; end S 55½" · end B 55½"; end S 50¼" · end S 48½" · end B 50¼" and 72½"; begin RF 50½"; end S 44½" · end B 48½" · begin RF 48½"; end S 40" · end B 68"; end all LF · begin RF 44½" · begin RF 40" · begin LF 40" · begin LF 44½" · begin B 68"; end all RF · begin LF 48½"; begin S 40" · end B 48½" · begin LF 50¼"; begin LF 55¼"; begin S 44½" · begin S 48½"

Make note of the number of rows worked since the CO edge. Place removable marker in first st at neck edge.

SHAPE NECK
DECREASE ROW (RS): Work to last 3 sts, ssk, k1—1 st decreased.
Repeat Decrease Row every 4 rows 10 (11, 10, 11, 12) (13, 12, 13, 14) more times—18 (21, 24, 25, 28) (31, 34, 36, 39) sts remain.
Work even until piece measures 26½ (26½, 27, 27, 27½) (27½, 28, 28, 28½)" [67.5 (67.5, 68.5, 68.5, 70) (70, 71, 71, 72.5) cm] from the beginning, ending with a WS row.

SHAPE SHOULDER
BO 4 (5, 6, 6, 7) (7, 8, 9, 9) sts at beginning of next 2 (3, 4, 3, 4) (1, 2, 4, 1) RS row(s), then 5 (6, 0, 7, 0) (8, 9, 0, 10) sts at beginning of next 2 (1, 0, 1, 0) (3, 2, 0, 3) RS rows. Make note of the number of rows worked since placing removable marker.

Right Front
Using smaller needles and Long-Tail Cast-On, CO 32 (36, 40, 42, 46) (50, 52, 56, 60) sts.
Begin 1×1 Rib; work 8 rows even.
Change to larger needles.
NEXT ROW (WS): P5 (6, 5, 7, 6) (5, 7, 8, 6), *p2tog, p7 (8, 5, 5, 6) (7, 7, 6, 7); repeat from * to end—29 (33, 35, 37, 41) (45, 47, 50, 54) sts remain.
SET-UP ROW: K1 (edge st; keep in St st), work Flowers Allover Chart (beginning

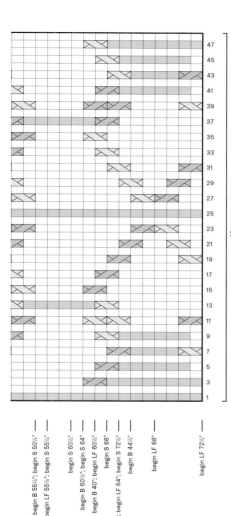

begin B 55¼"; begin S 50½"

begin LF 55¼"; begin S 55¼"

begin S 60½"

begin B 60½"; begin LF 60½"

begin B 40"; begin LF 60½"

begin S 68"

begin B 64"; begin LF 64"; begin S 72½"

begin B 44½"

begin LF 68"

begin LF 72½"

and ending as indicated in chart for your size), to last st, k1 (edge st; keep in St st). Work even until piece measures 16½ (16½, 17, 17, 17½) (17½, 18, 18, 18½)" [42 (42, 43, 43, 44.5) (44.5, 45.5, 45.5, 47) cm] from the beginning, ending with a WS row. Make note of the number of rows worked since the CO edge. Place removable marker in first st at neck edge.

SHAPE NECK

DECREASE ROW (RS): K1, k2tog, work to end–1 st decreased.
Repeat Decrease Row every 4 rows 10 (11, 10, 11, 12) (13, 12, 13, 14) more times–18 (21, 24, 25, 28) (31, 34, 36, 39) sts remain. Work even until piece measures 26½ (26½, 27, 27, 27½) (27½, 28, 28, 28½)" [67.5 (67.5, 68.5, 68.5, 70) (70, 71, 71, 72.5) cm] from the beginning, ending with a WS row. BO 4 (5, 6, 6, 7) (7, 8, 9, 9) sts at beginning of next 2 (3, 4, 3, 4) (1, 2, 4, 1) WS row(s), then 5 (6, 0, 7, 0) (8, 9, 0, 10) sts at beginning of next 2 (1, 0, 1, 0) (3, 2, 0, 3) WS row(s). Make note of the number of rows worked since placing removable marker.

Sleeves

Sew shoulder seams. Place removable markers 6½ (7, 7½, 8, 8½) (9, 9½, 10, 10½)" [16.5 (18, 19, 20, 21.5) (23, 24, 25, 26.5) cm] down from each shoulder seam on fronts and back. **NOTE:** The distance between the markers is approximately 1" (2.5 cm) wider than the top of the sleeve. This makes the sleeve lie flat and keeps it from bulging at the top.
With RS facing, using larger needles, pick up and knit 36 (40, 42, 46, 48) (52, 54, 58, 60) sts between markers. Do not join; work back and forth in rows.
Purl 1 row.
SET-UP ROW (RS): K1 (edge st; keep in St st), work Flowers Allover Chart (beginning and ending as indicated in chart for your size), to last st, k1 (edge st; keep in St st).
Work 21 (13, 9, 9, 5) (1, 1, 5, 1) row(s) even.

SHAPE SLEEVE

DECREASE ROW (RS): K1, k2tog, work to last 3 sts, ssk, k1–2 sts decreased.
Repeat Decrease row every 22 (14, 10, 10, 10) (8, 8, 6, 6) rows 2 (4, 5, 5, 6) (8, 8, 10, 11) times–30 (30, 30, 34, 34) (34, 36, 36, 36) sts remain.
Work even until piece measures 16" (40.5 cm) from pick-up row, ending with a RS row.
Change to smaller needles.
Purl 1 row.
Work 8 rows in 1×1 Rib, ending with a WS row.
BO all sts in pattern.

FINISHING

Block as desired.
Sew side and sleeve seams.

LEFT FRONT BAND/COLLAR

Using smaller needles and Long-Tail Cast-On, CO 9 sts.
SET-UP ROW (WS): K1, [p1, k1] 3 times, p2.
NEXT ROW: K2, [p1, k1] 3 times, k1.
Repeat the last 2 rows until you have worked the same number of rows as for the left front to removable marker, ending with a WS row. Place a removable marker in first st on RS.
ROW 1 (RS): K2, M1L, *p1, k1; repeat from * to last st, k1–1 st increased.
ROW 2: *K1, p1; repeat from * to last 2 sts, p2.
ROW 3: K3, *p1, k1; repeat from * to last st, k1.
ROW 4: Repeat Row 2.
ROW 5: K2, M1PL, *k1, p1; repeat from * to last 2 sts, k2–1 st increased.
ROW 6: *K1, p1; repeat from * to last st, p1.
ROW 7: K2, *p1, k1; repeat from * to last st, k1.
ROW 8: Repeat Row 6.
Repeat Rows 1–8 five more times–21 sts.
Work even until you have worked the same number of rows as for the left front from removable marker to final BO, ending with a RS row. Work even for 2 (2, 2¼, 2¼, 2¼) (2½, 2½, 3, 3)" [5 (5, 5.5, 5.5, 5.5) (6.5, 6.5, 7.5, 7.5) cm] more, ending with a WS row.
DECREASE ROW (RS): [K4, k2tog] 3 times, k3–18 sts remain.
Knit 7 rows.
Cut yarn and transfer sts to st holder or waste yarn.
Sew left front band/collar to left front, aligning removable marker on band with removable marker on left front, and ending at center back neck. Place removable markers for buttons in the center of the band: the first 1" (2.5 cm) up from CO edge, the last at the first band increase row, and the remaining 3 evenly spaced between.

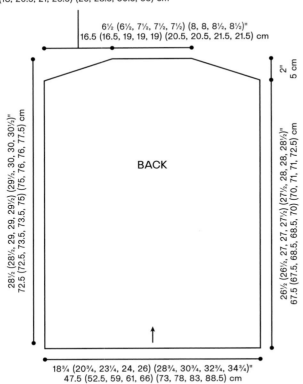

6 (7, 8, 8¼, 9¼) (10¼, 11¼, 12, 13)"
15 (18, 20.5, 21, 23.5) (26, 28.5, 30.5, 33) cm

6½ (6½, 7½, 7½, 7½) (8, 8, 8½, 8½)"
16.5 (16.5, 19, 19, 19) (20.5, 20.5, 21.5, 21.5) cm

2"
5 cm

28½ (28½, 29, 29, 29½) (29½, 30, 30, 30½)"
72.5 (72.5, 73.5, 73.5, 75) (75, 76, 76, 77.5) cm

BACK

26½ (26½, 27, 27, 27½) (27½, 28, 28, 28½)"
67.5 (67.5, 68.5, 68.5, 70) (70, 71, 71, 72.5) cm

18¾ (20¾, 23¼, 24, 26) (28¾, 30¾, 32¾, 34¾)"
47.5 (52.5, 59, 61, 66) (73, 78, 83, 88.5) cm

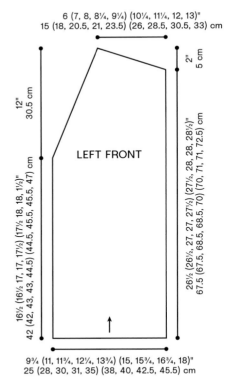

6 (7, 8, 8¼, 9¼) (10¼, 11¼, 12, 13)"
15 (18, 20.5, 21, 23.5) (26, 28.5, 30.5, 33) cm

2"
5 cm

12"
30.5 cm

LEFT FRONT

16½ (16½, 17, 17, 17½) (17½, 18, 18, 1½)"
42 (42, 43, 43, 44.5) (44.5, 45.5, 45.5, 47) cm

26½ (26½, 27, 27, 27½) (27½, 28, 28, 28½)"
67.5 (67.5, 68.5, 68.5, 70) (70, 71, 71, 72.5) cm

9¾ (11, 11¾, 12¼, 13¾) (15, 15¾, 16¾, 18)"
25 (28, 30, 31, 35) (38, 40, 42.5, 45.5) cm

RIGHT FRONT BAND/COLLAR

Using smaller needles and Long-Tail Cast-On, CO 9 sts.

SET-UP ROW (WS): P2, [k1, p1] 3 times, k1.

NEXT ROW: K2, [p1, k1] 3 times, k1.

Repeat the last 2 rows until you have worked the same number of rows as for the right front to removable marker on right front, ending with a WS row, and working buttonholes to correspond with button markers on the left band, as follows:

BUTTONHOLE ROW (RS): K2, p1, ssk, yo, k1, p1, k2.

Place a removable marker in first st on RS.

ROW 1 (RS): K2, p1, *k1, p1; repeat from * to last 2 sts, M1R, k2–1 st increased.

ROW 2: P3, *k1, p1; repeat from * to last st, k1.

ROW 3: Repeat Row 3.

ROW 4: P3, *k1, p1; repeat from * to last st, k1.

ROW 5: K2, p1, *k1, p1; repeat from * to last 3 sts, k1, M1PR, k2–1 st increased.

ROW 6: P2, *k1, p1; repeat from * to last st, k1.

ROW 7: K2, *p1, k1; repeat from * to last st, k1.

ROW 8: Repeat Row 7.

Repeat Rows 1–8 five more times–21 sts. Work even until you have worked the same number of rows as for the right front from removable marker to final BO, ending with a WS row. Work even for 1¾ (1¾, 2¼, 2¼, 2¼) (2½, 2½, 2¾, 2¾)" [4.5 (4.5, 5.5, 5.5, 5.5) (6.5, 6.5, 7, 7) cm] more, ending with a WS row.

DECREASE ROW (RS): [K4, k2tog] 3 times, k3–18 sts remain.

Knit 7 rows.

Do not cut yarn. With WSs of left and right collars together (seam will be on the RS), join collars using smaller needles and 3-Needle Bind-Off (see Special Techniques, page 270).

Sew right front band/collar to right front, aligning removable marker on band with removable marker on right front, and ending at center back neck.

Sew side and sleeve seams. Sew on buttons to correspond to buttonholes. Substitute charts from other chapters as long as their PSS (Percentage of Stockinette Stitch) is about 90. See page 7 to learn more about Percentage of Stockinette Stitch (PSS) and substituting twisted stitches. You'll have to determine the starting and ending points of your chart, using the number of stitches specified for each piece.

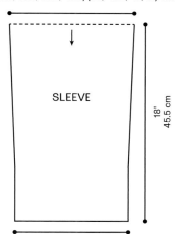

12 (13¼, 14, 15¼, 16) (17¼, 18, 19¼, 20)"
30.5 (33.5, 35.5, 38.5, 40.5) (44, 45.5, 49, 51) cm

SLEEVE

18"
45.5 cm

10 (10, 10, 11¼, 11¼) (11¼, 12, 12, 12)"
25.5 (25.5, 25.5, 28.5, 28.5) (28.5, 30.5, 30.5, 30.5) cm

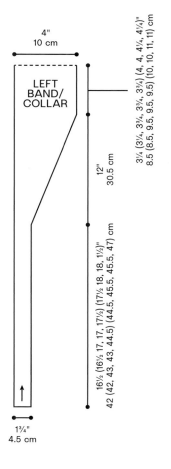

4"
10 cm

LEFT
BAND/
COLLAR

3¼ (3¾, 3¾, 3¾, 3¾) (4, 4, 4¼, 4¼)"
8.5 (8.5, 9.5, 9.5, 9.5) (10, 10, 11, 11) cm

12"
30.5 cm

16½ (16½, 17, 17, 17½) (17½, 18, 18, 18½)"
42 (42, 43, 43, 44.5) (44.5, 45.5, 45.5, 47) cm

1¾"
4.5 cm

GRANDPOPS

Romantic Pullover

Knit flat in pieces from the bottom up, this simple, loose-fitting pullover is made special by adding a balloon sleeve to the extended shoulders and by expanding the central pattern stitch. The result is feminine in a very modern way.

SIZES
To fit bust 30 (34, 38, 42, 46) (50, 54, 58, 62)" [76 (86.5, 96.5, 106.5, 117) (127, 137, 147.5, 157.5) cm]

FINISHED MEASUREMENTS
32½ (37, 40, 44½, 48½) (53, 56, 60½, 64½)" [82.5 (94, 101.5, 113, 123) (134.5, 142, 153.5, 164) cm] bust

YARN
Quince & Co. Crane [50% super kid mohair/50% South African superfine merino; 208 yards (190 meters)/100 grams]: 5 (6, 6, 7, 7) (8, 9, 10, 10) skeins Quanah

NEEDLES
One pair straight needles, size US 4 (3.5 mm)

One pair straight needles, size US 6 (4 mm)

One 16" (40 cm) long circular needle, size US 4 (3.5 mm)

Change needle size if necessary to obtain correct gauge.

NOTIONS
Stitch markers

GAUGES
22 sts and 28 rows = 4" (10 cm) in St st, using larger needles

23 sts and 32 rows = 4" (10 cm) in Smocking Grow, using larger needles

STITCH PATTERNS
2×2 RIB
(multiple of 4 sts + 2; 2-row repeat)
ROW 1 (RS): K2, *p2, k2; repeat from * to end.
ROW 2: P2, *k2, p2; repeat from * to end.
Repeat Rows 1 and 2 for pattern.

SMOCKING GROW (#66)
(panel of 10 sts; one 10-st panel added to each side of pattern every 16 rows; 16-row repeat)
ROW 1 (RS): K2, p6, k2.
ROW 2 AND ALL WS ROWS: Purl.
ROW 3: Repeat Row 1.
ROW 5: K1, RT twice, LT twice, k1.
ROW 7: RT twice, k2, LT twice.
ROW 9: P3, k4, p3.
ROW 11: Repeat Row 9.
ROW 13: LT twice, k2, RT twice.
ROW 15: K1, LT twice, RT twice, k1.
ROW 16: Purl.
Repeat Rows 1–16 between markers for pattern.

PATTERN NOTES
This top is worked from the bottom up in pieces, then the shoulders are sewn together. The sleeves are picked up from the armhole edges and worked back and forth in rows to the cuffs.

The stitch pattern begins with 10 stitches in the center of the piece, then markers are shifted 10 stitches toward each edge with every 16-row pattern repeat, adding 20 new stitches to the pattern every 16 rows.

Back
Using smaller needles and Long-Tail Cast-On (see Special Techniques, page 270), CO 90 (102, 110, 122, 134) (146, 154, 166, 178) sts.

Begin 2×2 Rib (beginning with Row 2); work even until piece measures 3" (7.5 cm) from the beginning, ending with a WS row.

Change to larger needles and St st; work even until piece measures 5" (13 cm) from the beginning, ending with a WS row.

SET-UP ROW (RS): K40 (46, 50, 56, 62) (68, 72, 78, 84), pm, work Smocking Grow over 10 sts, pm, knit to end.

Continuing to work sts between markers in pattern and remainder of sts in St st, work even through Row 16 of pattern.

EXPANSION ROW (RS): Knit to 10 sts before first marker, pm for beginning of new pattern panel, work Smocking Grow to marker, sm, work as established to last marker, sm, work Smocking Grow over 10 sts, pm for end of new pattern panel, knit to end (10 sts added to pattern on each side).

CONTINUE PATTERN EXPANSION AND SHAPE UNDERARM GUSSET
NOTE: Pattern expansion and underarm gusset shaping are worked at the same time; please read entire section through before beginning.

Continuing to work sts between markers in pattern and remainder of sts in St st, work even through Row 16 of pattern.

Repeat Expansion Row on next row, then every 16 rows once more (70 sts between outisde markers).

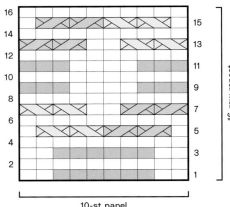

16-row repeat

10-st panel

AT THE SAME TIME, when piece measures 9 (9½, 10, 10, 10½) (11, 11½, 11½, 12)" [23 (24, 25.5, 25.5, 26.5) (28, 29, 29, 30.5) cm] from the beginning, begin underarm gusset shaping, as follows:
INCREASE ROW (RS): K2, M1L, work to last 2 sts, M1R, k2–2 sts increased.
Repeat Increase Row every RS row 10 more times–112 (124, 132, 144, 156) (168, 176, 188, 200) sts.
Using Cable Cast-On (see Special Techniques, page 270), CO 6 sts at beginning of next 2 rows–124 (136, 144, 156, 168) (180, 188, 200, 212) sts.
Work even until piece measures 5½ (5½, 6, 6, 6) (6½, 6½, 7, 7)" [14 (14, 15, 15, 15,) (16.5, 16.5, 18, 18) cm] from end of gusset shaping, ending with a WS row.

SHAPE SHOULDERS AND NECK
NOTE: Shoulder and neck shaping are worked at the same time, beginning with shoulder shaping; please read entire section through before beginning.

Place marker at either side of center 18 (18, 24, 24) (24, 30, 30, 30) sts.
BO 7 (7, 8, 8, 9) (10, 10, 11, 12) sts at beginning of next 2 (14, 2, 14, 12) (10, 12, 10, 8) rows, then 6 (0, 7, 0, 8) (9, 9, 10, 11) sts at beginning of next 12 (0, 12, 0, 2) (4, 2, 4, 6) rows, and AT THE SAME TIME, beginning on Row 9 of shoulder shaping, begin neck shaping as follows:
NEXT ROW (RS): Work to second marker, join a second ball of yarn, BO center sts, work to end.
Working both sides at once, BO 5 sts at each neck edge twice.

Front
Work as for back until piece measures 4½ (4½, 5, 5, 5) (5½, 5½, 6, 6)" [11.5 (11.5, 12.5, 12.5, 12.5) (14, 14, 15, 15) cm] from end of underarm gusset shaping, ending with a WS row.

SHAPE NECK AND SHOULDERS
NOTE: Neck and shoulder shaping are

worked at the same time, beginning with neck shaping; please read entire section through before beginning.
NEXT ROW (RS): Work 58 (64, 65, 71, 77) (83, 84, 90, 96) sts, join a second ball of yarn, BO center 8 (8, 14, 14, 14) (14, 20, 20, 20) sts, work to end.
Working both sides at once, BO 3 sts at each neck edge 5 times and, AT THE SAME TIME, when piece measures 5½ (5½, 6, 6, 6) (6½, 6½, 7, 7)" [14 (14, 15, 15, 15) (16.5, 16.5, 18, 18) cm] from end of gusset shaping, ending with a WS row, BO 7 (7, 8, 8, 9) (10, 10, 11, 12) sts at beginning of next 2 (14, 2, 14, 12) (10, 12, 10, 8) rows, then 6 (0, 7, 0, 8) (9, 9, 10, 11) sts at beginning of next 12 (0, 12, 0, 2) (4, 2, 4, 6) rows.
Sew back and front shoulders.

Sleeves
With RS facing, using larger needles, pick up and knit 61 (61, 67, 67, 67) (73, 73, 77, 77) sts along armhole opening.

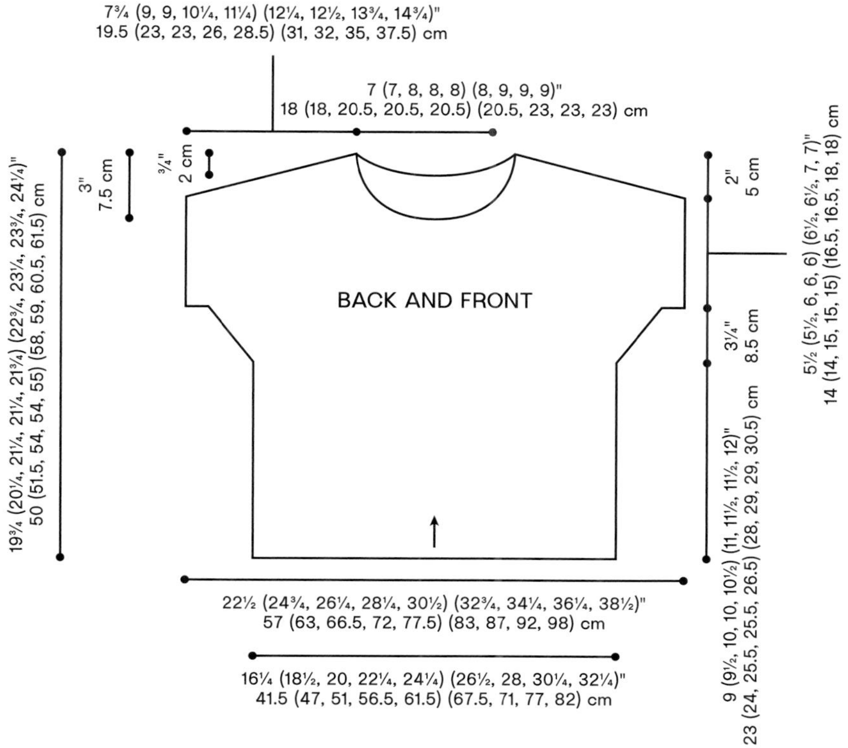
7¾ (9, 9, 10¼, 11¼) (12¼, 12½, 13¾, 14¾)"
19.5 (23, 23, 26, 28.5) (31, 32, 35, 37.5) cm
7 (7, 8, 8, 8) (8, 9, 9, 9)"
18 (18, 20.5, 20.5, 20.5) (20.5, 23, 23, 23) cm
19¾ (20¼, 21¼, 21¼, 21¾) (22¾, 23¼, 23¾, 24¼)"
50 (51.5, 54, 54, 55) (58, 59, 60.5, 61.5) cm
3"
7.5 cm
¾"
2 cm
BACK AND FRONT
2"
5 cm
3¼"
8.5 cm
9 (9½, 10, 10, 10½) (11, 11½, 11½, 12)"
23 (24, 25.5, 25.5, 26.5) (28, 29, 29, 30.5) cm
5½ (5½, 6, 6, 6) (6½, 6½, 7, 7)"
14 (14, 15, 15, 15) (16.5, 16.5, 18, 18) cm
22½ (24¾, 26¼, 28¼, 30½) (32¾, 34¼, 36¼, 38½)"
57 (63, 66.5, 72, 77.5) (83, 87, 92, 98) cm
16¼ (18½, 20, 22¼, 24¼) (26½, 28, 30¼, 32¼)"
41.5 (47, 51, 56.5, 61.5) (67.5, 71, 77, 82) cm

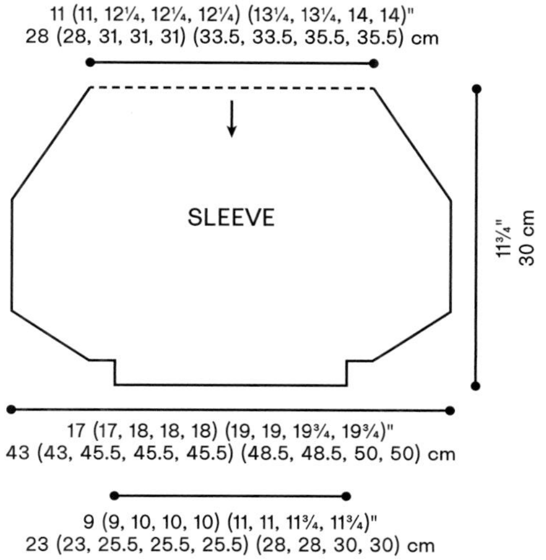
11 (11, 12¼, 12¼, 12¼) (13¼, 13¼, 14, 14)"
28 (28, 31, 31, 31) (33.5, 33.5, 35.5, 35.5) cm
SLEEVE
11¾"
30 cm
17 (17, 18, 18, 18) (19, 19, 19¾, 19¾)"
43 (43, 45.5, 45.5, 45.5) (48.5, 48.5, 50, 50) cm
9 (9, 10, 10, 10) (11, 11, 11¾, 11¾)"
23 (23, 25.5, 25.5, 25.5) (28, 28, 30, 30) cm

NEXT ROW (WS): P14 (14, 14, 14, 14) (14, 14, 16, 16), pm, [p11 (11, 13, 13, 13) (15, 15, 15, 15) sts, pm] 3 times, purl to end.
Knit 1 row, purl 1 row.

SHAPE SLEEVE

INCREASE ROW (RS): [Knit to marker, M1R, sm] twice, [knit to marker, sm, M1L] twice, knit to end—4 sts increased.
Repeat Increase Row every 4 rows 7 more times—93 (93, 99, 99, 99) (105, 105, 109, 109) sts.
Work even until piece measures 9" (23 cm) from pick-up row, ending with a WS row.
DECREASE ROW (RS): [Knit to 2 sts before marker, ssk, sm] twice, [knit to marker, sm, k2tog] twice, knit to end—4 sts decreased.
Repeat Decrease Row every RS row 7 more times—61 (61, 67, 67, 67) (73, 73, 77, 77) sts remain.
Change to smaller needles.
NEXT ROW (RS): *K3 (3, 3, 3, 3) (4, 4, 4, 4), k2tog; repeat from * to last 1 (1, 2, 2, 2) (1, 1, 5, 5) st(s), knit to end—49 (49, 55, 55, 55) (61, 61, 65, 65) sts remain.
Knit 1 row, purl 1 row.
BO all sts.

FINISHING

NECKBAND

With RS facing, using circular needle and beginning at right shoulder, pick up and knit 106 (106, 112, 112, 112) (112, 118, 118, 118) sts evenly around neck opening. Join for working in the rnd; pm for beginning of rnd. Purl 2 rnds. BO all sts purlwise.
Sew side and underarm seams.
Block as desired.

Substitute charts as long as the PSS is 90 and the stitch count is close. There are several related expanding stitches: Smocking Half Step (#65) and Smocking Fancy (#67), both variations of the original stitch used in this sweater, Smocking Grow (#66), as well as an allover version, Smocking (#64). No changes are needed when subbing in those three stitches. A more flexible alternative would be to choose a column that will start at the rib. Your panel can be quite a bit smaller or somewhat wider than the pattern shown with a little math on your part. Since our original pattern stitch has a PSS of 90, it is 90 percent the width of the same number of Stockinette stitches, if you replace a lot of pattern you'll want to reduce the number of stitches changed to Stockinette by about 10 percent. Remember that any change of stitch count will affect the shoulder shaping.

Michelle Sleeveless

A basic shell with an elegant self-finish at the armhole, worked as the armhole is shaped. While sometimes thought of as a fashion item to be worn with palazzo pants at a cocktail party, a sleeveless mock turtleneck is great layered under a cardigan or jacket for day and acts as a temperature regulator for those of us of a certain age. Remember, of course, that the neck ribbing can be extended to make a full turtleneck, or stop at 1" (4 cm) for a crew neckline.

SIZES
To fit bust 30 (34, 38, 42, 46) (50, 54, 58, 62)" [76 (86.5, 96.5, 106.5, 117) (127, 137, 147.5, 157.5) cm]

FINISHED MEASUREMENTS
33 (38½, 40½, 44, 48½) (53, 56½, 61, 65)" [84 (98, 103, 112, 123) (134.5, 143.5, 155, 165) cm] bust

YARN
Blue Sky Fibers Eco-Cashmere [50% recycled cashmere/50% virgin cashmere; 164 yards (150 meters)/50 grams]: 5 (5, 6, 7, 8) (8, 9, 10, 11) hanks Gold Rush

NEEDLES
One pair straight needles, size US 4 (3.5 mm)

One pair straight needles, size US 6 (4 mm)

One 16" (40 cm) long circular needle, size US 4 (3.5 mm)

Change needle size if necessary to obtain correct gauge.

NOTIONS
Stitch markers; removable stitch marker

GAUGE
23 sts and 32 rows = 4" (10 cm) in Blackwork, using larger needles

STITCH PATTERNS
1×1 RIB
(even number of sts; 1-row repeat)

ALL ROWS: *K1, p1; repeat from * to end.

BLACKWORK (#85)
(multiple of 18 sts + 3 (1, 7, 17, 11) (7, 17, 11, 5); 14-row repeat)

ROW 1 (RS): K2 (1, 1, 4, 1) (1, 4, 1, 0), LT 0 (0, 0, 1, 1) (0, 1, 1, 0) time(s), RT 0 (0, 1, 1, 1) (1, 1, 1, 1) time(s), k0 (0, 1, 1, 1) (1, 1, 1, 1), *LT, RT, k4, p1, k4, LT, RT, k1; repeat from * to last 1 (0, 3, 8, 5) (3, 8, 5, 2) st(s), k1 (0, 0, 0, 0) (0, 0, 0, 0), LT 0 (0, 1, 1, 1) (1, 1, 1, 1) time(s), RT 0 (0, 0, 1, 1) (0, 1, 1, 0) time(s), k0 (0, 1, 4, 1) (1, 4, 1, 0).

ROW 2: P1 (0, 3, 8, 5) (3, 8, 5, 2), *p9, k1, p8; repeat from * to last 2 (1, 4, 9, 6) (4, 9, 6, 3) st(s), p2 (1, 4, 9, 6) (4, 9, 6, 3).

ROW 3: K2 (1, 0, 5, 2) (0, 5, 2, 3), LT 0 (0, 1, 1, 1) (1, 1, 1, 0) time(s), k0 (0, 2, 2, 2) (2, 2, 2, 0), *k1, RT, k5, p1, k5, LT, k2; repeat from * to last 1 (0, 3, 8, 5) (3, 8, 5, 2) st(s), k1 (0, 1, 1, 1) (1, 1, 1, 2), RT 0 (0, 1, 1, 1) (1, 1, 1, 0) time(s), k0 (0, 0, 5, 2) (0, 5, 2, 0).

ROW 4: Repeat Row 2.

ROW 5: K1 (0, 1, 6, 3) (1, 6, 3, 0), RT 0 (0, 1, 1, 1) (1, 1, 1, 1) time(s), p1, *RT, k6, p1, k6, LT, p1; repeat from * to last 1 (0, 3, 8, 5) (3, 8, 5, 2) st(s), RT 0 (0, 1, 1, 1) (1, 1, 1, 1) time(s), k0 (0, 1, 6, 3) (1, 6, 3, 0).

ROW 6: P1 (0, 3, 8, 5) (3, 8, 5, 2), *k1, p8; repeat from * to last 2 (1, 4, 9, 6) (4, 9, 6, 3) sts, k1, 1 (0, 3, 8, 5) (3, 8, 5, 2) st(s).

ROW 7: K1 (0, 3, 3, 0) (3, 3, 0, 2), LT 0 (0, 1, 1) (0, 1, 1, 0) time(s), k0 (0, 0, 3, 3) (0, 3, 3, 0), p1, *k6, RT, k1, LT, k6, p1; repeat from * to last 1 (0, 3, 8, 5) (3, 8, 5, 2) st(s), k1 (0, 3, 3, 3) (3, 3, 3, 2), RT 0 (0, 0, 1, 1) (0, 1, 1, 0) time(s), k0 (0, 0, 3, 0) (0, 3, 0, 0).

ROW 8: P1 (0, 3, 8, 5) (3, 8, 5, 2), *k1, p17; repeat from * to last 2 (1, 4, 9, 6) (4, 9, 6, 3) st(s), k1, p1 (0, 3, 8, 5) (3, 8, 5, 2) st(s).

ROW 9: K1 (0, 3, 4, 1) (3, 4, 1, 2), LT 0 (0, 0, 1, 1) (0, 1, 1, 0) time(s), k0 (0, 0, 2, 2) (0, 2, 2, 0), p1, *k5, RT, k3, LT, k5, p1; repeat from * to last 1 (0, 3, 8, 5) (3, 8, 5, 2) st(s), k1 (0, 3, 2, 2) (3, 2, 2, 2), RT 0 (0, 0, 1, 1) (0, 1, 1, 0) time(s), k0 (0, 0, 4, 1) (0, 4, 1, 0).

ROW 10: Repeat Row 6.

ROW 11: K1 (0, 0, 3, 0) (0, 3, 0, 2), RT 0 (0, 0, 1, 1) (0, 1, 1, 0) time(s), LT 0 (0, 1, 1, 1) (1, 1, 1, 0) time(s), k0 (0, 1, 1, 1) (1, 1, 1, 0), p1, *k4, RT, LT, p1, RT, LT, k4, p1; repeat from * to last 1 (0, 3, 8, 5) (3, 8, 5, 2) st(s), k1 (0, 1, 1, 1) (1, 1, 1, 2), RT 0 (0, 1, 1, 1) (1, 1, 1, 0) time(s), LT 0 (0, 0, 1, 1) (0, 1, 1, 0) time(s), k0 (0, 0, 3, 0) (0, 3, 0, 0).

ROW 12: Repeat Row 6.

ROW 13: K1 (0, 1, 6, 3) (1, 6, 3, 0), RT 0 (0, 1, 1, 1) (1, 1, 1, 1) time(s), p1, *k3, RT, k3, p1, k3, LT, k3, p1; repeat from * to last 1 (0, 3, 8, 5) (3, 8, 5, 2) st(s), k1 (0, 0, 0, 0) (0, 0, 0, 0), RT 0 (0, 1, 1, 1) (1, 1, 1, 1) time(s), k0 (0, 1, 6, 3) (1, 6, 3, 0).

ROW 14: Repeat Row 6.

Repeat Rows 1–14 for pattern.

PATTERN NOTES
This top is worked in pieces from the bottom up, then sewn together. Stitches are cast on at the underarms to create the armhole edging.

When decreasing in Blackwork pattern, if there are not enough stitches to work a full twisted st, work the affected stitch in Stockinette stitch instead.

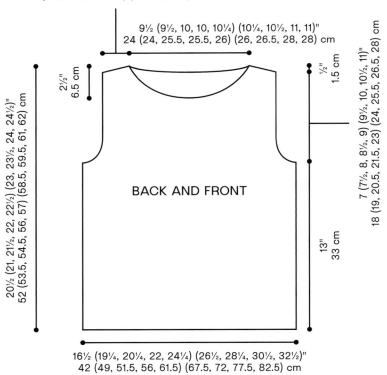

1¾ (1¾, 2½, 2½, 3¼) (3½, 3½, 4¼, 4½)"
4.5 (4.5, 6.5, 6.5, 8.5) (9, 9, 11, 11.5) cm

9½ (9½, 10, 10, 10¼) (10¼, 10½, 11, 11)"
24 (24, 25.5, 25.5, 26) (26, 26.5, 28, 28) cm

2½"
6.5 cm

½"
1.5 cm

7 (7½, 8, 8½, 9) (9½, 10, 10½, 11)"
18 (19, 20.5, 21.5, 23) (24, 25.5, 26.5, 28) cm

20½ (21, 21½, 22, 22½) (23, 23½, 24, 24½)"
52 (53.5, 54.5, 56, 57) (58.5, 59.5, 61, 62) cm

BACK AND FRONT

13"
33 cm

16½ (19¼, 20¼, 22, 24¼) (26½, 28¼, 30½, 32½)"
42 (49, 51.5, 56, 61.5) (67.5, 72, 77.5, 82.5) cm

Back

Using smaller needles and Long-Tail Cast-On (see Special Techniques, page 270), CO 102 (118, 126, 136, 148) (162, 174, 186, 198) sts.

Begin 1×1 Rib; work even until piece measures 1¼" (3 cm) from the beginning, ending with a RS row.

Change to larger needles.

NEXT ROW (WS): *P11 (13, 11, 12, 13) (14, 13, 14, 15), p2tog; repeat from * to last 11 (13, 9, 10, 13) (18, 9, 10, 11) sts, purl to end—95 (111, 117, 127, 139) (153, 163, 175, 187) sts remain.

SET-UP ROW: K1 (edge st; keep in St st), work Blackwork pattern (beginning and ending where indicated for your size if working from chart) to last st, k1 (edge st; keep in St st).

Work even until piece measures 13" (33 cm) from the beginning, ending with a WS row.

SHAPE ARMHOLES

NOTE: After working first armhole shaping row, with RS facing, place removable marker around base of st, 26 (34, 32, 37, 38) (43, 47, 48, 52) sts in from beginning of row (including sts CO for armhole edging) to mark beginning of armhole shaping.

SET-UP ROW 1 (RS): Using Cable CO (see Special Techniques, page 270), CO 6 sts for armhole edging, [k2, p1] twice across CO sts, work to end—101 (117, 123, 133, 145) (159, 169, 181, 193) sts.

SET-UP ROW 2: CO 6 sts for armhole edging, [p2, k4] across CO sts, work to last 7 sts, p1, k4, p2—107 (123, 129, 139, 151) (165, 175, 187, 199) sts.

DECREASE ROW 1 (RS): Slip 2 purlwise wyib, p1, k2, p1, ssk, work to last 8 sts, k2tog, p1, k2, p1, k2—2 sts decreased.

DECREASE ROW 2: Slip 2 purlwise wyif, k4, p2tog, work to last 8 sts, ssp, k4, p2—2 sts decreased.

Repeat the last 2 rows 4 (7, 6, 8, 9) (11, 12, 13, 15) more times—87 (91, 101, 103, 111) (117, 123, 131, 135) sts remain.

Repeat Decrease row 1 once.

NEXT ROW: Slip 2 purlwise wyif, k4, p1, work to last 7 sts, p1, k4, p2.

Repeat the last 2 rows 5 (7, 7, 8, 7) (8, 10, 9, 9) more times—75 (75, 85, 85, 95) (99, 101, 111, 115) sts remain.

Work even until piece measures 7 (7½, 8, 8½, 9) (9½, 10, 10½, 11)" [18 (19, 20, 21.5, 23) (24, 25.5, 26.5, 28) cm] from armhole-shaping marker, ending with a WS row.

SHAPE SHOULDERS AND NECK

NOTE: Shoulder and neck shaping are worked at the same time; please read entire section through before beginning. Place marker either side of center 25 (25, 27, 27, 29) (29, 31, 33, 33) sts.

NEXT ROW (RS): BO 5 (5, 7, 7, 9) (10, 10, 12,

13) sts, work to marker, join a second ball of yarn and BO center sts, work to end. Working both sides once, BO 5 (5, 7, 7, 9) (10, 10, 12, 13) sts at beginning of next 3 rows and AT THE SAME TIME, BO 5 sts at each neck edge 3 times.

Front

Work as for back until armholes measure 5 (5½, 6, 6½, 7) (7½, 8, 8½, 9)" [12.5 (14, 15, 16.5, 18) (19, 20.5, 21.5, 23) cm] from armhole-shaping marker, ending with a WS row—75 (75, 85, 85, 95) (99, 101, 111, 115) sts remain.

SHAPE NECK AND SHOULDERS

NOTE: Shoulder and neck shaping are worked at the same time; please read through entire section before beginning. Place marker at either side of center 21 (21, 23, 23, 25) (25, 27, 29, 29) sts.

NEXT ROW (RS): Work to marker, join a second ball of yarn and BO center sts, work to end—27 (27, 31, 31, 35) (37, 37, 41, 43) sts remain each side.

Working both sides at once, BO 4 sts at each neck edge twice, 3 sts once, then 2 sts once.

Work 1 WS even.

DECREASE ROW (RS): Work to 3 sts before left neck edge, ssk, k1; on right neck edge, k1, k2tog, work to end—1 st decreased each neck edge.

Repeat Decrease Row every RS row 3 more times.

AT THE SAME TIME, when armholes measure 7 (7½, 8, 8½, 9) (9½, 10, 10½, 11)" [18 (19, 20, 21.5, 23) (24, 25.5, 26.5, 28) cm] from armhole shaping marker, ending with a WS row, BO 5 (5, 7, 7, 9) (10, 10, 12, 13) sts at each armhole edge twice.

FINISHING

Sew shoulder seams.
Block as desired.

NECKBAND

With RS facing, using circular needle, beginning at center back neck, pick up and knit 124 (124, 128, 128, 132) (132, 136, 140, 140) sts evenly around neck opening. Join for working in the rnd; pm for beginning of rnd. Work in 1×1 Rib for 3½" (9 cm). BO all sts in pattern.
Sew side seams, sewing CO edge of armhole edging into side seam.

To substitute stitches, look for a (PSS) of 80. Wheat (#86) and Droplets (#87), both also from Chapter 5, would work well, as would Always (#93) from Chapter 6. If you don't mind 5 percent more width front and back, take a look at stitches with a PSS of 85. You'll have to figure the starting and ending points of your chart, using the number of stitches specified for each piece.

BLACKWORK

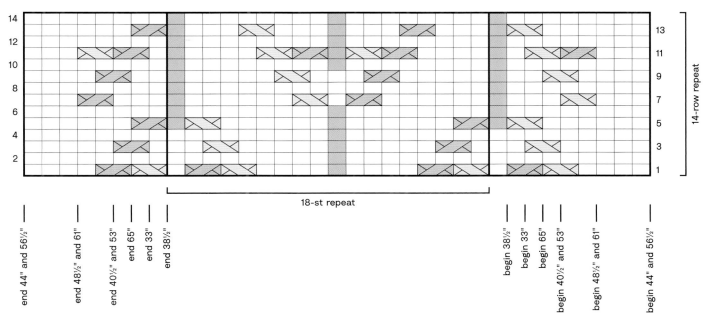

Cropped Cardi

Fitted and cropped to kiss the waistband, this abbreviated cardigan is perfect to highlight a shapely torso while providing warmth. The shorter length and larger gauge make it a quick project, kept interesting with twisted-stitch panels placed to avoid side seam and armhole shaping. The Deco Dragon pattern stitch is mirrored on the fronts and repeated on the back. A shaped stand collar is worked with short rows, while three-quarter-length sleeves are in balance with the cropped body.

SIZES
To fit bust 30 (34, 38, 42, 46) (50, 54, 58, 62)" [76 (86.5, 96.5, 106.5, 117) (127, 137, 147.5, 157.5) cm]

FINISHED MEASUREMENTS
31½ (35½, 39½, 43½, 47½) (50¼, 54¼, 58¼, 62¼)" [80 (90, 100.5, 110.5, 120.5) (127.5, 138, 148, 158) cm] bust, buttoned

YARN
Jill Draper Makes Stuff Valkill [100% Cheviot wool; 252 yards (230 meters)/4 ounces (113 grams)]: 3 (4, 4, 5, 5) (5, 6, 6, 7) skeins Luciferase

NEEDLES
One pair straight needles, size US 6 (4.25 mm)

One pair straight needles, size 8 (5 mm)

Change needle size if necessary to obtain correct gauge.

NOTIONS
Stitch markers; removable stitch markers; five 1" (25 mm) buttons

GAUGES
16 sts and 24 rows = 4" (10 cm) in St st, using larger needles

18 sts and 26 rows = 4" (10 cm) in Deco Dragon Right or Left, using larger needles

STITCH PATTERNS

2×2 RIB
(multiple of 4 sts + 2; 2-row repeat)

ROW 1 (RS): K2, *p2, k2; repeat from * to end.

ROW 2: P2, *k2, p2; repeat from * to end.

Repeat Rows 1 and 2 for pattern.

HALF TWISTED RIB
(odd number of sts; 2-row repeat)

ROW 1 (RS): K1, *k1-tbl, p1; repeat from * to last 2 sts, k1-tbl, k1.

ROW 2: *K1, p1; repeat from * to last st, k1.

Repeat Rows 1 and 2 for pattern.

DECO DRAGON RIGHT (#78)
(multiple of 22 sts + 1; 32-row repeat)

ROW 1 (RS): P1, *[k1-tbl, p1] 4 times, RT, p1, LT 5 times, p1; repeat from * to end.

ROW 2: Knit the knit sts and purl the purl sts as they face you.

ROW 3: P1, *k1-tbl, [p1, k1-tbl] 3 times, RT, k1, p1, k1-tbl, LT 4 times, k1, p1; repeat from * to end.

ROW 4: K1, *p8, k1, p1, k1, p4, k1, [p1, k1] 3 times; repeat from * to end.

ROW 5: P1, *[k1-tbl, p1] 3 times, RT twice, p1, k1-tbl, p1, LT 4 times, p1; repeat from * to end.

ROW 6: Repeat Row 2.

ROW 7: P1, *k1-tbl, [p1, k1-tbl] twice, RT twice, k1, [p1, k1-tbl] twice, LT 3 times, k1, p1; repeat from * to end.

ROW 8: K1, *p6, k1, [p1, k1] twice, p6, k1, [p1, k1] twice; repeat from * to end.

ROW 9: P1, *[k1-tbl, p1] twice, RT 3 times, p1, [k1-tbl, p1] twice, LT 3 times, p1; repeat from * to end.

ROW 10: Repeat Row 2.

ROW 11: P1, *k1-tbl, p1, k1-tbl, RT 3 times, k1, [p1, k1-tbl] 3 times, LT twice, k1, p1; repeat from * to end.

ROW 12: K1, *p4, k1, [p1, k1] 3 times, p8, k1, p1, k1; repeat from * to end.

ROW 13: P1, *k1-tbl, p1, RT 4 times, p1, [k1-tbl, p1] 3 times, LT twice, p1; repeat from * to end.

ROW 14: Repeat Row 2.

ROW 15: P1, *k1-tbl, RT 4 times, k1, [p1, k1-tbl] 4 times, LT, k1, p1; repeat from * to end.

ROW 16: K1, *p2, k1, [p1, k1] 4 times, p10, k1; repeat from * to end.

ROW 17: P1, *LT 5 times, p1, [k1-tbl, p1] 4 times, RT, p1; repeat from * to end.

ROW 18: Repeat Row 2.

ROW 19: P1, *k1-tbl, LT 4 times, k1, [p1, k1-tbl] 4 times, RT, k1, p1; repeat from * to end.

ROW 20: K1, *p4, k1, [p1, k1] 3 times, p8, k1, p1, k1; repeat from * to end.

ROW 21: P1, *k1-tbl, p1, LT 4 times, p1, [k1-tbl, p1] 3 times, RT twice, p1; repeat from * to end.

ROW 22: Repeat Row 2.

ROW 23: P1, *k1-tbl, p1, k1-tbl, LT 3 times, k1, [p1, k1-tbl] 3 times, RT twice, k1, p1; repeat from * to end.

ROW 24: K1, *p6, k1, [p1, k1] twice, p6, k1, [p1, k1] twice; repeat from * to end.

ROW 25: P1, *[k1-tbl, p1] twice, LT 3 times, p1, [k1-tbl, p1] twice, RT 3 times, p1; repeat from * to end.

ROW 26: Repeat Row 2.

ROW 27: P1, *k1-tbl, [p1, k1-tbl] twice, LT twice, k1, [p1, k1-tbl] twice, RT 3 times, k1, p1; repeat from * to end.

ROW 28: K1, *p8, k1, p1, k1, p4, k1, [p1, k1] 3 times; repeat from * to end.

ROW 29: P1, *[k1-tbl, p1] 3 times, LT, p1, k1-tbl, p1, RT 4 times, p1; repeat from * to end.

ROW 30: Repeat Row 2.

ROW 31: P1, *k1-tbl, [p1, k1-tbl] 3 times, LT, k1, p1, k1-tbl, RT 4 times, k1, p1; repeat from * to end.

ROW 32: K1, *p10, k1, p2, k1, [p1, k1] 4 times; repeat from * to end.

Repeat Rows 1–32 for pattern.

DECO DRAGON LEFT

(multiple of 22 sts + 1; 32-row repeat)

ROW 1 (RS): P1, *RT 5 times, p1, LT, p1, [k1-tbl, p1] 4 times; repeat from * to end.

ROW 2: Knit the knit sts and purl the purl sts as they face you.

ROW 3: P1, *k1, RT 4 times, k1-tbl, p1, k1, LT, [k1-tbl, p1] 4 times; repeat from * to end.

ROW 4: K1, *[p1, k1] 3 times, p4, k1, p1, k1, p8, k1; repeat from * to end.

ROW 5: P1, *RT 4 times, p1, k1-tbl, p1, LT twice, p1, [k1-tbl, p1] 3 times; repeat from * to end.

ROW 6: Repeat Row 2.

ROW 7: P1, *k1, RT 3 times, [k1-tbl, p1] twice, k1, LT twice, [k1-tbl, p1] 3 times; repeat from * to end.

ROW 8: K1, *[p1, k1] twice, p6, k1, [p1, k1] twice, p6, k1; repeat from * to end.

ROW 9: P1, *RT 3 times, p1, [k1-tbl, p1] twice, LT 3 times, p1, [k1-tbl, p1] twice; repeat from * to end.

ROW 10: Repeat Row 2.

ROW 11: P1, *k1, RT twice, [k1-tbl, p1] 3 times, k1, LT 3 times, [k1-tbl, p1] twice; repeat from * to end.

ROW 12: K1, *p1, k1, p8, k1, [p1, k1] 3 times, p4, k1; repeat from * to end.

ROW 13: P1, *RT twice, p1, [k1-tbl, p1] 3 times, LT 4 times, p1, k1-tbl, p1; repeat from * to end.

ROW 14: Repeat Row 2.

ROW 15: P1, *k1, RT, [k1-tbl, p1] 4 times, k1, LT 4 times, k1-tbl, p1; repeat from * to end.

DECO DRAGON RIGHT

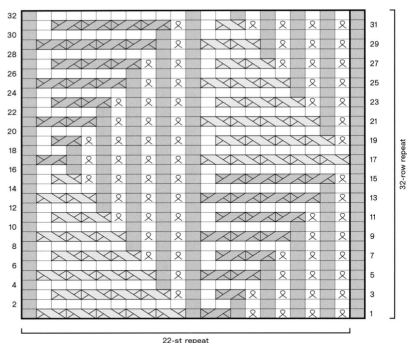

22-st repeat

32-row repeat

DECO DRAGON LEFT

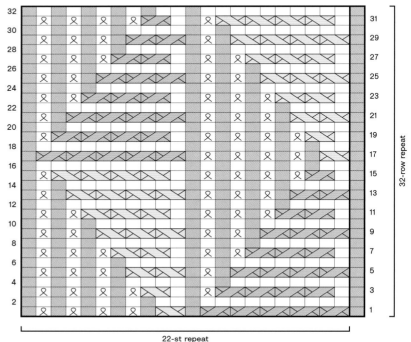

22-st repeat

32-row repeat

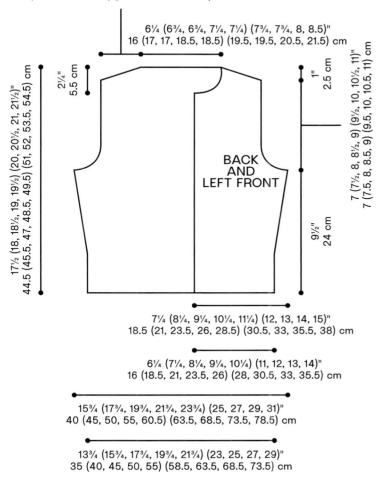

3 (3¼, 3¾, 4, 4½) (4½, 5, 5, 5¼)"
7.5 (8.5, 9.5, 10, 11.5) (11.5, 12.5, 12.5, 13.5) cm

6¼ (6¾, 6¾, 7¼, 7¼) (7¾, 7¾, 8, 8.5)"
16 (17, 17, 18.5, 18.5) (19.5, 19.5, 20.5, 21.5) cm

2¼"
5.5 cm

1"
2.5 cm

17½ (18, 18½, 19, 19½) (20, 20½, 21, 21½)"
44.5 (45.5, 47, 48.5, 49.5) (51, 52, 53.5, 54.5) cm

7 (7½, 8, 8½, 9) (9½, 10, 10½, 11)"
7 (7.5, 8, 8.5, 9) (9.5, 10, 10.5, 11) cm

BACK
AND
LEFT FRONT

9½"
24 cm

7¼ (8¼, 9¼, 10¼, 11¼) (12, 13, 14, 15)"
18.5 (21, 23.5, 26, 28.5) (30.5, 33, 35.5, 38) cm

6¼ (7¼, 8¼, 9¼, 10¼) (11, 12, 13, 14)"
16 (18.5, 21, 23.5, 26) (28, 30.5, 33, 35.5) cm

15¾ (17¾, 19¾, 21¾, 23¾) (25, 27, 29, 31)"
40 (45, 50, 55, 60.5) (63.5, 68.5, 73.5, 78.5) cm

13¾ (15¾, 17¾, 19¾, 21¾) (23, 25, 27, 29)"
35 (40, 45, 50, 55) (58.5, 63.5, 68.5, 73.5) cm

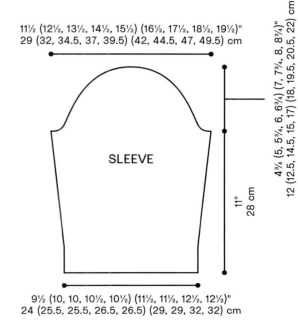

11½ (12½, 13½, 14½, 15½) (16½, 17½, 18½, 19½)"
29 (32, 34.5, 37, 39.5) (42, 44.5, 47, 49.5) cm

SLEEVE

4¾ (5, 5¾, 6, 6¾) (7, 7¾, 8, 8¾)"
12 (12.5, 14.5, 15, 17) (18, 19.5, 20.5, 22) cm

11"
28 cm

9½ (10, 10, 10½, 10½) (11½, 11½, 12½, 12½)"
24 (25.5, 25.5, 26.5, 26.5) (29, 29, 32, 32) cm

ROW 16: K1, *p10, k1, [p1, k1-tbl] 4 times, p2, k1; repeat from * to end.

ROW 17: P1, *LT, p1, [k1, p1] 4 times, RT 5 times, p1; repeat from * to end.

ROW 18: Repeat Row 2.

ROW 19: P1, *k1, LT, [k-tbl1, p1] 4 times, k1, RT 4 times, k1-tbl, p1; repeat from * to end.

ROW 20: K1, *p1, k1, p8, k1, [p1, k1] 3 times, p4, k1; repeat from * to end.

ROW 21: P1, *LT twice, p1, [k1-tbl, p1] 3 times, RT 4 times, p1, k1-tbl, p1; repeat from * to end.

ROW 22: Repeat Row 2.

ROW 23: P1, *k1, LT twice, [k1-tbl, p1] 3 times, k1, RT 3 times, [k1-tbl, p1] twice.

ROW 24: K1, *[p1, k1] twice, p6, k1, [p1, k1] twice, p6, k1; repeat from * to end.

ROW 25: P1, *LT 3 times, p1, [k1-tbl, p1] twice, RT 3 times, p1, [k1-tbl, p1] twice; repeat from * to end.

ROW 26: Repeat Row 2.

ROW 27: P1, *k1, LT 3 times, [k1-tbl, p1] twice, k1, RT twice, [k1-tbl, p1] 3 times; repeat from * to end.

ROW 28: K1, *[p1, k1] 3 times, p4, k1, p1, k1, p8, k1; repeat from * to end.

ROW 29: P1, *LT 4 times, p1, k1-tbl, p1, RT twice, p1, [k1-tbl, p1] 3 times; repeat from * to end.

ROW 30: Repeat Row 2.

ROW 31: P1, *k1, LT 4 times, k1-tbl, p1, k1, RT, [k1-tbl, p1] 4 times; repeat from * to end.

ROW 32: K1, [p1, k1] 4 times, p2, k1, p10, k1; repeat from * to end.

Repeat Rows 1–32 for pattern.

PATTERN NOTES

This cardigan is worked from the bottom up in pieces, then sewn together. When working neck shaping, if there are not enough stitches to work a full twisted stitch, work the affected stitch in Stockinette stitch instead.

Back

Using smaller needles and Long-Tail Cast-On (see Special Techniques, page 270), CO 58 (66, 74, 82, 90) (102, 110, 118, 126) sts.

Begin 2×2 Rib (beginning with Row 2); work even until piece measures 2" (5 cm) from the beginning, ending with a RS row. Change to larger needles.

Purl 1 row, increasing 2 (2, 2, 2, 2) (0, 0, 0, 0) sts evenly across—60 (68, 76, 84, 92) (102, 110, 118, 126) sts.

SET-UP ROW 1 (RS): K5 (9, 13, 17, 21) (4, 8, 12, 16), pm, work Deco Dragon Right over 23 (23, 23, 23, 23) (45, 45, 45, 45) sts, pm, k4, pm, work Deco Dragon Left over 23 (23, 23, 23, 23) (45, 45, 45, 45) sts, pm, knit to end.

SET-UP ROW 2: Purl to marker, sm, work Deco Dragon Left to marker, sm, p4, work Deco Dragon Right to marker, sm, purl to end.

Work 6 rows even.

SHAPE BODY

INCREASE ROW (RS): K2, M1L, work to last 2 sts, M1R—2 sts increased.

Repeat Increase Row every 8 rows 3 more times—68 (76, 84, 92, 100) (110, 118, 126, 134) sts.

Work even until piece measures 9½" (24 cm) from the beginning, ending with a WS row.

SHAPE ARMHOLES

BO 4 sts at beginning of next 0 (0, 0, 0, 0) (2, 2, 2, 2) rows, 3 sts at beginning of next 2 (2, 4, 4, 4) (4, 4, 4, 4) rows, then 2 sts at beginning of next 2 (2, 2, 2, 4) (2, 4, 6, 6) rows—58 (66, 68, 76, 80) (86, 90, 94, 102) sts remain.

DECREASE ROW (RS): K1, k2tog, work to last 3 sts, ssk, k1—2 sts decreased.

Repeat Decrease Row every RS row 1 (3, 2, 4, 4) (5, 5, 5, 7) more time(s)—54 (58, 62, 66, 70) (74, 78, 82, 86) sts remain.

Work even until armholes measure 7 (7½, 8, 8½, 9) (9½, 10, 10½, 11)" [18 (19, 20, 21.5, 23) (24, 25, 26.5, 28) cm], ending with a WS row.

SHAPE SHOULDERS

BO 5 (5, 6, 6, 7) (7, 8, 8, 8) sts at beginning of next 2 (4, 2, 4, 2) (4, 2, 4, 6) rows, then 4 (4, 5, 5, 6) (6, 7, 7, 0) sts at beginning of next 4 (2, 4, 2, 4) (2, 4, 2, 0) rows.

BO remaining 28 (30, 30, 32, 32) (34, 34, 36, 38) sts.

Left Front

Using smaller needles and Long-Tail Cast-On (see Special Techniques, page 270), CO 26 (30, 34, 38, 42) (46, 50, 54, 58) sts.

Begin 2×2 Rib (beginning with Row 2); work even for 2" (5 cm), ending with a RS row.

Change to larger needles.

Purl 1 row, increasing 2 (2, 2, 2, 2) (3, 3, 3, 3) sts evenly across—28 (32, 36, 40, 44) (49, 53, 57, 61) sts.

SET-UP ROW 1 (RS): K5 (9, 13, 17, 21) (4, 8, 12, 16), pm, work Deco Dragon Right over 23 (23, 23, 23, 23) (45, 45, 45, 45) sts.

SET-UP ROW 2: Work Deco Dragon Right to marker, sm, purl to end.

Work 6 rows even.

SHAPE BODY

INCREASE ROW (RS): K2, M1L, work to end—1 st increased.

Repeat Increase row every 8 rows 3 more times—32 (36, 40, 44, 48) (53, 57, 61, 65) sts.

Work even until piece measures 9½" (24 cm) from the beginning, ending with a WS row.

SHAPE ARMHOLE

BO 4 sts at beginning of next 0 (0, 0, 0, 0) (1, 1, 1, 1) RS row(s), 3 sts at beginning of next 1 (1, 2, 2, 2) (2, 2, 2, 2) RS row(s), then 2 sts at beginning of next 1 (1, 1, 1, 2) (1, 2, 3, 3) RS row(s)—27 (31, 32, 36, 38) (41, 43, 45, 49) sts remain.

DECREASE ROW (RS): K1, k2tog, work to end—1 st decreased.

Repeat Decrease row every RS row 1 (3, 2, 4, 4) (5, 5, 5, 7) more time(s)—25 (27, 29, 31, 33) (35, 37, 39, 41) sts remain.

Work even until armhole measures 5¾ (6¼, 6¾, 7¼, 7¾) (8¼, 8¾, 9¼, 9¾)" [14.5 (16, 17, 18.5, 19.5) (21, 22, 23.5, 25) cm, ending with a RS row.

SHAPE NECK AND SHOULDER

NOTE: Neck and shoulder shaping are worked at the same time, beginning with neck shaping; please read entire section through before beginning.

BO 0 (4, 4, 4, 4) (5, 5, 6, 7) sts at neck edge once, 3 sts 2 (1, 1, 2, 2) (2, 2, 2, 2) time(s), 2 sts 2 (2, 2, 1, 1) (1, 1, 1, 1) time(s), then 1 st twice. AT THE SAME TIME, when armhole measures 7 (7¼, 8, 8¼, 9) (9¼, 10, 10¼, 11)" [18 (19, 20.5, 21.5, 23) (24, 25.5, 26.5, 28) cm], ending with a WS row, BO 5 (5, 6, 6, 7) (7, 8, 8, 8) sts at armhole edge once, 4 (5, 5, 6, 6) (7, 7, 8, 8) sts once, then 4 (4, 5, 5, 6) (6, 7, 7, 8) sts once.

Right Front

Using smaller needles and Long-Tail Cast-On, CO 26 (30, 34, 38, 42) (46, 50, 54, 58) sts.

Begin 2×2 Rib (beginning with Row 2); work even until piece measures 2" (5 cm) from the beginning, ending with a RS row. Change to larger needles.

Purl 1 row, increasing 2 (2, 2, 2, 2) (3, 3, 3, 3) sts evenly across—28 (32, 36, 40, 44) (49, 53, 57, 61) sts.

SET-UP ROW 1 (RS): Work Deco Dragon Left over 23 (23, 23, 23, 23) (45, 45, 45, 45) sts, pm, k5 (9, 13, 17, 21) (4, 8, 12, 16).

SET-UP ROW 2: Purl to marker, sm, work Deco Dragon Left to end.

Work 6 rows even.

SHAPE BODY

INCREASE ROW (RS): Work to last 2 sts, M1R, k2—1 st increased.

Repeat Increase Row every 8 rows 3 more times—32 (36, 40, 44, 48) (53, 57, 61, 65) sts.

Work even until piece measures 9½" (5 cm) from the beginning, ending with a RS row.

SHAPE ARMHOLE

BO 4 sts at beginning of next 0 (0, 0, 0, 0) (1, 1, 1, 1) WS row(s), 3 sts at beginning of next 1 (1, 2, 2, 2) (2, 2, 2, 2) WS row(s), then 2 sts at beginning of next 1 (1, 1, 1, 2) (1, 2, 3, 3) WS row(s)—27 (31, 32, 36, 38) (41, 43, 45, 49) sts remain.

DECREASE ROW (RS): K1, k2tog, work to end—1 st decreased.

Repeat Decrease Row every WS row 1 (3, 2, 4, 4) (5, 5, 5, 7) more time(s)—25 (27, 29, 31, 33) (35, 37, 39, 41) sts remain. Work even until armhole measures 5¾ (6¼, 6¾, 7¼, 7¾) (8¼, 8¾, 9¼, 9¾)" [14.5 (16, 17, 18.5, 19.5) (21, 22, 23.5, 25) cm, ending with a WS row.

SHAPE NECK AND SHOULDER

NOTE: Neck and shoulder shaping are worked at the same time, beginning with neck shaping; please read entire section through before beginning.
BO 0 (4, 4, 4, 4) (5, 5, 6, 7) sts at neck edge once, 3 sts 2 (1, 1, 2, 2) (2, 2, 2, 2) time(s), 2 sts 2 (2, 2, 1, 1) (1, 1, 1, 1) RS time(s), then 1 st twice. AT THE SAME TIME, when armhole measures 7 (7¼, 8, 8¼, 9) (9¼, 10, 10¼, 11)" [18 (19, 20.5, 21.5, 23) (24, 25.5, 26.5, 28) cm], ending with a RS row, BO 5 (5, 6, 6, 7) (7, 8, 8, 8) sts at armhole edge once, 4 (5, 5, 6, 6) (7, 7, 8, 8) sts once, then 4 (4, 5, 5, 6) (6, 7, 7, 8) sts once.

Sleeves

Using smaller needles and Long-Tail Cast-On, CO 38 (38, 38, 42, 42) (42, 42, 46, 46) sts.
Begin 2×2 Rib (beginning with Row 2); work even until piece measures 2" (5 cm) from the beginning, ending with a RS row. Change to larger needles.
Purl 1 row, increasing 0 (2, 2, 0, 0) (4, 4, 4, 4) stitches evenly across—38 (40, 40, 42, 42) (46, 46, 50, 50) sts.
Work 10 (6, 6, 4, 6) (6, 2, 2, 4) rows even.

SHAPE SLEEVE

INCREASE ROW (RS): K2, M1L, work to last 2 sts, M1R, k2—2 sts increased.
Repeat Increase Row every 12 (10, 8, 6, 6) (6, 4, 4, 4) rows 3 (4, 2, 7, 2) (2, 11, 11, 8) times, then every 0 (0, 6, 0, 4) (4, 0, 2, 2) rows 0 (0, 4, 0, 7) (7, 0, 0, 5) times—46 (50, 54, 58, 62) (66, 70, 74, 78) sts.
Work even until piece measures 11" (28 cm) from the beginning, ending with a WS row.

SHAPE CAP

BO 3 sts at beginning of next 2 rows, then 2 sts at beginning of next 2 rows—36 (40, 44, 48, 52) (56, 60, 64, 68) sts remain.

DECREASE ROW (RS): K1, k2tog, work to last 3 sts, ssk, k1—2 sts decreased.
Repeat Decrease Row every RS row 1 (2, 2, 4, 5) (8, 8, 9, 8) more time(s), every 4 rows 4 (3, 3, 2, 2) (2, 2, 2, 2) times, then every RS row 0 (2, 4, 5, 6) (4, 6, 6, 9) times—24 (24, 24, 24, 24) (26, 26, 28, 28) sts remain.
Work 1 row even.
BO 2 sts at beginning of next 2 rows, then 3 sts at beginning of next 2 rows. BO remaining 14 (14, 14, 14, 14) (16, 16, 18, 18) sts.

FINISHING

Block as desired.
Sew shoulder seams.

BUTTON BAND

Using smaller needles, pick up and knit 63 (65, 67, 69, 71) (73, 75, 77, 79) sts along left front edge, picking up 1 full st in from edge.
Begin Half Twisted Rib, beginning with a WS row; work even for 1¼" (3 cm). BO all sts in pattern. Place removable markers for buttons in the center of the band; the first approximately 1" (2.5 cm) up from CO edge, the last just below top edge of band, and the remaining 3 evenly spaced between.

BUTTONHOLE BAND

Using smaller needles, pick up and knit 63 (65, 67, 69, 71) (73, 75, 77, 79) sts along right front edge, picking up 1 full st in from edge.
Begin Half Twisted Rib, beginning with a WS row; work 3 rows even.
BUTTONHOLE ROW (RS): Work to first marker, [yo, p2tog, work to next marker] 4 times, yo, p2tog, work to end.
Work even until band measures same as for button band. BO all sts in pattern.

COLLAR

With RS facing, using smaller needles and beginning at BO edge of button band, pick up and knit 73 (75, 75, 77, 77) (79, 79, 81, 83) sts along neck edge, ending at BO edge of buttonhole band.

SHAPE COLLAR

NOTE: Collar is shaped using German Short Rows (see Special Techniques, page 270).
SHORT ROW 1 (WS): Work Half Twisted Rib, beginning with a WS row, to last 2 sts, turn.
SHORT ROW 2: DS, work to last 2 sts, turn.
SHORT ROW 3: DS, work to 1 st before DS from previous WS row, turn.
SHORT ROW 4: DS, work to 1 st before DS from previous RS row, turn.
SHORT ROWS 5–8: Repeat Short Rows 3 and 4 twice.
SHORT ROW 9: Work in pattern to end, closing each DS as you come to it.
SHORT ROW 10: Work to end, closing each remaining DS as you come to it.
BO all sts in pattern.
Sew in sleeves. Sew side and sleeve seams. Sew on buttons to correspond to buttonholes.

Look for columns of about twenty-three stitches or an allover pattern that fits in twenty-four stitches. The PSS of Deco Dragon is 80, but stitches with a PSS of 85 will work fine. Wheat (#86) has a PSS of 80 and can be worked over 21 stitches; add one reverse Stockinette stitch to each end for a perfect substitution. Plaid Medium (#16), with a PSS of 85, is close enough. One repeat plus one edge st is worked over 19 stitches. Add two reverse Stockinette stitches at each end to make the panel 23, matching the original.

Topper

An expanding Stockinette stitch center sets the stitch panels and outer panels on a tilt. More of a tabard than a true pullover, the underarm seams are sewn together only at the ribbing, leaving the sides open. Self-finished i-cord edges worked as you knit, the lack of neck and shoulder shaping, and knitting the shoulders together rather than sewing them means once those tiny seams in the ribbing are done, you are done.

SIZES
To fit bust 30 (34, 38, 42, 46) (50, 54, 58, 62)" [76 (86.5, 96.5, 106.5, 117) (127, 137, 147.5, 157.5) cm]

FINISHED MEASUREMENTS
31 (34½, 38½, 43, 47) (50½, 54½, 59, 63)" [78.5 (87.5, 98, 109, 119.5) (128.5, 138.5, 150, 160) cm] waist

YARN
Nature's Luxury On Stage [50% merino wool/30% mulberry silk/20% baby camel; 328 yards (300 meters)/100 grams]: 2 (3, 3, 3, 4) (4, 4, 5, 5) skeins Color II Volo

NEEDLES
One 24" (60 cm) long or longer circular needle, size US 3 (3.25 mm)

One spare needle in any style, size US 3 (3.25 mm), for 3-Needle Bind-Off

Change needle size if necessary to obtain correct gauge.

NOTIONS
Stitch markers

GAUGE
26 sts and 38 rows = 4" (10 cm) in St st

STITCH PATTERNS
2×2 RIB
(multiple of 4 sts + 2; 2-row repeat)
ROW 1 (RS): K2, *p2, k2; repeat from * to end.
ROW 2: P2, *k2, p2; repeat from * to end.
Repeat Rows 1 and 2 for pattern.

DAMASK
(panel of 19 sts; 24-row repeat)
ROW 1 (RS): K1-tbl, p6, k5, p6, k1-tbl.
ROWS 2, 4, AND 6: P1-tbl, k1, p15, k1, p1-tbl.
ROW 3: K1-tbl, p1, LT, k2, LT, k3, RT, k2, RT, p1, k1-tbl.
ROW 5: K1-tbl, p1, k1, LT, k2, LT, k1, RT, k2, RT, k1, p1, k1-tbl.
ROW 7: K1-tbl, p1, k2, LT, k2, p1, k1-tbl, p1, k2, RT, k2, p1, k1-tbl.
ROWS 8, 10, 12, 14, 16, AND 18: P1-tbl, p7, k1, p1-tbl, k1, p7, p1-tbl.
ROW 9: K1-tbl, LT, k2, LT, k1, p1, k1-tbl, p1, k1, RT, k2, RT, k1-tbl.
ROW 11: K1-tbl, k1, LT, k2, LT, p1, k1-tbl, p1, RT, k2, RT, k1, k1-tbl.
ROW 13: K1-tbl, k2, p6, k1-tbl, p6, k2, k1-tbl.
ROW 15: K1-tbl, k1, RT, k2, RT, p1, k1-tbl, p1, LT, k2, LT, k1, k1-tbl.
ROW 17: K1-tbl, RT, k2, RT, k1, p1, k1-tbl, p1, k1, LT, k2, LT, k1-tbl.
ROW 19: K1-tbl, p1, k2, RT, k2, p1, k1-tbl, p1, k2, LT, k2, p1, k1-tbl.
ROW 20: P1-tbl, k1, p7, p1-tbl, p7, k1, p1-tbl.
ROW 21: K1-tbl, p1, k1, RT, k2, RT, k1, LT, k2, LT, k1, p1, k1-tbl.
ROW 22: P1-tbl, k1, p15, k1, p1-tbl.
ROW 23: K1-tbl, p1, RT, k2, RT, k3, LT, k2, LT, p1, k1-tbl.
ROW 24: Repeat Row 22.
Repeat Rows 1–24 for pattern.

PATTERN NOTES
This topper is worked from the bottom up in two identical pieces, which are joined at the shoulders using the 3-Needle Bind-Off. The sides are sewn along the ribbing only, leaving the remainder of the sides open.
The piece is worked back and forth in rows. The circular needle is used to accommodate the large number of stitches; do not join.

Back
Using Long-Tail Cast-On (see Special Techniques, page 270), CO 106 (118, 130, 146, 158) (170, 182, 198, 210) sts.
Begin 2×2 Rib (beginning with Row 2); work even until piece measures 2" (5 cm) from the beginning, ending with a RS row. Purl 1 row.
SET-UP ROW 1 (RS): Slip 2 purlwise wyib, p1, k14 (19, 25, 31, 36) (39, 43, 49, 53), p2, pm, work Damask over 19 sts, pm, p2, k2, pm, k22 (24, 24, 28, 30) (36, 40, 44, 48), pm, k2, p2, pm, work Damask over 19 sts, pm, p2, k14 (19, 25, 31, 36) (39, 43, 49, 53), p1, k2.
SET-UP ROW 2: Slip 2 purlwise wyif, k3, purl to 4 sts before marker, k4, sm, work to marker, sm, k4, sm, purl to marker, sm, k4, sm, work to marker, sm, k4, purl to

last 5 sts, k3, p2.
Work 4 rows even.

SHAPE SIDES

INCREASE ROW (RS): [Work to marker, sm] 3 times, k2, M1L, knit to 2 sts before marker, M1R, k2, sm, work to end—2 sts increased.

*Repeat Increase Row every 6 rows once, then every 4 rows once—4 sts increased.

Repeat from * 11 more times—156 (168, 180, 196, 208) (220, 232, 248, 260) sts.
Work even until piece measures 15½ (16, 16, 17, 17) (17½, 17½, 18, 18)" [39.5 (40.5, 40.5, 43, 43) (44.5, 44.5, 45.5, 45.5) cm] from the beginning, ending with a RS row. Cut yarn and transfer sts to spare circular needle; set aside.

Front

Work as for back, leaving sts on the needle; do not cut yarn.

FINISHING

With WSs of front and back together (seam will be on the RS) and with back facing you and yarn attached to front, join right shoulders together from armhole edge to first marker using 3-Needle Bind-Off (see Special Techniques, page 270); using standard BO, BO sts purlwise across front neck to next marker (removing marker to BO last neck st). Cut yarn and transfer last st from right needle back to left needle. With WS facing, rejoin yarn to beginning of back neck; using standard BO, BO sts knitwise to marker (removing marker to BO last neck st); transfer last st from right needle back to left needle. Using 3-Needle Bind-Off, join left shoulders together to end.
Sew side seams from CO edge to top of ribbing, leaving the remainder of the armholes open.
Block as desired.

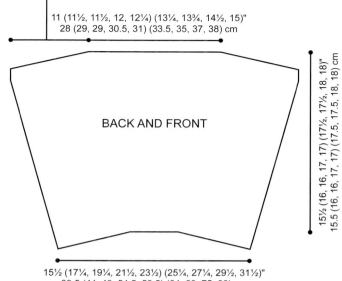

6 (6¾, 7¾, 8¾, 9½) (10, 10½, 11½, 12)"
15 (17, 19.5, 22, 24) (25.5, 26.5, 29, 30.5) cm

11 (11½, 11½, 12, 12¼) (13¼, 13¾, 14½, 15)"
28 (29, 29, 30.5, 31) (33.5, 35, 37, 38) cm

BACK AND FRONT

15½ (16, 16, 17, 17) (17½, 17½, 18, 18)"
15.5 (16, 16, 17, 17) (17.5, 18, 18) cm

15½ (17¼, 19¼, 21½, 23½) (25¼, 27¼, 29½, 31½)"
39.5 (44, 49, 54.5, 59.5) (64, 69, 75, 80) cm

DAMASK

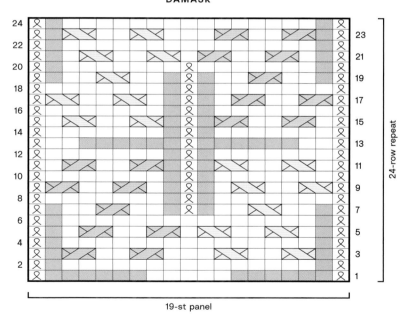

19-st panel

24-row repeat

The number of stitches involved in the stitch panels is so small, for this small gauge, that you can ignore PSS without changing the effect or size of your finished piece a discernible amount. To keep the proportions similar to the original, look for a panel, or an allover stitch that can be worked as a panel, of about 18–21 stitches, like Cherries (#91) or Eyelet Zigzag (#102). Remember to adjust the number of stitches above the ribbing if your stitch count changes.

Hat & Mitts

Sharing the same abstract X and O motif, the fitted cap is knit in the round and the fingerless mitts are knit flat. I felt each was the best technique for its project. The hat has seven repeats of the chart, each tapering to form a head-hugging dome, while the mitts utilize the chart twice, filled in with a bit of ribbing. Keeping it easy, the thumb hole is simply a gap in the seam left unsewn.

FINISHED MEASUREMENTS

HAT: 19½" (49.5 cm) circumference

MITTS: 7¾" (19.5 cm) hand circumference

YARN

Neighborhood Fiber Co. Studio DK [100% superwash merino; 275 yards (251.5 meters)/4 ounces (114 grams)]: 2 hanks Hollins Market

NEEDLES

HAT: Needle(s) in preferred style for small circumference knitting in the rnd, size US 2 (2.75 mm)

Needle(s) in preferred style for small circumference knitting in the rnd, size US 4 (3.5 mm)

Change needle size if necessary to obtain correct gauge.

MITTS: One pair straight needles, size US 2 (2.75 mm)

One pair straight needles, size US 4 (3.5 mm)

Change needle size if necessary to obtain correct gauge.

NOTIONS

Stitch markers

GAUGES

HAT: 26 sts and 36 rows = 4" (10 cm) in Hugs & Kisses, using larger needle(s)

One 18-st repeat of Hugs & Kisses = 2¾" (7 cm) wide, using larger needle(s)

MITTS: 23 sts and 34 rows = 4" (10 cm) in St st, using larger needle(s)

One 19-st panel of Hugs & Kisses = 3⅛" (8 cm) wide, using larger needle(s)

49 rows of Hugs & Kisses for Mitts = 5¼" (13.5 cm) long, using larger needle(s)

STITCH PATTERNS

1×1 RIB

(even number of sts; 1-row/rnd repeat)

ALL ROWS/RNDS: *K1, p1; repeat from * to end.

HUGS & KISSES FOR HAT

(multiple of 18 sts, decreases to multiple of 1 st; 59 rnds)

RND 1: *P3, k3, RT, p1, LT, p3, k4; repeat from * to end.

RND 2, 4, 6, 8, 10, 12, AND 14: *P3, k11, p3; repeat from * to end.

RND 3: *P3, k2, RT, k1, p1, k1, LT, k2, p4; repeat from * to end.

RND 5: *P3, k1, RT, k2, p1, k2, LT, k1, p4; repeat from * to end.

RND 7: *P3, RT, k3, p1, k3, LT, p4; repeat from * to end.

RND 9: *P4, k4, p1, k4, p5; repeat from * to end.

RND 11: *P3, LT, k3, p1, k3, RT, p4; repeat from * to end.

RND 13: *P3, k1, LT, k2, p1, k2, RT, k1, p4; repeat from * to end.

RND 15: *P3, k2, LT, k1, p1, k1, RT, k2, p4; repeat from * to end.

RNDS 16, 18, 20, 22, 24, 26, 28, 30, 32, AND 34: *K17, p1; repeat from * to end.

RND 17: *LT twice, k2, LT, p1, KRT, k2, RT twice, p1; repeat from * to end.

RND 19: *K1, LT twice, k3, p1, k3, RT twice, k1, p1; repeat from * to end.

RND 21: *K2, LT twice, k2, p1, k2, RT twice, k2, p1; repeat from * to end.

RND 23: *K3, LT twice, k1, p1, k1, RT twice, k3, p1; repeat from * to end.

RND 25: *K4, p9, k4, p1; repeat from * to end.

RND 27: *K3, RT twice, k1, p1, k1, LT twice, k3, p1; repeat from * to end.

RND 29: *K2, RT twice, k2, p1, k2, LT twice, k2, p1; repeat from * to end.

RND 31: *K1, RT twice, k3, p1, k3, LT twice, k1, p1; repeat from * to end.

RND 33: *RT twice, k2, RT, p1, LT, k2, LT twice, p1; repeat from * to end.

RND 35: *P3, k2, RT, k1, p1, k1, LT, k2, p4; repeat from * to end.

RND 36: *P3, k11, p4; repeat from * to end.

RND 37: *P2tog, p1, k1, RT, k2, p1, k2, LT, k1, p1, ssp, p1; repeat from * to end—2 sts decreased.

RND 38: *P2, k11, p3; repeat from * to end.

RND 39: *P2, RT, k3, p1, k3, LT, p3; repeat from * to end.

RND 40: Repeat Rnd 38.

RND 41: *Ptog, p1, [k4, p1] twice, ssp, p1; repeat from * to end—2 sts decreased.

RND 42: *P1, k11, p2; repeat from * to end.

RND 43: *P1, LT, k3, p1, k3, RT, p2; repeat from * to end.

RND 44: Repeat Rnd 42.

RND 45: *K2tog, LT, k2, p1, k2, RT, ssk, p1; repeat from * to end—2 sts decreased.

RND 46: *K11, p1; repeat from * to end.

RND 47: *K2, LT, k1, p1, k1, RT, k2, p1; repeat from * to end.

RND 48: Repeat Rnd 46.

RND 49: *Ssk, k1, LT, p1, RT, k1, k2tog, p1; repeat from * to end—2 sts decreased.

RND 50: *K9, p1; repeat from * to end.

RND 51: *Ssk, k2, p1, k2, k2tog, p1; repeat from * to end—2 sts decreased.

RND 52: *K7, p1; repeat from * to end.

RND 53: *Ssk, k1, p1, k1, k2tog, p1; repeat from * to end—2 sts decreased.

RND 54: *K5, p1; repeat from * to end.

RND 55: *Ssk, p1, k2tog, p1; repeat from * to end—2 sts decreased.

RND 56: *K3, p1; repeat from * to end.

RND 57: *Ssk twice, p1; repeat from * to end—2 sts decreased.

RND 58: *K2, p1; repeat from * to end.

RND 59: *Ssk, p1; repeat from * to end—2 sts decreased.

HUGS & KISSES FOR MITTS

(panel of 19 sts; 49 rows)

ROW 1 (RS): *P4, k3, RT, p1, LT, k3, p4; repeat from * to end.

ROWS 2, 4, 6, 8, 10, 12, AND 14: *K4, k11, k4; repeat from * to end.

ROW 3: *P4, k2, RT, k1, p1, k1, LT, k2, p4; repeat from * to end.

ROW 5: *P4, k1, RT, k2, p1, k2, LT, k1, p4; repeat from * to end.

ROW 7: *P4, RT, k3, p1, k3, LT, p4; repeat from * to end.

ROW 9: *P5, k4, p1, k4, p5; repeat from * to end.

ROW 11: *P4, LT, k3, p1, k3, RT, p4; repeat from * to end.

ROW 13: *P4, k1, LT, k2, p1, k2, RT, k1, p4; repeat from * to end.

ROW 15: *P4, k2, LT, k1, p1, k1, RT, k2, p4; repeat from * to end.

ROWS 16, 18, 20, 22, 24, 26, 28, 30, 32, AND 34: *K1, p17; repeat from * to end.

ROW 17: *P1, LT twice, k2, LT, p1, RT, k2, RT twice, p1; repeat from * to end.

ROW 19: *P1, k1, LT twice, k3, p1, k3, RT twice, k1, p1; repeat from * to end.

ROW 21: *P1, k2, LT twice, k2, p1, k2, RT twice, k2, p1; repeat from * to end.

ROW 23: *P1, k3, LT twice, k1, p1, k1, RT twice, k3, p1; repeat from * to end.

ROW 25: *P1, k4, p9, k4, p1; repeat from * to end.

ROW 27: *P1, k3, RT twice, k1, p1, k1, LT twice, k3, p1; repeat from * to end.

ROW 29: *P1, k2, RT twice, k2, p1, k2, LT twice, k2, p1; repeat from * to end.

ROW 31: *P1, k1, RT twice, k3, p1, k3, LT twice, k1, p1; repeat from * to end.

ROW 33: *P1, RT twice, k2, RT, p1, LT, k2, LT twice, p1; repeat from * to end.

ROWS 35–47: Repeat Rows 3–15.

ROW 48: Repeat Row 2.

ROW 49: *P4, k3, LT, p1, RT, k3, p4; repeat from * to end.

SPECIAL TECHNIQUES
RIB CABLED CAST-ON
(FOR HAT AND LEFT MITT)

Make a loop (using a slipknot) with the working yarn and place it on the left-hand needle (first stitch cast on), knit into slipknot, draw up a loop but do not drop stitch from left-hand needle; place new loop on left-hand needle; *insert the tip of the right-hand needle from behind the needle into the space between the last 2 stitches on the left-hand needle and draw up a loop, insert the tip of the right-hand needle from the front into the space between the last 2 stitches on the left-hand needle and draw up a loop; place the loop on the left-hand needle. Repeat from * for remaining stitches to be CO, or for casting on at the end of a row in progress. Do not join.

ROW 1 (RS): *K1, slip 1 purlwise wyib; repeat from * to end.

ROW 2: *K1, slip 1 purlwise wyif; repeat from * to end.

Turn work to RS, ready to begin as instructed.

RIB CABLED CAST-ON
(FOR RIGHT MITT)

Make a loop (using a slipknot) with the working yarn and place it on the left-hand needle (first stitch cast on), purl into slipknot, draw up a loop but do not drop stitch from left-hand needle; place new loop on left-hand needle; * insert the tip of the right-hand needle from the front into the space between the last 2 stitches on the left-hand needle and draw up a loop, insert the tip of the right-hand needle from behind the needle into the space between the last 2 stitches on the left-hand needle and draw up a loop; place the loop on the left-hand needle. Repeat from * for remaining stitches to be CO, or for casting on at the end of a row in progress. Do not join.

ROW 1 (RS): *Slip 1 purlwise wyib, k1; repeat from * to end.

ROW 2: *Slip 1 purlwise wyif, k1; repeat from * to end.

Turn work to RS, ready to begin as instructed.

PATTERN NOTES

The hat is worked in the round. The mitts are worked back and forth, then the side edges are sewn together, leaving an opening for the thumb.

Hat

NOTE: Use your preferred method of working in the rnd.

Using smaller needle(s) and Rib Cabled Cast-On (see Special Techniques, above) or your preferred cast-on, CO 126 sts. Join for working in the rnd, being careful not to twist sts; pm for beginning of rnd. Work in 1x1 Rib until piece measures 1½" (4 cm).

Change to larger needle(s); knit 1 rnd. Work Rnds 1–59 of Hugs & Kisses for Hat—7 sts remain after Rnd 59. Cut yarn, leaving a long tail. Thread tail through remaining sts, pull tight, and fasten off.

HUGS & KISSES FOR HAT

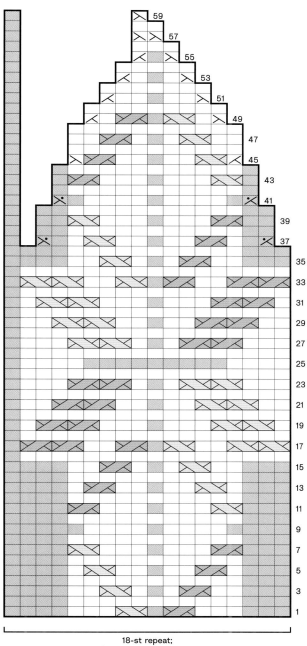

18-st repeat;
decreases to 1-st repeat

HUGS & KISSES FOR MITTS

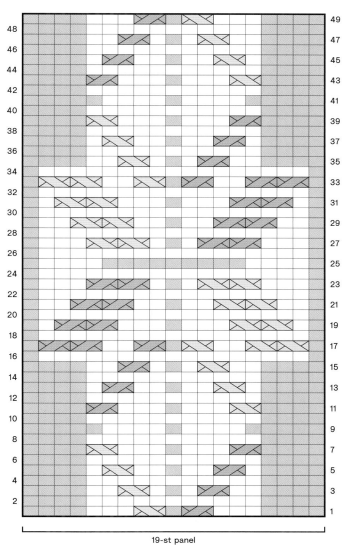

19-st panel

FINISHING

Block as desired.

Mitts

LEFT MITT

Using smaller needles and Rib Cabled Cast-On or your preferred cast-on, CO 50 sts.

Work in 1×1 Rib for 1" (2.5 cm), ending with a RS row.

Change to larger needles; purl 1 row.

ROW 1 (RS): K2, p1, k1, pm, work Hugs & Kisses for Mitts across 19 sts, pm, [k1, p1] twice, k1, pm, work Hugs & Kisses for Mitts across 19 sts, pm, k1, p1, k1.

ROW 2: P1, k1, p1, sm, work to marker, sm, [k1, p1] twice, k1, sm, work as established to marker, sm, p1, k1, p2.

Work even through Row 49 of pattern.

Change to smaller needles; purl 1 row.

Work in 1×1 Rib for 1" (2.5 cm).

BO all sts in pattern.

RIGHT MITT

Using smaller needles and Rib Cabled Cast-On, CO 50 sts.

Work in 1×1 Rib for 1" (2.5 cm), ending with a RS row.

Change to larger needles; purl 1 row.

ROW 1 (RS): K1, p1, k1, pm, work Hugs & Kisses for Mitts across 19 sts, pm, [k1, p1] twice, k1, pm, work Hugs & Kisses for Mitts across 19 sts, pm, k1, p1, k2.

ROW 2: P2, k1, p1, pm, work Hugs & Kisses for Mitts across 18 sts, pm, [k1, p1] 3 times, pm, work Hugs & Kisses for Mitts across 18 sts, pm, [k1, p1] twice.

Work even through Row 49 of pattern.

Change to smaller needles; purl 1 row.

Work in 1×1 Rib for 1" (2.5 cm).

BO all sts in pattern.

FINISHING

Sew side edges together, leaving a 1½" (4 cm) opening below the top ribbing for thumb hole.

Block as desired.

The original stitch for the mitts is a 17-stitch column with an additional purl at each end and has a PSS of 90. So, look for a column of 17 to 19 stitches with a PSS that is close. One repeat of an allover pattern might work too. For example, Blackwork (#85) makes a great substitution if you replace the first and last stitches with reverse Stockinette. A PSS of 80 means it will pull in 10 percent more, which shouldn't be a problem, since the ribs in the mitt allow enough give. A 16-stitch column can work too with a little more fiddling, reducing the number of stitches after the bottom rib.

The hat requires more advanced substitution. The same 16- or 17-stitch patterns with a purl added to each end to make 18 or 19 stitches will work at the start of the hat. You then need to manipulate and change the stitch pattern to fit in the wedge shape formed while decreasing. I've provided an empty wedge, with the decreases included, on page 258.

Basic Pullover

Neither tight nor loose, short nor long, this basic crewneck pullover is made special by the pattern stitch you knit into it. Lengthen the neck ribbing if you'd like a mock or turtleneck. The straight body is easily lengthened or shortened to fit your style, and the pattern is added in a panel on both the body and the sleeves, allowing plenty of room for customized shaping, if you'd like it, without having to decrease or increase in pattern.

SIZES
To fit bust 30 (34, 38, 42, 46) (50, 54, 58, 62)" [76 (86.5, 96.5, 106.5, 117) (127, 137, 147.5, 157.5) cm]

FINISHED MEASUREMENTS
32½ (36, 40½, 44, 48½) (52, 56½, 60, 64½)" [82.5 (91.5, 103, 112, 123) (132, 143.5, 152.5, 164) cm] bust

YARN
Brooklyn Tweed Arbor [100% American Targhee Wool; 145 yards (132 meters)/50 grams]: 8 (8, 9, 10, 11) (12, 13, 14, 15) skeins Morandi

NEEDLES
One pair straight needles, size US 3 (3.25 mm)

One pair straight needles, size US 5 (3.75 mm)

One 16" (40 cm) long circular needle, size US 3 (3.25 mm)

Change needle size if necessary to obtain correct gauge.

NOTIONS
Stitch markers

GAUGE
22 sts and 32 rows = 4" (10 cm) in St st, using larger needles

STITCH PATTERNS

FLAT 2×2 RIB
(multiple of 4 sts + 2; 2-row repeat)

ROW 1 (RS): K2, *p2, k2; repeat from * to end.

ROW 2: P2, *k2, p2; repeat from * to end.

Repeat Rows 1 and 2 for 2×2 Rib.

CIRCULAR 2×2 RIB
(multiple of 4 sts; 1-rnd repeat)

ALL RNDS: K1, p2, *k2, p2; repeat from * to last st, k1.

OPEN PYRAMIDS (#103)
(multiple of 30 sts + 1; 32-row repeat)

ROW 1 (RS): K1, *k1, [RT, k1] twice, k2tog, yo, k3, k2tog, yo, k1, yo, ssk, k3, yo, ssk, [k1, LT] twice, k2; repeat from * to end.

ROW 2 AND ALL WS ROWS: Purl.

ROW 3: K1, *[RT, k1] twice, k2tog, yo, k13, yo, ssk, k1, [LT, k1] twice; repeat from * to end.

ROW 5: K1, *yo, ssk, RT, k1, k2tog, yo, k15, yo, ssk, k1, LT, k2tog, yo, k1; repeat from * to end.

ROW 7: K1, *k1, RT, k1, k2tog, yo, k17, yo, ssk, k1, LT, k2; repeat from * to end.

ROW 9: K1, *RT, k1, k2tog, yo, k19, yo, ssk, k1, LT, k1; repeat from * to end.

ROW 11: K1, *yo, ssk, k2tog, yo, k21, yo, ssk, k2tog, yo, k1; repeat from * to end.

ROW 13: K1, *k1, k2tog, yo, k23, yo, ssk, k2; repeat from * to end.

ROW 15: K1, * k2tog, yo, k25, yo, ssk, k1; repeat from * to end.

ROW 17: K1, *yo, ssk, k3, yo, ssk, [k1, LT] twice, k3, [RT, k1] twice, k2tog, yo, k3, k2tog, yo, k1; repeat from * to end.

ROW 19: K1, *k6, yo, ssk, [k1, LT] twice, k1, [RT, k1] twice, k2tog, yo, k7; repeat from * to end.

ROW 21: K1, *k7, yo, ssk, k1, LT, k2tog, yo, k1, yo, ssk, RT, k1, k2tog, yo, k8; repeat from * to end.

ROW 23: K1, *k8, yo, ssk, k1, LT, k3, RT, k1, k2tog, yo, k9; repeat from * end.

ROW 25: K1, *k9, yo, ssk, k1, LT, k1, RT, k1, k2tog, yo, k10; repeat from * to end.

ROW 27: K1, *k10, yo, ssk, k2tog, yo, k1, yo, ssk, k2tog, yo, k11; repeat from * to end.

ROW 29: K1, *k11, yo, ssk, k3, k2tog, yo, k12; repeat from * to end.

ROW 31: K1, *k12, yo, ssk, k1, k2tog, yo, k13; repeat from * to end.

ROW 32: Purl.

Repeat Rows 1–32 for pattern.

PATTERN NOTES
This pullover is worked from the bottom up in pieces, then sewn together. When working neck and sleeve cap shaping, if there are not enough stitches to work a full twisted stitch, or to work a yarnover without its corresponding decrease, work the affected stitch in Stockinette stitch instead.

Back
Using smaller needles and Long-Tail Cast-On (see Special Techniques, page 270), CO 98 (110, 122, 134, 146) (158, 170, 182, 194) sts.

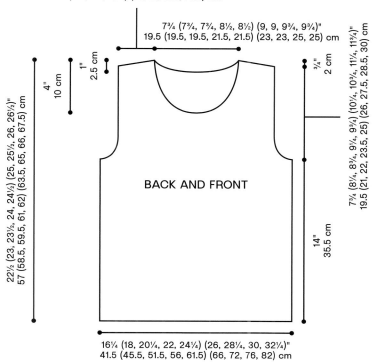

3 (3, 3, 3½, 3½) (4, 4¾, 5, 5¾)"
7.5 (7.5, 7.5, 9, 9) (10, 12, 12.5, 14.5) cm
7¾ (7¾, 7¾, 8½, 8½) (9, 9, 9¾, 9¾)"
19.5 (19.5, 19.5, 21.5, 21.5) (23, 23, 25, 25) cm
22½ (23, 23½, 24, 24½) (25, 25½, 26, 26½)"
57 (58.5, 59.5, 61, 62) (63.5, 65, 66, 67.5) cm
4"
10 cm
1"
2.5 cm
¾"
2 cm
7¾ (8¼, 8¾, 9¼, 9¾) (10¼, 10¾, 11¼, 11¾)"
19.5 (21, 22, 23.5, 25) (26, 27.5, 28.5, 30) cm
BACK AND FRONT
14"
35.5 cm
16¼ (18, 20¼, 22, 24¼) (26, 28¼, 30, 32¼)"
41.5 (45.5, 51.5, 56, 61.5) (66, 72, 76, 82) cm
12¼ (13, 14¼, 15, 16¼) (17, 18, 19, 20¼)"
31 (33, 36, 38, 41.5) (43, 45.5, 48.5, 51.5) cm
5½ (5¼, 5½, 6, 6¾) (7¼, 8, 8¼, 8½)"
14 (13.5, 14, 15, 17) (18.5, 20.5, 21, 21.5) cm
SLEEVE
18"
45.5 cm
9¼ (9¼, 10, 10, 10) (11, 11, 12¼, 12¼)"
23.5 (23.5, 25.5, 25.5, 25.5) (28, 28, 31, 31) cm

Begin Flat 2×2 Rib (beginning with Row 2); work even until piece measures 2" (5 cm) from the beginning, ending with a RS row. Change to larger needles.

NEXT ROW (WS): P8 (9, 10, 12, 12) (8, 14, 10, 7), *p2tog, p8 (7, 8, 7, 8) (8, 8, 8, 9); repeat from * to last 0 (2, 2, 5, 4) (0, 6, 2, 0) sts, purl to end—89 (99, 111, 121, 133) (143, 155, 165, 177) sts remain.

SET-UP ROW 1: K14 (4, 10, 15, 6) (11, 17, 7, 13), pm, work Open Pyramids over 61 (91, 91, 91, 121) (121, 121, 151, 151) sts, pm, knit to end.

SET-UP ROW 2: Purl to marker, sm, work to marker, sm, purl to end.

Work even until piece measures 14" (35.5 cm) from the beginning, ending with a WS Row.

SHAPE ARMHOLES

BO 4 sts at beginning of next 0 (0, 2, 2, 2) (2, 2, 2, 2) rows, 3 sts at beginning of next 2 (2, 4, 4, 4) (4, 6, 6, 8) rows, then 2 sts at beginning of next 2 (4, 4, 4, 8) (8, 8, 8, 8) rows—79 (85, 83, 93, 97) (107, 113, 123, 129) sts remain.

DECREASE ROW (RS): K1, k2tog, work to last 3 sts, ssk, k1—2 sts decreased.

Repeat Decrease Row every RS row 1 (3, 2, 3, 5) (6, 5, 6, 6) more time(s)—75 (77, 77, 85, 85) (93, 101, 109, 115) sts remain.

Work even until armholes measure 7½ (8, 8½, 9, 9½) (10, 10½, 11, 11½)" [19 (20.5, 21.5, 23, 24) (25.5, 26.5, 28, 29) cm], ending with a WS row.

SHAPE NECK AND SHOULDERS

NOTE: Neck and shoulder shaping are worked at the same time, beginning with neck shaping; please read entire section through before beginning.

NEXT ROW (RS): Work 28 (29, 29, 31, 31) (34, 38, 40, 43) sts, join a second ball of yarn, BO center 19 (19, 19, 23, 23) (25, 25, 29, 29) sts, work to end.

Working both sides at once, BO 4 sts at each neck edge 3 times. AT THE SAME TIME, beginning on third row of neck shaping, BO 6 (6, 6, 7, 7) (8, 9, 10, 10) sts at each armhole edge 1 (2, 2, 1, 1) (1, 2, 1, 2) time(s), then 5 (5, 5, 6, 6) (7, 8, 9, 11) sts 2 (1, 1, 2, 2) (2, 1, 2, 1) time(s).

Front

Work as for back until armholes measure 4½ (5, 5½, 6, 6½) (7, 7½, 8, 8½)" [11.5 (12.5, 14, 15, 16.5) (18, 19, 20.5, 21.5) cm], ending with a WS row—75 (77, 77, 85, 85) (93, 101, 109, 115) sts remain.

SHAPE NECK

NEXT ROW (RS): Work 30 (31, 31, 33, 33) (36, 40, 42, 45) sts, join a new ball of yarn and BO center 15 (15, 15, 19, 19) (21, 21, 25, 25) sts, work to end. Working both sides at once, BO 4 sts at each neck edge once, 3 sts once, then 2 sts once.

NECK DECREASE ROW (RS): Work to 3 sts before left neck edge, ssk, k1; on right

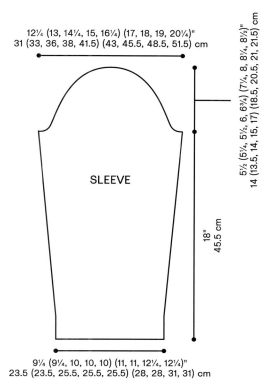

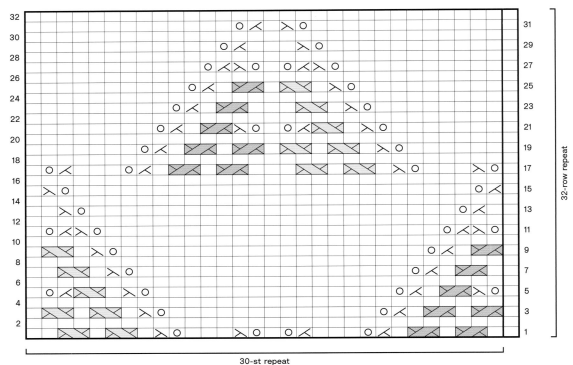

30-st repeat

32-row repeat

neck edge, k1, k2tog, work to end—1 st decreased each neck edge.
Repeat Neck Decrease row 4 more times—16 (17, 17, 19, 19) (22, 26, 28, 31) sts remain each shoulder.
Work even until armholes measure 7¾ (8¼, 8¾, 9¼, 9¾) (10¼, 10¾, 11¼, 11¾)" [19.5 (21, 22, 23.5, 25) (26, 27.5, 28.5, 30) cm], ending with a WS row.

SHAPE SHOULDERS
BO 6 (6, 6, 7, 7) (8, 9, 10, 10) sts at each armhole edge 1 (2, 2, 1, 1) (1, 2, 1, 2) time(s), then 5 (5, 5, 6, 6) (7, 8, 9, 11) sts 2 (1, 1, 2, 2) (2, 1, 2, 1) time(s).

Sleeves
Using smaller needles and Long-Tail Cast-On, CO 50 (50, 54, 54, 54) (58, 58, 66, 66) sts.
Begin Flat 2×2 Rib (beginning with Row 2); work even until piece measures 2" (5 cm) from the beginning, ending with a RS row.

Change to larger needles.
Purl 1 row, increasing 1 (1, 1, 1, 1) (3, 3, 1, 1) stitch(es) evenly across—51 (51, 55, 55, 55) (61, 61, 67, 67) sts.
SET-UP ROW 1 (RS): K10 (10, 12, 12, 12) (15, 15, 18, 18), pm, work Open Pyramids over 31 sts, pm, knit to end.
SET-UP ROW 2: Purl to marker, sm, work Open Pyramids to marker, sm, purl to end.
Work 12 (8, 6, 6, 4) (4, 4, 4, 2) rows even.

SHAPE SLEEVE
INCREASE ROW (RS): K2, M1L, work to last 2 sts, M1R, k2—2 sts increased.
Repeat Increase Row every 14 (12, 10, 8, 6) (6, 6, 6, 4) rows 7 (9, 11, 13, 16) (7, 18, 18, 9) more times, then every 0 (0, 0, 0, 0) (8, 0, 0, 6) rows 0 (0, 0, 0, 0) (8, 0, 0, 12) times—67 (71, 79, 83, 89) (93, 99, 105, 111) sts.
Work even until piece measures 18" (46 cm), from the beginning, ending with a WS row.

SHAPE CAP
BO 2 (3, 3, 3, 3) (3, 3, 4, 4) sts at beginning of next 4 (2, 2, 2, 2) (2, 4, 2, 2) rows, then 0 (2, 2, 2, 2) (2, 0, 3, 3) sts at beginning of next 2 rows—59 (61, 69, 73, 79) (83, 87, 91, 97) sts remain.
DECREASE ROW (RS): K1, k2tog, work to last 3 sts, ssk, k1—2 sts decreased.
Repeat Decrease Row every RS row 15 (15, 17, 19, 21) (23, 25, 27, 29) more times—27 (29, 33, 33, 35) (35, 35, 35, 37) sts remain.
Work 1 row even.
BO 2 (2, 2, 2, 3) (3, 3, 3, 3) sts at beginning of next 4 (4, 2, 2, 4) (4, 4, 4, 2) rows, then 0 (0, 3, 3, 0) (0, 0, 0, 4) sts at beginning of next 2 rows.
BO remaining 19 (21, 23, 23, 23, 23, 23, 23) sts.

FINISHING
Sew shoulder seams.

NECKBAND
With RS facing, using circular needle and beginning at center back neck, pick up and knit 100 (100, 100, 108, 108) (116, 116, 124, 124) sts evenly around neck opening. Join for working in the rnd; pm for beginning of rnd. Work in Circular 2×2 Rib for 1¼" (3 cm). BO all sts in pattern.
Sew in sleeves. Sew side and sleeve seams.
Block as desired.

Most of the stitches with eyelets (Chapter 7) don't pull in at all. With a PSS of 100, their gauge is the same as the Stockinette gauge, and that's the case here. For an easy substitution without eyelets, look for patterns with a lot of Stockinette stitch in the background, like Seahook (#77) or Rune (#40). Not only will they have a close PSS (95), but the Stockinette backgrounds also allow for a smooth transition where the panel ends and the Stockinette begins. Try sprinkling Single Flowers (#57) across the surfaces for a less structured design. When surrounded by a lot of Stockinette, the PSS of 85 won't really matter.

The pattern is worked in a panel flanked by Stockinette stitch on either side, avoiding the armhole shaping. You can match the number of stitches in the panel or come short. Be careful, if you'd like to make the panel wider, that your panel fits into the number of stitches remaining after the armhole shaping is complete. On the sleeves, the panel needs to fit into the number of stitches above the cuff.

Shortie

A little something to wear over your sleeveless dresses for modesty or warmth, this loose-fitting cardigan with narrow sleeves layers well. The openwork pattern highlights the fronts and continues onto the collar. While not written to be on the back, the gauge is the same as the Stockinette gauge, so you can use it on the back as well, if you'd like. The construction is identical to the much longer Sketch Coat (page 232), and either can easily be knit to any length to suit your needs.

SIZES
To fit bust 30 (34, 38, 42, 46) (50, 54, 58, 62)" [76 (86.5, 96.5, 106.5, 117) (127, 137, 147.5, 157.5) cm]

FINISHED MEASUREMENTS
36½ (40, 44½, 48, 52½) (56, 60½, 64, 68½)" [92.5 (101.5, 113, 122, 133.5) (142, 153.5, 162.5, 174) cm] bust, with fronts overlapped

YARN
Blue Sky Fibers Alpaca Silk [50% alpaca/50% silk; 146 yards (133 meters)/50 grams]: 7 (7, 8, 9, 9) (10, 11, 12, 13) hanks #129 Amethyst

NEEDLES
One pair straight needles, size US 2 (2.75 mm)

One pair straight needles, size US 4 (3.5 mm)

One spare needle in any style, size US 5 (3.5 mm), for 3-Needle Bind-Off

Change needle size if necessary to obtain correct gauge.

NOTIONS
Stitch markers; removable stitch markers; stitch holder or waste yarn

GAUGES
26 sts and 36 rows = 4" (10 cm) in St st, using larger needles

26 sts and 36 rows = 4" (10 cm) in Open Lattice, using larger needles

STITCH PATTERNS
2×2 RIB
(multiple of 4 sts + 2; 2-row repeat)
ROW 1 (RS): K2, *p2, k2; repeat from * to end.
ROW 2: P2, *k2, p2; repeat from * to end.
Repeat Rows 1 and 2 for pattern.

OPEN LATTICE (#106)
(multiple of 4 sts + 2; 8-row repeat)
ROW 1 (RS): K1, *RT, LT; repeat from * to last st, k1.
ROW 2: P1, *ssp, yo twice, p2tog; repeat from * to last st, p1.
ROW 3: LT, *(k1, p1) into double yo, LT; repeat from * to end.
ROW 4: Purl.
ROW 5: K1, *LT, RT; repeat from * to last st, k1.
ROW 6: P1, yo, p2tog, ssp, *yo twice, p2tog, ssp; repeat from * to st, yo, p1.
ROW 7: K1, p1, RT, *(k1, p1) into double yo, RT; repeat from * to last 2 sts, k2.
ROW 8: Purl.
Repeat Rows 1–8 for pattern.

PATTERN NOTES
The back and fronts of this cardigan are worked from the bottom up in pieces, then the shoulders are sewn together and the neck extensions are worked to the center back neck, joined using 3-Needle Bind-Off, then sewn in place. The sleeves are picked up from the armhole edges and worked back and forth in rows to the cuffs.
When working shoulder shaping, if there are not enough stitches to work a full twisted stitch, work the affected stitch in Stockinette stitch instead.

Back
Using smaller needles and Long-Tail Cast-On (see Special Techniques, page 270), CO 118 (130, 142, 154, 170) (182, 194, 206, 222) sts.
Begin 2×2 Rib (beginning with Row 2); work even until piece measures 2" (5 cm) from the beginning, ending with a WS row.
Knit 1 row, increasing 0 (0, 2, 2, 0) (0, 2, 2, 0) sts evenly across—118 (130, 144, 156, 170) (182, 196, 208, 222) sts.
Change to larger needles and St st; work even until piece measures 11 (11, 11½, 11½, 12) (12½, 13, 13, 13½)" [28 (28, 29, 29, 30.5) (32, 33, 33, 34.5) cm] from the beginning, ending with a WS row.

SHAPE SHOULDERS
BO 4 (5, 6, 6, 7) (8, 9, 10, 10) sts at beginning of next 2 (8, 10, 2, 4) (8, 12, 16, 2) rows, then 5 (6, 7, 7, 8) (9, 10, 0, 11) sts at beginning of next 14 (8, 6, 14, 12) (8, 4, 0, 14) rows.
BO remaining 40 (42, 42, 46, 46) (46, 48, 48, 48) sts.

Left Front
Using smaller needles and Long-Tail Cast-On, CO 61 (69, 77, 81, 89) (97, 105, 109, 117) sts.
SET-UP ROW (WS): Slip 2 purlwise wyif, k1, work in 2×2 Rib (beginning with Row 2) to end.
NEXT ROW: Work to last 3 sts, sts, p1, k2.

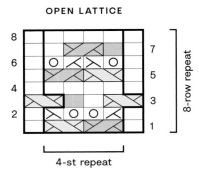

OPEN LATTICE

8-row repeat

4-st repeat

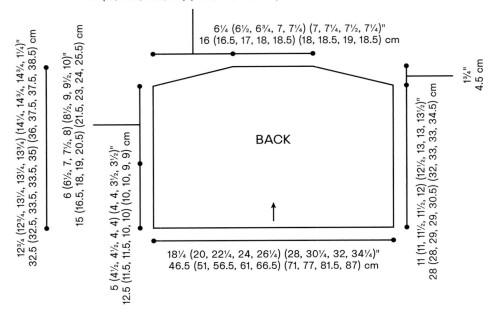

6 (6¾, 7¾, 8½, 9½) (10½, 11½, 12¼, 13½)"
15 (17, 19.5, 21.5, 24) (26.5, 29, 31, 34.5) cm

6¼ (6½, 6¾, 7, 7¼) (7, 7¼, 7½, 7¼)"
16 (16.5, 17, 18, 18.5) (18, 18.5, 19, 18.5) cm

1¾"
4.5 cm

BACK

12¾ (12¾, 13¼, 13¼, 13¾) (14¼, 14¾, 14¾, 1¼)"
32.5 (32.5, 33.5, 33.5, 35) (36, 37.5, 37.5, 38.5) cm

6 (6½, 7, 7½, 8) (8½, 9, 9½, 10)"
15 (16.5, 18, 19, 20.5) (21.5, 23, 24, 25.5) cm

5 (4½, 4½, 4, 4) (4, 4, 3½, 3½)"
12.5 (11.5, 11.5, 10, 10) (10, 10, 9, 9) cm

18¼ (20, 22¼, 24, 26¼) (28, 30¼, 32, 34¼)"
46.5 (51, 56.5, 61, 66.5) (71, 77, 81.5, 87) cm

11 (11, 11½, 11½, 12) (12½, 13, 13, 13½)"
28 (28, 29, 29, 30.5) (32, 33, 33, 34.5) cm

Work even until piece measures 2" (5 cm) from the beginning, ending with a RS row. Change to larger needles.

NEXT ROW (WS): Slip 2 purlwise wyif, k1, purl to end, increasing 0 (1, 0, 0, 0) (1, 0, 1, 0) st(s) or decreasing 0 (0, 0, 0, 1) (0, 1, 0, 0) st(s)—61 (70, 77, 81, 88) (98, 104, 110, 117) sts.

SET-UP ROW 1 (RS): K24 (25, 24, 24, 27) (29, 27, 29, 28), pm, work Open Lattice to last 3 sts, p1, k2.

SET-UP ROW 2: Slip 2 purlwise wyif, k1, work to marker, sm, purl to end.

Work even until piece measures 11 (11, 11½, 11½, 12) (12½, 13, 13, 13½)" [28 (28, 29, 29, 30.5) (32, 33, 33, 34.5) cm] from the beginning, ending with a WS row.

SHAPE SHOULDER

BO 4 (5, 6, 6, 7) (8, 9, 10, 10) sts at beginning of next 1 (4, 5, 1, 2) (4, 6, 8, 1) RS row(s), then 5 (6, 7, 7, 8) (9, 10, 0, 11) sts at beginning of next next 7 (4, 3, 7, 6) (4, 2, 0, 7) RS rows—22 (26, 26, 26, 26) (30, 30, 30, 30) sts remain.

SHAPE NECK EXTENSION

SET-UP ROW 1 (WS): Slip 2 purlwise wyif, k1, work as established to last st, p1.

SET-UP ROW 2: K1, work to last 3 sts, p1, k2.

Work even until piece measures 3 (3¼, 3¼, 3½, 3½) (3½, 3¾, 3¾, 3¾)" [7.5 (8.5, 8.5, 9, 9) (9, 9.5, 9.5, 9.5) cm] from end of shoulder shaping, ending with a RS row. Cut yarn, leaving a 6" (15 cm) tail and transfer sts to st holder or waste yarn.

Right Front

Using smaller needles and Long-Tail Cast-On, CO 61 (69, 77, 81, 89) (97, 105, 109, 117) sts.

SET-UP ROW (WS): Work in 2x2 Rib (beginning with Row 2) to last 3 sts, k1, p2.

NEXT ROW: Slip 2 purlwise wyib, p1, work in 2×2 Rib to end.

Work even until piece measures 2" (5 cm) from the beginning, ending with a RS row. Change to larger needles.

NEXT ROW (WS): Purl to last 3 sts, increasing 0 (1, 0, 0, 0) (1, 0, 1, 0) st(s) or decreasing 0 (0, 0, 0, 1) (0, 1, 0, 0) st(s), k1,

p2—61 (70, 77, 81, 88) (98, 104, 110, 117) sts.

SET-UP ROW 1 (RS): Slip 2 purlwise wyib, p1, work Open Lattice over 34 (42, 50, 54, 58) (66, 74, 78, 86) sts, pm, knit to end.

SET-UP ROW 2: Purl to marker, sm, work to last 3 sts, k1, p2.

Work even until piece measures 11 (11, 11½, 11½, 12) (12½, 13, 13, 13½)" [28 (28, 29, 29, 30.5) (32, 33, 33, 34.5) cm] from the beginning, ending with a RS row.

SHAPE SHOULDER

BO 4 (5, 6, 6, 7) (8, 9, 10, 10) sts at beginning of next 1 (4, 5, 1, 2) (4, 6, 8, 1) WS row(s), then 5 (6, 7, 7, 8) (9, 10, 0, 11) sts at beginning of next next 7 (4, 3, 7, 6) (4, 2, 0, 7) WS rows—22 (26, 26, 26, 26) (30, 30, 30, 30) sts remain.

SHAPE NECK EXTENSION

SET-UP ROW 1 (RS): P1, work as established to last 3 sts, k1, p2.

SET-UP ROW 2: Slip 2 purlwise wyib, p1, work to last st, k1.

Work even until piece measures 3 (3¼, 3¼, 3½, 3½) (3½, 3¾, 3¾, 3¾)" [7.5 (8.5,

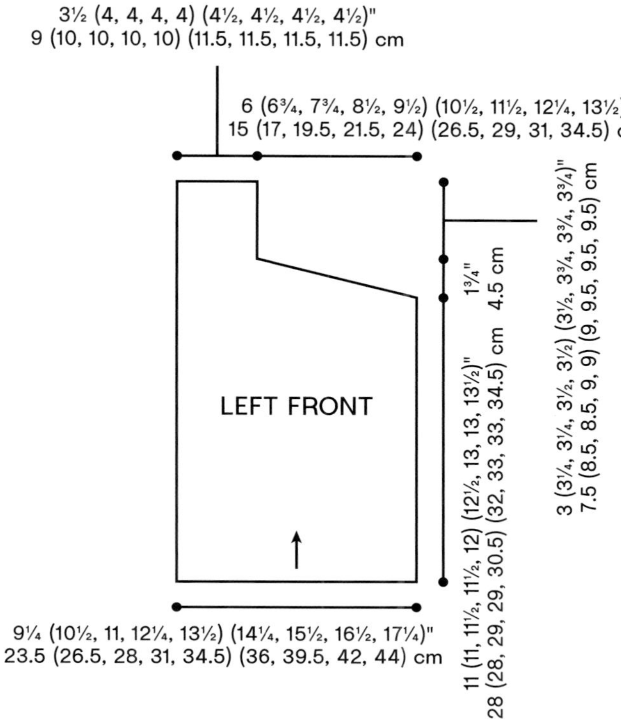
3½ (4, 4, 4, 4) (4½, 4½, 4½, 4½)"
9 (10, 10, 10, 10) (11.5, 11.5, 11.5, 11.5) cm
6 (6¾, 7¾, 8½, 9½) (10½, 11½, 12¼, 13½)"
15 (17, 19.5, 21.5, 24) (26.5, 29, 31, 34.5) cm
LEFT FRONT
1¾"
4.5 cm
3 (3¼, 3¼, 3½, 3½) (3½, 3¾, 3¾, 3¾)"
7.5 (8.5, 8.5, 9, 9) (9, 9.5, 9.5, 9.5) cm
11 (11, 11½, 11½, 12) (12½, 13, 13, 13½)"
28 (28, 29, 29, 30.5) (32, 33, 33, 34.5) cm
9¼ (10½, 11, 12¼, 13½) (14¼, 15½, 16½, 17¼)"
23.5 (26.5, 28, 31, 34.5) (36, 39.5, 42, 44) cm

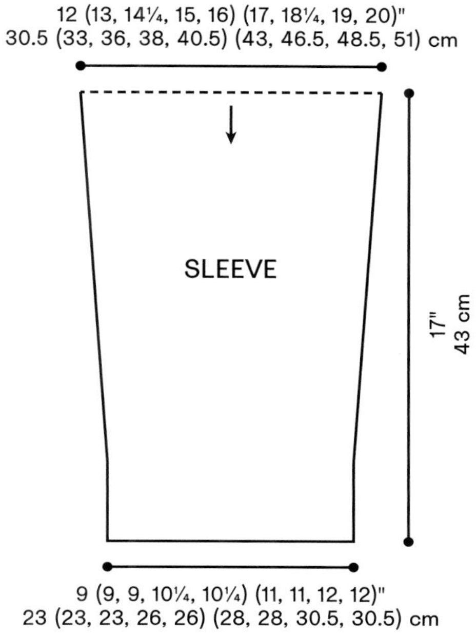
12 (13, 14¼, 15, 16) (17, 18¼, 19, 20)"
30.5 (33, 36, 38, 40.5) (43, 46.5, 48.5, 51) cm
SLEEVE
17"
43 cm
9 (9, 9, 10¼, 10¼) (11, 11, 12, 12)"
23 (23, 23, 26, 26) (28, 28, 30.5, 30.5) cm

8.5, 9, 9) (9, 9.5, 9.5, 9.5) cm] from end of shoulder shaping, ending with a WS row. Leave sts on the needle; do not cut yarn.

JOIN NECK EXTENSIONS

With WSs of neck extensions together (seam will be on the RS) and using larger needles and yarn attached to right front neck extension, join extensions using 3-Needle Bind-Off (see Special Techniques, page 270). Sew shoulder seams. Sew joined neck extensions to back neck edge.

Sleeves

Place removable markers 6 (6½, 7, 7½, 8) (8½, 9, 9½, 10)" [15 (16.5, 18, 19, 20.5) (21.5, 23, 24, 25.5) cm] down from each shoulder seam on fronts and back.
With RS facing, using larger needles, pick up and knit 78 (84, 92, 98, 104) (110, 118, 124, 130) sts between markers. Do not join; work back and forth in rows.
Begin St st; work 9 (9, 7, 7, 5) (5, 3, 3, 3) rows even.

SHAPE SLEEVE

DECREASE ROW (RS): K2, k2tog, knit to last 4 sts, ssk, k2–2 sts decreased.
Repeat Decrease Row every 8 (8, 6, 6, 4) (4, 2, 2, 2) row 9 (12, 16, 15, 18) (18, 22, 22, 25) more times–58 (58, 58, 66, 66) (72, 72, 78, 78) sts remain.
Work even until piece measures 14" (35.5 cm) from pick-up row, ending with a RS row.
Change to smaller needles.
NEXT ROW (WS): *Purl 5 (5, 5, 5, 5) (5, 5, 4, 4), p2tog; repeat from * to last 2 (2, 2, 10, 10) (2, 2, 6, 6) sts, purl to end–50 (50, 50, 58, 58) (62, 62, 66, 66) sts remain.
Change to 2×2 Rib; work even for 3" (7.5 cm), ending with a WS row.
BO all sts in pattern.

FINISHING

Sew side and sleeve seams.
Block as desired.

Most of the stitches with eyelets (Chapter 7) don't pull in at all. With a PSS of 100, their gauge is the same as the Stockinette gauge, and that's the case here. For an easy substitution without eyelets, look for patterns with a close PSS (95), like Carp (#45).

If you'd prefer to use a stitch that pulls in more (with a lower PSS), you may want to throw in a few extra stitches. For example, if my pattern stitch panel has 58 stitches (varies with the size) and I want to use X & O Lattice (#59), which has a PSS of 80, without any additional stitches the panel will be 20 percent narrower than I want it to be. I need 11 or 12 stitches to add back 20 percent of 58 (in St st gauge), which brings my panel to 70 stitches. Now let's see how X & O Lattice (#59) fits in 70 stitches. The repeat is 14 sts + 2. Repeating the 14 stitches five times brings me up to 70 stitches. I can either leave out the 2 edge stitches or add 2 more stitches to my panel. Either will be fine; it won't change the look of the pattern stitch very much. Remember to add the new stitches in above the ribbing as well as at the end, distributing them between the shoulder shaping and collar.

Extreme Yoke Pullover

The yoke itself is not extreme, only the pattern stitch, because there are twists on every round. The lack of resting rows is easier, however, in the round, because you can always see what you are doing. Short rows are worked under the yoke, bringing the front neckline down. The elegant, lightweight yarn used to knit this pullover knits up faster than you might think and is a joy to wear.

SIZES
To fit bust 30 (34, 38, 42, 46) (50, 54, 58, 62)" [76 (86.5, 96.5, 106.5, 117) (127, 137, 147.5, 157.5) cm]

FINISHED MEASUREMENTS
32 (36¼, 40¼, 44¼, 48¼) (52¼, 56¼, 60¼, 64¼)" [81.5 (92, 102, 112.5, 122.5) (132.5, 143, 153, 163) cm] bust

YARN
Quince & Co. Tern [75% American wool/25% silk; 221 yards (202 meters)/50 grams]: 6 (7, 7, 8, 9) (10, 11, 12, 12) hanks Terra Cotta

NEEDLES
Two 24" long or longer circular needles, size US 2 (2.75 mm)

Needle(s) in preferred style for small circumference knitting in the rnd, size US 2 (2.75 mm)

Change needle size if necessary to obtain correct gauge.

NOTIONS
Stitch markers; stitch holder or waste yarn; removable stitch markers; one double-pointed needle size US 2 (2.75 mm) or smaller

GAUGE
29 sts and 42 rows = 4" (10 cm) in St st

STITCH PATTERNS

FLAT GARTER RIB
(multiple of 6 sts + 8; 2-row repeat)

ROW 1 (RS): *K2, p1; repeat from * to last 2 sts, k2.

ROW 2: K3, *p2, k4; repeat from * to last 5 sts, p2, k3.

Repeat Rows 1 and 2 for pattern.

CIRCULAR GARTER RIB
(multiple of 6 sts; 2-rnd repeat)

RND 1: K1, *p1, k2; repeat from * to last 2 sts, p1, k1.

RND 2: P2, *k2, p4; repeat from * to last 4 sts, k2, p2.

Repeat Rnds 1 and 2 for pattern.

SASHIKO COMPACT
(multiple of 22 sts, decreases to multiple of 8 sts; 47 rnds)

NOTE: On Rnds 1, 5, 7, 11, 15, 19, 21, 25, 34, and 37, after working first LT or RT of the rnd, place beginning-of-rnd marker between the 2 sts of the LT or RT.

RND 1: *LT (at beginning of rnd only, reposition beginning-of-rnd marker to between these 2 sts), k20; repeat from * to last st, k1.

RND 2: *LT, k18, RT; repeat from * to end.

RND 3: *K1, LT, k16, RT, k1; repeat from * to end.

RND 4: *RT, LT, k14, RT, LT; repeat from * to end; slip last st worked back to left-hand needle, ready to work it with first st of Rnd 5.

RND 5: *LT (at beginning of rnd only, reposition beginning-of-rnd marker to between these 2 sts), RT, LT, k12, RT, LT; repeat from * to last st, k1.

RND 6: *RT, k2, LT, k10, RT, k2, LT; repeat from * to end; slip last st worked back to left-hand needle, ready to work it with first st of Rnd 7.

RND 7: *LT (at beginning of rnd only, reposition beginning-of-rnd marker to between these 2 sts), k4, LT, k8, RT, k4; repeat from * to last st, k1.

RND 8: *LT, k4, LT, k6, RT, k4, RT; repeat from * to end.

RND 9: *K1, [LT, k4] twice, RT, k4, RT, k1 repeat from * to end.

RND 10: *K2, LT, k4, LT, k2, RT, k4, RT, k2; repeat from * to last 22 sts, k2, LT, k4, LT, k2, RT, k4, RT, k1; do not work last st; it will be worked with first st of Rnd 11.

RND 11: *LT (at beginning of rnd only, reposition beginning-of-rnd marker to between these 2 sts), k2, LT, k4, LT, RT, k4, RT, k2; repeat from * to last st, k1.

RND 12: *LT, k2, LT, k4, RT, k4, RT, k2, RT; repeat from * to end.

RND 13: *K1, [LT, k2] twice, RT, LT, [k2, RT] twice, k1; repeat from * to end.

RND 14: *[K2, LT] twice, RT, LT twice, [RT, k2] twice; repeat from * to last 22 sts, [k2, LT] twice, RT, LT twice, RT, k2, RT, k1; do not work last st; it will be worked with first st of Rnd 15.

RND 15: *LT (at beginning of rnd only, reposition beginning-of-rnd marker to between these 2 sts), [k2, LT] twice, RT, LT, [RT, k2] twice; repeat from * to last st, k1.

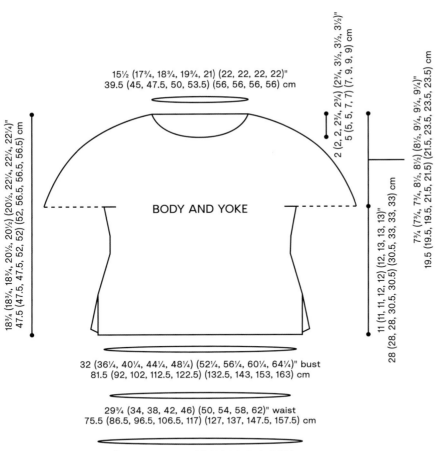

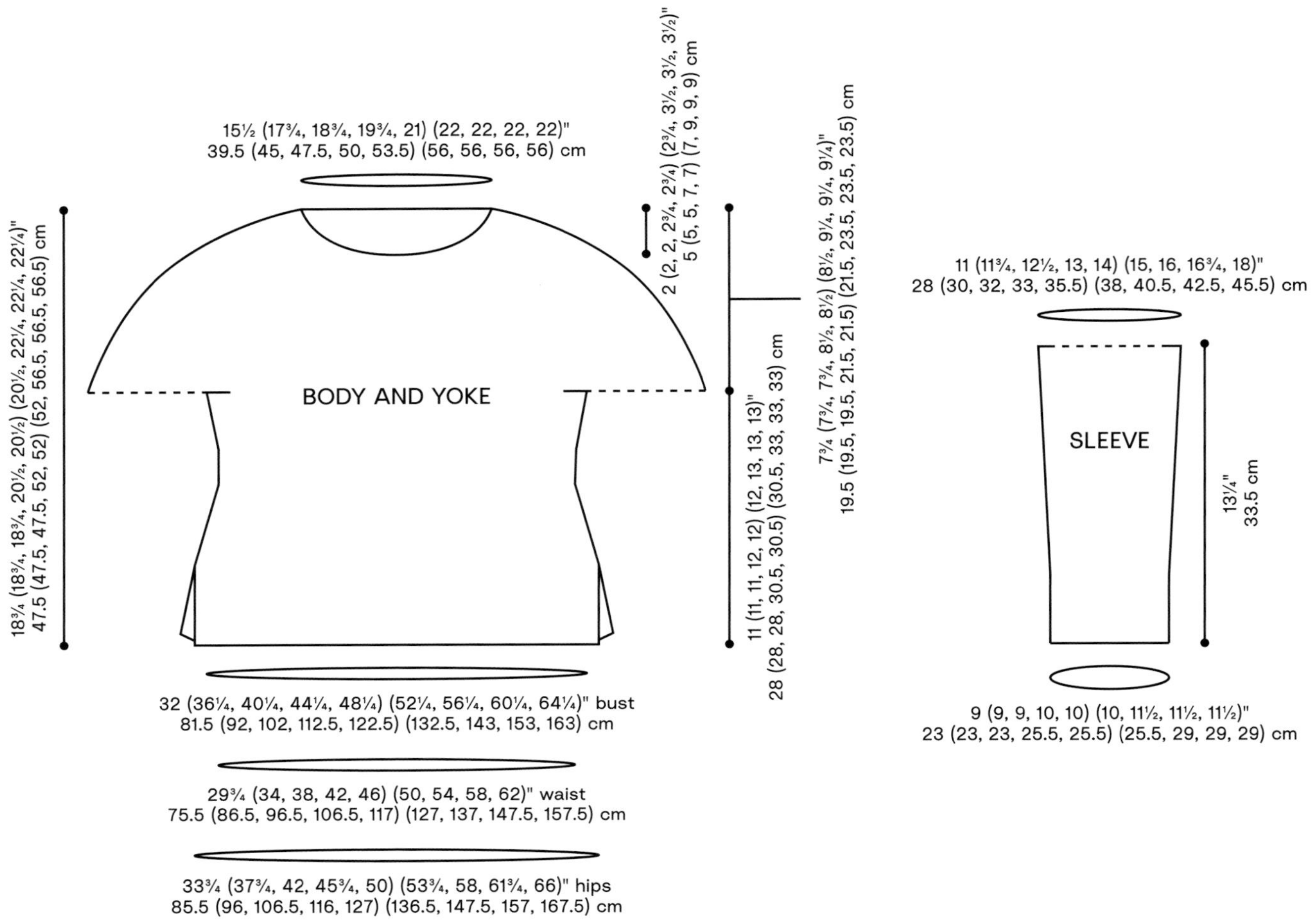

15½ (17¾, 18¾, 19¾, 21) (22, 22, 22, 22)"
39.5 (45, 47.5, 50, 53.5) (56, 56, 56, 56) cm

2 (2, 2, 2¾, 2¾) (2¾, 3½, 3½, 3½)"
5 (5, 5, 7, 7) (7, 9, 9, 9) cm

7¾ (7¾, 7¾, 8½, 8½) (8½, 9¼, 9¼, 9¼)"
19.5 (19.5, 19.5, 21.5, 21.5) (21.5, 23.5, 23.5, 23.5) cm

11 (11, 11, 12, 12) (12, 13, 13, 13)"
28 (28, 28, 30.5, 30.5) (30.5, 33, 33, 33) cm

18¾ (18¾, 18¾, 20½, 20½) (20½, 22¼, 22¼, 22¼)"
47.5 (47.5, 47.5, 52, 52) (52, 56.5, 56.5, 56.5) cm

BODY AND YOKE

32 (36¼, 40¼, 44¼, 48¼) (52¼, 56¼, 60¼, 64¼)" bust
81.5 (92, 102, 112.5, 122.5) (132.5, 143, 153, 163) cm

29¾ (34, 38, 42, 46) (50, 54, 58, 62)" waist
75.5 (86.5, 96.5, 106.5, 117) (127, 137, 147.5, 157.5) cm

33¾ (37¾, 42, 45¾, 50) (53¾, 58, 61¾, 66)" hips
85.5 (96, 106.5, 116, 127) (136.5, 147.5, 157, 167.5) cm

11 (11¾, 12½, 13, 14) (15, 16, 16¾, 18)"
28 (30, 32, 33, 35.5) (38, 40.5, 42.5, 45.5) cm

SLEEVE

13¼" cm
33.5 cm

9 (9, 9, 10, 10) (10, 11½, 11½, 11½)"
23 (23, 23, 25.5, 25.5) (25.5, 29, 29, 29) cm

RND 16: *[LT, k2] 3 times, RT, [k2, RT] twice; repeat from * to end.

RND 17: *K1, LT, [k2, LT] twice, RT, [k2, RT] twice, k1; repeat from * to end.

RND 18: *RT, [LT, k2] twice, RT, [k2, RT] twice, LT; repeat from * to end; slip last st worked back to left-hand needle, ready to work it with first st of Rnd 19.

RND 19: *RT (at beginning of rnd only, reposition beginning-of-rnd marker to between these 2 sts), RT, LT, k2, LT, k4, RT, k2, RT, LT; repeat from * to last st, k1.

RND 20: *RT, k2, [LT, k2] twice, [RT, k2] twice, LT; repeat from * to end; slip last st worked back to left-hand needle, ready to work it with first st of Rnd 21.

RND 21: *LT (at beginning of rnd only, reposition beginning-of-rnd marker to between these 2 sts), k4, LT, k2, LT, RT, k2, RT, k4; repeat from * to last st, k1.

RND 22: *LT, k4, LT, k2, RT, k2, RT, k4, RT; repeat from * to end.

RND 23: *K1, [LT, k4] twice, RT, k4, RT, k1; repeat from * to end.

RND 24: *K2, LT, k4, LT, k2, RT, k4, RT, k2; repeat from * to last 22 sts, k2, LT, k4, LT, k2, RT, k4, RT, k1; do not work last st; it will be worked with first st of Rnd 25.

RND 25: *LT (at beginning of rnd only, reposition beginning-of-rnd marker to between these 2 sts), k2, LT, k4, LT, RT, k4, RT, k2; repeat from * to last st, k1.

RND 26: *LT, k2, LT, k4, RT, k4, RT, k2, RT; repeat from * to end.

RND 27: *K1, [LT, k2] twice, RT, LT, [k2, RT] twice, k1; repeat from * to end.

RND 28: *[K2, LT] twice, RT, LT twice, [RT, k2] twice; repeat from * to end.

RND 29: *K3, LT, k2, LT, RT, LT, RT, k2, RT, k3; repeat from * to end.

RND 30: *Ssk, k2, [LT, k2] twice, [RT, k2] twice, k2tog; repeat from * to end—2 sts decreased.

RND 31: *LT, [k2, LT] twice, RT, [k2, RT] twice; repeat from * to end.

RND 32: *K1, [LT, k2] twice, RT, [k2, RT] twice, k1; repeat from * to end.

RND 33: *[K2, LT] twice, k4, [RT, k2] twice; repeat from * to last 20 sts, [k2, LT] twice, k4, RT, k2, RT, k1; do not work last st; it will be worked with first st of Rnd 34.

RND 34: *RT (at beginning of rnd only, reposition beginning-of-rnd marker to between these 2 sts), RT, [LT, k2] twice, RT, k2, RT, LT; repeat from * to last st, k1.

RND 35: *RT twice, LT, k2, LT, RT, k2, RT, LT, RT; repeat from * to end.

RND 36: *K2tog, k3, LT, [k2, RT] twice, k3, ssk; repeat from * to end; slip last st worked back to left-hand needle, ready to work it with first st of Rnd 37—2 sts decreased.

RND 37: *LT (at beginning of rnd only, reposition beginning-of-rnd marker to between these 2 sts), k4, LT, k4, RT, k4; repeat from * to last st, k1.

RND 38: *LT, k4, LT, k2, RT, k4, RT; repeat from * to end.

RND 39: *K1, LT, k4, LT, RT, k4, RT, k1; repeat from * to end.

RND 40: *K2tog, LT, k4, RT, k4, RT, ssk; repeat from * to end—2 sts decreased.

RND 41: *K2, [LT, k2, RT] twice, k2; repeat from * to end.

RND 42: *K1, k2tog, LT, RT, LT twice, RT, ssk, k1; repeat from * to end—2 sts decreased.

RND 43: *K3, [LT, RT] twice, k3; repeat from * to end.

RND 44: *K2, k2tog, LT, k2, RT, ssk, k2; repeat from * to end—2 sts decreased.

RND 45: *K4, LT, RT, k4; repeat from * to end.

RND 46: *K3, k2tog, RT, ssk, k3; repeat from * to end—2 sts decreased.

RND 47: *K3, k2tog, ssk, k3; repeat from * to end—2 sts decreased.

PATTERN NOTES

The body of this pullover begins with separate back and front hems, which are then joined and the body is worked in the round to the underarms, with waist and bust shaping. The sleeves are worked in the round to the underarms, then the body and sleeves are joined and the yoke is worked in the round to the neck, with short-row shaping to shape the back neck.

When working Sashiko Compact, the beginning-of-round marker shifts numerous times; to make it easier to reposition the marker, you may wish to use a removable marker instead of a ring marker to mark the beginning of the round.

Back Hem

Using circular needle and Long-Tail Cast-On (see Special Techniques, page 270),

SASHIKO COMPACT

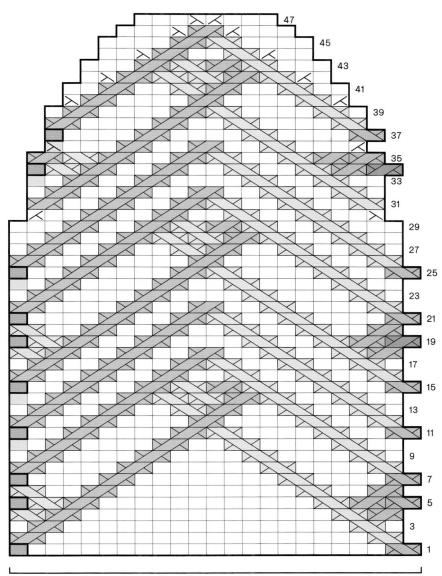

22-st repeat;
decreases to 8-st repeat

On last repeat of rnd only, do not work this st; it will be worked with the first st of the following rnd. On all preceding repeats, knit this st.

On last repeat of rnd only, knit this st; on all preceding repeats, omit this st.

On last repeat of rnd only, k2tog, slip st back to left-hand needle where it will be worked with the first st of the following rnd. On all preceding repeats, work as k2tog.

On first repeat of rnd only, after working LT, replace beginning-of-rnd marker in center of LT. On all following repeats, work as LT.

On first repeat of rnd only, after working RT, replace beginning-of-rnd marker in center of RT. On all following repeats, work as RT.

On last repeat of rnd only, after working LT, slip 1 st back to left-hand needle, ready to work it with the first st of the following rnd. On all preceding repeats, work as LT.

CO 134 (146, 158, 176, 188) (200, 218, 230, 248) sts. Do not join; work back and forth in rows.
Purl 1 WS row.
Begin Flat Garter Rib; work even until piece measures 2¾" (7 cm) from the beginning, ending with a WS row. Cut yarn, leaving sts on the needle.

Front Hem

Work as for back hem. Do not cut yarn.

Body

JOINING ROW (RS): With RS facing, slip last 2 sts of back hem to dpn and hold behind front hem. Using yarn attached to front sts, *k2tog (1 front st together with 1 back st from dpn), pm, k2tog (1 front st together with 1 back st from dpn); k10 (16, 30, 20, 29) (49, 34, 46, 34), [k2tog, k10 (16, 29, 17, 29) (47, 28, 43, 28)] 10 (7, 4, 8, 5) (3, 6, 4, 7) times*; slip first 2 sts of back hem to dpn and hold behind front hem, repeat from * to * once more, k1 (you should now be at beginning-of-rnd marker)—244 (274, 304, 332, 362) (390, 420, 448, 478) sts.
Knit 5 (5, 5, 9, 9) (9, 13, 13, 13) rnds.

SHAPE WAIST

WAIST DECREASE RND: [K2, k2tog, knit to 4 sts before marker, ssk, k2, sm] twice—4 sts decreased.
Repeat Waist Decrease Rnd every 6 rnds 6 more times—216 (246, 276, 304, 334) (362, 392, 420, 450) sts remain.
Work even until piece measures 8½ (8½, 8½, 9½, 9½) (9½, 10½, 10½, 10½)" [21.5 (21.5, 21.5, 24, 24) (24, 26.5, 26.5, 26.5) cm] from the beginning.

SHAPE BUST

INCREASE RND: [K2, M1L, knit to 2 sts before marker, M1R, k2, sm] twice—4 sts decreased.
Repeat Increase Rnd every 6 rnds 3 more times—232 (262, 292, 320, 350) (378, 408, 436, 466) sts remain.
Work even until piece measures 11 (11, 11, 12, 12) (12, 13, 13, 13)" [28 (28, 28, 30.5, 30.5) (30.5, 33, 33, 33) cm] from the beginning, ending 8 (9, 9, 10, 10) (10, 11, 11,

11) sts before beginning-of-rnd marker.
DIVIDING RND: [BO 16 (18, 18, 20, 20) (20, 22, 22, 22) sts for underarm (removing marker), work to 8 (9, 9, 10, 10) (10, 11, 11, 11) sts before marker] twice, knit to end—100 (113, 128, 140, 155) (169, 182, 196, 211) sts remain each for front and back.
Do not break yarn; leave sts on needle and set aside.

Sleeves

Using needle(s) in preferred style for small circumference knitting in the rnd and Long-Tail Cast-On, CO 72 (72, 72, 78, 78) (78, 90, 90, 90) sts. Join for working in the rnd, being careful not to twist sts; pm for beginning of rnd.
Begin Circular Garter Rib; work even until piece measures 2¾" (7 cm) from the beginning.
NEXT RND: K5 (5, 5, 6, 6) (6, 7, 7, 7), [k2tog, k10 (10, 10, 11, 11) (11, 13, 13, 13)] 5 times, k2tog, knit to end—66 (66, 66, 72, 72) (72, 84, 84, 84) sts remain.
Begin St st (knit every rnd); work 10 rnds even.

SHAPE SLEEVE

INCREASE RND: K2, M1L, knit to last 2 sts, M1R, k2—2 sts increased.
Repeat Increase Rnd every 14 (8, 6, 8, 6) (4, 4, 4, 4) rnds 6 (3, 2, 8, 14) (9, 3, 12, 22) more times, then every 0 (10, 8, 10, 0) (6, 6, 6, 0) rnds 0 (6, 9, 2, 0) (8, 12, 6, 0) times—80 (86, 90, 94, 102) (108, 116, 122, 130) sts.
Work even until piece measures 13¼" (33.5 cm) from the beginning, ending 8 (9, 9, 10, 10) (10, 11, 11, 11) sts before beginning-of-rnd marker.
DIVIDING RND: BO 16 (18, 18, 20, 20) (20, 22, 22, 22) sts for underarm (removing marker), knit to end—64 (68, 72, 74, 82) (88, 94, 100, 108) sts remain. Cut yarn and transfer sts to st holder or waste yarn.
Repeat for second sleeve, leaving sts on needle(s).

Yoke

JOINING RND: Using yarn attached to body, *knit across 64 (68, 72, 74, 82) (88,

94, 100, 108) sts left sleeve sts, pm, knit across 100 (113, 128, 140, 155) (169, 182, 196, 211) front sts, pm*; repeat from * to * for right sleeve and back—328 (362, 400, 428, 474) (514, 552, 592, 638) sts. Join for working in the rnd; pm for beginning of rnd.
Knit 1 rnd.
DECREASE RND: *K10 (16, 7, 6, 4) (7, 6, 4, 5) sts, [k2tog, k19 (32, 12, 10, 6) (6, 7, 11, 10) sts] 2 (1, 4, 5, 9) (9, 9, 7, 8) time(s), k2tog, k10 (16, 7, 6, 4) (7, 5, 3, 5), sm, k7 (18, 7, 6, 9) (1, 6, 7, 9), [k2tog, k12 (36, 14, 12, 6) (9, 12, 13, 14)] 6 (2, 7, 9, 17) (15, 12, 12, 12) times, k2tog, k7 (17, 7, 6, 8) (1, 6, 7, 8), sm; repeat from * once more—308 (352, 374, 396, 418) (462, 506, 550, 594) sts remain.

SHAPE BACK NECK

NOTE: Neck is shaped using German Short Rows (see Special Techniques, page 270).
Place removable marker to either side of 23 (22, 22, 22, 23) (23, 23, 23, 22) center front sts.
SHORT ROW 1 (RS): Knit to removable marker, turn.
SHORT ROW 2 (WS): DS, purl to removable marker, turn.
SHORT ROW 3: DS, knit to 3 sts before DS from previous RS row, turn.
SHORT ROW 4: DS, purl to 3 sts before DS from previous WS row, turn.
Repeat Short Rows 3 and 4 eight (8, 8, 12, 12) (12, 16, 16, 16) more times.
SHORT ROW 5: Knit to beginning-of-rnd marker.
Knit 1 rnd, closing each DS as you come to it.
K18 (10, 16, 0, 7) (21, 13, 6, 21), place marker for new beginning-of-rnd.
Begin Sashiko Compact; when you get to the center front, sts 1 and 2 of the pattern should be roughly centered (you may be 1 st off to either side).
Work even through Rnd 47 of pattern (removing all markers except beginning-of-rnd marker on Rnd 2); 112 (128, 136, 144, 152) (168, 184, 200, 216) sts remain when pattern is complete.

SIZES 52¼ AND 60¼"
[132.5 AND 153 CM] ONLY:
NEXT RND: *[K2tog, k– (–, –, –, –) (19, –, 3, –); repeat from * to end—160 sts remain.

SIZES 56¼ AND 64¼"
[143 AND 163 CM] ONLY:
NEXT RND: *K2tog, k– (–, –, –, –) (–, 5, –, 1), [k2tog, k– (–, –, –, –) (–, 6, –, 2)] – (–, –, –, –) (–, 2, –, 6) times; repeat from * to end—160 sts remain.

ALL SIZES:
Work 1" (2.5 cm) even.
BO all sts.

FINISHING
Sew underarm seams.
Block as desired.

There is no easy substitution here. To swap stitches for the yoke, you'll need to draw your chosen stitch into the yoke wedge on page 258. The pattern stitch needs to fill or almost fill the chart. Look for a PSS of 80–90. This may seem like a wide range, but I've found it works fine.

EXTREME YOKE PULLOVER

Sketch Coat

A simple silhouette becomes the canvas for textures and lines of twisted stitches. Easy to wear and uncomplicated to knit. The self-finished front edge continues around the neck-hugging collar. Knitters experienced with steeks may want to knit this one in the round, with steeks for the front opening and armholes. For the rest of us, though, the pattern is written flat, in easy-to-manage pieces.

SIZES
To fit bust 30 (34, 38, 42, 46) (50, 54, 58, 62)" [76 (86.5, 96.5, 106.5, 117) (127, 137, 147.5, 157.5) cm]

FINISHED MEASUREMENTS
36 (40, 44, 48, 52) (56, 60, 64, 68)" [91.5 (101.5, 111.5, 122, 132) (142, 152.5, 162.5, 172.5) cm] bust

YARN
Brooklyn Tweed Shelter [100% American Targhee-Columbia wool; 140 yards (128 meters)/50 grams]: 10 (11, 12, 13, 14) (15, 16, 17, 19) skeins Barn Owl

NEEDLES
One pair straight needles, size US 5 (3.75 mm)

One pair straight needles, size US 7 (4.5 mm)

Change needle size if necessary to obtain correct gauge.

NOTIONS
Stitch markers; removable stitch markers; stitch holder or waste yarn

GAUGE
21½ sts and 28 rows = 4" (10 cm) in Sketch, using larger needles

35-st repeat from Sketch measures 6½" (16.5 cm) wide, using larger needles

STITCH PATTERNS
2×2 RIB
(multiple of 4 sts + 2; 2-row repeat)

ROW 1 (RS): K2, *p2, k2; repeat from * to end.

ROW 2: P2, *k2, p2; repeat from * to end.

Repeat Rows 1 and 2 for pattern.

SKETCH (#115)
Note: Pattern is worked from charts only; work swatch from Sketch (page 146).

PATTERN NOTES
The back and fronts of this coat are worked from the bottom up in pieces, then the shoulders are sewn together and the neck extensions are worked to the center back neck, joined using 3-Needle Bind-Off, then sewn in place. The sleeves are picked up from the armhole edges and worked back and forth in rows to the cuffs.

When shaping shoulders in charted pattern, if there are not enough stitches to work a full twisted stitch, work the affected stitch in Stockinette stitch instead.

Back
Using smaller needles and Long-Tail Cast-On (see Special Techniques, page 270), CO 106 (118, 130, 142, 154) (166, 178, 190, 202) sts.

Begin 2×2 Rib (beginning with Row 2); work even until piece measures 3" (7.5 cm) from the beginning, ending with a RS row.

Change to larger needles.

NEXT ROW (WS): P7 (7, 8, 4, 4) (4, 4, 4, 9), [p2tog, p13 (15, 12, 9, 10) (11, 12, 13, 11)] 6 (6, 8, 12, 12) (12, 12, 12, 14) times, p2tog, purl to end—99 (111, 121, 129, 141) (153, 165, 177, 187) sts remain.

SET-UP ROW: K1 (edge st; keep in St st), work Sketch Chart (beginning and ending as indicated in chart for your size), to last st, k1 (edge st, keep in St st). Work even until piece measures 29" (73.5 cm) from the beginning, ending with a WS row.

SHAPE SHOULDERS
BO 4 (5, 6, 6, 7) (8, 9, 9, 10) sts at beginning of next 4 (8, 12, 4, 10) (12, 14, 4, 8) rows, then 5 (6, 7, 7, 8) (9, 0, 10, 11) sts at beginning of next 10 (6, 2, 10, 4) (2, 0, 10, 6) rows.

BO remaining 33 (35, 35, 35, 39) (39, 39, 41, 41) sts.

Left Front
Using smaller needles and Long-Tail Cast-On, CO 53 (61, 69, 73, 77) (85, 93, 97, 105) sts.

SET-UP ROW (WS): Slip 2 purlwise wyif, k1, work in 2×2 Rib, beginning with Row 2, to end.

NEXT ROW: Work to last 3 sts, p1, k2. Work even until piece measures 3" (7.5 cm) from the beginning, ending with a RS row. Change to larger needles.

NEXT ROW (WS): Slip 2 purlwise wyif, k1, p7 (4, 4, 4, 6) (5, 4, 6, 5), [p2tog, p15 (10, 6, 8, 10) (8, 7, 8, 7)] 2 (4, 7, 6, 5) (7, 9, 8, 10) times, p2tog, purl to end—50 (56, 61,

6¼ (7, 8, 8¾, 9½) (10½, 11¾, 12¾, 13½)"
16 (18, 20.5, 22, 24) (26.5, 30, 32.5, 34.5) cm

6 (6¾, 6½, 6½, 7¼) (7½, 7¼, 7½, 7¾)"
15 (17, 16.5, 16.5, 18.5) (19, 18.5, 19, 19.5) cm

2"
5 cm

7¼ (7¾, 8, 8½, 9¼) (9¾, 10, 10¾, 11¼)"
18.5 (19.5, 20.5, 21.5, 21.5, 23.5) (25, 25.5, 27.5, 28.5) cm

31"
78.5 cm

21¾ (21¼, 21, 20½, 19¾) (19¼, 19, 18¼, 17¾)"
55 (54, 53.5, 52, 50) (49, 48.5, 46.5, 45) cm

BACK

29"
73.5 cm

18½ (20¾, 22½, 24, 26¼) (28½, 30¾, 33, 34¾)"
47 (52.5, 57, 61, 66.5) (72.5, 78, 84, 88.5) cm

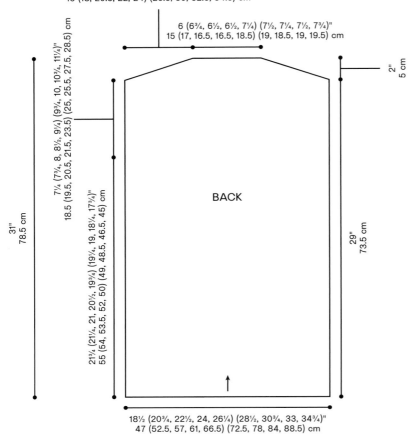

3¼ (3¼, 3¼, 3½, 3¾) (3¾, 3¾, 3¾, 4)"
8.5 (8.5, 8.5, 9, 9.5) (9.5, 9.5, 9.5, 10) cm

6 (6¾, 6½, 6½, 7¼) (7½, 7¼, 7½, 7¾)"
15 (17, 16.5, 16.5, 18.5) (19, 18.5, 19, 19.5) cm

2"
5 cm

3¼ (3¼, 3¼, 3¼, 3¾) (3¾, 3¾, 4, 4)"
8.5 (8.5, 8.5, 8.5, 9.5) (9.5, 9.5, 10, 10) cm

LEFT FRONT

29"
73.5 cm

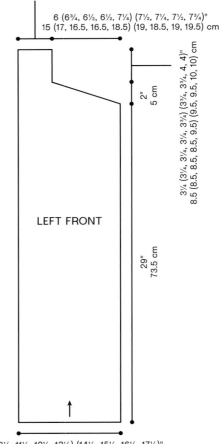

9¼ (10½, 11¼, 12¼, 13¼) (14¼, 15½, 16¼, 17½)"
23.5 (26.5, 28.5, 31, 33.5) (36, 39.5, 41.5, 44.5) cm

13½ (14½, 15¼, 16, 17½) (18½, 19¼, 20½, 21½)"
34.5 (37, 38.5, 40.5, 44.5) (47, 49, 52, 54.5) cm

SLEEVE

16"
40.5 cm

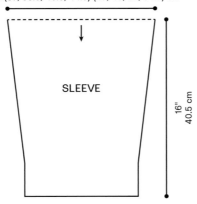

10½ (10½, 11¼, 11¼, 12) (12, 12, 12¾, 12¾)"
26.5 (26.5, 28.5, 28.5, 30.5) (30.5, 30.5, 32.5, 32.5) cm

66, 71) (77, 83, 88, 94) sts remain.

SET-UP ROW: K1 (edge st; keep in St st), work Sketch Chart (beginning and ending as indicated in chart for your size), to last 3 sts, p1, k2.

Work even until piece measures 29" (73.5 cm) from the beginning, ending with a WS row.

SHAPE SHOULDER

BO 4 (5, 6, 6, 7) (8, 9, 9, 10) sts at beginning of next 2 (4, 6, 2, 5) (6, 7, 2, 4) RS rows, then 5 (6, 7, 7, 8) (9, 0, 10, 11) sts at beginning of next 5 (3, 1, 5, 2) (1, 0, 5, 3) RS row(s)—17 (18, 18, 19, 20) (20, 20, 20, 21) sts remain.

SHAPE NECK EXTENSION

SET-UP ROW (WS): Slip 2 purlwise wyif, k1, work to last st, p1 (edge st; keep in St st). Work even until piece measures 3¼ (3¼, 3¼, 3¼, 3¾) (3¾, 3¾, 4, 4)" [8.5 (8.5, 8.5, 8.5, 9.5) (9.5, 9.5, 10, 10) cm] from end of shoulder shaping, ending with a WS row. Cut yarn, leaving a 6" (15 cm) tail; transfer sts to st holder or waste yarn.

Right Front

Using smaller needles and Long-Tail Cast-On, CO 53 (61, 69, 73, 77) (85, 93, 97, 105) sts.

SET-UP ROW (WS): Work in 2×2 Rib, beginning with Row 2, to last 3 sts, k1, p2.

NEXT ROW: Slip 2 purlwise wyib, p1, work to end.

Work even until piece measures 3" (7.5 cm), ending with a RS row.

Change to larger needles.

NEXT ROW (WS): P7 (4, 4, 4, 6) (5, 4, 6, 5), [p2tog, p15 (10, 6, 8, 10) (8, 7, 8, 7)] 2 (4, 7, 6, 5) (7, 9, 8, 10) times, p2tog, purl to last 3 sts, k1, p2—50 (56, 61, 66, 71) (77, 83, 88, 94) sts remain.

SET-UP ROW: Slip 2 purlwise wyib, p1, work Sketch Chart (beginning and ending as indicated in chart for your size), to last st, k1 (edge st; keep in St st).

Work even until piece measures 29" (73.5 cm) from the beginning, ending with a WS row.

SHAPE SHOULDER

BO 4 (5, 6, 6, 7) (8, 9, 9, 10) sts at beginning of next 2 (4, 6, 2, 5) (6, 7, 2, 4) WS rows, then 5 (6, 7, 7, 8) (9, 0, 10, 11) sts at beginning of next 5 (3, 1, 5, 2) (1, 0, 5, 3) WS row(s)—17 (18, 18, 19, 20) (20, 20, 20, 21) sts remain.

SHAPE NECK EXTENSION

SET-UP ROW 1 (RS): K1 (edge st, keep in St st), work to last 3 sts, k1, p2.

SET-UP ROW 2: Slip 2 purlwise wyib, p1, work to last st, k1.

Work even until piece measures 3¼ (3¼, 3¼, 3¼, 3¾) (3¾, 3¾, 4, 4)" [8.5 (8.5, 8.5, 8.5, 9.5) (9.5, 9.5, 10, 10) cm] from end of shoulder shaping, ending with a WS row. Leave sts on the needle; do not cut yarn.

JOIN NECK EXTENSIONS

With WSs of neck extensions together (seam will be on the RS) and using larger needles and yarn attached to right front neck extension, join extensions using 3-Needle Bind-Off (see Special Techniques, page 270). Sew shoulder seams. Sew joined neck extensions to back neck edge.

Sleeves

Place removable markers 7¼ (7¾, 8, 8½, 9¼) (9¾, 10, 10¾, 11¼)" [18.5 (19.5, 20.5, 21.5, 23.5) (25, 25.5, 27.5, 28.5) cm] down from each shoulder seam on fronts and back. NOTE: The distance between the markers is approximately 1" (2.5 cm) wider than the top of the sleeve. This makes the sleeve lie flat and keeps it from bulging at the top.

With RS facing, using larger needles, pick up and knit 72 (78, 82, 86, 94) (100, 104, 110, 116) sts between markers. Do not join; work back and forth in rows. Purl 1 row.

SET-UP ROW (RS): K1 (edge st; keep in St st), work Sketch Chart (beginning and ending as indicated in chart for your size), to last st, k1 (edge st, keep in St st). Work 11 (9, 9, 7, 7) (7, 5, 5, 5) rows even.

SHAPE SLEEVE

DECREASE ROW (RS): K1, k2tog, work to last 3 sts, ssk, k1—2 sts decreased.

Repeat Decrease Row every 10 (8, 8, 6, 6) (6, 4, 4, 4) rows 6 (5, 5, 12, 8) (2, 18, 17, 14) times, then every 8 (6, 6, 0, 4) (4, 2, 2, 2) rows 1 (5, 5, 0, 6) (15, 1, 3, 9) time(s)—56 (56, 60, 60, 64) (64, 64, 68, 68) sts remain.

Work even until piece measures 13" (33 cm) from the beginning, ending with a RS row.

Change to smaller needles.

Purl 1 row, increasing 2 sts evenly across—58 (58, 62, 62, 66) (66, 66, 70, 70) sts.

Change to 2×2 Rib; work even for 3" (7.5 cm), ending with a WS row.

BO all sts in pattern.

FINISHING

Sew side and sleeve seams.

Block as desired.

Switch out charts from other chapters, as long as their PSS is about 85. A handful of my favorite stitches that would be easy to substitute here are Diamonds Allover (#5), Plaid Medium (#16), Triplet Weave Filled (#26), and Rattan Filled (#61). You will have to determine the starting and ending points of your chart, using the number of stitches specified for each piece.

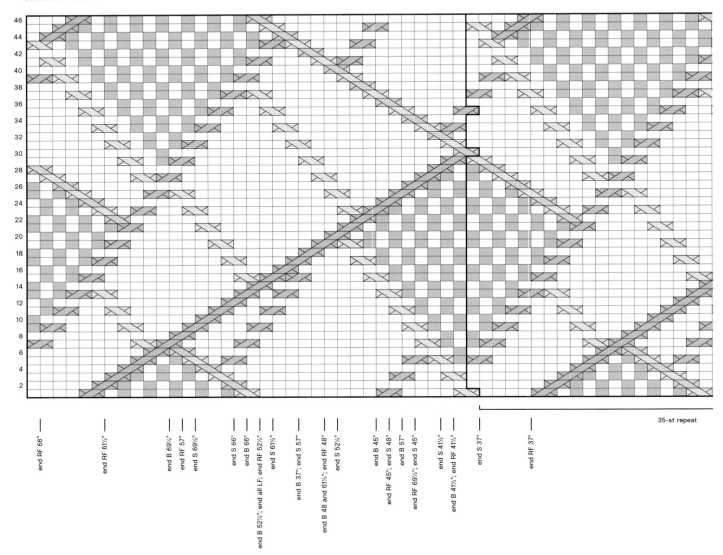

35-st repeat

end RF 66"

end RF 61½"

end B 69½"
end RF 57"
end S 69½"

end S 66"
end B 66"
end B 52½"; end all LF; end RF 52½"
end S 61½"

end B 37"; end S 57"

end B 48 and 61½"; end RF 48"
end S 52½"

end B 45"
end RF 45"; end S 48"
end B 57"
end RF 69½"; end S 45"
end S 41½"
end B 41½"; end RF 41½"

end S 37"

end RF 37"

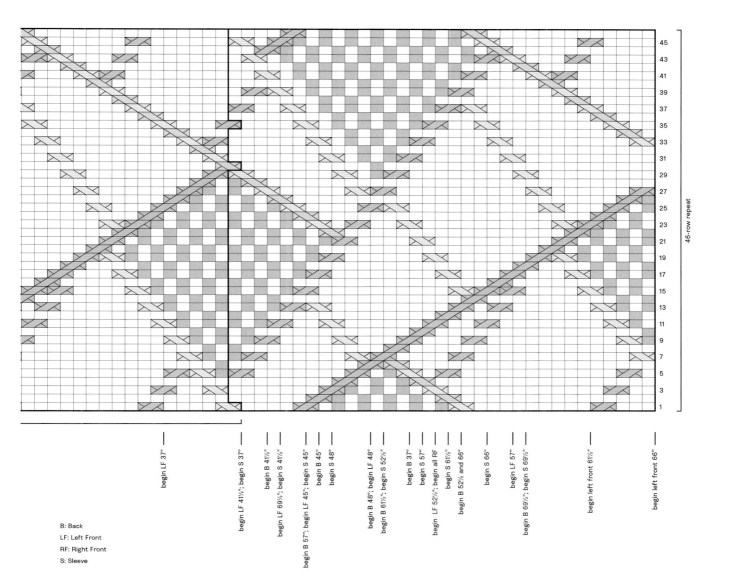

45
43
41
39
37
35
33
31
29
27
25
23
21
19
17
15
13
11
9
7
5
3
1

46-row repeat

B: Back
LF: Left Front
RF: Right Front
S: Sleeve

begin LF 37"
begin LF 41½"; begin S 37"
begin B 41½"
begin LF 69½"; begin S 41½"
begin B 57"; begin LF 45"; begin S 45"
begin B 45"
begin S 48"
begin B 48"; begin LF 48"
begin B 61½"; begin S 52½"
begin B 37"
begin S 57"
begin LF 52½"; begin all RF
begin S 61½"
begin B 52½ and 66"
begin S 66"
begin LF 57"
begin B 69½"; begin S 69½"
begin left front 61½"
begin left front 66"

Snowflake Scarf

Five identical hexagons, each started on the outside edge and decreasing to the center, combine to make an interesting and versatile scarf. While the hexagons here are attached in a row, forming a straight line, you might experiment with attaching the shapes along a different edge, making a large V formation or curving them into a crescent. The Garter stitch worked into the beginning of each piece means that there is no added finishing, and since the pieces are attached as you go, there is no sewing either.

FINISHED MEASUREMENTS
HEXAGON: Approximately 11" (28 cm) wide (point to point) × 9½" (24 cm) long (flat edge to flat edge)

SCARF: Approximately 11" (28 cm) wide × 47½" (120.5 cm) long

YARN
Blue Sky Fibers Spud & Chloë Fine [80% superwash wool/20% silk; 248 yards (227 meters)/65 grams]: 3 hanks #7810 Lipstick

NEEDLES
One 24" (60 cm) long circular needle, size US 3 (3.25 mm)

Needle(s) in preferred style for small circumference knitting in the rnd, size US 3 (3.25 mm)

Change needle size if necessary to obtain correct gauge.

NOTIONS
Stitch markers

GAUGE
28 sts and 36 rows = 4"/10 cm in St st

STITCH PATTERN
WATER LILY (#118)
(multiple of 39 sts, decreases to multiple of 1 st; 51 rnds)
RND 1: *P1, k2tog, knit to 2 sts before marker, ssk; repeat from * to end—2 sts decreased.

RND 2: *P1, knit to marker; repeat from * to end.

RND 3: *P1, k17, RT, knit to marker; repeat from * to end.

RND 4: Repeat Rnd 1.

RND 5: *P1, k15, LT, RT, knit to marker; repeat from * to end.

RND 6: Repeat Rnd 2.

RND 7: *P1, k2tog, k14, RT, knit to 2 sts before marker, ssk; repeat from * to end—2 sts decreased.

RND 8: Repeat Rnd 2.

RND 9: *P1, k14, RT, LT, knit to marker; repeat from * to end.

RND 10: Repeat Rnd 1.

RND 11: *P1, k12, RT twice, LT, knit to marker; repeat from * to end.

RND 12: Repeat Rnd 2.

RND 13: *P1, k2tog, k9, [RT, LT] twice, knit to 2 sts before marker, ssk; repeat from * to end—2 sts decreased.

RND 14: Repeat Rnd 2.

RND 15: *P1, k9, RT, LT, RT twice, LT, knit to marker; repeat from * to end.

RND 16: Repeat Rnd 1.

RND 17: *P1, k7, [RT, LT] 3 times, knit to marker; repeat from * to end.

RND 18: Repeat Rnd 2.

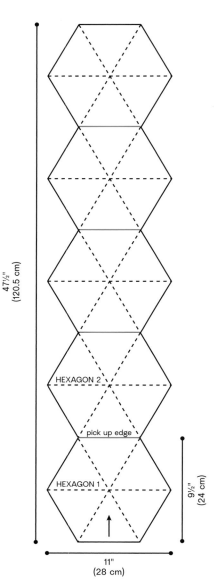

47½"
(120.5 cm)

HEXAGON 2

pick up edge

HEXAGON 1

9½"
(24 cm)

11"
(28 cm)

RND 19: *P1, k2tog, k4, RT, LT, RT, k2, LT, RT, LT, k4, ssk; repeat from * to end—2 sts decreased.

RND 20: Repeat Rnd 2.

RND 21: *P1, k4, RT, LT, RT, k4, LT, RT, LT, k4; repeat from * to end.

RND 22: Repeat Rnd 1.

RND 23: *P1, k2, RT, LT, RT, k6, LT, RT, LT, k2; repeat from * to end.

RND 24: Repeat Rnd 2.

RND 25: *P1, k2tog, k1, LT, RT, LT, k4, RT, LT, RT, k1, ssk; repeat from * to end—2 sts decreased.

RND 26: Repeat Rnd 2.

RND 27: *P1, k1, LT, RT, k2, LT, k2, RT, k2, LT, RT, k1; repeat from * to end.

RND 28: Repeat Rnd 1.

RND 29: *P1, k1, [RT, k4, LT] twice, k1; repeat from * to end.

RND 30: Repeat Rnd 2.

RND 31: *P1, k2tog, k6, LT, knit to 2 sts before marker, ssk; repeat from * to end—2 sts decreased.

RND 32: Repeat Rnd 2.

RND 33: *P1, k6, RT, LT, knit to marker; repeat from * to end.

RND 34: Repeat Rnd 1.

RND 35: *P1, k4, RT, k2, LT, k4; repeat from * to end.

RND 36: Repeat Rnd 2.

RND 37: *P1, k2tog, k1, RT, k4, LT, k1, ssk; repeat from * to end—2 sts decreased.

RND 38: Repeat Rnd 2.

RND 39: *P1, k1, RT, k6, LT, k1; repeat from * to end.

RNDS 40 AND 41: Repeat Rnds 1 and 2.

RND 42: Repeat Rnd 2.

RNDS 43-48: Repeat Rnds 1 and 2 three times.

RND 49: *P1, k2tog, ssk; repeat from * to end—2 sts decreased.

RND 50: *P1, k2; repeat from * to end.

RND 51: *P3tog; repeat from * to end—2 sts decreased.

PATTERN NOTES

The scarf begins with a single hexagon worked in the round. For each following hexagon, you will cast on stitches for

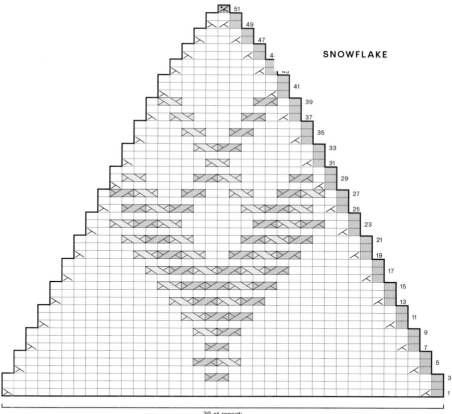

SNOWFLAKE

39-st repeat;
decreases to 1-st repeat

five sides, then pick up stitches from one side of the previous hexagon.
Use Long-Tail Cast-On for all cast-on stitches in this pattern.

Hexagon 1

Using circular needle and Long-Tail Cast-On (see Special Techniques, page 270), [CO 41 sts, pm] 6 times—246 sts. Join for working in the rnd, being careful not to twist sts; last marker placed is beginning-of-rnd marker.

SET-UP RND: [P1, knit to marker] 6 times. Purl 1 rnd.

DECREASE RND: [P1, k2tog, knit to 2 sts before marker, ssk] 6 times—234 sts remain.
Purl 1 rnd.

NEXT RND: [P1, knit to marker] 6 times. Begin Snowflake. Work even until pattern is complete—6 sts remain.
Cut yarn, leaving a long tail. Thread tail through remaining sts, pull tight, and fasten off.

Hexagon 2

Using circular needle, [CO 41 sts, pm] 5 times, then pick up and knit 41 sts along one edge of Hexagon 1, pm—246 sts. Complete as for Hexagon 1.

Hexagons 3, 4, and 5

Using circular needle, [CO 41 sts, pm] 5 times, then pick up and knit 41 sts along the edge opposite the attached edge of previous Hexagon, pm—246 sts. Complete as for Hexagon 1.

FINISHING

Block as desired.

Any of the ten charts in Chapter 9 can be used in this pattern without any other changes.

Hexagon Pullover

One large hexagon, embellished with a repeated, snowflake-like pattern, becomes the front of this roomy pullover. Another forms the back. The innate geometry here makes the slant of raglan sleeves the natural choice. Knit from the outside in, the seamless hexagon is picked up along the raglan edges of the sleeves and the slanted edges of triangular side inserts. Echoing the angles found throughout the sweater, the neck and bottom edges are finished off with mitered ribbing.

SIZES
To fit bust 30 (34, 38, 42, 46) (50, 54, 58, 62)" [76 (86.5, 96.5, 106.5, 117) (127, 137, 147.5, 157.5) cm]

FINISHED MEASUREMENTS
36 (40, 43, 48, 53) (56, 60, 65, 68)" [91.5 (101.5, 109, 122, 134.5) (142, 152.5, 165, 172.5) cm] bust

YARN
mYak Baby Yak Medium [100% baby yak; 125 yards (117 meters)/50 grams]: 9 (10, 11, 12, 13) (14, 16, 17, 19) skeins Mustard

NEEDLES
One pair straight needles, size 4 (3.5 mm)

One 16" (40 cm) long circular needle, size US 4 (3.5 mm)

Needle(s) in preferred style for small circumference circular knitting in the rnd, size US 6 (4 mm)

One 32" (80 cm) long circular needle, size US 6 (4 mm)

Change needle size if necessary to obtain correct gauge.

NOTIONS
Stitch markers

GAUGE
21 sts and 32 rows = 4" (10 cm) in St st, using larger needles

STITCH PATTERNS

2×2 RIB
(multiple of 4 sts + 2; 2-row repeat)

ROW 1 (RS): K2, *p2, k2; repeat from * to end.

ROW 2: P2, *k2, p2; repeat from * to end.

Repeat Rows 1 and 2 for 2x2 Rib.

DROID (#122)
(multiple of 39 sts, decreases to a multiple of 1 st; 51 rnds)

Place a marker between pattern repeats.

RND 1: *P1, k2tog, k7, LT, k16, RT, knit to 2 sts before marker, ssk; repeat from * to end—2 sts decreased.

RND 2: *P1, knit to marker; repeat from * to end.

RND 3: *P1, k9, LT, k2, RT, k6, LT, k2, RT, knit to marker; repeat from * to end.

RND 4: *P1, k2tog, knit to 2 sts before marker, ssk; repeat from * to end—2 sts decreased.

RND 5: *P1, k9, LT, RT, LT k4, RT, LT, RT, knit to marker; repeat from * to end.

RND 6: *P1, k12, p2, k6, p2, knit to marker; repeat from * to end.

RND 7: *P1, k2tog, k8, LT, p2, LT, k2, RT, p2, RT, knit to 2 sts before marker, ssk; repeat from * to end—2 sts decreased.

RND 8: *P1, k11, p3, k4, p3, knit to marker; repeat from * to end.

RND 9: *P1, k8, RT, LT, p2, LT, RT, p2, RT, LT, knit to marker; repeat from * to end.

RND 10: *P1, k2tog, k10, p3, k2, p3, knit to 2 sts before marker, ssk; repeat from * to end—2 sts decreased.

RND 11: *P1, k6, RT, k2, [LT, p2] twice, RT, k2, LT, knit to marker; repeat from * to end.

RND 12: *P1, k12, p2, k2, p2, knit to marker; repeat from * to end.

RND 13: *P1, k2tog, k3, RT, k4, [LT, RT] twice, k4, LT, k3, ssk, repeat from * to end—2 sts decreased.

RND 14: *P1, k13, p2, knit to marker; repeat from * to end.

RND 15: *P1, k3, RT, [k2, RT] twice, p2, RT, [k2, LT] twice, k3; repeat from * to end.

RND 16: *P1, k2tog, k11, p2, knit to 2 sts before marker, ssk; repeat from * to end—2 sts decreased.

RND 17: *P1, k3, [LT, RT] 5 times, k3; repeat from * to end.

RND 18: *P1, k6, p2, [k2, p2] 3 times, knit to marker; repeat from * to end.

RND 19: *P1, k2tog, k2, [LT, p2] 4 times, RT, k2, ssk; repeat from * to end—2 sts decreased.

RND 20: *P1, k5, p2, [k2, p2] 3 times, knit to marker; repeat from * to end.

RND 21: *P1, k4, [LT, RT] 4 times, k4; repeat from * to end.

RND 22: *P1, k2tog, k9, p2, knit to 2 sts before marker, ssk; repeat from * to end—2 sts decreased.

RND 23: *P1, k4, RT, k2, RT, p2, RT, k2, LT, k4; repeat from * to end.

RND 24: *P1, k10, p2, knit to marker; repeat from * to end.

RND 25: *P1, k2tog, k5, [RT, LT] twice, knit to 2 sts before marker, ssk; repeat from * to end—2 sts decreased.

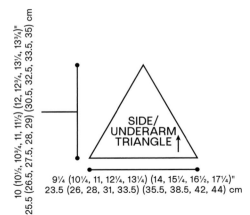

SIDE/
UNDERARM
TRIANGLE ↑

10 (10½, 10¾, 11, 11½) (12, 12¾, 13¼, 13¾)" cm
25.5 (26.5, 27.5, 28, 29) (30.5, 32.5, 33.5, 35) cm

9¼ (10¼, 11, 12¼, 13¼) (14, 15¼, 16½, 17¼)"
23.5 (26, 28, 31, 33.5) (35.5, 38.5, 42, 44) cm

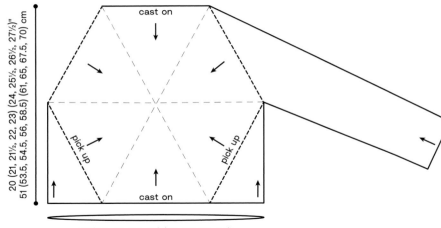

cast on

pick up   pick up

cast on

20 (21, 21½, 22, 23) (24, 25½, 26½, 27½)"
51 (53.5, 54.5, 56, 58.5) (61, 65, 67.5, 70) cm

36 (40, 43, 48, 53) (56, 60, 65, 68)"
91.5 (101.5, 109, 122, 134.5) (142, 152.5, 165, 172.5) cm

RND 26: Repeat Rnd 2.

RND 27: *P1, k5, RT, [k2, LT] twice, knit to marker; repeat from * to end.

RND 28: Repeat Rnd 4.

RND 29: *P1, k3, RT, k2, RT, LT, k2, LT, k3; repeat from * to end.

RND 30: *P1, k8, p2, knit to marker; repeat from * to end.

RND 31: *P1, k2tog, RT, k2, LT, p2, RT, k2, LT, ssk; repeat from * to end—2 sts decreased.

RND 32: *P1, k7, p2, knit to marker; repeat from * to end.

RND 33: *P1, [RT, k4, LT] twice; repeat from * to end.

RND 34: Repeat Rnd 4.

RND 35: *P1, k6, LT, knit to marker; repeat from * to end.

RND 36: Repeat Rnd 2.

RND 37: *P1, k2tog, k3, RT, LT, k3, ssk; repeat from * to end—2 sts decreased.

RND 38: *P1, k5, p2, knit to marker; repeat from * to end.

RND 39: *P1, k3, RT, p2, LT, k3; repeat from * to end.

RND 40: *P1, k2tog, k2, p4, k2, ssk, repeat from * to end—2 sts decreased.

RND 41: *P1, k1, RT, p4, LT, k1; repeat from * to end.

RND 42: *P1, k3, p4, k3; repeat from * to end.

RND 43: *P1, k2tog, LT, p2, RT, ssk; repeat from * to end—2 sts decreased.

RND 44: *P1, k3, p2, k3; repeat from * to end.

RND 45: *P1, k2tog, LT, RT, ssk; repeat from * to end—2 sts decreased.

RND 46: Repeat Rnd 2.

RND 47: *P1, k2tog, LT, ssk; repeat from * to end—2 sts decreased.

RND 48: Repeat Rnd 2.

RND 49: *P1, k2tog, ssk, repeat from * to end—2 sts decreased.

RND 50: *P1, k2; repeat from * to end.

RND 51: *P3tog; repeat from * to end—2 sts decreased.

PATTERN NOTES

This pullover begins with two side/underam triangles. The back and front each consist of a hexagon, for which the stitches are either picked up from the side triangles and sleeve caps or cast on. Each hexagon is worked from the outside edge in to the center. Stitches are picked up in separate sections for the bottom ribbing, and each section is worked down separately.

Side/Underarm Triangles (make 2)

Using larger straight needles and Long-Tail Cast-On (see Special Techniques, page 270), CO 48 (54, 58, 64, 70) (74, 80, 86, 90) sts.

Begin St st; purl 1 row.

SHAPE TRIANGLE

You will be working decreases on both RS and WS rows, as instructed below. Work Decrease Rows as follows:

RS DECREASE ROWS: K1, k2tog, knit to last 3 sts, ssk, k1—2 sts decreased.

WS DECREASE ROWS: P1, ssp, purl to last 3 sts, p2tog, p1—2 sts decreased.

Work decreases on RS and/or WS row as follows:

*Work Decrease Row (RS or WS) once—2 sts decreased.

Work 3 (3, 3, 2, 2) (2, 2, 2, 2) rows even.

Repeat from * 12 (7, 4, 27, 25) (25, 25, 23, 23) more times—22 (38, 48, 8, 18) (22, 28, 38, 42) sts remain.

**Work Decrease Row (RS or WS) once—2 sts decreased.

Work 2 (2, 2, 1, 1) (1, 1, 1, 1) row(s) even.

Repeat from ** 8 (16, 21, 1, 6) (8, 11, 16, 18) more times—4 sts remain.

BO all sts.

Sleeves

Using smaller straight needles and Long-Tail Cast-On, CO 50 (50, 54, 54, 54) (58, 58, 66, 66) sts.

Begin 2×2 Rib (beginning with Row 2); work even until piece measures 3" (7.5 cm) from the beginning, ending with a RS row.

Change to larger needles.

Begin St st; purl 1 row.

SHAPE SLEEVE

INCREASE ROW (RS): K2, M1L, knit to last 2 sts, M1R, k2—2 sts increased.

Repeat Increase Row every 28 (14, 12, 8, 6) (6, 4, 6, 4) rows 1 (4, 5, 11, 4) (4, 1, 8, 4) more time(s), then every 30 (16, 14, 0, 8) (8, 6, 8, 6) rows 2 (2, 2, 0, 8) (8, 14, 5, 12) times—58 (64, 70, 78, 80) (84, 90, 94, 100) sts.

Work even until piece measures 17" (43 cm) from the beginning, ending with a WS row.

SHAPE CAP

DECREASE ROW (RS): K1, k2tog, knit to last 3 sts, ssk, k1—2 sts decreased.

Repeat Decrease Row every 4 rows 13 (12, 12, 9, 10) (10, 9, 8, 8) more times, then every 13 (17, 20, 27, 27) (29, 33, 36, 39) times—4 sts remain.

Work 2 rows even.

NEXT ROW (WS): P2tog twice.

BO remaining 2 sts.

Back

Note: Use Cable Cast-On (see Special Techniques, page 270) for all CO sts in this section.

With RS of one side/underarm triangle facing, using larger circular needle and beginning at BO edge of triangle, pick up and knit 47 (53, 57, 63, 69) (73, 79, 85, 89) sts along left edge of triangle (ending at CO edge), pm; turn to WS and and CO 47 (53, 57, 63, 69) (73, 79, 85, 89) sts, turn to RS, pm; pick up and knit 47 (53, 57, 63, 69) (73, 79, 85, 89) sts along right edge of second side/underarm triangle (beginning at CO edge of triangle and ending at BO edge), pm; pick up and knit 47 (53, 57, 63, 69) (73, 79, 85, 89) sts along right edge of first sleeve cap, pm; turn to WS and CO 47 (53, 57, 63, 69) (73, 79, 85, 89) sts, turn to RS, pm; pick up and knit 47 (53, 57, 63, 69) (73, 79, 85, 89) sts along left edge of second sleeve cap, pm for beginning of rnd—282 (318, 342, 378, 414) (438, 474, 510, 534) sts. Join for working in the rnd.

Knit 1 rnd.

SHAPE HEXAGON

NOTE: Change to needle(s) in preferred style for small circumference knitting in the rnd when necessary for the number of sts on needle(s).

DECREASE RND: *K1, k2tog, knit to 3 sts before marker, ssk, k1, sm; repeat from * to end—12 sts decreased; 2 sts decreased between markers.

Knit 6 (4, 3, 3, 2) (2, 2, 2, 2) rnds.

Repeat the last 7 (5, 4, 4, 3) (3, 3, 3, 3) rnds 3 (3, 7, 0, 10) (10, 10, 8, 8) more times—234 (270, 246, 366, 282) (306, 342, 402, 426) sts remain; 39 (45, 41, 61, 47) (51, 57, 67, 71) sts remain between markers.

SIZES 40, 43, 48, 53, 56, 60, 65, AND 68" [101.5, 109, 122, 134.5, 142, 152.5, 165, AND 172.5 CM] ONLY:
Repeat Decrease Rnd once.
Knit – (3, 2, 2, 1) (1, 1, 1, 1) rnd(s).
Repeat the last – (4, 3, 3, 2) (2, 2, 2, 2) rnds – (2, 0, 10, 3) (5, 8, 13, 15) more times—39 sts remain.

ALL SIZES:
Begin Droid; work even through Rnd 51 of pattern—6 sts remain when pattern is complete. Cut yarn, leaving a long tail. Thread tail through remaining sts, pull tight, and fasten off.

Front

Work as for back.

FINISHING

Block as desired.

BOTTOM RIB
With RS facing and using smaller straight needles, pick up and knit 52 (56, 60, 64, 68) (76, 80, 84, 88) sts along CO edge of one side/underarm triangle.

SET-UP ROW (WS): P3, *k2, p2; repeat from * to last st, p1.

ROW 1: K2, ssk, work to last 4 sts, k2tog, k2—2 sts decreased.

ROWS 2, 3, AND 4: Knit the knit sts and

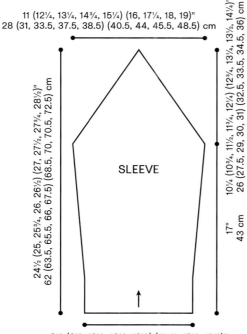

11 (12¼, 13¼, 14¾, 15¼) (16, 17¼, 18, 19)"
28 (31, 33.5, 37.5, 38.5) (40.5, 44, 45.5, 48.5) cm

24½ (25, 25¼, 26, 26½) (27, 27½, 27¾, 28½)"
62 (63.5, 65.5, 66, 67.5) (68.5, 70, 70.5, 72.5) cm

SLEEVE

10¼ (10¾, 11½, 11¾, 12¼) (12¾, 13¼, 13½, 14¼)"
26 (27.5, 29, 30, 31) (32.5, 33.5, 34.5, 36) cm

17"
43 cm

9½ (9½, 10¼, 10¼, 10¼) (11, 11, 12½, 12½)"
24 (24, 26, 26, 26) (28, 28, 32, 32) cm

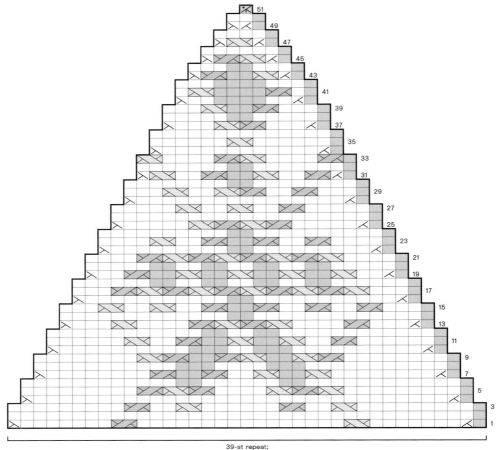

39-st repeat;
decreases to 1-st repeat

purl the purl sts as they face you.
Repeat Rows 1–4 two more times, then
repeat Row 2 once more—48 (52, 56, 60,
64) (72, 76, 80, 84) sts remain.
BO all sts in pattern.
Repeat for second side/underarm
triangle and the CO edge of the bottom
triangle in each hexagon.

**SIZES 53, 56, 60, 65 AND 68" [134.5,
142, 152.5, 165 AND 172.5 CM] ONLY:**
Sew shoulder seams for – (–, –, –, 1¼)
(1½, 2½, 3¼, 4)" [– (–, –, –, 3) (4, 6.5, 8.5,
10) cm] on each side.

ALL SIZES:
NECKBAND
With RS facing, using smaller circular
needle and beginning at top center of
sleeve or at shoulder seam, *pick up and
knit 52 (56, 60, 68, 68) (72, 72, 72, 72) sts
along neck edge to opposite sleeve or
shoulder seam, pm; repeat from * once
more—104 (112, 120, 136, 136) (144, 144,
144, 144) sts. Join for working in the rnd;
pm for beginning of rnd.

**SIZES 36 AND 40" [91.5 AND 101.5 CM]
ONLY:**
SET-UP RND: [K1, p2, *k2, p2; repeat from
* to 1 st before marker, k1] twice.
Work 7 rnds even.

**SIZES 43, 48, 53, 56, 60, 65, AND 68"
[109, 122, 134.5, 142, 152.5, 165, AND
172.5 CM] ONLY:**
RND 1: [K1, p2, *k2, p2; repeat from * to 1
st before marker, k1] twice.
RND 2: [Ssk, work to 2 sts before marker,
k2tog] twice—4 sts decreased.
Repeat Rnds 1 and 2 three more times— –
(–, 104, 120, 120) (128, 128, 128, 128) sts
remain.

ALL SIZES:
BO all sts in pattern.
Sew sleeve seams.

*Any of the ten charts in Chapter 9 can
be used in this pattern without any
other changes.*

PART III

DESIGNING YOUR OWN

The last part of this book is dedicated to getting designers interested in making up their own twisted-stitch patterns and giving them some tools to work with. First, I talk about my process of gathering and working with outside inspirations. Then I include some tools to help with planning out new stitch patterns: knitter's proportioned graph paper and diagonal grids. Finally, a series of ten lessons range from the basics of pattern design to details pertaining specifically to twisted stitches.

CHAPTER 10

Getting Started

In a world of infinite possibilities, getting started can be a challenge. I like to narrow my choices by making a framework of starting points. Specialty grids will help you wrap your head around the initial planning of patterns, from all diagonal to multidirectional grids. For the next step, actually charting a pattern, there is a page of knitter's proportioned graph paper to use for pattern planning if you are not charting with a computer drawing program. To further help you along, I've compiled a library of elements to remind you of some of the possible lines, horizontals, and verticals you might use to build your new pattern.

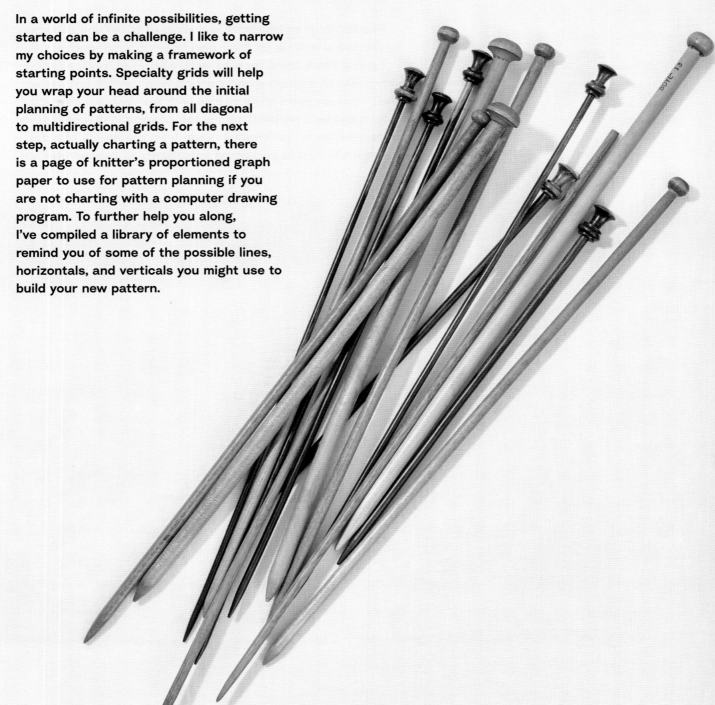

INSPIRATION

In planning this book, I spent many happy hours perusing Pinterest and looking to other arts and crafts as starting points for designs. I found a good deal of inspiration in textiles—blackwork and Sashiko embroideries, quilting and patchwork, woven damasks and twills. Just as inspiring were less related crafts like tile designs, brickwork, wallpaper, origami, and architectural ornament. Gathering inspirational photos and examining them for similarities before separating them into organized folders helped me to focus my ideas. When I wanted to get started, I dove in, chose an inspiration, and began playing with the pattern. As I

charted and test knit, the patterns inevitably changed and became something new. I can't stress enough how much an unhurried attitude helps with pattern-stitch inventions. My favorite way to work is to indulge in intense spates of working on new ideas, finishing some and leaving others to ferment. Don't throw ideas away if they are not working the first time you try. Give it a rest and come back to the idea hours, days, or months later. You may find yourself looking at the problem from a completely different angle, able to overcome the stumbling block.

LIBRARY OF ELEMENTS

Here is a visual library of elements you can use as a starting point when
making up new twisted stitches. From top to bottom:

HORIZONTAL LINES

RIGHT SLANTING LINES

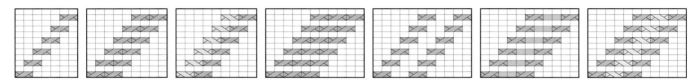

LEFT SLANTING LINES

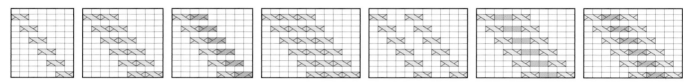

ACUTE LINES (TWISTS WORKED EVERY ROW)

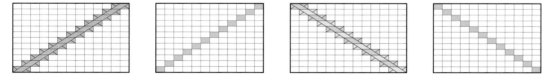

VERTICAL LINES

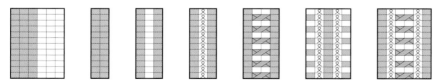

FILLS OR BACKGROUNDS

PLANNING GRIDS

Knitter's Grid

All the charts in this book are shown on a knitter's proportioned grid. As with Stockinette stitch, twisted stitches are shorter than they are wide, so a charting on a grid of similar proportions gives a more accurate picture of the final knitted outcome. Here is a page of grid for you to work on. Please feel free to photocopy this page.

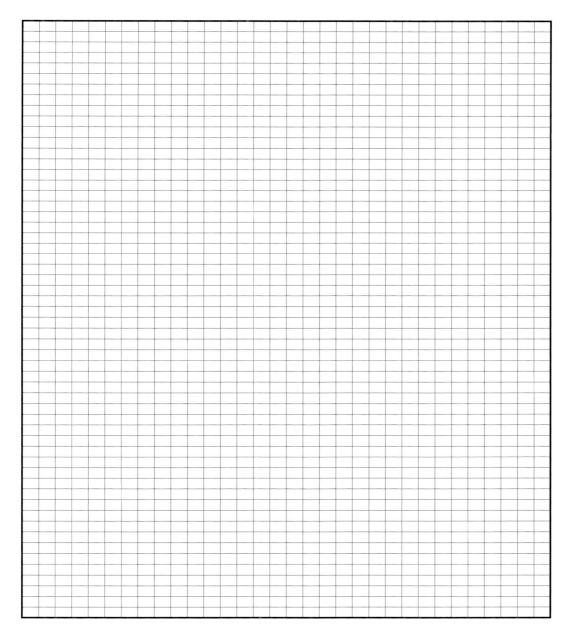

Diagonal Grid

Use this page to plan diagonal twisted-stitch designs. After you've planned your design, re-create the pattern with RT and LT symbols on knitter's graph paper. Then knit your swatch to test out the new idea. Please feel free to photocopy the grid page. To give you an idea of how to begin, here is an example of a pattern being planned on a diagonal grid.

Diagonal + Horizontal Grid

Use this page to plan twisted-stitch designs with both diagonal and horizontal elements. After you've planned your design, re-create the pattern on knitter's graph paper. Then knit your swatch to test out the new idea. Please feel free to photocopy this page.

Diagonal + Vertical Grid

Use this page to plan twisted-stitch designs with both diagonal and vertical elements. After you've planned your design, re-create the pattern on knitter's graph paper. Then knit your swatch to test out the new idea. Please feel free to photocopy this page.

Multidirectional Grid

Use this page to plan twisted-stitch designs with diagonal, horizontal, and vertical elements. After you've planned your design, re-create the pattern on knitter's graph paper. Then knit your swatch to test out the new idea. Please feel free to photocopy this page.

Design Your Own Specialty Shapes

Place your own twisted stitches or stitches from this book in these charts to make new versions of the Hat (page 212), Extreme Yoke Pullover (page 227), Snowflake Scarf (page 238), and Hexagon Pullover (page 242). Check each garment pattern for the intended gauge.

HAT CHART

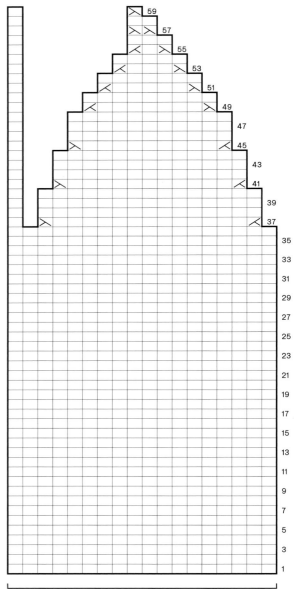

18-st repeat;
decreases to 1-st repeat

YOKE CHART

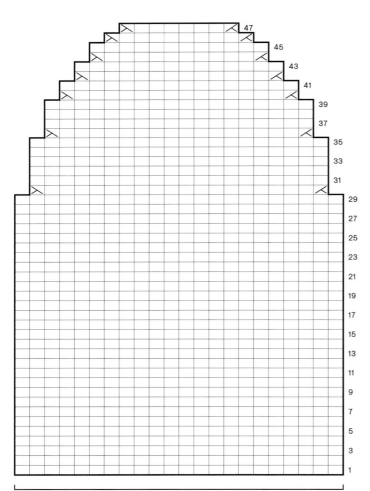

22-st repeat;
decreases to 8-st repeat

HEXAGON CHART

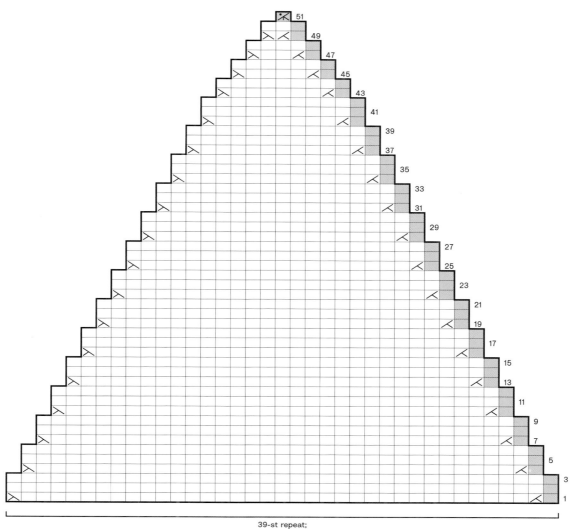

51
49
47
45
43
41
39
37
35
33
31
29
27
25
23
21
19
17
15
13
11
9
7
5
3
1

39-st repeat;
decreases to 1-st repeat

CHAPTER 11

Ten Lessons

In these ten lessons I share a few of the tricks
I've learned while developing twisted pattern
stitches. It's not a step-by-step guide but, instead,
a collection of ideas that you may find useful
on your design journey. Some lessons are about
design details, some are about planning concepts,
and some are insights into my design process.

1 TURNING CORNERS

With twisted stitches, the easiest and most expected way to make a corner after completing a line of twists in one direction is to simply reverse direction and start traveling in the opposite direction on the next right-side row. This makes a slightly rounded corner as seen in Zirconia (#10). For a crisp, very angular turn, again on the next right-side row, start the line that travels in the opposite direction one stitch before or after the end of the first diagonal (Diamond [#1]). Alternatively, as illustrated by Droplets (#87), add a few straight rows before switching direction, for a much curvier, rounded transition.

ZIRCONIA

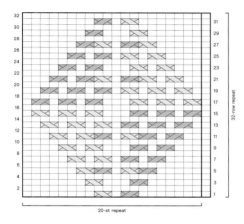

32-row repeat

20-st repeat

DIAMOND

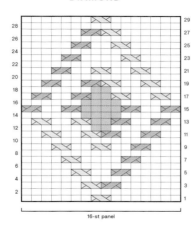

16-st panel

DROPLETS

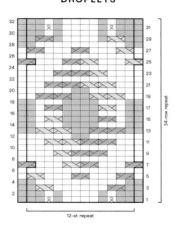

34-row repeat

12-st repeat

While diagonal lines stand out quite nicely against a Stockinette background, vertical lines need help getting noticed. The mini cables in the center of Starburst (#73) are clearly defined, while the mini cable in the center of Spire (#75), with no reverse Stockinette, is very subtle. You may choose to add extra definition to the outside edges near a corner as well, as in Stack (#6). I try to add the least amount of reverse Stockinette needed to achieve my goal. As I mentioned before, swatching is the key to success with decisions like these.

STARBURST

SPIRE

STACK

③ SCALE

Experiment with the size of your pattern. Once you have put together a pattern you like, don't be content to stop there. Try larger and smaller versions of your composition. You may end up preferring one of the other iterations, or you may be pleased with all three (or more).

Be sure to keep charts for all your trials. Even if these stitches are not what you are looking for now, you don't know when the ideas might come in handy or trigger another new idea when you look back on them in the future. Plaid Medium (#16) was my initial pattern in that series. Keeping the center the same size while expanding the diagonals resulted in Plaid Vast (#15), while reducing the number of diagonals, shortening them, and reducing the center all served to compress the pattern and resulted in Plaid Small (#52).

PLAID MEDIUM

PLAID VAST

PLAID SMALL

4 **TAKING AWAY**

Carve away at an allover pattern to reveal new variations. Here the pattern Smocking (#64) fills the entire surface of the knitting. Take away pattern from the bottom to reveal a narrow beginning, expanding to full width (Smocking Grow [#66]). Then carve pattern from the interior, and the result is a more baroque and lacy pattern (Smocking Fancy [#67]). Many more patterns are waiting to be revealed as offspring of the original allover pattern. The easiest way to find and document new variations is to make a page full of the allover pattern on a computer's drawing program, duplicate the page, and begin removing elements or partial elements. Often the new pattern in turn reveals the next new variation. When explorations feel as if they are at a dead end, start anew with the original allover pattern.

SMOCKING

SMOCKING GROW

SMOCKING FANCY

5 **LINE WEIGHT**

If you find your design looking a little thin, in need of emphasis, or calling out for some variation, try changing the line weight by doubling the lines. Single Flowers (#57) illustrates the difference between single diagonal lines and doubled, in both the large and the small versions of the geometric blooms.

6 **EVOLUTION**

When I am designing, one pattern often morphs into the next. Sometimes this happens with small changes, like extending a few lines, adding a twist, or reversing directions. Check out Diagonal Columns (#33), Braids (#34), and Mini Os (#35) to see how little changes transform one column into the next. The evolution from Twirl (#68) to Blanket Star (#71) and Big Star (#72) is less obvious. It took me a chunk of time to perfect the three parallelograms that combine to make Twirl, so it occurred to be that I might profit from the work already done by reusing those shapes. It was fun to recombine them in my drawing program, and to my surprise, Arrows (#70), Blanket Star, and Big Star were ultimately the results of my playing around.

ARROWS

BLANKET STAR

BIG STAR

After you've charted a pattern that is meant to repeat multiple times, be sure to test the repeat by duplicating the repeating part of the chart and placing it next to and on top of the original. If it works in these two directions, you are all set. I've caught a lot of serious errors this way.

BLACKWORK

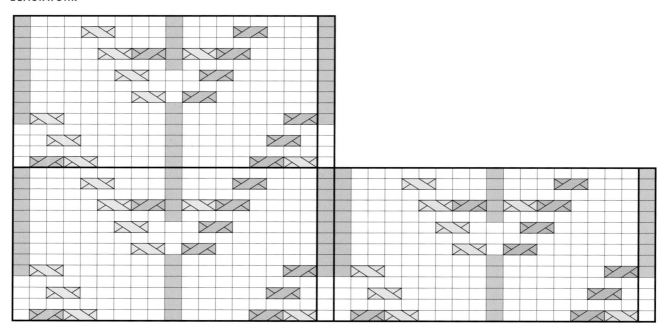

PATTERN DESIGN

One motif can be the seed of many ideas. To illustrate my point, let's start with a pyramid-shaped motif, cycle through some age-old concepts, and create new designs as we go.

+ The single pyramid motif is stacked to become a column in Pyramid Columns (#8).

+ Mirror the same pyramid along the horizontal axis, and it becomes the diamond shape in Zirconia (#10).

+ Separate the two halves of the pyramid, and repeat each half off to the sides to make Pyramid Split (#11).

+ Now take the columns of smaller triangles we just made and drop every other column down by half the number of rows in the repeat (that's called a half drop), and you have Pyramid Half Drop (#9).

You begin to see how this could go on forever. I'll show you two more iterations, each with special considerations, in the next two lessons.

PYRAMID COLUMNS

ZIRCONIA

PYRAMID SPLIT

PYRAMID HALF DROP

(9) TAKE ONE MORE STEP

Let's go back to using pyramids as the building block for new compositions. In my first attempt, shown in the chart below, I placed the pyramids in a true checkerboard arrangement, as if there were a rectangle drawn around each motif, with no overlap. I could see without even knitting that the design was too spread out, making it, to my eye, a bit boring. Moving the pyramids closer together, with fewer stitches between them, as in Pyramids Overlap (#7), at right, solved the problem.

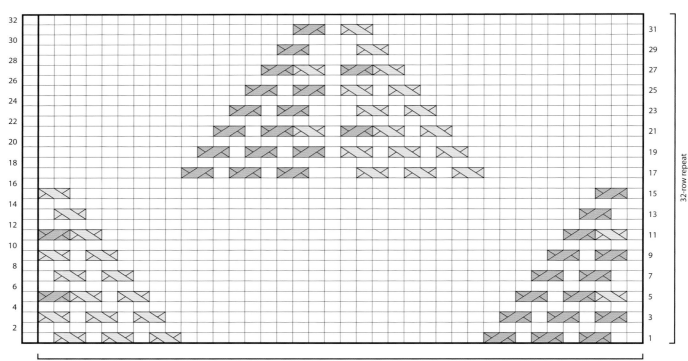

38-st repeat

32-row repeat

10 IT SHOULD BE EASIER

Look back at Triangle Half Drop (#12, page 30). When I first saw the chart, I immediately thought, *What if the long diagonals lined up to become one really long line? Wouldn't that look cool?* So I tried. Keeping the 10-stitch repeat, I began to put the idea in chart form and became discouraged. The rows didn't repeat until 80 rows were complete, which was rather ungainly. I am sure there is a mathematical way to figure out how to make the repeat work, but I started playing around, adding stitches between the motifs instead of calculating. I got lucky early. Adding 2 stitches and making the pattern a 12-stitch repeat created a pattern that repeats every 48 rows, rather than every 80 rows. This reminds me of one of my favorite pieces of design advice: Think of something and then make it easier.

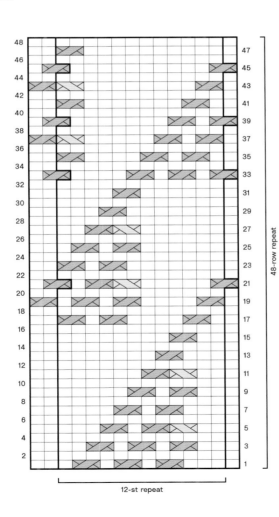

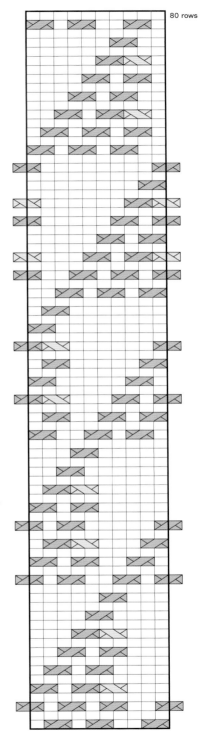

ABBREVIATIONS

BO Bind off

CO Cast on

K1-TBL Knit 1 stitch through the back loop.

K2TOG Knit 2 stitches together.

K3TOG Knit 3 stitches together.

K Knit

LT (LEFT TWIST—RS ROWS) Slip 1 stitch knitwise, slip a second stitch knitwise, slip both stitches back to the left-hand needle in their new orientation (just as for the beginning of ssk); knit into the back of the second stitch (approaching from the back), then knit into the back of both stitches and slip both from the needle. (Combination knitters, see pages 10 and 11).

LT (LEFT TWIST—WS ROWS) Slip 1 st knitwise, slip a second st knitwise, slip both sts back to left-hand needle in their new orientation (just as for the beginning of ssk); purl into the back of both sts together (approaching from the back), then into the back of the first st only and slip both sts from needle. (Combination knitters, see pages 10 and 11).

M1L (MAKE 1—LEFT SLANTING) With the tip of the left-hand needle inserted from front to back, lift the strand between the 2 needles onto the left-hand needle; knit the strand through the back loop to increase 1 stitch.

M1P OR M1PR (MAKE 1 PURLWISE—RIGHT SLANTING) With the tip of the left-hand needle inserted from back to front, lift the strand between the 2 needles onto the left-hand needle; purl the strand through the front loop to increase 1 stitch.

M1PL (MAKE 1 PURLWISE—LEFT SLANTING) With the tip of the left-hand needle inserted from front to back, lift the strand between the 2 needles onto the left-hand needle; purl the strand through the back loop to increase 1 stitch.

M1R (MAKE 1—RIGHT SLANTING) With the

tip of the left-hand needle inserted from back to front, lift the strand between the 2 needles onto the left-hand needle; knit the strand through the front loop to increase 1 stitch.

MB Make bobble (as instructed).

P1-TBL Purl 1 stitch through the back loop.

P2TOG Purl 2 stitches together.

P3TOG Purl 3 stitches together.

PM Place marker

P Purl

RND(S) Round(s)

RS Right side

RT (RIGHT TWIST—RS ROWS) K2tog leaving the original sts on left-hand needle, then knit the first st only and slip both sts from needle. (Combination knitters, see pages 10 and 11).

RT (RIGHT TWIST—WS ROWS) Purl into second st leaving the original sts on left-hand needle, then purl into the first and second sts together and slip both sts from needle. (Combination knitters, see pages 10 and 11).

SM Slip marker

SSK (SLIP, SLIP, KNIT) Slip the next 2 stitches to the right-hand needle one at a time as if to knit; return them to the left-hand needle one at a time in their new orientation; knit them together through the back loops.

SSP (SLIP, SLIP, PURL) Slip the next 2 stitches to the right-hand needle one at a time as if to knit; return them to the left-hand needle one at a time in their new orientation; purl them together through the back loops.

ST(S) Stitch(es)

TBL Through the back loop

WS Wrong side

WYIB With yarn in back

WYIF With yarn in front

YO Yarnover

SPECIAL TECHNIQUES

3-NEEDLE BIND-OFF

Place the sts to be joined onto two same-size needles; hold the pieces to be joined with the right sides facing each other and the needles parallel, both pointing to the right. Holding both needles in your left hand, using working yarn and a third needle the same size or one size larger, insert third needle into first st on front needle, then into first st on back needle; knit these two sts together; *knit next st from each needle together (two sts on right-hand needle); pass first st over second st to BO one st. Repeat from * until one st remains on third needle; cut yarn and fasten off.

CABLE CAST-ON

Make a loop (using a slipknot) with the working yarn and place it on the left-hand needle (first stitch cast on), knit into slipknot, draw up a loop but do not drop stitch from left-hand needle; place new loop on left-hand needle; *insert the tip of the right-hand needle into the space between the last 2 stitches on the left-hand needle and draw up a loop; place the loop on the left-hand needle. Repeat from * for remaining stitches to be cast on. .Can also be used to cast on at the end of a row in progress.

GERMAN SHORT ROWS

Work to specified turning point, then turn work. Slip 1 stitch purlwise to right-hand needle with yarn in front. Pull yarn over top of needle to back, creating a double stitch (DS) on the right-hand needle. If the next stitch to be worked is a knit stitch, leave yarn at back, and keep yarn tight when working the first stitch to ensure the double stitch stays in place. If the next stitch to be worked is a purl stitch, bring yarn to the front, ready to work the next stitch. When short rows are completed, or when working progressively longer short rows, knit or purl the two legs (the one created by taking the yarn over the needle and the original slipped stitch) of the double stitch together. When counting stitches, always count the double stitch as a single stitch.

LONG-TAIL CAST-ON
Leaving tail with about 1" (2.5 cm) of yarn for each stitch to be cast on, make a slipknot in the yarn and place it on the right-hand needle, with the tail to the front and the working end to the back. Insert the thumb and forefinger of your left hand between the strands of yarn so that the working end is around your forefinger, and the tail end is around your thumb "slingshot" fashion; *insert the tip of the right-hand needle into the front loop on the thumb, hook the strand of yarn coming from the forefinger from back to front, and draw it through the loop on your thumb; remove your thumb from the loop and pull on the working yarn to tighten the new stitch on the right-hand needle; return your thumb and forefinger to their original positions, and repeat from * for remaining stitches to be cast on.

Acknowledgments

DURING THE WRITING OF THIS BOOK, I relied on the sample knitters not only to knit the garments, but to patiently and intelligently catch the problems with my original instructions as well. Thanks for your invaluable help: Janet D'Alesandre, Patricia McMullen, Nancy Brown, Lynn Marlow, Elke Probst, Martha Wissing, and Barbara Khouri.

I am so grateful for the talents brought to this book by Caroline Goddard's photography and Emily Nora O'Neil's styling. They are a formidable team, bringing their intelligence, knowledge, and a like-minded aesthetic to this project. My gratitude and thanks also go to models Jordan Blackwell and Lilly Turmelle.

Thanks again to Barbara Khouri for grading all the garments, a task I do not care to do and one at which she happily excels. The book would not be possible without the efforts and technical editing talents of Sue McCain, whom I have had the pleasure to work with for many years. Thanks also to my editor, Shawna Mullen, who shares my unusual fascination with coelacanths.

Special thanks to my husband, John Ranta, for the many dinners he cooked, the many hours he watched mysteries with me while I knit, the many groans he endured during the writing process, and especially for the grandchildren he brought into my life. Thanks to those six amazing grandchildren, Loki, Edith, Ollie, June, Atticus, and Tobi, now ages four through nine, who share with me their love of science, reading, storytelling, fishing, and camping. They are my favorite companions for roasting marshmallows, making messes with clay, kayaking, finger knitting, and eating birthday cake.

EDITOR Shawna Mullen
DESIGNER Sarah Gifford
PRODUCTION MANAGER Kathleen Gaffney

Library of Congress Control Number:
2020931033

ISBN: 978-1-4197-4756-4
eISBN: 978-1-64700-012-7

Text copyright © 2021 Norah Gaughan
Photographs by Caroline Goddard

Cover © 2021 Abrams

Printed and bound in China
10 9 8 7 6 5 4 3 2 1

Abrams books are available at special
discounts when purchased in quantity
for premiums and promotions as well as
fundraising or educational use. Special
editions can also be created to specification.
For details, contact
specialsales@abramsbooks.com
or the address below.

ABRAMS
The Art of Books

195 Broadway
New York, NY 10007
abramsbooks.com